MENACHEM BEGIN AND THE ISRAEL-EGYPT PEACE PROCESS

PERSPECTIVES ON ISRAEL STUDIES

S. Ilan Troen, Natan Aridan, Donna Divine, David Ellenson, and Arieh
Saposnik, editors

Sponsored by the Ben-Gurion Research Institute for the Study of Israel and
Zionism of the Ben-Gurion University of the Negev and the Schusterman
Center for Israel Studies of Brandeis University

MENACHEM BEGIN AND THE ISRAEL-EGYPT PEACE PROCESS

Between Ideology and Political Realism

Gerald M. Steinberg and Ziv Rubinovitz

Indiana University Press

This book is a publication of

Indiana University Press
Office of Scholarly Publishing
Herman B Wells Library 350
1320 East 10th Street
Bloomington, Indiana 47405 USA

iupress.org

First paperback edition 2025

First printing 2019

The Library of Congress cataloged the original edition as follows:

Names: Steinberg, Gerald M., author. | Rubinovitz, Ziv, author.
Title: Menachem Begin and the Israel-Egypt peace process: between ideology
    and political realism / Gerald M. Steinberg and Ziv Rubinovitz.
Description: Bloomington, Indiana : Indiana University Press, [2019]
Series: Perspectives on Israel studies | Includes bibliographical references and index.
Identifiers: LCCN 2018049713 (print) | LCCN 2018050671 (ebook) |
    ISBN 9780253039552 (e-book) | ISBN 9780253039521 (cl : alk. paper)
Subjects: LCSH: Begin, Menachem, 1913-1992 | Prime ministers—Israel—
    Biography. | Israel—Foreign relations—Egypt. | Egypt—Foreign relations—
    Israel. | Arab-Israeli conflict—1973-1993—Diplomatic history.
Classification: LCC DS126.6.B33 (ebook) |
    LCC DS126.6.B33 S74 2019 (print) | DDC 956.04—dc23
LC record available at https://lccn.loc.gov/2018049713

ISBN 978-0-253-07127-9 (pbk.)

Citizens of Israel, when you hear these words, it will be morning. It will be an early hour and the sun will rise on the land of our Forefathers and Sons.

Will we be able to come to you within a few days and sing along, "We have brought peace unto you"?

This I can tell you: As we have made every possible human effort to bring it, we will continue so that every one of us can say, "Peace has come to our people and our land, not only for the current generation but also for generations to come."

With God's help, together we will accomplish this goal and will be blessed with good days of construction, brotherhood, and understanding. May this be God's will.

Prime Minister Menachem Begin, speaking in Hebrew to the citizens of Israel, at the signing ceremony of the Camp David Accords at the White House, September 17, 1978

Contents

Preface

THE SUCCESSFUL NEGOTIATION of a peace treaty between Israel and Egypt and the fact that this treaty has held for four decades are remarkable achievements in the realm of diplomacy and international relations. While many other attempts to negotiate viable peace agreements have sought to emulate this success, including for the unresolved parts of the Arab-Israel conflict, most have failed. The central question that we and many other authors who have examined the negotiations between Menachem Begin and Anwar Sadat have sought to answer is: Why? What were the key factors that led to success, and how can these be repeated in other cases?

Although the story of these negotiations has been told many times, a central part has largely been missing—specifically, the perspectives and strategies of Prime Minister Begin. In this volume, we reexamine and reassess these events—from the initial secret meetings leading to Sadat's dramatic arrival in Jerusalem and through the pivotal Camp David summit and the final signatures on the treaty.

To understand Begin's views and policies as prime minister and the story of the negotiations with Egypt, we need to go back and trace their evolution. Thus, after providing some background on Begin's early years and as leader of the Irgun underground, we begin our study with the May–June crisis preceding the 1967 Arab-Israeli War, during which Begin joined the National Unity Government under Prime Minister Levi Eshkol. Begin's participation in the events and debates beginning before the war, and continuing in its aftermath, particularly regarding the future of the occupied territories, were central in the formation of his policies during the crucial peace negotiations with Egypt.

Our analysis primarily focuses on Begin, who did not write memoirs or grant many interviews after leaving office. And while many of the other players, including senior Israeli ministers, published their versions, these were mostly personal accounts in which Begin's role as chief negotiator and decision maker was diminished, whether by design or oversight.

In any political or social process as complex as peace negotiations between two longtime enemies, the histories that are written are likely to reflect particular perspectives while neglecting others. In addition to the Israeli memoirs, the American participants, including President Jimmy Carter, have published extensively on these events, particularly regarding the Camp David summit of September 1978. The interpretation of central issues, including the relationship between Begin and Carter, has been largely shaped by the latter's extensive diaries and public statements, as well as the memoirs of Carter's aides.

While this practice is understandable, it leaves the historical record incomplete and inaccurate. One of the major differences concerns the emphasis regarding the two central strands in the negotiations—one focusing on Egyptian-Israeli bilateral issues, summarized as "land for peace," and the other on the Palestinian dimension, which was ultimately dealt with through an agreement to negotiate a nonterritorial form of autonomy. The Israeli histories tend to focus on the Egyptian-Israeli strand, while the American histories and analyses give more attention to the difficult negotiations on autonomy between Begin and Carter. In some ways, these two sets of emphasis present quite different versions of the events. In addition, for both groups, the image of Begin was secondhand, meaning that they relied on what other actors—Carter, Secretary of State Cyrus Vance, Foreign Minister Moshe Dayan, and Defense Minister Ezer Weizman—said about the Israeli prime minister's goals, priorities, and strategies.

As a result, our first objective in undertaking the research that led to this publication was to fill the major gap in the historical record and to compare the existing accounts from Americans, Israelis, Egyptians, and others with the evidence that presents Begin's point of view. Of course, we do not pretend to be able to write a memoir or diary in place of the ones that Begin never wrote, but we are able to raise questions and provide some answers based on a very detailed and comprehensive analysis of Begin's own words and actions during this period.

In this process, we have benefited from numerous Israeli and American government documents and records that have become available in recent years, almost four decades after the events themselves. Begin's powerful and eloquent voice is now accessible through protocols and other documents that record and summarize the meetings, negotiation sessions, and internal debates, and we have given it the attention we believe it deserves. The full texts of the relevant documents are available on the dedicated website created to accompany this publication, at this link: https://www.begincenter .org.il/menachem-begin-israel-egypt-peace-process-ideology -political-realism/.

In filling in the missing history and in reviewing and comparing the documents to the existing accounts and analyses, we expected to find many instances where we could corroborate the established narratives, as well as point out and perhaps even settle significant contradictions. With a negligible portion of the material at the Israel State Archives that remains classified—official American documentation from the Camp David summit is sparse—the presentation in this volume is an important and necessary correction to the existing histories and scholarship.[1] Similarly, by reexamining the events of forty years ago in the light of the new archival material, we are able to reconsider the main conclusions that have been drawn regarding the factors that led to the successful outcome.

The main arguments concerning Israeli policies and Begin's role, as found in the existing histories and analyses of the Egyptian-Israeli peace negotiations, and not internally consistent, can be summarized as follows:

1. Menachem Begin was an inflexible negotiator whose personality, based on personal history and experience, and obsessively focused on the Holocaust, created major obstacles to agreement.

2. Begin's Zionist Revisionist ideology and his self-image as Ze'ev Jabotinsky's heir reinforced these personality obstacles, particularly on the Palestinian dimension of the negotiations.

3. In pursuing a peace agreement with Sadat, Begin abandoned his previous ideological positions, in large part under the withering pressure of Carter and his administration.

4. Begin's overemphasis on formalistic legalistic dimensions prevented pragmatic interest-based positions and created additional obstacles.

5. After the initial meeting, Begin and Sadat clashed constantly and intensely, making it impossible for them to negotiate constructively.

6. President Carter was able to overcome these obstacles through careful manipulation of the negotiation process, including avoiding joint meetings involving Begin and Sadat, particularly during the Camp David summit.

7. Much of the progress made after periods of stalemate and coming close to the collapse of the talks, including at Camp David, was the result of the flexible policies and willingness to compromise of the other Israelis—particularly Foreign Minister Dayan, Defense Minister Weizman, and (outgoing) Attorney General Aharon Barak.

8. At Camp David, Begin was isolated and withdrawn—a "prime minister under siege"—as reflected in the title and theme of one of the major books on the process, published by a senior Israeli journalist.[2]

9. Begin had strong domestic political backing for the agreements (both after Camp David and the final treaty), but he exaggerated the criticism in the Knesset and in other venues to gain concessions in the negotiations.

10. After reluctantly accepting the concessions made at Camp David, Begin had buyer's remorse and sought to revise the terms of the framework agreement, particularly on autonomy.

11. According to Carter and most of the American officials, because of Begin, a historic opportunity for a comprehensive peace that would end the entire Middle East conflict, based on a solution for the Palestinians, was missed.

In attempting to address, question, and, where justified, expand on these issues and theories, as well as adding new theories and lessons, we begin with

Begin's personal and political history. In understanding the policies toward peace with Egypt and related issues that he pursued with great vigor from his first day as prime minister following the 1977 elections, it is necessary to examine his early policies and approaches. The main biographical events, including the period of his leadership of the Irgun underground and then the Herut party, as well as his long stint as head of the opposition in the Knesset, are briefly summarized in the introduction.

In chapter 1, we examine Begin's actions, statements, and policies as a member of the National Unity Government, beginning immediately before the 1967 war until his resignation in 1970. In this period, Begin developed clear approaches on the potential for a peace agreement with Egypt, as well as on the requirements as he saw them regarding the future status of Judea and Samaria (as he consistently referred to the West Bank). His many statements on these issues were made in cabinet meetings, Knesset debates, appearances before Herut party frameworks (some closed sessions and some open), media interviews, and elsewhere. This rich record of Begin's statements and positions provides an essential baseline for examining his activities and policies as prime minister a decade later. On this basis, we can test the theory that Begin changed his views substantially and abandoned much of his ideological framework as prime minister.

In 1970, after three years, Begin took the Gahal bloc out of the Unity Government, citing basic policy differences over Prime Minister Golda Meir's decision to accept the US-brokered ceasefire agreement with Egypt to end the War of Attrition, which included terms he rejected—namely the acceptance of UN Security Council Resolution 242 as the basis for the next steps in Middle East peacemaking. But Begin was also positioning himself and Gahal for a run at the leadership in elections scheduled for October 1973. The earthquake of the 1973 Yom Kippur War intervened, and when the delayed elections took place, Gahal, now renamed the Likud, had made substantial gains, but not enough to defeat the Alignment, and remained in the opposition. Nevertheless, Begin recognized a positive gradual change in the new Knesset, with a majority of members of the Knesset (MKs)—including many from the Alignment—who objected to Israeli withdrawal from Judea and Samaria.

Chapter 2 continues with the background, covering the period until the May 17, 1977, elections, including the campaign. In this period, we see further development of Begin's concepts of peace and his view of Egypt. Prior to the campaign, the documentation for this chapter comes largely from regular Knesset and party speeches, as well as numerous newspaper columns. In the months leading to the elections, Begin was busy giving speeches at rallies around the country, although toward the end, he had a heart attack and was hospitalized.

In this chapter, we also examine the domestic political framework in which Begin operated, including the factors that led to the unprecedented and revolutionary election outcome that brought the Likud bloc, with Herut at the center, to power for the first time. These included the decline of the Labor-led bloc due to a combination of corruption, the ongoing impact of public anger over the Yom Kippur War, and internal leadership battles. The rise of a significant third bloc—Dash (the Democratic Movement for Change), which itself consisted of three different subparties—also contributed to putting Begin into the prime minister's office. These domestic political factors are essential in understanding the framework and limitations that constrained Begin's flexibility during the negotiations.

Chapters 3 through 8 are the heart of the book, starting with the immediate attention that Begin gave to reports that Sadat had signaled an interest in reaching an accommodation and ending with the signing and implementation of the treaty. These chapters present the recently released Israeli and American documentation covering each of the critical phases, summits, and crises, allowing us in chapter 9 to reexamine the various theories and conclusions on the basis of this new information. In this final chapter, we also consider the implications of the history, as enriched by the perspective focusing on Begin's role.

However, we are not revisionists. Our history and analysis are anchored in the protocols of discussions and memoranda that were written in real time, without the hindsight that later authors had in writing of an achievement that was already in hand. And with the prime minister back in the center of the events, the previous narratives are shown to be incomplete.

Through this fresh analysis, we add significantly to the understanding of how peace between Israel and Egypt was achieved in the late 1970s and how Begin led Israel through this unique achievement. The lessons from Begin's careful tailoring of the peace treaty remain relevant and serve as important guides for diplomats, negotiators, and third parties.

Notes

1. The editorial note in the *Foreign Relations of the United States 1977–1980*, vol. 9, document 26, states, "No memoranda of conversation or official records of the substance of [the US delegation] conversations, or indeed any of the internal discussions of the U.S. delegation, have been found. This dearth of official documentation also extends to the negotiations themselves and reflects the idiosyncratic recordkeeping of the U.S. delegation at Camp David."

2. Benziman, *Prime Minister under Siege.*

Acknowledgments

THIS BOOK IS the fruit of more than fifteen years of research, beginning with the seed planted by the late Harry Hurwitz, a close confident of Menachem Begin's and the first head of the center built in Jerusalem to honor Begin's accomplishments. Hurwitz recognized that while the 1979 peace treaty with Egypt was Begin's outstanding accomplishment as prime minister, no detailed history or analysis of his role had been published. And while numerous previously classified documents were expected to become available, particularly from the Israeli sources, these had yet to be examined and included in a published history.

At Harry's request, and with the backing of the late Yechiel Kadishai, who accompanied Begin throughout his political career, I (Gerald Steinberg) agreed to undertake this task as part of my academic work on international negotiation and diplomacy. The process was painfully slow for all involved as I began to review every available source, read every published book and article, and collect the documents. To seriously explain the story of Begin at Camp David, it was not enough to start in November 1977 with Sadat's visit to Jerusalem or even with Begin's first role in government as a minister in the National Unity Government formed on the eve of the 1967 war, but I had to go back to his ideological roots in the Zionist Revisionist Movement, to his experience leading the Irgun underground, and to twenty-six years as head of the opposition in the Knesset.

After I sent students recruited from classes at Bar Ilan University (particularly Shaul Weisband), to copy reams of newspaper articles in Hebrew and English in order to distill Begin's words and to collect transcripts of speeches from party meetings, Knesset plenaries, and declassified protocols of cabinet meetings, the outline of the book gradually took shape. Interns assisted with proofreading sources (Abby Hayton) and with early drafts of chapters (Itai Bavli). While our efforts could not take the place of the memoirs that Begin never wrote or the diary he did not keep, these sources provided the closest equivalent.

The frequent and none-too-gentle queries from Herzl Makov and Dr. Moshe Fuksman-Sha'al from the Begin Center, who followed the project closely for many years and provided funds for research travels, were essential in completing this book. With their encouragement, Ziv Rubinovitz joined the research project, first as a graduate student, and then a post-doc, and finally as he took academic positions. Ziv became a partner and coauthor and meticulously collected the documents as they were declassified at the Israel State Archives and at the Carter Library. Being among the first scholars to review these documents, we were fortunate to get a better sense of the dilemmas, analyses, and concessions that faced Begin and his colleagues and to read Begin's views without filters. The flood of archival material allowed us to evaluate the accuracy of previous accounts, and in numerous sessions, we transformed the outlines and rough drafts into detailed chapters, sorting out the many contradictions in the different memoirs and interviews and separating credible sources from imagined or secondhand narratives.

It took a long time to trace, obtain, and study the endless number of documents for this book. From the Israel State Archives, we benefited from the many items that were declassified in recent years, including protocols of meetings, letters, and other documents available. We are grateful to Dr. Louise Fischer, who provided vital advice and direction, sharing knowledge based on her own research and expertise, and to the Reading Room staff for their help during numerous sessions.

In addition, the staff of the Menachem Begin Heritage Center provided enormous assistance, including making oral histories and documentation available. At the Begin Center Archives, we thank Iris Berlatzky and Yossi Barnea for their assistance in the earlier stages of this project and, in recent years, Rami Shtivi and his assistants and interns.

Many of the documents and related material were obtained from the Jimmy Carter Presidential Library in Atlanta, Georgia. The expertise and goodwill of the excellent archival team at the Carter Library, led by Albert Nason and Keith Shuler, made the visits and correspondence highly productive, constructive, and pleasant.

We also thank our many colleagues and friends for their good advice and for sharing knowledge and experience. In helping us navigate the publication process, Ilan Troen and Natan Aridan were very helpful, and in the final stages, the anonymous reviewers at the Indiana University Press, as well as our editors—Dee Mortensen, Paige Rasmussen, Nancy Lightfoot, and Julia Turner—gave us important feedback and guidance.

Finally, we thank our patient families—among the Steinbergs, my parents and teachers, Anne and Henry; my wife and inspiration, Connie; and our four children, Hadara, Sygall, Yael, and Binyamin, who grew up with my seemingly unending Begin project hovering in the background; and for the Rubinovitzs, my father, Dr. Chaim Rubinovitz, and his partner, Tanya; my sister, Maayan, her spouse, Amir, and their daughter, Ori; and my mother, Prof. Nili Rubinovitz-Grossman, who passed away and would have been delighted to see the completion of this book.

May the peace treaty that Menachem Begin and Anwar Sadat negotiated and signed almost forty years ago serve as an example for us and for all those who follow.

MENACHEM BEGIN AND
THE ISRAEL-EGYPT PEACE PROCESS

Introduction

Begin's Ideological Core

To understand Menachem Begin, a central leader of the Revisionist wing of Zionism, it is necessary to understand and examine the substance and strength of his ideological commitment.

While a full treatment of Begin's ideological foundations, beginning with his education in Brest-Litovsk (part of Russia when he was born in 1913) and the flight to Vilna in advance of the Nazi invasion, followed by the years in the Irgun underground and as leader of Herut, is beyond the scope of this book, some background is necessary. Begin was raised in a politically involved family, where the nascent Zionist movement was central. He was heavily influenced by the Revisionist Zionist philosophy of Ze'ev Jabotinsky, whom he heard as a high school student, and joined the Betar Youth Movement from the HaShomer HaTza'ir left-leaning youth movement. As a follower of Jabotinsky, Begin absorbed and highlighted the centrality of national rebirth, the restoration of Jewish sovereignty, the need for a Jewish fighting force (originally embodied during World War I in the Jewish Legion), and the concept of *hadar*—dignity. In addition, his talent for inspiring oratory led him to leadership positions in the movement; as a young man in Poland, Begin became a major Revisionist figure.[1]

Begin's interests and talents led him to Warsaw University, where he studied law, and he continued his activities in Betar. In 1939, following the Nazi invasion of Poland, he and his wife, Aliza, fled to Vilna (Vilnius, Lithuania). Later, his parents and one of his brothers, who were in Brest, were taken and murdered by the Nazis. On a deeply personal basis, the shadow of the Holocaust was always present in Begin's life.

In 1940, he was arrested, and repeatedly interrogated by the People's Commissariat for Internal Affairs (abbreviated NKVD in Russian). In his autobiography covering this period, *White Nights*, Begin recounts the interrogation sessions and incarceration in the Soviet Gulag from 1940 to 1942, highlighting his Zionist commitment and other ideological principles.[2]

Begin was released in May 1942 with all Poles who joined the Free Polish Army of General Wladyslav Anders, and he arranged to be sent to Italy as part of the British-led anti-Nazi alliance. Soon afterward, while stationed in Palestine, he was released for an unlimited time and went underground to become leader of the Revisionist underground force, known as the Irgun (Irgun Zvai Leumi,

Etzel).[3] This period, which continued until the 1948 declaration of the State of Israel, and the war that accompanied these developments are covered in his auto-biographical book *The Revolt*.[4] Begin was constantly in hiding, part of the time in disguise. He ordered numerous operations from the underground and later testified that that era was the most challenging in his life, more than being Israel's prime minister. During these years, he was on top of the British list of "wanted persons in Palestine."

In 1952, Begin published his principles in a booklet entitled *Basic Outlines of Our Life-Worldview and Our National Outlook*. These are general concepts derived directly from liberal and nationalist frameworks. The section on liberalism deals with freedom of the individual, social reform, and the supremacy of law. The nationalist section that is most important to this discussion covers the liberation of the homeland and the return to Zion, reestablishing the nation.

The territorial dimension began with the core Zionist objective of liberating the Jewish homeland—Eretz Israel. According to Begin, "Not only the national vision, but indeed real experience teaches us that liberation of the homeland is a program that is possible to realize quickly in our days and not a 'hallucination' for the future generations."[5] But unlike David Ben-Gurion and the Labor Zionist wing, Revisionists in general, and Begin in particular, rejected pragmatic compromises, as decided in the case of the UN Partition Plan in 1947. Thus, Begin thundered, "As is well known, the Jewish Agency desired truly and innocently the partition of the country by 'peaceful means' as set out in the United Nations' program which was accepted, in its entirety, happily and with rejoicing by all the circles of the Jewish Agency."[6]

Begin wrote this in 1952, just three years after the War of Independence ended painfully, without Israeli control over the Old City of Jerusalem, Judea and Samaria, and Gaza. Begin saw the results as unfinished business that needed correction. The correction came eighteen years later in the form of the Six-Day War and its outcome. Israel took control over Jerusalem, Judea, Samaria, and Gaza—the missing parts of Eretz Israel as Begin saw it. This image was in sharp contrast to the one that dominated the international community and also circulated among many Israelis who had begun to accept the transformation of armistice lines into permanent and acknowledged borders.

The de facto boundaries of Eretz Israel had changed throughout history many times, and the Hebrew Bible presents two significantly different sets of borders.[7] But while Begin was a religious person in many aspects of his life, he did not attempt to realize the biblical boundaries per se. Begin, like many of his contemporaries, viewed the lines established by the League of Nations in 1920 and the British Mandate for Palestine as the modern version of Eretz Israel. Hence, the border between Mandatory Palestine and Egypt was drawn from the Gulf of Aqaba/Eilat to Rafah as early as 1906.[8] This is known as the international border, and in the aftermath, this was the agreed border between Israel and Egypt, with minor corrections.[9]

In 1922, Britain divided Palestine and established Transjordan on the East Bank of the Jordan River, which has become known since its independence in 1946 as the Hashemite Kingdom of Jordan. Begin rejected the legitimacy of this partition of the land, but by the time he became prime minister, he had come to terms with this reality. While the Jordan River was initially envisioned as the center of the future independent country in Palestine, as early as 1922, it became the eastern perimeter of Mandatory Palestine. The symbol of the Etzel (the Irgun), which Begin commanded in the underground from 1943 to 1948, reflected his concept in that Jordan does not exist in it.[10] From this perspective, any piece of this territory that was removed from the Jewish protostate was already a painful concession. While many right-wing politicians stated that "Jordan is Palestine," thus implying that it should become the Palestinian state (after replacing the Hashemites), Begin rejected this slogan, arguing that the Jewish people also had a right to Jordan, so suggesting that Jordan belongs to the Palestinians undermines the Jewish claim.

Begin accepted—long before 1977—the political reality of Jordan's existence. If he had any reservations on its legality, he kept them to himself. However, although he called on King Hussein to make peace with Israel and pressed Jordan to join the peace process and particularly the autonomy talks in which a significant role awaited Jordan, he was the only Israeli prime minister during Hussein's forty-seven years of reign who did not meet with him at all.

In this period, Begin slowly started to identify the idea of Eretz Israel with the territory west of the Jordan River.[11] As Arye Naor explains, the ceasefire lines of 1949 were widely understood among Israelis as the territorial status quo, and Begin's early calls for military action to capture territory beyond the ceasefire lines did not resonate.[12] Amir Goldstein attributes this to Begin's pragmatic politics: avoiding a decline in public support while attempting to negotiate the establishment of a political alignment with the General Zionists, which led to the formation of the Gahal bloc.[13]

However, Begin saw the outcome of the 1967 war as a correction of a major historical error.[14] As a result, at no point would he be willing to concede what he perceived as Israel's legal and political right to demand sovereignty over the West Bank and Gaza. It was on this core position that Jimmy Carter, more than Sadat, sought to change Begin's mind, and, as the record showed, Carter failed; Begin's ideological commitment to Jewish sovereignty over Judea and Samaria was unshakable. This was not a matter of stubbornness, pessimism, or other personality and psychological traits, as understood by the Americans, but rather of fundamental principle.

Begin's ideological convictions were not limited to Eretz Israel and the Jewish people's right to sovereignty over it. He also held strong views on individual liberty—the party's name was Herut, "freedom" or "liberty" in Hebrew. He sought to end the continuation of martial law that Israel imposed on its Arab citizens from 1948 to 1966. This principle was also one of the foundations of Begin's autonomy plan in 1977, in which he sought a path to provide civil liberties to the Palestinians while maintaining Israeli sovereignty and security control. However, Begin also saw grave peril in Palestinian statehood that could—and, in his view, would—become a mortal danger to Israel.

Begin as a Pragmatic Leader

Begin's background, including his legal education, imprisonment by the Soviets, and leadership of the Irgun in its fight against the British for Jewish independence, as well as his experience as a student of Jabotinsky, was also reflected in a strong emphasis on liberal democratic principles as he understood them. He recognized and frequently articulated the need for an appropriate political and legal framework for the Palestinian inhabitants of the territories (Judea and Samaria). Israel could not annex the land without granting the inhabitants citizenship, a solution Begin rejected for fear of undermining the Jewish character of the Israeli state. Deporting (transferring) them was out of the question.

Therefore, Begin embraced autonomy as an acceptable compromise. The Palestinians would control their civic life but without independent foreign relations or sovereign territory. Autonomy was an attempt to mediate between core ideological principles and the pragmatism that emerged beginning in 1967, when Begin joined the Unity Government.

In a sense, this compromise between ideology and realism followed the precedent set by Ben-Gurion and Mapai. Naor recalls that Ben-Gurion also believed the Jews had historical rights to Eretz Israel, but he preferred territorial compromise (reflected in the Yishuv's acceptance of the plans to partition the land long before Israel was established) to realize political control in whatever territory was possible. At the time, Begin and Herut confronted Mapai and opposed all compromise.[15] But unlike Ben-Gurion and Mapai, Begin insisted on the rights to Eretz Israel wherever Israel had control (i.e., Judea, Samaria, and Gaza), whereas Mapai accepted further compromise, extending to the disputed territories west of the Jordan River.

Begin as Decision Maker: 1967 to 1979

Menachem Begin's appointment as minister without portfolio on June 5, 1967, with the outbreak of the war, was the first time that he had national responsibility as a cabinet member. This also gave him public legitimacy and governmental experience that contributed to his elevation to prime minister a decade later.

Israel's decisive victory made his presence in the cabinet room significant in terms of the ongoing development and implementation of policy following the conflict. The secret decision—to which Begin made a major contribution—confirmed a week after the ceasefire declared that the Sinai Peninsula, taken from Egypt, and the Golan Heights, captured from Syria, were to be regarded as deposits for peace with these two countries.

However, from the beginning, Begin rejected calls to apply this formula to the other occupied territories—Judea, Samaria (the West Bank, captured from Jordan), and the Gaza Strip (also captured from Egypt). He was not alone in this position, and the Eshkol government accepted it. From Begin's perspective, the negotiations with Egypt a decade later, when he was prime minister, applied this decision to the letter. He was willing to return control over the entire Sinai Peninsula to Egypt (in contrast to Labor, which sought to annex the eastern coast) but refused to relinquish a square inch (or millimeter) of the West Bank or Gaza.

Throughout this period, Begin demonstrated a strong commitment to leadership—he was a decisive decision maker and did not delegate core decisions but rather the opposite. As the unchallenged leader (for the most part) of the Irgun underground, Begin emerged with strong personal allegiance and, on this basis, was also the largely uncontested leader of Herut in the Knesset and then the head of the wider bloc that became Gahal and Likud.

As a minister beginning in 1967, during and after the war, Begin actively and repeatedly pressed initiatives, and if he was thwarted in one avenue, he tried and often succeeded through another one. Throughout this period, his determination to gain support for his policies was evident in his powerful rhetoric and his actions. Although he had a different and more complex environment as prime minister and depended on getting majority approval in the cabinet, as well as depending on the cooperation of powerful personalities such as Moshe Dayan and Ezer Weizman to execute policy decisions, he succeeded in this process.

Begin as Politician

In Israel, as a parliamentary democracy based on multiparty coalitions, the government is not simply a reflection of the prime minister or under his control. Many of the politicians who occupy the cabinet seats have their own power base, and usually all of them are MKs. Each one has his or her own agenda and calculations, unlike cabinet members in American administrations, who serve "at the pleasure of the president,"[16] often without an independent political base. It is usually difficult for the prime minister to remove or replace a minister other than due to moral and ethical infractions. If a dissenting minister is from the prime minister's party, he or she can create difficulties in the Knesset or the party. And if the minister is from a coalition partner, replacing him or her requires reaching understandings with that party so that it will not leave the coalition.

On many occasions during the negotiations, Begin concluded that President Carter seemed to misunderstand the fundamental dynamics of the Israeli political system. The US president consistently acted in ways that made it difficult for Begin to maneuver between the international players (the United States, Israel's patron and only ally, doing most of the demanding and exerting the pressure) and a complex domestic political reality. His coalition was fractured, particularly as this was the first time in Israel's history that the country directly confronted the difficult choices for peace. Begin could cajole and use his political capital to threaten, but he could not force his own views and policies on the cabinet, the Knesset, or the public; instead, he needed to convince them and advocate for their approval—and Begin's core constituency, which shared his ideology and passion but did not have the responsibilities of national leadership, was the most difficult to convince.

Thus, ideology and realpolitik, at the domestic and international levels, are both vital for the understanding of Begin's actions, suggestions, and concessions during the negotiations. As the responsible decision maker for the nation, Begin faced difficult pragmatic dilemmas that many of his followers did not comprehend, and they could not accept the concessions he made. This, in turn, caused Begin major political difficulties, particularly within the Likud. Begin often presented to Carter the intense opposition that he faced, requesting more understanding of his situation, usually without success. From Carter's perspective, Begin was simply using domestic politics to justify refusal to make additional compromises and concessions.

Negotiation Theories and Their Limits

In the negotiations from 1977 to 1979 involving Israel, Egypt, and the United States, as presented in the following chapters, several theories and frameworks are useful for the analysis of events. These are also important in addressing the various theories and questions regarding the outcome and the implications for future peace processes.

We begin with the two-level game approach of Robert Putnam, who discusses the interaction between domestic and international levels that the negotiator must deal with.[17] The peace process between Israel and Egypt vividly demonstrates this analytical model, although it applies more to the Israeli side than the Egyptian due to the different political structures.

Regarding the American role, Carter also maneuvered between the domestic and international levels. He feared losing support from the Jewish community as he pressured Israel. Sadat—although he eventually paid the highest price with his own life, in part for signing the treaty—imposed the deal on Egypt as the head of an authoritarian regime. Sadat's domestic political concerns seemed mostly related to members of his own entourage, and at specific points he needed to force them to accept his actions with the goal of securing what he saw as the ultimate objective: the return of full Egyptian sovereignty over the Sinai. In the process, two of Sadat's foreign ministers resigned in protest. Although this was not an

Egyptian domestic issue, Sadat also had to deal with the Arab world, where he had played a leading role until his trip to Jerusalem in November 1977.

Moving from the structural to the individual approach in international negotiations, Kenneth Stein's important history of Israeli-Arab talks from 1973 through 1978 (with a final chapter covering the next twenty years, through the Oslo framework) is entitled *Heroic Diplomacy*. As the title implies, Stein focuses on the key players and the molders of history—Kissinger, Sadat, Begin, and Carter. According to this model, the contributions of each individual, examined in detail, made possible the breakthrough agreement between Egypt and Israel. When Sadat replaced Nasser, the former's combination of vision and pragmatism, coupled with his "background, flamboyance, disdain for foreign control, secretive style, and impatience redirected Egypt's orientation."[18]

Similarly, in Stein's analysis, Begin was essential to the success of the negotiations, based on his mind-set that focused on one question: "Is it good or bad for the Jewish people?" That assessment, along with his immersion "in every detail and legality associated with policies, politics and processes of negotiations," was vital to reaching an agreement with Sadat. As opposition to the peace process mounted on both sides, "Begin and Sadat remained steadfast in seeing agreements made between their two countries."[19]

But according to Stein, like most analysts, Sadat and Begin "could not effectively work together without an intermediary"—a role that, in this analysis, was filled by Carter. The American president had "a penchant to find solutions" to problems, as well as an "impatience for its resolution." According to this "heroic leader" model, "Carter's personal commitment and unyielding zeal to impel a negotiated outcome was unequaled."[20]

In the following chapters, the support for these claims is tested based on the available evidence, which now includes the voluminous Israeli documentation. While Carter was indeed energetic in pursuing peace and clearly displayed a strong commitment to a successful outcome, we will compare two different frameworks for assessing the role: (1) as the vital intermediary and (2) as a primary adversary in negotiations with Begin, particularly on the Palestinian dimension.

In examining the claims that psychological factors played a major role in determining the process and outcome, we will consider the evidence regarding the theories and models of negotiation that incorporate and emphasize these dimensions, notably in the work of Herbert Kelman, Louis Kriesberg, and many others.[21]

In contrast to these theories that focus on individuals and personalities, the realist approach to international politics and diplomacy highlights the role of interests and other factors. From this perspective, the ability of Sadat and Begin to reach an agreement is seen as resulting from the fact that the terms fulfilled the interests of both leaders and their nations and that evidence as well as explanations focusing on personality and cultural clashes are overstated.

In terms of theories of third-party intervention and negotiation processes, the fact that the talks between Israel and Egypt took place directly rather than via intermediaries, as in the case of Kissinger's shuttle diplomacy a few years earlier, is also significant. When Carter took office, he envisioned and pursued a regional and comprehensive approach in which the great powers, including the Soviet Union, would broker a deal. However, one of the first points of agreement between Sadat and Begin was the realization that Carter's formula was a dead end that would not result in agreement. Later, when the differences and crises arose in the negotiations, the Americans returned as important actors, but Carter's emphasis on reaching a comprehensive agreement was rebuffed.

At the same time, the applicability of ripeness models of international negotiation would appear to be useful in the analysis of the Egyptian-Israeli process and outcome. As developed by William Zartman and others, the concept of ripeness posits a conflict dynamic in which a "mutually hurting stalemate" (or, in a few cases, an "enticing opportunity") leads to political accommodation through negotiations.[22] This theory emphasizes the role of leaders rather than of societal or cultural factors and is rooted in game theory and rational analysis, as distinct from social psychology. As detailed in this volume, this approach is consistent with Begin's leadership and decision-making throughout the negotiations with Sadat and Carter.

However, in many cases, the factors that are central to this theory are subjective and based on perceptions; ripeness can often be discerned only in retrospect, after agreements are signed and implemented and the conflict is ended or reduced significantly.

Although the opening of direct negotiations at the final phase of the 1973 Yom Kippur War, through the active mediation of Henry Kissinger, is consistent with the mutual stalemate approach, it is not clear that the process involving Begin and Sadat and the resulting peace treaty are largely attributable to ripeness. The immediate and intense crisis on both sides that accompanied the 1973 war had abated, and the separation of forces agreements of 1974 and 1975 were holding. When Begin took office in 1977, there was no immediate crisis in terms of relations with Egypt.

Nevertheless, Begin was clearly aware of both the dangers of renewed conflict, and, perhaps more importantly, he and Sadat repeatedly articulated the framework of a mutual enticing opportunity. The leaders of both countries referred to the importance of reaching a peace agreement in terms of national interest and recognized the unique historical opportunity that existed at the time. In addition (and returning to the domestic arena and the two-level game), Begin was also cognizant of the impact that reaching a peace agreement with Egypt would have on his political legacy.

The negotiations and successful outcome were by no means inevitable, and the fact that they took place and resulted in agreement based on mutual interests is relatively unusual in international relations. Violent conflicts such as between Egypt and Israel do not always move toward resolution, even when the costs of continuing conflict endanger the survival of the regimes. The Balkans conflict of the 1990s, which eventually led to the replacement of the Serbian regime, among others, is a case in point, as is the completed destruction of the Tamil leadership in the Sri Lankan conflict.

Thus, there is a great deal to be learned from this case study and from the additional perspectives based on the analysis of the Israeli documentation and the emphasis on Begin's role.

Methodological Note

Our book comes out at a late stage in the historiography of the peace process, long after the memoirs of participants in the process, most of whom have passed away, and journalistic accounts that came out soon after the events from reporters who covered the process, based on interviews with a few of the central participants.[23] It also comes after several thorough academic studies of the process, which were usually based on publicized accounts and media reports, while later ones had some of the declassified primary sources.[24]

However, new histories and analyses were made possible by the massive declassification of documents by the American National Archives (NARA) in the form of two large volumes of the *Foreign Relations of the United States* (*FRUS*) from Carter's term (volumes 8 and 9), the Carter Presidential Library in Atlanta, Georgia, and the Israel State Archives.[25] Our analysis, which focuses on the Israeli perspective in general and on Begin's role in particular, was made possible by access to these documents.

As noted throughout the text, in examining the documents, we compare their contents with the existing evidence and narratives, often resulting in inconsistencies and contradictions. In these sections, when the protocols, cables, and assessments made at the time are not consistent with the other versions, we give the primary sources priority over the narratives. Of course, given the differing versions, the reader is free to reach different conclusions. We do not claim that our history is the final version or that it is necessarily the correct one, but rather we see it as an important contribution to understanding these unique events and Menachem Begin's essential role and accomplishment.

Notes

1. See also Gordis, *Menachem Begin*; Shilon, *Menachem Begin*.
2. Begin, *White Nights*.
3. Hoffman, *Anonymous Soldiers*, 123–24.

4. Begin, *Revolt*.

5. Begin, *Basic Outlines of Our Life-Worldview and Our National Outlook*, 32.

6. Begin, *Basic Outlines of Our Life-Worldview and Our National Outlook*, 32–33.

7. Wazana, *All the Boundaries of the Land*.

8. Ben-Bassat and Ben-Artzi, "Collision of Empires as Seen from Istanbul."

9. On the modern definitions of boundaries for Palestine/Eretz Israel, see Biger, *Boundaries of Modern Palestine, 1840–1947*.

10. Gruweis-Kovalsky, "Map as an Official Symbol and the 'Greater Israel' Ideology."

11. A. Goldstein, "Crisis and Development," 120; Shelef, "From 'Both Banks of the Jordan' to the 'Whole Land of Israel.'"

12. Naor, *Greater Israel*, 100.

13. A. Goldstein, "Crisis and Development," 120.

14. As Naor points out, Begin made a clear distinction in summer 1967—following the war—between "Western Eretz Israel," which was under the control of the State of Israel, and other regions of the Promised Land that weren't. He did not argue based on historical rights sovereignty over the Hashemite Kingdom of Jordan, and he also did not demand to implement Israel's sovereignty over the Sinai or Golan Heights, although they were under Israeli control. Naor, *Greater Israel*, 67.

15. Naor, *Greater Israel*, 185.

16. John P. Deeben, "Serving at the Pleasure of the President," *Prologue Magazine* 37, no.4 (Winter 2005).

17. Putnam, "Diplomacy and Domestic Politics."

18. Stein, *Heroic Diplomacy*, 3.

19. Stein, *Heroic Diplomacy*, 25–27.

20. Stein, *Heroic Diplomacy*, 26, 37, 43.

21. Kelman, "Political Psychology of the Israeli-Palestinian Conflict"; Kriesberg, "Mediation and the Transformation of the Israeli-Palestinian Conflict"; Steinberg, "Limits of Peacebuilding Theory."

22. Zartman, "Ripeness"; Zartman, *Ripe for Resolution*.

23. From Israel's side, Dayan, *Breakthrough*; Weizman, *Battle for Peace*; Ben-Elissar, *No More War*; Rubinstein, *Paths of Peace*; Tamir, *Soldier in Search of Peace*. From Egypt, el-Sadat, *In Search of Identity*; Boutros-Ghali, *Egypt's Road to Jerusalem*; Fahmy, *Negotiating for Peace in the Middle East*. From the United States, J. Carter, *Keeping Faith*; Vance, *Hard Choices*; Brzezinski, *Power and Principle*. Journalistic accounts include Haber, Schiff, and Yaari, *Year of the Dove*; Marcus, *Camp David*; Benziman, *Prime Minister under Siege*.

24. Bar-Siman-Tov, *Israel and the Peace Process, 1977–1982*; Quandt, *Camp David*; Stein, *Heroic Diplomacy*; Telhami, *Power and Leadership in International Bargaining*; Spiegel, *The Other Arab-Israeli Conflict*; Touval, *The Peace Brokers*; among others.

25. Howard, *Foreign Relations of the United States* [hereafter cited as FRUS], 1977–1980, vol. 8, Arab-Israeli Dispute, January 1977–August 1978; Howard, *FRUS*, 1977–1980, vol. 9, Arab-Israeli Dispute, August 1978–December 1980; Strieff, *Jimmy Carter and the Middle East*.

1 The Six-Day War and the Emergence of Begin's Approach to Peace

1967–70

THE MOMENTOUS EVENTS surrounding the 1967 Six-Day War marked a fundamental change in Menachem Begin's role in Israeli politics and the policymaking process. For the two decades of Israeli independence prior to this crisis, Herut, as a political movement, and Begin, as an individual, had been totally excluded from the structure of government. The legacy of the bitter rivalries of the underground and prestate years left political, psychological, and societal rifts. Under Ben-Gurion and, later, Eshkol, the dominant Mapai leadership refused to even consider coalition governments with Herut.

However, in time, the gaps narrowed, and the common objectives and shared experiences eroded the legacy of the historical clashes. Despite the boycott from Israel's elite, Begin's reputation grew as an effective parliamentarian and a knowledgeable member of the Knesset's Foreign Affairs and Defense Committee. As Israel faced the gravest crisis since 1948, Prime Minister Levi Eshkol was perceived as hesitant and lacking resolve. Conditions were prime for expanding the governing coalition, giving Begin an important opening.

The crisis had many origins, including great power politics related to Cold War competition, conflicts over water, domestic political processes in the Arab states (particularly in Syria), and inter-Arab dynamics. The combination of these factors seemed to be propelling the Arab armies, which had been unified under Egyptian command, toward another war to annihilate Israel. Nasser's sudden expulsion of the UN buffer forces in the Sinai, the massing of Egyptian forces along the border, the closing of the Red Sea to Israeli shipping, mobilization of the Syrian army, and the rhetoric of war and threat of destruction in Nasser's speeches all seemed to point to an imminent confrontation.[1]

During the weeks of tension and crisis preceding the war, Israelis prepared themselves, and the political mood was bleak. On June 1, the Rafi Party (including Moshe Dayan and Shimon Peres), which had splintered from Mapai in 1965, as well as the Gahal bloc, led by Menachem Begin—both opposition parties—joined to form a National Unity Government.[2] Dayan was appointed defense minister, and Begin became minister without portfolio and, more importantly, a member of the Ministerial Defense Committee.[3] In agreeing to join the Unity Government, Begin reversed an early decision from the beginning of the 1960s in which he declared his opposition to this framework, which he viewed as contrary to the norms of democracy.[4]

For members of Gahal, and for Begin in particular, these events marked a number of important transformations. The prohibition on including Begin in coalition governments imposed by Ben-Gurion was gone, and Herut leaders were now able to play a direct role in decision-making at the highest levels. The energetic Begin, fifty-four at the time, quickly became involved in important policy decisions prior to, during, and after the war that began on June 5, 1967. When Begin became prime minister in 1977, his actions and views reflected many of the positions that he took during the three years in which he served in the Unity Government

As head of the opposition in the Knesset during the developing crisis, Begin kept a relatively low profile. As Nasser "tightened the noose around Israel's neck," Begin was not yet a government minister and was excluded from formal decision-making. However, in a move that echoed the 1940 wartime decision by the British Conservative leadership to install Churchill in place of Chamberlin, Begin quietly went to his archrival, Ben-Gurion, who had retired as prime minister in 1963 and since then remained a member of the Knesset as part of Rafi. During that meeting, Begin reportedly appealed to the "Old Man" to preside over a War Cabinet (i.e., replacing Eshkol) to reassure and lead the nation on the brink of what was expected to be a terrible war. While there are different versions of this meeting and Ben-Gurion's response to Begin, the initiative set a broader process in motion.[5]

Others, including some from the National Religious Party, led by Minister of Interior Haim Moshe Shapira, joined in pressing Eshkol to establish a wall-to-wall unity government. According to the journalist Eric Silver, Begin insisted on Dayan's appointment as minister of defense and on including Rafi in any unity coalition. Yechiel Kadishai recalled that Begin was "less concerned with Dayan's activist reputation than with ensuring as wide a span of unity as possible. In the end, Eshkol yielded to the clamor of public opinion, and to Begin."[6]

The new cabinet met on June 1,[7] and Begin gave his first speech as a minister, invoking Jewish history and the centrality of national survival.[8] Throughout this period, Begin—as a member of the Knesset Committee on Foreign Affairs and Defense and then as a cabinet minister—spoke out in favor of a preemptive strike. This position reflected the high regard that Begin always held for the Israel Defense Forces (IDF) as well as his view that to survive, the Jewish nation must be able to use their military power. On this strategic basis, and despite very different political and ideological views, Begin developed a close working relationship with Yigal Allon, and together they formed the more "hawkish" wing of the unity cabinet.[9]

However, Begin also argued repeatedly that Jewish sovereignty in the Land of Israel is based on what he referred to as a historical right, in contrast to the right of force. In a speech to the fourth Herut committee conference on October 1, 1956, he criticized Ben-Gurion's government for justifying Israel's territorial gains in the 1948 War of Independence (beyond the territory determined by the UN Partition Plan) by relying on military success: "This answer destroys ["assassinates" in the original Hebrew] not only the truth, it destroys the essence of our existence. It is a presumption of a small, power-intoxicated nation, on physical power that we do not possess. Right versus power or power versus right? What is the true Hebrew philosophy, since the ancient days and until now?" When Herut establishes a new government, Begin continued, it will tell the world that "there is no 'occupation' or 'expansion' but a historical restoration of a right that was trampled and deprived by force."[10]

Eleven years later, on the eve of war, Begin's faith in military power had increased significantly, although during the cabinet meeting on June 4, he suggested sending Mossad head Meir Amit to Paris, London, and Washington to gain support and delay the war by several more days.[11] But in the final vote, Begin supported the decision to attack.

Begin's Role in Decision-Making during the War

Operational decisions in war are usually made by the prime minister, minister of defense, and chief of staff, while other ministers receive updates and participate in the cabinet meetings on broader political and strategic issues. Thus, on June 4, 1967, the government delegated Defense Minister Dayan and Chief of Staff Yitzhak Rabin to decide when to launch the preemptive strike. But once the war began on June 5, Begin pressed the government and military to move quickly in achieving central objectives. He focused on Jerusalem, seeing the fighting as an opportunity to reverse the loss of the Old City and the destruction of the Jewish Quarter in the 1948 War of Independence. (In 1969, at a dedication of a memorial to members of the Irgun Zvai Leumi (IZL), Begin criticized the decision in 1948 to forgo more attempts to retake the Jewish Quarter: "Israel should not have felt bound by ceasefire as long as the other side was still violating it. . . . We could even then have liberated the Old City and reached the Jordan River. . . . If Israelis had been successful then no one today would speak of an occupied city or of occupied territory . . . but twenty years from now no one will speak of occupied city or occupied territory."[12])

On the first day of fighting, after signs of Jordanian collapse, Begin (along with Allon) urged the liberation of the Old City and Jewish Jerusalem, arguing with opponents concerned about the political costs of such a move, including fear of worldwide Christian protests and possible military intervention by the Soviet

Union. According to Silver, Begin sent his close confident Yechiel Kadishai to intercept Eshkol at the Knesset and request an urgent cabinet meeting on Jerusalem, to which the prime minister agreed.[13] The meeting, focusing on Jerusalem, was held in the Knesset's underground shelter while the building was under Jordanian artillery attack. This was described later as "perhaps the most important cabinet meeting Jerusalem ever held."[14]

Begin began with a dramatic declaration: "This is the hour of our political test. . . . We must attack the Old City in response both to the unheeded warnings we sent Hussein as well as to the Jordanian shelling." Others, including Allon and even Mordechai Bentov from the far-left Mapam party, agreed with Begin, but Eshkol and Foreign Minister Abba Eban urged a more cautious approach. Eshkol adjourned the meeting without a decision to act but with the recognition that this was not the final word and "an opportunity has perhaps been created to recapture the Old City."[15] According to Silver, "the meeting voted unanimously to take the Old City," but out of concern regarding possible damage to the sacred sites, the army was ordered to encircle it in the hope that the Jordanian forces would surrender.[16]

During the session of the Ministerial Defense Committee on June 6 (day two of the war), Begin warned of political efforts centered in the United Nations to reach an immediate ceasefire (to be enforced by the United States and, more worryingly, the Soviet Union). If this occurred, Begin advised that "we are liable to remain outside the walls of Jerusalem as we did in 1948." He even called for a march led by the country's leaders through the armistice lines and directly to the Western Wall to reestablish Jewish rights and presence at this sacred religious site.[17]

By that evening, Israeli forces had captured parts of the Jordanian-controlled West Bank, had surrounded Jerusalem to prevent the arrival of reinforcements, and were moving into position around the Old City, including the Western Wall and the Temple Mount. At the same time, the Arab states and their supporters demanded a UN Security Council resolution ordering a ceasefire. Making the most of his new role, the peripatetic Begin camped out in the almost deserted King David Hotel in Jerusalem, located along the 1949 armistice lines, and walked the streets nearby, observing the action and military preparations.[18] After listening to the 4:00 a.m. BBC news, Begin reportedly called Defense Minister Dayan, urging him to accelerate the operation to recapture Jerusalem and noting, "The Security Council's decision changes the whole situation. . . . We must not wait a second more."[19] Dayan told Begin to contact Eshkol, and after apologizing for waking him, Begin asked the prime minister to convene an emergency cabinet meeting no later than 7:00 a.m.[20] (According to Silver, Begin called Eshkol first, and the prime minister told him to speak to Dayan; after gaining the defense minister's support of an immediate operation to take Jerusalem, he returned to Eshkol.[21])

Israeli ground and air forces, under strict instructions to avoid damage to holy sites, provided support for the operation in Jerusalem, which began at 6:00 a.m. Within a few hours, and before the UN Security Council could act, Israel had taken the Old City and returned the Western Wall and Temple Mount to Jewish control.

Begin immediately initiated discussions on rebuilding the Jewish Quarter, which had been desecrated and was left in ruins after the 1948 war and during the following two decades of Jordanian control, in which time no Jews were allowed to set foot in the Old City.[22] In a cabinet meeting immediately after the ceasefire on June 11, Begin introduced legislation under the heading "Jerusalem—Capital of Israel." Many members of the government supported this proposal, including the dovish Abba Eban. Begin also objected to the use of the term "annexation" with regard to the Old City, stating that Jerusalem had been liberated, not occupied.[23] Applying the same logic, he later rejected the idea of the annexation of Judea, Samaria, and Gaza to Israel, claiming that these are parts of the homeland and one does not annex one's homeland.[24]

Begin was also a member of the "Golan lobby" and supported Dayan's decision to reverse his earlier stand against attacking Syria.[25] While this operation was taking place, some members of the Ministerial Defense Committee sought to halt the advance, angrily noting that in an earlier meeting, held during the night prior to the attack, the committee had decided against authorizing the IDF to undertake this mission. Begin joined Allon, Yisrael Galili, and others in rejecting this criticism and defended Dayan and Eshkol for using their authority legitimately. He observed, "In the days of Maria Theresa [in the Austro-Hungarian Empire] there was a law that said that if a soldier broke discipline but performed an act of bravery, he would get both a demerit and a medal."[26]

Begin's Role in Postwar Diplomacy

After the ceasefire, the government's focus shifted to diplomacy. Many Israelis believed that the Arab states would now recognize that they had no choice but to accept the permanence of Israel and agree to negotiate peace agreements with the Jewish state. Dayan said that he was "waiting for the phone to ring" with an offer to begin negotiations.[27]

Begin naturally had strong views on these issues, agreeing in general to the principle of "land for peace" with Egypt and Syria while emphasizing the centrality of peace treaties rather than temporary armistice agreements as in the past. Like other Israeli leaders, Begin was determined to avoid a repetition of the 1949 experience, in which territory captured by Israel was relinquished as part of limited ceasefire agreements while Arab commitments to negotiate permanent treaties were subsequently ignored. This time, to regain land, Begin insisted that Egypt and Syria sign full-fledged peace treaties.

As the scale of the Arab defeat unfolded, the Soviet Union demanded an emergency session of the UN Security Council that would order Israel to withdraw from all of the newly occupied territories. The United States considered the options and asked for Israel's views regarding postwar negotiations. Thus, immediately after the war ended, Israel was pressed to develop a coherent policy.[28]

The cabinet held several closed sessions between June 15 and 19, 1967, to form a reply to Washington and to instruct Eban prior to his scheduled speech at the United Nations.[29] Begin was first to speak in the Ministerial Committee for Security Affairs on June 15, stating a readiness to return Sinai to Egypt as part of a peace treaty—but not unconditionally. He argued that the Gaza Strip must become an integral part of Israel (he did not use the word "annexation"); Sinai must be demilitarized, and an Israeli force must remain in Sharm El Sheikh; and Egypt must acknowledge Israel's right to use the Suez Canal. Begin was willing to return the Golan Heights to Syria if this area were demilitarized.

Regarding Jordan, Begin supported a peace treaty with King Hussein but only as the ruler of the eastern bank of the Jordan River. Begin's willingness to make peace with Hussein was a deviation from his party's long-held position that Jordan was an illegitimate country, illegally torn off from mandatory Palestine. But this postwar position is less surprising than Begin's policy during the war, when he supported Eshkol's letter to Hussein offering restraint if Jordan's military stayed out of the conflict. This signaled implicit acceptance of the status quo (which Begin had rejected for eighteen years), including Hashemite control over the West Bank and even in Jerusalem's Old City.[30] But now, given the results of the war, he declared that the State of Israel must be seen as encompassing all of Eretz Israel. The Arab population in the West Bank would be given residence status for seven years, after which they would have to decide whether to become Israeli citizens or to emigrate. Begin believed that during this seven-year period, a massive expansion in the Jewish population would create a majority in these areas. He spoke optimistically about an economic union between Israel and Jordan and again erased the long-term Herut position that claimed "both banks of the Jordan" for Israel. Regarding the refugees currently in the Gaza Strip, Begin called for settling them in El-Arish in the Sinai.[31]

Begin, like other Israeli leaders, was trying to adjust quickly to the new strategic reality, largely based on his realist approach but also integrating and adjusting the ideological component. This dualism, which was reflected in his rejection of the "land for peace" equation for the West Bank and Gaza, would later become a major source of confrontations with foreign leaders before and during his tenure as prime minister. In 1967, as a member of the government for the first time and wishing to play a major role, Begin accepted the necessary compromises while trying to maintain the core Revisionist ideology. This careful balancing was reflected in his decision to sign the June 19 resolution offering to exchange the Sinai and the Golan Heights for full peace agreements while excluding the territory wrested from Jordanian control. Begin was not alone in these views, but on the Palestinian issue, he stood out in basing his position on Ze'ev Jabotinsky's writings.

In this central session, which laid out the postwar political and diplomatic framework, Begin was the first to speak and set the terms for the discussion; others related to his ideas, some supporting and some opposed, with many nuances. In the next stage, the cabinet debated a written summary of the main positions but could not resolve the Jordanian issue; therefore, it does not appear in the official memorandum. The only partial reference can be seen in the brief mention of the refugee issue, noting that "peace in the Middle East will open options for regional cooperation to solve the refugee problem."[32] On Egypt and Syria, the "land for peace" formula was consistent with Begin's position.

Although not a Revisionist by any measure, Allon had much stronger views than Begin on Jordan. He opposed seeking a peace agreement, arguing that "we must forget nostalgia concerning the Hashemite House—Abdullah (Hussein's grandfather) fooled us."[33] He called for annexing Judea, including Jerusalem and the northwest coast of the Dead Sea, and making Samaria (the northern West Bank) a semi-independent entity. In addition, he proposed the Jordan Valley should be settled by Jews as a defensive barrier between Samaria and Jordan. Concerning Egypt and Syria, Allon's view was similar to Begin's, but he wanted to adjust the border with Syria by adding the sources of the Baniyas River to Israel (to prevent renewed attempts to divert them). Eban did not accept Allon's views on border changes but agreed with Begin and Allon regarding Egypt.

Dayan predicted that Egypt and Syria would reject Israel's offer and joined Begin and Allon in viewing the Jordan River as Israel's eastern border. He said that the West Bank would be "under martial law," and there would be no concessions.

On the other side, several ministers favored an immediate effort to reach a political solution with Jordan, and others saw the West Bank as a "deposit" to be returned eventually—wholly or partially—to Jordan. Dayan repeatedly spoke about realism, rejecting claims that Israel could force a political arrangement unilaterally in the West Bank, and argued that a basis for discussions with Hussein existed. In this context, Eshkol did not take a position.[34]

On June 18, as the closed discussions were ongoing within the cabinet, Begin made a public statement before party supporters in Tel Aviv, declaring that "if there is no peace treaty between Israel and its neighbors, or willingness to make such a treaty, we will not surrender any territory conquered by the Defense Forces." He highlighted the conditions "necessary to prevent any threat to our security in the future." However, even if such terms were forthcoming, Begin announced, "It is simply unthinkable that we would return an inch of eastern Eretz

Israel . . . to Jordan. . . . If we display necessary courage, the fruit of victory will remain in our hands." Addressing demands from the Soviet Union that Israel return immediately to the 1949 armistice lines, he emphasized, "We are not the Jews you remember from the pogroms. . . . We are a new nation that will not bow its head before any power."[35]

The next day (June 19), the cabinet debate continued, reaching a consensus on the Egyptian and Syrian dimensions but leaving the future status of Judea and Samaria unresolved. After a close vote (10 to 9) in favor of proposing peace treaties with Egypt and Syria based on the international border and Israel's security needs (to which Dayan objected, warning that he would change his vote and demand to retain the Golan Heights), a special ministerial committee was appointed. The committee formulated a proposal to seek treaties with Egypt and Syria based on the international borders of mandatory Palestine, which would include demilitarization of the Sinai and the Golan, free navigation in the Suez Canal [vis-à-vis Egypt], and a guarantee of unobstructed water flow from Syria into the Jordan River.[36] The agreed proposal did not include Judea and Samaria, and Jerusalem was to remain Israel's permanent undivided capital, excluded in any "land for peace" discussions.[37] This proposal was approved unanimously.[38]

The text was sent to Foreign Minister Eban, who had left for the United States and—according to his autobiography—presented it to Secretary of State Dean Rusk, Ambassador Arthur Goldberg, Undersecretary Eugene Rostow, Assistant Secretary Joseph Sisco, and others. Eban wrote that the Americans were astounded by Israel's willingness to give up the territory so soon after their sweeping victory in return for a permanent peace. According to Eban, the United States reluctantly presented the proposal to the governments of Egypt and Syria, who rejected the terms, demanding unconditional withdrawal.[39] Later, Eban's description was questioned, and critics argue that he created the myth of Israel's generous peace proposal.[40]

In these critical discussions, Begin introduced many of the arguments and themes that he would use and repeat in later debates and negotiations, including those with Carter and at Camp David. He reemphasized the distinction between the Judea and Samaria districts of the West Bank, on the one hand, and the other territories (the Sinai and Golan), on the other. He noted that Israel captured the Sinai and the Golan primarily for security reasons but that Judea and Samaria were fundamentally different. Jordanian control from 1948 to 1967, he noted, was the result of illegal seizure through the use of force and occupation.[41] Some ministers, including Dayan, favored Palestinian autonomy, but Begin disagreed intensely, arguing that "the concept of autonomy will lead to a Palestinian state," which was unacceptable.[42] (A decade later, as prime minister, Begin would be confronted with this support for autonomy. The 1967 version referred to an entity with a clear territorial definition. Ten years later, Begin's autonomy proposal was nonterritorial, referring to individuals—in this case, Palestinians in the West Bank—and excluding Jerusalem, fearing that any territorial dimension to such an autonomy would end in statehood, which he opposed fiercely.) According to aide and military secretary Yisrael Lior, in several private conversations Eshkol expressed a readiness to accept the establishment of a Palestinian state in Judea and Samaria.[43]

Begin also rejected the political segmentation in Judea and Samaria: "There is not just one canton. There are cantons, and if we agree to an Arab canton, we will have to accept a Jewish canton too. . . . We cannot offer the world an Arab canton, and we must eliminate this term from our discussion, because it might force us to cantonize Eretz Israel. If we establish cantons in Nablus, Jenin and Tul Karem, is it possible to explain why we did not establish a canton in Gaza?"[44]

Begin was also firmly against the autonomy plan favored by Dayan because, he stated, "I believe the term autonomy leads to a Palestinian state by the very essence of the issue. . . . If we say autonomy, it's an invitation for an independent-Arab-Palestinian state." Again, it seems that Begin's opposition to autonomy was based on the terms that Israel would offer, fearing plans that included territorial dimensions that would then be difficult, if not impossible, to reverse. He was also firmly against handing territory over to King Hussein's control: "Is it for this that we have gone to war? It is a fact that one could have shelled the central area of Israel from Kalkilya. Why shouldn't it happen again?"[45]

Begin, unlike Dayan, claimed it was up to Israel to deal with the refugee issue while rejecting proposals to transfer refugees from the Gaza Strip to the West Bank: "I don't understand how one can offer to transfer 200 thousand refugees from the Gaza Strip to somewhere else. Will that solve the problem?" He considered proposing to settle them in El Arish, as Yigal Allon suggested: "Once the entire People of Israel sought a solution in El Arish; why is it inappropriate?"[46]

Reuven Pedatzur, who closely analyzed secondary reports of the cabinet meeting (before the protocols were declassified), concluded that Begin refused to support any plan that yielded Israel's control over the West Bank, but he had no formula of his own. He based his demand to keep Judea and Samaria on security reasons, not historical or religious ones: "As to Western Eretz Israel, I prefer to say that Israel's sovereignty reaches the Jordan River rather than to say the Jordan River is the border."[47]

On July 26, 1967, Begin spoke at a Herut meeting, saying that government policy was to achieve peace treaties with security assurances, but until such treaties were achieved, Israel would not move from its current position. He said Arab demands to return captured territories were irrelevant since Israel was acting to defend itself, and therefore the territorial changes were not illegal as the Arabs claimed. Regarding the Arab population, Begin said that Zionism demanded a Jewish majority in Israel, not a single-ethnic state.[48]

On August 14, the cabinet held a discussion on permanent borders. Dayan suggested building four military camps in the Samaria hills, but not in the Palestinian cities, so the bases would not prevent the implementation of the autonomy plan. Begin accepted the suggestion but criticized Dayan for calling the Jordan River a security border instead of a political one.[49] Ironically, a decade later, as prime minister, during his presentation of the autonomy plan to the Carter administration, Begin himself referred to the Jordan River as Israel's security border and not its political one.

While Begin held fast to most of his core beliefs on autonomy, he tried out different details as the debate continued. According to Avidan, the subject was discussed in a later cabinet meeting (no date available but before December 1967), and Begin again referred to Judea and Samaria as part of Eretz Israel and raised the idea of granting the Palestinians temporary citizenship. He said he was against a binational state but also mentioned that Zionism never objected to a biethnic state. However, he did not explain this statement.[50] In December 1967, Begin declared, "Not only do we stay, but we settle and make a stronghold from the positions and areas the IDF had reached while overcoming aggression six months ago."[51]

At the time, this view reflected a consensus in the cabinet, particularly after the Khartoum Conference in August 1967. This meeting of the Arab League set Arab policy toward Israel for the following years. The final statement included the three "noes": no peace, no recognition, and no negotiations. In a speech before the Herut leadership on October 24, 1967, Begin referred to the Khartoum declaration as reinforcing the government decision to maintain the status quo, justified by international law as well as Israeli security and rights.[52]

Foreign Minister Eban was one of Begin's sharpest opponents regarding retaining control over the West Bank, noting that by 1985 the Palestinians would comprise 40 percent of Israel's population. He also rejected an independent Palestinian entity, preferring to return the territories to Jordanian control, although ensuring that the Jordan River would be the security border (meaning no Arab armies in the West Bank), and holding Jerusalem. Begin responded, claiming that "accepting [Eban's plan] will be the first time since the destruction of the Second Temple that we divide Eretz Israel. . . . A year ago we were willing to make peace based on the Armistice Lines, but now, [the idea] that we offer or agree to divide [the land] shivers my heart." In an unusual personal statement, Begin continued, "I admit I espouse sentiment."[53]

Begin also demanded a revision in the June 19 decision regarding Egypt, arguing that Egypt's acquisition of surface-to-surface rockets required holding on to the Sinai. He added, "I dream of peace negotiations with the Arabs, but the treaty itself does not ensure peace. If Hussein returns to the West Bank, there is danger of [building] an Arab military force—an annihilation danger. Maybe not

[in] one year or even five, but we must consider our grandchildren." He asked the IDF chief of staff whether a security border existed west of the Jordan River, answering his own question: "We must not move a single step from the river—on security grounds."[54]

The December 1967 discussions were held to craft guidelines for Eshkol's meetings with President Johnson the following month. The long discussions did not result in any fundamental agreement among the members of the cabinet. Begin's was one of various views expressed during the discussions. Eventually, the cabinet prepared a document for Eshkol with four separate opinions reflecting the views of Begin, Dayan, Allon, and Zalman Aran (minister of education). The peace initiative of June 19 received diluted attention and was largely removed from the document.[55]

On July 30, 1967, by unanimous vote, the cabinet adopted a resolution declaring that "Israeli forces would not withdraw from the ceasefire lines except as a result of direct negotiations with the Arab countries concerned."[56] Begin's views were largely referred to in this position. Immediately afterward, the government formulated a proposal to Egypt and Syria that included withdrawal to the international borders, demilitarization of the Sinai and Golan, and a full and formal peace settlement. This proposal was summarily rejected by the Arabs and accompanied by the demand for full and unconditional Israeli withdrawal.[57]

Begin was also deeply involved in formulating Israeli policy regarding UN Security Council Resolution 242, seeking to avoid a formal commitment to withdrawal. In an interview published in 1970, after he had left the Unity Government, Begin stated, "Three times it was proposed to the Cabinet to use the word 'withdrawal' and the Cabinet refused. . . . The Prime Minister was asked by one of my colleagues in the Cabinet what the difference was. . . . [Eshkol replied:] 'If we say withdrawal, then we're committed to it. If we say [re]deployment of forces, then Eban will interpret the way he thinks right, and Begin will interpret it the way he thinks right.'"[58] Later, Begin rejected "[re]deployment of forces" as suggesting preparation for war, replacing the term with "disposition of forces." According to Begin, "Withdrawal means moving backwards. . . . In disposition there is no movement. It will be decided by the borders, as determined in the peace treaty."[59]

In the months after the war, Begin, like other Israelis, understood that the Arab leaders were not likely to accept the Israeli terms of exchanging "land for peace." The internal debates on the terms of possible negotiations and borders with Egypt and Syria lost their urgency.

At the same time, Begin criticized what he saw as weakness among some government ministers and declared that Israel need not apologize for defending itself against its enemies while the Arab leaders continue to declare their intention "to annihilate us."[60] Begin cited the frequent calls by Arab leaders for the destruction of Israel. For example, in December 1967, upon returning from a trip to Moscow, Nasser repeated the Khartoum formula.[61] Begin compared Nasser's declarations to Nazi propaganda, noting that such speeches were clear evidence that despite talk of peace, the Arabs' "sole purpose is the complete destruction of Israel."[62] This was familiar ground to Begin, resonating in terms of his personal experience and understanding of history—particularly Jewish history.

In December 1967, Begin noted, "In view of Nasser's declared policy of refusing to come to terms with Israel, it is no longer a mere assumption but a definite conclusion that Israel will not only stay, but will settle in occupied areas."[63] Recalling his legal training, Begin declared, "According to international law there is no obligation to withdraw from ceasefire lines until a peace treaty is signed."[64] Begin insisted that since Israel had responded to Arab aggression, "it has the right, under international law to make territorial adjustments . . . after the war until peace treaties are signed."[65] Begin also emphasized the importance of the Israeli presence in Sinai, particularly on security grounds.[66] In the event of a fundamental change in Arab policy with respect to Israel and readiness to negotiate peace treaties, the principle of "land for peace" remained acceptable. But until such a fundamental change took place, settlement activity would continue and expand.

In contrast, with respect to the West Bank, even with a basic change in Arab policy and the willingness to exchange land for peace, this territory was not part of the potential negotiation package. Begin often repeated that Judea and Samaria "are integral parts of the Land of Israel and there is no question about returning them," regardless of political developments or an eventual end to Arab rejectionism.[67] In September 1967, when the first outposts of the Etzion bloc outside of Jerusalem were reestablished (they were Jewish settlements prior to being overrun in the 1948 war), Herut released a statement of congratulations.[68] One year later, in September 1968, Begin said at a party meeting, "Settlement in the administrated areas is not only our right. Intensifying such settlement is also a duty and imperative for our national security."[69] Begin not only supported the establishment of new Jewish settlements, but he also called for Jewish suburbs (*krayot*) within Arab cities such as Jericho, Bethlehem, Ramallah, and Gaza.[70]

On these issues, Begin's rhetoric reflected a strong sentimental attachment to the land, reinforced by his ideological commitment and the moral or legal justifications as he understood them. As minister without portfolio and a second-tier, albeit influential, member of the government, he could afford to go beyond weighing policy options based on a realist cost-benefit approach.

"The Land of Our Forefathers"

Begin was not religious, but unlike the leaders of Mapai, including Dayan, Allon, Eshkol, and Eban, he was also not a strong secularist. Instead, as a Jewish traditionalist, Begin invoked the language of Jewish history and traditional texts, including the Hebrew Bible, with which he was very familiar, and appealed to religious and secular Israelis alike. His view of history and the role of the Jewish nation was strongly shaped by the cultural and religious heritage and was reflected in his positions on Jerusalem and the territories in Eretz Israel—the Land of Israel.

The drafting of policy on Jerusalem immediately after the war was assigned to Foreign Minister Eban, NRP leader and Minister of Religious Affairs Zerach Warhaftig, and Begin. Begin's red lines were clear and consistent: Israel "does not claim unilateral control or exclusive jurisdiction in the holy places of Christianity and Islam" and is prepared to give "appropriate expression" to this principle in the event of a peace agreement.[71] But for Begin, as for most Israelis, including Eban and Warhaftig, the return to sacred Jerusalem, containing the Jewish Quarter, the Western Wall, and the Temple Mount, was not negotiable in any form.[72]

In December 1968, when discussions of the "Jordanian option" intensified as Mapai, and Allon in particular, began to float different ideas, Begin demanded, "We must stop talking about returning territory to King Hussein. These territories were returned to the people of Israel."[73] On another occasion, Begin responded fiercely and sardonically to criticism of the government's policy of "freeing our ancestral heritage" and advised the head of left-wing Mapam, which strongly opposed all settlements, to apologize to the patriarchs Abraham, Isaac, and Jacob as well as Moses the Lawgiver. "It is peculiar after so many years to hear a Zionist leader talking in such a manner. After all, did not all Zionist youth movements sing of returning to the land of our forefathers?"[74] In cabinet discussions, Begin declared that withdrawal without a treaty was unthinkable: "The Coalition would not have remained in existence for a single minute had it taken a decision to withdraw. . . . The Land of Israel is ours forever."[75]

At the same time, Begin did not ignore the arguments against settlement in the administered territories of Eretz Israel and, in particular, the demographic threat that the addition of a large Arab population in the areas under Israeli control would overwhelm the Jewish majority. His responses, particularly on demography, were again largely emotional and historical. In a speech to a group of students in Jerusalem, Begin stated that "no other nation in the world ever voluntarily relinquished part of its homeland because of a so-called demographic problem. Why should our nation whose very soul is bound up in Eretz Israel down through the ages and through every dispersion be the one to do that? . . . Right is the bedrock of our presence in this country. Our faith in this right is the source of our return. . . . If we stand by our rights, they will stand by us." He also declared that "the demographic problem can be solved by maintaining the large majority which we have built up in western Eretz Israel."[76] He also believed the demographic issue could be solved by encouraging large-scale Jewish immigration (*aliyah*), as well as increasing the Israeli birthrate (based on a French model).

He did not call for annexation of all of the occupied territories, repeating that "one does not annex one's own territory."[77] Later, Begin declared that the Herut movement has "always advocated the right of the Jewish People to all of the Land of Israel."[78] In April 1969, he explicitly called for the application of Israeli law in the territories.[79]

Begin's Responses to International Pressure

The intense international efforts to catalyze Middle East peace negotiations following the war in 1967 had major impacts on Israeli government policies in general and on Begin's policies in particular. The first major effort was conducted within the framework of the UN Security Council, leading to the adoption of Resolution 242 on November 22, 1967. The British ambassador to the United Nations, Lord Caradon (Hugh Foot), led the negotiations, and the text included a declaration that the acquisition of territory by war was unacceptable; called for Israeli withdrawal from occupied territories linked to the "acknowledgement of the sovereignty, territorial integrity and political independence of every State in the area and their right to live in peace within secure and recognized boundaries free from threats or acts of force"; specified the need for free navigation in international water, a solution to the refugee problem, and guaranteeing the safety and political freedom of "every state in the area." The resolution also called for the appointment of a UN special representative to promote the application of these proposals.[80]

The adoption of Resolution 242 became a central issue. Egypt's President Nasser formally announced public acceptance of the terms while also endorsing the opposite, pledging that "what was taken by force will be returned by force."[81] Jordan also accepted the terms, and Syria denounced both Egypt and Jordan for this position. The Israeli cabinet was divided, with some favoring acceptance, others calling for qualified adoption, and others, including Begin and Allon, opposed. For Begin, the use of the term "withdrawal" rather than "disposition" was enough to invalidate this resolution as the basis for negotiations.

Following the initial rejection of UNSRC 242 by Israel and Syria, the UN secretary general appointed Gunnar Jarring (a Swedish diplomat) as the special negotiator. Jarring held a series of separate meetings with Israeli and Arab officials but made no progress. He saw his mandate as limited to indirect discussions and not facilitating face-to-face negotiations, as Israel had demanded.[82]

In May 1968, an Egyptian source leaked information that was published in the international press claiming that Jarring had sent a letter to UN Secretary General U Thant, saying that both sides had agreed to accept the full terms of Resolution 242. (In fact, Jarring's letter suggested a draft text, but after the Israeli rejection, it was never sent to the secretary general. Egypt's response is not known.) At the same time, Israel's UN ambassador, Yosef Tekoa, gave a speech that indicated Israel had accepted Resolution 242, and the press reported that Eban had informed Jarring.[83] In response, Gahal ministers Begin and Yosef Sapir met with Eshkol and demanded to know if this was indeed the case, and if so, who had authorized this decision. Eshkol and Eban explained that this was a necessary tactical move to ensure that the Arabs could not present themselves as the "peace-loving side" while Israel was portrayed as refusing to even discuss the resolution.[84] They further explained that Israel only accepted the resolution as a "call for just peace with agreed and safe borders" but had not committed itself to any details regarding implementation. Begin and Sapir were also concerned with the impression that Israel was prepared to accept the Jarring Plan, to which Eshkol responded that while officials had agreed to meet with Jarring, it was made clear to him that no decisions would be made unless an Arab representative agreed to attend the meeting.[85]

Many ministers (including Dayan, Allon, the NRP representatives, and others) criticized Eban's role on this issue, arguing that the full cabinet, and not only the prime minister, should have been consulted before Tekoa made this announcement. At the end of this debate, the government resolved that (a) the letter received from Jarring did not commit Israel, and (b) a peace treaty could only be achieved via direct talks. This resolution satisfied Gahal, and the National Unity Government was saved for the time being.[86]

On May 26, 1968, the Ninth Herut Convention was opened in the Old City of Jerusalem, not far from the Temple Mount. In his speech, Begin recalled the cabinet decision that "the only solution for establishing lasting peace in the Middle East is the signing of a peace treaty between Israel and the Arab States. A peace treaty can only be achieved by direct negotiations between the parties. . . . That is the policy of the National Unity Government, and that will remain its policy."[87] He hinted at the disagreements within the cabinet, saying there was no foreign policy of the minister of foreign affairs nor a security policy of the minister of defense but rather a policy of the government of Israel.

Begin proudly pointed to the role that Gahal played in demanding a full peace treaty at cabinet meetings, and after the government adopted the concept, this became official policy. Since there were "misunderstandings," he explained, "Not only does the idea of peace treaty not require any advance notice of concessions, but a peace treaty may lay down basic territorial changes. The defeat of an aggressor and the repulsion of aggression are international law. These are international precedents." Begin concluded his speech with the Herut "Declaration of the Rights of the Jewish People to its Homeland, to Liberty, Security and Peace," including a statement that no previous partition of Eretz Israel was legal but rather a result of colonial collusion or an act of violence (Article C) and that widespread settlement in Judea, Samaria and Gaza, the Golan Heights, and the Sinai was vital for assuring the nation's security (Article H).[88]

The cabinet conflict over Jarring's proposals intensified. Eban and Eshkol strongly favored discussions and negotiations on this basis, but Begin restated his opposition to indirect talks and to declarations on withdrawal from Judea and Samaria. However, Begin and the Gahal faction avoided triggering the breakup of the National Unity Government. In the Knesset, when the two-member Free Center Party (which broke off from Herut) called for a vote of no-confidence on this issue, Begin and Gahal were forced to choose between supporting the opposition's criticism regarding negotiations with Jarring, thereby resigning from the government, or supporting the government despite the intense disagreement. Gahal voted with the coalition.[89] According to Sofer, journalists close to Begin reported that "he was playing a major role in shaping a policy opposed to withdrawal, and was thwarting all initiatives that entailed renunciation by Israel of territories occupied in the war."[90]

Prime Minister Levi Eshkol died suddenly on February 26, 1969, and Golda Meir formed a new government on March 17.[91] The guidelines of Meir's coalition included the statement, drafted by Begin, that in the absence of a peace treaty, Israel would not return "to the vulnerable armistice lines and pre-1967 conditions, and will strengthen its hold in the territories according to its national security and development interest and needs."[92] Begin respected Golda Meir as a "proud Jewess" and approved of her stands on political matters.[93]

In October 1969, Israelis went to the polls to elect a new Knesset. The Alignment received fifty-six seats—the largest single-party outcome in Israel's history, while Gahal held its previous support at twenty-six seats. During the negotiations on forming a new coalition, Begin spoke to the Herut leadership. He said there were three agreed issues, allowing people with various views to sit together on the cabinet:

1. Peace treaties, and not alternative arrangements.
2. In the absence of a peace arrangement, Israel will remain on the armistice lines.
3. The June 4, 1967, line will never return.[94]

Golda Meir also agreed to say on the Knesset plenum, "Our forefathers' patrimony was liberated," using Begin's language at his request. Thus, on both substance and symbolism, Begin was seen as expanding his influence in the government.

During this period, the War of Attrition with Egypt escalated, and casualties mounted, bringing intensified negotiations for a ceasefire and greater pressure for an Israeli withdrawal. In May 1969, Begin stated that "the government was unanimous that without a directly negotiated peace treaty, Israeli forces will continue to hold the present lines and that Israel will never return to the June 4, 1967, lines."[95]

Begin's position was clear and consistent: only direct negotiations between government representatives would be acceptable, in contrast to the system of proximity talks used by UN mediator Ralph Bunche in 1949 during the Rhodes talks and as part of the Jarring approach. If the Arabs were ready for peace, reasoned Begin, they would talk directly to Israelis leaders. In addition, Begin declared that the government's pursuit of peace would have to be "in accordance with the decisions of the Knesset and the government since the Six Day War" (meaning no return to the 1948–49 ceasefire lines).[96]

In late 1969, following the major escalation of the fighting between Israel and Egypt, the Nixon administration became directly involved in the search for a diplomatic solution. This activity was led by Secretary of State William Rogers, who presented a new proposal on December 9, 1969. The Rogers Initiative took UNSCR 242 and the Jarring Plan as starting points and called for Israeli withdrawal from Sinai as part of an agreement to include partial demilitarization based on Israel's security requirements and unobstructed passage through the Suez Canal. The framework also called for negotiations on the future status of Gaza and Sharm-El-Sheikh. On December 18, the United States added a section including Israeli withdrawal from most of the West Bank, Jordanian sovereignty in east Jerusalem, and a solution for the refugee issue based on return or monetary compensation (as specified in UN Resolution 194, December 11, 1948). The new regime in Jerusalem would ensure unobstructed access to the sacred sites for all (including Jews, in contrast to the situation between 1949 and 1967).

The leaders of Israel and Egypt rejected the initial version of the initiative, while Jordan announced acceptance. Rogers presented a revised version in June 1970, proposing indirect Egyptian-Israeli negotiations, under Jarring's auspices, with the objective of achieving a peace treaty based on UNSCR 242. As a first step, Rogers called for a ceasefire in the War of Attrition, to be monitored by the United States. The Egyptians, who initially rejected this option, accepted it on July 31, and under heavy American pressure, as well as mounting casualties, Prime Minister Golda Meir's government debated the options and finally voted to accept the revised Rogers Plan.[97] As a result, the Israeli government agreed for the first time to the word "withdrawal" rather than "redeployment" in an official document.

Throughout the discussions on the Rogers Plan, the participation of Begin and Gahal in the government became increasingly problematic, and the disagreements with leading "doves" such as Abba Eban grew. For Begin, proposals to return to the dangerous pre-1967 ceasefire lines were totally anathema; he noted that the United Nation's goal was to force Israel back to the 1949 line with "minor adjustments."[98] In arguing against the proposal, Begin declared, "For 18 years Israel was divided and no peace treaty was forthcoming. Up to the Six Day War we lost 7,011 people and over 14,000 were wounded. The Rogers Plan would only push Israel back into this unacceptable situation, without bringing lasting peace."[99] He also rejected the argument that if Israel were seen as rejecting the various peace proposals, it would lead to diplomatic isolation and international criticism: "I think people in Israel should liberate themselves from this irrational fear of imagery. I have never heard of a people forgoing fundamental national interests in order to improve their public relations image."[100] To Begin, the achievements of the 1967 war demonstrated that Israel was no longer in need of external protection. "We should make it clear we refuse to be anybody's wards. If there are security problems we should solve them ourselves."[101]

Despite the earlier cooperation with Yigal Allon, Begin also rejected the peace framework Allon had proposed. The Allon Plan was based on a treaty that would transfer control of Palestinian cities in Judea and Samara back to Jordan while maintaining Israeli control of the unpopulated and desert areas of strategic importance, including the Jordan Valley. Although discussed for many years and widely supported within the Labor Party, the Allon Plan was never formally adopted.[102] In May 1970, Begin warned that if the government adopted the Allon Plan, Gahal would resign, and he argued repeatedly that withdrawal to the 1967 lines would not bring peace.[103]

In public appearances, Begin described the support for the Rogers Plan as a "fatal mistake. . . . The cry must go forth that the Homeland is in danger. . . . I have the same sense of impending danger threatening our people that Jabotinsky had when he warned our people in 1939 of the impending horrors. He was ignored and those who ignored him were destroyed."[104] If Israel agreed to "hand Samaria and Judea back to Hussein. . . [Yasir] Arafat and [George] Habash will follow. . . . We will then have Katyushas aimed at Jerusalem and light artillery pointing at our main centers of population."[105] Quoting Abba Eban from an earlier period in which the foreign minister declared that "when I look at June 4, 1967, borders I see Auschwitz before my eyes," Begin noted that "the Arabs insist on nothing less than these borders."[106] Israeli compromise and concessions on security were unthinkable to him.

Begin repeatedly condemned Golda Meir, Abba Eban, and other leaders for agreeing to consider any withdrawal (or redeployment) without a peace treaty. This situation, he warned, would lead to even greater dangers. "There was no mention of Nasser either recognizing or making peace yet Israel was obligated to withdraw to the 1949 Armistice Lines, with the Egyptian ruler still intent on pushing Israel back to 1947 lines."[107] Claims that real peace talks between Israel and Egypt could be conducted through Dr. Jarring or any other go-between were only "an illusion."[108] Later, he warned that "there can be no short cut to peace with people who seek our annihilation as a people and a state."[109]

Beyond emphasizing the dangers that returning to the pre-war situation would pose, he returned to the focus on Jewish history, further conflating his political identity with this theme: "How can we be false to our ancient heritage? How can we divide again our ancient homeland? How can we sign a promissory note to hand over our Homeland to foreign rulers? We will never sign."[110]

On August 4, Begin led Gahal out of the Unity Government and back into opposition, declaring that he could not be expected to renounce what he had believed
all his life.[111] According to Yechiel Kadishai, Gahal's leadership approved the resignation decision, even though, at the last minute, the government agreed to Finance
Minister Pinhas Sapir's proposal that Gahal's ministers be allowed to vote against the
ceasefire proposal and the withdrawal and still keep their six cabinet portfolios.[112]

On August 12, 1970, in his first speech before the Knesset as head of opposition, Begin denounced the situation in which Egypt, the United States, and the
Soviet Union participated while drafting the ceasefire terms, but Israel would not
be allowed to propose any changes. He warned that "we are going towards one of
the two: an arrangement alongside war, or war with no arrangement."[113] Begin
announced that any framework that allowed Hussein to place his soldiers or police in Judea and Samaria would be catastrophic as the PLO would follow without
being bound by the agreement. Begin again warned that most of Israel would be
under artillery threat. He attacked the cabinet for accepting terms of a "peace
initiative" that did not even include real Arab recognition of Israel but rather a
passive acknowledgment of its existence. And he compared UNSCR 242 to the
Rogers Plan to show that the terms of reference for Israel had become worse.

Begin went on to state that four of the five permanent members of the Security Council would demand acceptance of their views on Israel's future borders.
Russia and France wanted Israel to return to the June 4, 1967, lines, while Britain
and the United States backed "minor modifications" or insubstantial alterations,
agreed upon by both sides.[114] In contrast, Begin said there was a consensus in the
cabinet that in negotiations, Israel would demand to hold to the Jordan River,
Sharm El Sheikh, Gaza, the Golan Heights, Jerusalem, and Gush Etzion as a minimum for a future settlement.

He declared that Gahal could not sign a paper calling for "withdrawal from
territories occupied in the 1967 conflict" because it meant giving up Judea and
Samaria, or at least most of these territories. Begin implied that the United States
was doing to Israel what Britain did to Czechoslovakia in 1938 by demanding "a
plain acceptance" of the coerced terms, and after Czechoslovakia was surren-
dered, Britain and France noted the "great sacrifice . . . in the cause of peace."
Israel was given the same terms, and the identical words were currently used.[115]

Begin's Views of Relations with the United States

Begin's emphasis on the importance of Israel's position as an independent and
sovereign state capable of defending itself was a major theme throughout his
tenure in the National Unity Government. This position, which reflected a core
Revisionist principle, differed significantly from the view of the majority of the
cabinet members, who continued to hold the stance espoused by Ben-Gurion

on the need for Israel to closely coordinate its policies with the great powers. This perspective was based on realpolitik and the acknowledgment that Israel remained very small, isolated, and vulnerable geographically, demographically, and politically.

On this basis, Begin was very critical of the tendency of Israeli leaders to bow to US pressure, declaring that the outcome of the 1967 crisis and war had demonstrated that Israel could stand on its own. Although he was an Americophile and greatly admired US democracy, he would censure American leaders for positions and policies that he deemed as reflecting weakness, particularly regarding Israel.

Thus, in the context of the diplomatic struggles following the 1967 war and the various proposals that had been formulated in Washington, Moscow, and Cairo, Begin decried what he saw as a process that turned the Israeli government into a passive recipient.[116] "It is a pity," he said, "to have to be involved in a struggle between the big powers—but this does not detract from the fact that we have a right to the Land of the Bible."[117]

In this context, he denounced the cooperation between the United States and the Soviet Union as an illusory plan in which Washington would support Moscow's interests in Middle East negotiations, and, in return, the Soviets would help the United States in ending the Vietnam War. Even if it were feasible, Begin declared that the US president could not morally allow Israel to be returned to the dangers that existed from "the June 4, 1967" borders. He called on the Jews of the United States to protest against this unjust pressure.[118]

In December 1968, Begin stated at a party gathering that Israel would not allow a repeat of the mistakes of 1956–57, when "all those engaged in US policy making of the Eisenhower administration forced Israel to withdraw from Sinai without peace."[119] Begin recalled that although the United States had guaranteed peace as part of that agreement, the Americans did not honor this pledge in 1967.[120]

When the Nixon administration took office in January 1969, Begin's concerns increased, particularly as Secretary of State William Rogers led the efforts to press Israel to relinquish Judea and Samaria. Many Israelis viewed this administration as particularly unsympathetic, both to Jews and to Israelis. (Indeed, as the secret White House recordings later revealed, Nixon and many of his top aides held anti-Semitic views, despite the presence of Henry Kissinger and other Jews in key positions.)

According to Begin, the Rogers Plan was "an international scandal," and its supporters in the Israeli government were guilty of abandoning the hard-won sovereignty that was the core goal of Zionism. "Nobody asks Israel what it thinks anymore, because this state is no more than a toy in the international game of power politics." Accepting the Rogers Plan "would give Washington the go ahead to sign Israel's name to whatever it wished."[121] Begin also invoked the difficulties that the United States was having in the Vietnam War, warning that if the

American peace plan was accepted, "Israel's main cities could suffer the same fate as those of Southern Vietnam" and would be faced with "Saigonization." By standing up to these pressures and defending its vital national interests, Begin declared, Israel would earn the respect of the Americans.[122]

This position and the broader tendency to emphasize Israeli sovereign equality among the nations and, when necessary, challenge American pressures further separated Begin from most Israeli public figures. In the Israeli domestic political context, this issue also added to the factors that distinguished him from the Labor Party leadership as he returned to the opposition.

Conclusions

The years that Begin served in the unity governments led by Levi Eshkol and Golda Meir were central in translating his core principles and ideology into political policies. He had broken through a major barrier, demonstrating his ability to contribute significantly to the nation's leadership both in war and in pursuing peace. In this process, he established the legitimacy of an alternative leadership that would not threaten the survival of the country and would present policies that had considerable popular support. Indeed, as Begin's rivals on the Israeli Left, including Mapam, had warned, the inclusion of Gahal in the government was, in a sense, a Trojan horse that provided access to power and could not be reversed.

In another analysis, historian Shlomo Aronson wrote that the events and decisions during this period reflected Begin's strong influence: "Guilt feelings toward the Arabs—typical of the left . . . —were replaced by a new-old set of 'rights.'" In his rejection of demands that Israel return to the prewar armistice lines, and his bitter criticism of the United States' and the international community's inaction as the Arabs prepared to attack, Begin highlighted the "'right of the lone defender' who had managed to help himself against open aggression. If he had not managed, he would have been totally annihilated for nobody would have rescued him."[123]

Furthermore, Begin articulated the view that Israel had an "'historical' and strategic right to some of these territories," which were used "as a bridgehead for a deadly attack against Israel's heartland," and as a result, Arab rights were forfeited. Begin articulated the views of many Israelis who had fled from Arab countries and held a "more 'hawkish'" position.[124]

Between 1967 and 1970, starting before the war and ending with the government's acceptance of the Rogers Plan, Begin cemented the foundations of his political platform that led him and the Likud to victory in the 1977 elections. In addition, the pillars of Begin's policies as prime minister and, in particular, the core principles that guided him in the negotiations with Egyptian president Anwar Sadat and US president Jimmy Carter were all evident during this early period. Following the decisive military victory, the national consensus became significantly more hawkish, including many Labor Party leaders and voters who believed in the Greater Israel concept, although based more on security and secular factors than was the case for Begin.

Begin's three-year participation in the National Unity Government not only gave him the needed experience and legitimacy to mount a serious challenge for the position of prime minister but also led to the formation of several alliances, some short-lived, and others long lasting. He worked closely with Yigal Allon and Moshe Dayan, creating the foundations on which Begin appointed Dayan as foreign minister in 1977.

The experience in the cabinet and in helping to formulate Israel's negotiating positions after the war was particularly important regarding the issue of autonomy for the Palestinians. In 1967, Begin quickly and totally rejected every autonomy proposal, arguing that this would lead to a Palestinian state, but in the debate, he also heard other positions. A decade later, as prime minister, his position had changed, and he strongly pushed for autonomy, which became incorporated into the Camp David Accords in 1978.[125]

One explanation for this change is that in 1967, Begin was concerned that if the Labor government adopted the autonomy plan, he and the other Gahal minister, Yosef Sapir, would not be able to prevent this new situation from leading to a Palestinian state and a loss of Israeli sovereignty over Judea and Samaria.

From another perspective, it is argued that Begin's position on autonomy did not change. His mentor, Ze'ev Jabotinsky, had proposed autonomy for the Arabs of Palestine—within the future Jewish state. This framework was based on Eastern European models and termed "cultural autonomy" to be applied to the population but without any territorial dimension or qualities related to national sovereignty. Begin did not object to this framework while he was a member of the Unity Government, and when he became prime minister a decade later, the concept had not changed (although the reference to cultural autonomy was dropped).

Notes

1. For a detailed analysis of the origins of this war, see Oren, *Six Days of War.*
2. Ben-Gurion did not join the coalition and became an independent MK, leaving Rafi with nine MKs with Moshe Dayan and Shimon Peres as the leaders.
3. Nakdimon, *Toward H-Hour*; Gluska, *Israeli Military and the Origins of the 1967 War*; Yossi Goldstein, *Eshkol*; Shapira, *Yigal Allon, Native Son*, 309–12 (on the Allon-Dayan race for defense), and others (all in Hebrew) for details on the formation of the unity government and the struggle for the defense portfolio.
4. Sofer, *Begin*, 89.
5. Oren, *Six Days of War*, 134–35. According to Eric Silver, Ben-Gurion was not interested (Silver, *Begin*, 128). But both Preuss, in *Begin in Power*, and Haber, in "*Hayom Tifrotz*

Milchama," report that Ben-Gurion agreed to Begin's initiative, while Eshkol immediately rejected the effort to oust him.

6. Silver, *Begin*, 128.

7. The National Unity Government was officially established on June 5, the morning the war broke out, with the inauguration of the new ministers. All prior meetings were technically unofficial.

8. Oren, *Six Days of War*, 148.

9. Silver, *Begin*, 130.

10. Menachem Begin, "With the change of government—what shall we do?" speech by the chairman of the Herut Party at the opening of its fourth national convention, 1.10.1956, 18–19, Begin Center Archives (BCA), OP-132 [Hebrew].

11. Amir Goldstein, "Menachem Begin during the Six Day War and the Rebirth of the Israeli Right"; Tom Segev, *1967*, 336.

12. "Memorial to I.Z.L. Dead in Attack on New Gate," *Jerusalem Post*, July 17, 1969.

13. Silver, *Begin*, 131.

14. Oren, *Six Days of War*, 207; Haber, *Hayom Tifrotz Milchama*, 231.

15. Oren, *Six Days of War*, 208.

16. Silver, *Begin*, 131.

17. Oren, *Six Days of War*, 232.

18. Silver, *Begin*, 131–32.

19. Oren, *Six Days of War*, 242. In another version of these events, Begin called Eshkol and then Dayan. See Benziman, *Jerusalem*, 20; Tom Segev, *1967*, 352; Yossi Goldstein, *Eshkol*, 571. Benziman wrote that Begin called Dayan regarding the UN decision, and Dayan suggested that Begin talk with Eshkol. Begin called Eshkol, and then Eshkol agreed to call a meeting.

20. Oren, *Six Days of War*, 242–43; Haber, *Hayom Tifrotz Milchama*, 236–37.

21. Silver, *Begin*, 132; Goldstein, *Eshkol*, 571.

22. The prohibition on entry to Jordanian-controlled Jerusalem was not limited to Jews but also extended to Israeli Arabs: "In June 1967, Israel's Muslim citizens were able to access al-Haram al-Sharif after a 19-year period of exclusion during Jordanian rule in East Jerusalem" (Reiter, *Jerusalem and Its Role in Islamic Solidarity*, 130).

23. Oren, *Six Days of War*, 242–43; Haber, *Hayom Tifrotz Milchama*, 236–37.

24. Menachem Begin, "[We] Don't Want Annexation, But . . . " *Maariv*, February 18, 1972 [Hebrew].

25. Sofer, *Begin*, 89; Bader, *Knesset and Me*, 197–98.

26. Oren, *Six Days of War*, 292.

27. Oren, 315. In secret meetings from June 15 to 19, 1967, the cabinet agreed to propose peace and to offer the return of the Sinai Peninsula and the Golan Heights in exchange for comprehensive treaties with Egypt and Syria, respectively: "In contrast, the consensus was that 'Judea and Samaria' would not be returned to Jordan, and that the Gaza Strip was to be annexed." Based on Meir Avidan, "June 19, 1967: The Government of Israel Hereby Decides," *Davar*, June 2, 5, and 19, 1987.

28. For further details, see Raz, "Generous Peace Offer That Was Never Offered."

29. The full protocols of the government discussions are available at the Israel State Archives, files A 8164/7, A 8164/8, A 8164/9.

30. Eshkol's message to Hussein, June 5, 1967: "We are engaged in defensive fighting on the Egyptian sector, and we shall not engage ourselves in any action against Jordan, unless

Jordan attacks us. Should Jordan attack Israel, we shall go against her with all our might" (*IMFA* 1–2: 1947–1974, section XI: The Six-Day War, document 16; see also Goldstein, *Eshkol*, 570–71). Amir Goldstein, in "Menachem Begin during the Six Day War" (141–42), discusses Begin's support of the message and cites Minister Yisrael Galili's aide who recalled that Galili informed Begin, Dayan, and Allon of the message to Hussein before it was sent and that Begin even suggested to amend the message to promise that Israel's government will indefinitely accept the armistice line. But he also records Begin's own denial about six weeks before he passed away in a letter to Mordechai Motta Gur: "I did not know in advance of [the] message to King Hussein. I learned of it [later] in my activity in the National Unity Government." The letter to Gur is printed in Naor and Lammfromm, *Menachem Begin*, 640–41.

31. Avidan, "June 19, 1967," June 2, 1987.

32. Avidan.

33. Avidan.

34. Avidan.

35. "Party Leaders Talk of Peace Offensive," *Jerusalem Post*, June 18, 1967; "Begin: We Will Not Move without a Peace Treaty," *Haaretz*, June 18, 1967.

36. On October 31, 1968, the government added the condition that Sharm El Sheikh remain under Israeli control with territorial continuity to Israel (Avidan, "June 19, 1967"; Pedatzur, *Triumph of Embarrassment*). One year later, Eshkol reinforced the change, instructing Eban to stress to the US administration that "a secure border between Israel and Egypt necessitates changes in the former international border, including—obviously—keeping the Gaza Strip in Israel, continuing the Israeli control over Sharm El Sheikh with territorial connection to Israel and other vital security arrangements. These decisions (of October 31, 1968) of the government replace the declaration of June 19, 1967" (Eshkol telegram to Eban [New York], November 5, 1968; Lammfromm and Tsoref, *Levi Eshkol*, 649; Raz, "Generous Peace Offer," 96).

37. Shomron (Samaria) was the biblical name of one of the capital cities of the Kingdom of Israel. It was not the name of the mountainous region north of Jerusalem, which Samaria is now understood to mean. The name *Samaria* (*Shomron* in Hebrew) was decided in 1967, as presented in "The West Bank, Judea and Samaria, or Judea and Ephraim: How Was the Name Judea and Samaria Decided?" Israel State Archives (ISA), http://israelidocuments.blogspot .co.il/2016/01/blog-post_26.html (January 27, 2016) [Hebrew]. The terms *Judea* and *Samaria* were also used during the Mandate period to describe different regions in the Partition Plan (UNGA 181, November 29, 1947). See http://mfa.gov.il/MFA/ForeignPolicy/Peace/Guide /Pages/UN%20General%20Assembly%20Resolution%20181.aspx (accessed September 11, 2017).

38. Under this plan, Gaza would be annexed by Israel and the refugees would be resettled around the region (Oren, *Six Days of War*, 313–14).

39. Eban, *Autobiography*, 435–36.

40. Raz, "Generous Peace Offer."

41. See Bartal, *Fedayeen Emerge*, 3–5; Tovy, *Israel and the Palestinian Refugee Issue*, 87–106; Freundlich, *Documents on the Foreign Policy of Israel* 5 (1950): 285–86.

42. Oren, *Six Days of War*, 314.

43. Haber, *Hayom Tifrotz Milchama*, 293.

44. Pedatzur, *Triumph of Embarrassment*, 52.

45. Pedatzur, 52.

46. Pedatzur, 53.

47. Pedatzur, 52.

48. Speech at Herut Center meeting, July 26, 1967, BCA, OP-82 [Hebrew].

49. Avidan, "June 19, 1967," June 5, 1987, 19.

50. Avidan, 19. In an article in *Maariv* in June 1976, Begin explained that in a binational state, the parliament divided in half between the two nations of the state, regardless of their demographic ratios. Menachem Begin, "Facts vs. Illusion and Misleading," *Maariv* (June 18, 1976): 18 [Hebrew].

51. Avidan, "June 19, 1967."

52. Menachem Begin, "The Political and Security Situation (Lecture at the Herut Council)—in Three Parts," *Hayom*, October 25, 1967, 3, BCA, YM-196710.

53. Avidan, "June 19, 1967."

54. Avidan.

55. Avidan, 22.

56. "Government's opinion: Israel will hold on to all of the territories for a long while," *Haaretz* (July 31, 1967) [Hebrew].

57. Aronson, *Conflict and Bargaining in the Middle East*, 86.

58. Silver, *Begin*, 133–34

59. Silver, *Begin*, 134.

60. "Israel Owes No Apology to Arabs," *Jerusalem Post*, February 16, 1968.

61. Dan Margalit, "Begin: We Are Staying, Fortifying and Settling," *Haaretz*, December 8, 1967 [Hebrew].

62. "Begin: The Egyptian Description Is Like Inciting Stories," *Haaretz*, July 28, 1969 [Hebrew]; "Begin: Returning Territory Means Giving It Away," *Jerusalem Post*, December 8, 1968.

63. "Begin: Israel Settling Areas," *Jerusalem Post*, December 8, 1967.

64. No title, *Jerusalem Post*, October 25, 1968.

65. "Begin: Cairo Denials of Suez Canal Accord 'Falsehood,'" *Jerusalem Post*, June 7, 1968.

66. "Begin: There Is No Place for Another Partition of the Country," *Haaretz*, December 21, 1967 [Hebrew].

67. "Begin: No Question of Returning Land," *Jerusalem Post*, January 2, 1968.

68. "Herut Center Blesses the Beginning of Settlement," *Haaretz*, September 28, 1967 [Hebrew].

69. "Begin Calls for Rapid Settlement," *Jerusalem Post*, September 19, 1968.

70. Begin, in an answer to a question (Sheilta) in the Knesset, January 1, 1969, *Divrey Hakneset* 53 [Hebrew].

71. Silver, *Begin*, 133. Dayan as defense minister had full authority over all the territories captured during the war, and he acted quickly. On June 8, one day after the Old City was captured, he entered the Temple Mount and ordered the Israeli flag to be removed from it, as well as IDF personnel. Dayan also pledged to keep all holy places open, with the Muslim Waqf responsible for the mosques, including the Dome of the Rock. The cabinet, including Begin, was not consulted. Shragai, *The Temple Mount Conflict*, 18–27.

72. Begin lobbied in the Knesset for the unification of Jerusalem law. This legislation declared Israel's legal jurisdiction and widened its municipal territory. Thirteen years later, in 1980, when Begin was prime minister, the Knesset accepted the basic law "Jerusalem Capital of Israel," which stated that all national institutions must be located in Jerusalem.

73. "Begin: Returning Territory Means Giving It Away," *Jerusalem Post*, December 8, 1968.

74. "Begin Raps Mapam's Disloyalty Charges," *Jerusalem Post*, April 8, 1969.

75. "Land of Israel Forever," *Jerusalem Post*, July 22, 1969.

76. "Begin: Must Disregard Demographic Problem," *Jerusalem Post*, December 11, 1968.

77. Menachem Begin, Opening statement of Herut's 11th conference, Binyanei Hauma, December 17, 1972, BCA, OP–192 [Hebrew].

78. "Herut to Campaign to Save Democracy," *Jerusalem Post*, May 30, 1969.

79. S. Samet, "Begin: Israeli Law to Be Applied in the Territories," *Haaretz*, April 21, 1969 [Hebrew].

80. UN Security Council Resolution 242, available online: https://unispal.un.org/DPA/DPR/unispal.nsf/0/7D35E1F729DF491C85256EE700686136 (accessed August 25, 2018). See also Medzini, *Israel's Foreign Relations*. On Gunnar Jarring's mission, see Touval, *Peace Brokers*, 134–64. The French text of UNSCR refers to withdrawal from "the occupied territories," and the implication of this difference in comparison with the English version is the subject of intense debate. See Abu Odeh, Elaraby, Rosenne, Ross, Rostow, and Turner, *UN Security Council Resolution 242*.

81. Heikal, *Road to Ramadan*, cited by Aronson, *Conflict and Bargaining in the Middle East*, 89.

82. Touval, *Peace Brokers*, 134–164.

83. Touval, 145; "The Government Will Decide That Eban's and Tekoa's Announcements Are Valid," *Haaretz*, May 20, 1968 [Hebrew]; Yosef Harif, "Last-Minute Attempt to Prevent a Governmental Crisis," *Maariv*, May 19, 1968 [Hebrew].

84. *Davar* correspondent, "The Government Will Discuss Today the Dispute over the Statement by Israel's Representative to UN," *Davar*, May 20, 1968, 1 [Hebrew].

85. Harif, "Last-Minute Attempt,"; *Davar* correspondent. "The Government Will Discuss Today the Dispute over the Statement by Israel's Representative to UN," *Davar*, May 20, 1968, 1 [Hebrew].

86. "Eshkol Will Meet Today with Gahal Leaders Begin and Sapir, Attempting to Avoid Government Crisis," *Haaretz*, May 19, 1968 [Hebrew]; "Government Will Decide Today," *Haaretz*, May 20, 1968 [Hebrew]; "Begin—Situation in the Unity Government Restored," *Haaretz*, May 22, 1968 [Hebrew].

87. Address of Minister without Portfolio Mr. Menachem Begin at the Opening Rally of the 9th Herut Convention, on the 28th Iyar 5728 (May 26, 1968), BCA, OP 192.

88. Address of Minister without Portfolio Mr. Menachem Begin at the Opening Rally of the 9th Herut Convention, on the 28th Iyar 5728 (May 26, 1968), BCA, OP 192.

89. *Haaretz*, February 11, 1969.

90. Sofer, *Begin*, 89; Silver, *Begin*, 130–141; Haber, *Menachem Begin*, 262–85; Shlomo Nakdimon, "Begin Is Doing In the Government," *Yediot Aharonot*, November 8, 1968; Geula Cohen, "Why I Am in a National Unity Government," (interview with Menachem Begin), *Maariv*, June 20, 1969 [Hebrew]; Nakdimon, "The Scars of the Past Don't Affect the Present," *Yediot Aharonot*, June 12, 1969 [Hebrew]; Oren, *Six Days of War*, 314.

91. Yigal Allon was acting prime minister until Meir formed her government. On March 8, the War of Attrition broke out with massive artillery exchange across the Suez Canal.

92. "Final Accord Seen Today on New Cabinet Coalitions," *Jerusalem Post*, March 13, 1969. See also "Begin satisfied with G. Meir," *Haaretz*, March 14, 1969 [Hebrew]; Golan and Nakdimon, *Begin*, 226.

93. Iris Berlatzky, Begin Heritage Center oral documentation project: Interview with Yechiel Kadishai, October 2, 2002, BCA [Hebrew]; Temko, *To Win or to Die*, 176; Grosbard, *Menachem Begin*, 153. Avi Shilon claims that clashes from the prestate underground period remained sources of friction between Begin and Meir (Shilon, *Menachem Begin*, 210).

94. Herut Center, March 16, 1969, 19, BCA, OP-84 [Hebrew].

95. "Begin: Government Subscribes Only to Peace Treaty," *Jerusalem Post*, May 14, 1969.

96. "Begin on Changes in Policy Programme," *Jerusalem Post*, March 16, 1969.

97. Carmel, *It's All Politics*, 2:1018.

98. "Tension High in Secret Vote by Gahal Centre," *Jerusalem Post*, August 1970.

99. "Eban and Begin Carry on Slonging Match," *Jerusalem Post*, June 7, 1970.

100. *Jerusalem Post*, July 26, 1970.

101. *Jerusalem Post*, August 30, 1970.

102. Shapira, *Yigal Allon*, 312–16, regarding the Allon Plan's political stand.

103. "Begin: Should the Allon Plan Be Accepted, We Shall Leave the Government," *Haaretz*, May 3, 1970 [Hebrew]; "Gahal Would Quit if 'Certain Things' Voted," *Jerusalem Post*, June 4, 1970; "Begin Explains Under Which Conditions Will Gahal Resign from the Government," *Haaretz*, June 4, 1970 [Hebrew].

104. "Begin Calls for National Resistance to Withdrawal," *Jerusalem Post*, August 3, 1970.

105. "Tension High in Secret Vote."

106. "Begin, Galili, Raphael Speak on Conditions," *Jerusalem Post*, November 27, 1970. Begin's reference to Eban is a frequently cited paraphrase. Eban's words, as published in an interview with the German weekly *Der Spiegel* (January 27, 1969), referred to the dangers of the pre–June 4, 1967, borders as raising memories of Auschwitz among Israelis (Mann, *It's Inconceivable*, 65).

107. "Tension High in Secret Vote."

108. *Jerusalem Post*, August 30, 1970.

109. "Weizman Seems Assured of High Herut Post," *Jerusalem Post*, November 13, 1970.

110. "Begin Calls for National Resistance to Withdrawal."

111. Menachem Begin, "The Wholeness of the Nation and the Wholeness of the Land," speech before the National Council of the Herut movement, April 23, 1970, BCA, OP-133 [Hebrew]; *Devrei HaKnesset*, August 4, 1970; Dan Margalit, "Begin's Mistake," *Haaretz*, August 17, 1972 [Hebrew]; Bader, *The Knesset and Me*, 225–27, cited in Sofer, *Begin*, 90.

112. Berlatzky, interview with Kadishai.

113. Begin's speech in the Knesset, August 12, 1970, *Divrei HaKnesset* 58:2864 [Hebrew].

114. Gold, "U.S. Policy toward Israel in the Peace Process: Negating the 1967 Lines and Supporting Defensible Borders," 8.

115. Speech at Knesset debate regarding the prime minister's address about the cabinet decision over the American peace initiative, August 4, 1970, *Divrei HaKnesset* 58:2762–66 [Hebrew].

116. "Tension High in Secret Vote"; speech at Knesset debate, August 4, 1970, *Divrei HaKnesset*, vol. 58 [Hebrew].

117. "Begin Urges US Jews to Influence Nixon," *Jerusalem Post*, August 23, 1970.

118. Begin's speech in the Knesset, August 12, 1970, *Divrei HaKnesset* 58 [Hebrew].

119. "Begin Would Resist Bad US Policy," *Jerusalem Post*, December 19, 1968.

120. "Begin: Government Subscribes Only to Peace Treaty," *Jerusalem Post*, May 14, 1969.

121. Begin's speech in the Knesset, August 12, 1970, *Divrei Haknesset* 58 [Hebrew]; "Begin Charges US with Deception," *Jerusalem Post*, August 13, 1970.

122. "Begin Warns of Danger of Withdrawal," *Jerusalem Post*, August 21, 1970. In later speeches Begin said Israel was actually a very important player for the Americans regarding the Vietnam War due to the closure it forced in the Suez Canal.

123. Aronson, *Conflict and Bargaining in the Middle East*, 83.

124. Aronson, 83–84.

125. Prof. Arieh Eldad, a former MK from the National Unity faction, discussed apparent changes in the views of right-wing leaders when they become prime ministers (Eldad, *How Things Are Seen from Here*). On Begin, he argues that the changes took place long before becoming prime minister, and it was intentional to make Begin more likable to the center and moderates, enabling them to eventually support him and make him prime minister.

2 Return to Opposition
1970–77

After resigning from the National Unity Government in August 1970 and returning to opposition, Begin continued to press his ideological agenda and political objectives. He published a biweekly column in the *Maariv* daily newspaper and spoke widely on the questions of war and peace, repeatedly accusing the Labor-dominated government of sacrificing Israel's interests in the wake of its acceptance of the terms of the Rogers Plan. In addition, he addressed the conditions for peace with Egypt in public sessions of the Herut Central Committee. Thus, Begin's ideas regarding a peace agreement with Egypt continued to evolve in this period.

Begin was also busy managing and building up the Gahal political framework, which was transformed into the larger Likud bloc in 1973. Support for this expansion came from Ariel Sharon, who joined the Gahal leadership as a representative of the Liberal Party in July 1973. Sharon urged the formation of a center-right bloc, which Begin accepted, leading to the establishment of Likud in September of that year in preparation for the elections scheduled for October. In defining the goals of the Likud bloc, Begin stressed the primary objective of "creating a majority in the Knesset that would reject any plan and proposal to redivide the Land of Israel."[1]

On this basis, the Likud's preliminary platform statements on foreign and defense policy for the 1973 elections were very similar to the Gahal platform from the previous election campaign in 1969. Indeed, some of the sections referring to peace and foreign relations policy were copied without change. However, following the earthquake of the war and the delay in the elections, the focus of the campaign changed fundamentally. The Labor Alignment came out on top again but with less support than before (fifty-one seats instead of fifty-six in 1969), while Begin's Likud increased by 50 percent, from twenty-six seats in 1969 to thirty-nine in 1973. A few months later, after the release of the Agranat Commission report on responsibility for the war's failures, Golda Meir resigned, and Yitzhak Rabin became prime minister. But Rabin's government was fragile, beset by indecision and scandal, thus creating the foundation for Likud's electoral triumph in 1977.

During the three years between his resignation from Golda Meir's government, the Yom Kippur War, and the elections that followed, Begin was

consistent, repeating the points that he made upon leaving the Unity Government. Justifying the campaign that he initiated while in the cabinet, he sought
public support for his views. Begin's central theme was that the territorial gains
Israel had obtained in combat could only be relinquished in exchange for a full
peace. He firmly rejected any withdrawal in the context of intermediate agreements, such as the Rogers Plan: "We had a rule accepted by all parties: without
peace agreements—no movement. . . . A few months ago the rule was broken
when we [the government] said we are willing to discuss withdrawal even without peace agreements, but rather as a consequence of the discussion over the
opening of the (Suez) Canal."[2]

Following the war, the diplomatic focus shifted to negotiation of the separation agreements between Israel and Egypt. The first agreement (Sinai I) was
signed on January 18, 1974, and the second was signed on September 4, 1975, after
several crises between Israel and the United States. Both agreements involved
Israeli withdrawal from territory without a formal peace agreement with Egypt
or the establishment of diplomatic relations.

The period between the 1973 war and the 1977 elections was characterized
by growing support for Likud and Begin's increased visibility and impact on the
Israeli political and policy debate. His views on war and peace, the irrevocable
"right of the Jewish people to the Land of Israel," the centrality of settlements,
UN Security Council Resolution 242 and the land for peace formula, interim
arrangements, functionalist approaches for division of sovereignty and control,
and other core issues were presented in contrast to those of the Labor Alignment.

But though this debate was important in the Israeli context, it barely reg-
istered outside, so that when Likud emerged victorious from the 1977 elections
and Begin became prime minister, the policies that he advocated were largely
unknown, including in the United States. The foundation for the policies that
Begin followed in the context of the negotiations with President Sadat beginning
in July 1977 was created and flowed directly from his frequently stated positions
throughout this period.

Begin's Concept of Peace and Opposition to the Rogers Plan

Begin's opposition to the Rogers Plan and the dangers to Israel's security that he
saw were major themes in his speeches and writing during this period (August
1970 to 1973). Immediately after resigning from the government, Begin expanded
his criticism of the adoption of the American-sponsored ceasefire agreement with
additional vigor as head of the opposition. He declared, "Gahal left the government following this wretched decision, for which we could not accept responsibility, from a moral, historical or political perspective. For the dissolution [of the
government], it is necessary to bless all those who sought this in the Labor Party.
For many months, they claimed that Gahal was responsible for tying the hands of

the government and halting peace initiatives."[3] A month later, in another column published in *Maariv*, Begin wrote:

> Take the well-known slogan: Peace for land. Those who have clung to it failed to pay attention, and as a result, did not know that it totally contradicts reality. The territories are in our hands, as we generally claim, but in whose hands is peace? The Jewish people, in its entirety . . . desires peace with the Arabs in the Land of Israel and the wider region. The Arabs have refused to uphold [the peace] and refuse to make it. That is the truth. An observer can regret this refusal, or condemn it, or justify it. But he cannot deny it, unless he wishes to close his eyes to the facts.[4]

In July 1973, two and a half months before the war, Begin spoke about his requirements for a peace agreement. He distinguished among three concepts: the conditions of peace, peaceful relations, and a peace treaty. In his analysis, he referred positively to the de facto peaceful relations between Israel and Jordan, which evolved informally, particularly after 1967. At the same time, Begin emphasized that the integrity of the Land of Israel is equivalent to peace, because it provides security, which is the basic requirement for peace.[5]

Begin continued to attack the Labor government for naively promoting a false peace while also accusing the Egyptians and Anwar Sadat, in particular, of only pretending to be interested in peace. Writing again in *Maariv* in 1971, Begin warned:

> An Israeli political offensive will not be possible or effective as long as peoples and governments have the impression that Sadat truly and honestly wants a peace treaty with Israel. . . . During February, our official spokesmen, apparently for the purposes of internal propaganda, announced that Sadat's response to Dr. Jarring included something new, and even revolutionary. For the first time, supposedly, the Egyptian President said that he was ready to "enter" into a peace agreement with Israel. . . . It is a deception. Sadat, like Nasser, refers to a peace treaty with two conditions that turn any agreement into a travesty, peace into mockery. . . . First, the implementation of the withdrawal to the June 4, 1967 lines; and second, a solution to the problem of the Palestinian people.[6]

"Earthquake"—The Yom Kippur War

The 1973 Yom Kippur War shattered the country and undermined confidence in the Labor Alignment leadership. Immediately after the war ended and the scope of the disaster became clear in terms of the number of deaths and injuries, demonstrations and demands for investigations began.

Since leaving the Unity Government in August 1970, Begin had warned continuously of the disastrous consequences of the government's acceptance of the Rogers Plan, and now he could claim that these predictions were accurate.[7] In particular, he reminded Israelis that Sadat was indeed preparing for war, and Israeli passivity in the wake of ceasefire violations allowed Egypt to move its antiaircraft batteries to positions that allowed for surprise attacks. As head of the opposition, Begin highlighted the lack of military vigilance that preceded the war. In his view, the war was a self-inflicted disaster resulting from a "missed opportunity" that could and should have been avoided by mobilizing the forces on time and attacking before being attacked.[8] Had these measures been taken, Begin declared, they would have renewed Israel's deterrence and brought long-lasting stability to the area.[9] Speaking in the Knesset on October 23, 1973, Begin asked:

> How did it happen that Israel's intelligence services were so seriously mistaken in their estimation of the situation . . . ? I maintain that the responsibility is the Government's. The intelligence services are a governmental branch. . . . A responsible government examines intelligence assessments critically, and does not simply accept them unquestioningly.... That is the duty of a statesman. . . . This was irresponsible.... The enemy was massing its forces along the borders ... and the Government persuaded not only itself but also the Americans that there was no danger of war.[10]

The question of whether Israel should have launched a preemptive strike on October 6, 1973, occupied many scholars and policy makers. As expected from the leader of the opposition, Begin argued that Israel should have attacked as in 1967. But that was hindsight and omits the pressures from Washington against preemption.[11]

Emphasizing a familiar and central theme regarding limited ceasefires and interim agreements, Begin went on to criticize the absence of a direct link between the US-brokered ceasefire agreement and formal peace negotiations:

> We have been told that the Americans are committed to linking this ceasefire with direct peace negotiations. . . . But you must ask yourselves first whether the enemy accepts this link. . . . The crucial question is . . . will undertaking to implement Resolution 242, to repartition part of the Land of Israel, to withdraw, bring peace, a peace agreement, or not . . . ? I say that there is no chance that this will happen. . . . The enemy stated yesterday that he did not accept any connection between the sections, demanding first that 242 be implemented. . . . This means that the enemy does not have to do anything . . . since the implementation begins with Israel's withdrawal. . . . Where is the agreement, then? Where is peace? If the Government agrees, heaven forefend, there will be withdrawal, but there will be no peace, because, as you have said, there will be no withdrawal to the borders of 4 June 1967.[12]

Answering criticism from the Labor Alignment over opposition to the Rogers Plan and ceasefire, Begin recalled, "In August 1970 I warned the Knesset that we were headed for war . . . noting that the Egyptians had violated the ceasefire in a way which seriously threatened our security and future."[13]

The delayed 1973 election campaign took place in the shadow of the war—the "earthquake"—and issues of war and peace were a central focus of the campaign. Begin had a positive and cooperative relationship with Golda Meir, and they agreed in general on the implacable hostility of the Arab world.[14] But as the leader of the opposition, he demanded the replacement of the leadership that was responsible for the Yom Kippur War.[15]

In response, the Labor Alignment redoubled its condemnations of Begin as an extreme right-wing leader who refused to compromise and whose actions and policies, if accepted, would block any peace initiative in the region.[16] In refuting the claim that "the path of the Likud will lead the country to war," Begin declared that even without Gahal in the coalition, none of the peace initiatives succeeded. Begin stressed the argument that the Arab countries were not interested in peace and if the Likud won the election, it would form a unity government to deal with threats.[17]

Elections were held on December 31, 1973; the Labor Alignment received fifty-one seats (five fewer than in the previous Knesset), and the Likud bloc took thirty-nine, marking a substantial increase. This was a major political achievement for Begin and a significant milestone toward breaking the Alignment's dominance.

When the new government was presented to the Knesset in March 1974, Begin again responded as the head of the opposition. His speech stressed many of his familiar themes, calling for "educating the youth on our right to the Holy Land and campaigning overseas on this issue." He declared his support for "equal rights and free choice of citizenship to the Israeli Arabs" and housing and employment for the refugees under Israel's jurisdiction. Begin also demanded accelerated settlement activity in Judea and Samaria, repeating the major positions in the Likud platform, which declared that "the right of the Jewish people to the Land of Israel is not open to dispute." The platform also noted the eternal yearning and search for peace with the Arab states, the central importance of Jewish settlement, and equal rights for all citizens of the state without differentiation.[18]

This postwar government did not last long, and Golda Meir resigned in the wake of the Agranat Report and the continuing criticism of the government's responsibility for the Yom Kippur War. In response, Begin called for a responsible leadership that would "heal the nation's wounds, lead it out of its confusion, overcome the tragedy of the Jewish people and ensure its future and freedom in the Land of Israel."[19] Golda Meir was replaced by former IDF chief of staff Yitzhak Rabin in June 1974, who held office until 1977. Begin's speech on the occasion of this change was very similar to his declaration attacking Meir's government three months earlier.[20]

Policy Pronouncements

In his Knesset speeches and *Maariv* columns, Begin continued to emphasize these views and policy prescriptions. In his bid to establish political legitimacy after decades in opposition and in the wake of the labels of extremism, Begin emphasized his and Likud's commitment to peace, referring to the accusation of their being opposed to peace as a "blood libel."[21]

Based on the argument that "the Land of Israel belongs to the Jewish people," Begin repeatedly presented his policies on peace negotiations and the risk of war.[22] He ridiculed what he saw as the contradiction in Rabin's rejection of proposals to return full control of the Golan Heights to Syria and his willingness to withdraw from Judea and Samaria. And in the wake of Rabin's declaration that maintaining control of the Golan was preferable to a peace treaty with Syria, Begin asked how he (Begin) could be criticized for taking the same position regarding Judea and Samaria.[23] "Everyone already knows that the Prime Minister is ready to transfer control of territory in Judea and Samaria to Hussein" and to share functional responsibility with Jordan. According to Begin, this was a "moral atrocity"; no other nation had "sent an invitation for an agreed invasion."[24] He charged that Rabin's peace policies, which were not based on treaties but rather on interim arrangements, would result in another war.

Responding to the Alignment's attacks on his policies, Begin noted they were based on claims that:

> while perhaps we do not want to renew the fighting and the cycle of violence, our policies . . . will lead to this. Labor, they say, is ready to return territory to the Arabs, although not everything. In this way, it is possible to reach an agreement with the Arabs, and in this way, to prevent another war. But the Arabs will not accept the Likud's position, but would return to the strategy of violence. But what does reality tell us? . . . Those who would claim that the Arab states would agree on the based on Israeli control over part of the territory, on any front, are knowingly misleading the nation.[25]

Attacking the government's policies and debates over American-brokered disengagement initiatives following the 1973 war and Kissinger's shuttle diplomacy, he argued that the government was deceiving the people. The Arab leaders had declared many times that the only acceptable treaty included full withdrawal to the 1967 lines and a solution to the refugee problem, which, in Begin's view, meant that a peace treaty in the near future was impossible.[26] In July 1975, Begin criticized the Rabin government's weakness in the negotiations for a second Sinai withdrawal agreement:

> Concession followed concession. We offered Egypt land access to the oil fields of Abu-Rudeis. They said it wasn't enough, and as for the passages, they demanded we give them up entirely. The Americans told us to do as Egypt demanded. These concessions were justified as necessary in order to prevent confrontation with America. . . . We are demanded to surrender to our enemies by our friends. No doubt, the Munich spirit leads these pressures. A small nation is struggling to live. Its enemies want to push it out of defensive

positions in order to endanger its independence. A friend then arrives, adopts the enemy's demands, "explains" that the surrender is in his and "the world's" interests; therefore, he requires to accept the hostile demand as is.[27]

In December 1973, shortly before the postponed elections in Israel, the United States convened a short and unproductive meeting in Geneva, in which the representatives of Egypt, Jordan, and Israel participated, but it lost any importance when the Syrians failed to attend. Israeli leaders were wary of international conferences, in which they would be isolated and pressured by the superpowers and the Arab states. The agreement to participate in the Geneva Conference was the result of Kissinger's intense pressure.

Begin attacked involvement in these negotiations as extremely dangerous for Israel, reemphasizing the principle he had articulated after the 1967 war of "no withdrawal without a peace treaty."[28] While Begin called for rejection of US pressure for concessions, he emphasized the importance of maintaining positive relations with the Americans.[29] He recognized the impact of Israel's slipping image and support abroad resulting from the Arab political assault and called for an information campaign to explain Israel's policies.[30] In his intense opposition to any consideration of Palestinian sovereignty, Begin rejected the use of the term "Palestinians" in referring to the Arabs of the Land of Israel and described the PLO not as a liberation organization but a murderous gang.[31]

> In order to prevent the horrors we have seen [the Holocaust], we must release ourselves from two mistakes. One is moral and political. We should stop referring to the murderous Palestinians or even terrorists, and should not accept the name they are given in broadcasts in the international media. We shall call them in their real name: The Nazi organizations of the Arab states, and we shall try to penetrate this true description of the murderous organizations to world public opinion. Second—and that is the essence—we should no longer have a theory or practice of retaliation. We should fight the Nazi organizations of the Arab states until they are disarmed or paralyzed of any ability to kill Jews.[32]

In his newspaper column, he recalled the first interim agreement in January 1974, condemning the terms in which the Israeli withdrawal took place without any Egyptian commitment to peace and "even without any Egyptian interest in peace. . . . Simply presented, it is clear that none of our concessions is accepted as it is offered, introduced or promised. Not only in Cairo or Moscow, but also in Washington we are told: 'Not enough, concede more, or else . . .' The warning was fulfilled. The assumption that it will lead to an agreement was proven imaginary. Here is the paradox: Those who boast of their realism were hallucinating, while those who were accused of ignoring reality saw very clearly."[33]

Begin cited the frequent declarations from the Egyptian government that claimed that their main objective in the negotiations was to allow for the strengthening of military capabilities. He quoted an official publication that declared, "Egypt will continue in a political and military campaign to the liberation of all of the occupied territories and guaranteeing of the full rights of the Palestinian refugees."[34]

In *Maariv*, Begin mocked the concept of nonbelligerence for one year: "A 'high-level official' in the Secretary of State's entourage said on board of his plane that he may offer a one-year non-belligerence agreement. Splendid! We shall withdraw at least 50 kilometers from the Mitla and Gidi passages for one year of non-belligerence. In other words, after twelve months the phrase 'non' will drop off of 'non-belligerence,' and the second part will be activated, with our pre-permission!"[35]

Begin also rejected the government's claim that a second agreement, negotiated through the Americans, would lead to peace and that it was proof of Egypt's desire for an accord. He recalled Yigal Allon's statement before the Yom Kippur War that "Egypt had no more option of war" and Moshe Dayan's assessment at the same time that "there will be no war for the next 10 years."[36] In many of his speeches and articles, he included Holocaust analogies, such as comparing Arafat to Hitler, the PLO to the Nazis, and withdrawal proposals to the Munich accord.

In March 1975, US secretary of state Henry Kissinger arrived for a second phase of shuttle diplomacy between Israel and Egypt. Begin's opposition to interim and partial agreements intensified, arguing that they would bring neither peace nor security.[37] Begin demanded that Egypt end the state of war between the two countries as a precondition for negotiations.[38] This was also the government's position, but Sadat refused to end the state of war for a partial—and rather limited—Israeli withdrawal. Sadat would only give a vague promise that Egypt would not take advantage of the returned territory to launch an attack. The United States guaranteed that Sadat would keep his word. But this was far below Israel's minimum threshold and became a major reason for the failure of Kissinger's effort in March.

Kissinger and President Gerald Ford then increased the pressure on Israel, including a painful reassessment of Middle East policy. After six months, the Americans and Israelis formulated a new plan in which Israel would withdraw to the eastern entrance to the Sinai passes and Egypt would regain control of their western entrance. The passes themselves would be controlled by US civilians and include early-warning stations that both Israel and Egypt would build.[39]

In a report to his Herut faction during the reassessment crisis, Begin said that Rabin had promised to reject the Egyptian and American demands, and in response, Begin pledged support.[40] However, in the summer, when Rabin accepted Sadat's conditions, Begin criticized this decision and also denounced Kissinger.[41]

Begin had an alternative approach to peace, which he presented to the Herut Central Committee in January 1975, perhaps reflecting a realization that with his growing political influence and the possibility of becoming prime minister, he needed to go beyond opposition. The framework incorporated and elaborated on the elements he had been emphasizing for years. The basis for negotiations required a complete ceasefire between Israel and its neighbors—meaning Egypt and Jordan. Any agreement must include a declaration ending "the state of war." Begin's proposed framework would incorporate "all the issues between the nations, most important the borders and refugees and their property—Arabs and Jews alike." This initiative would be made public so that if the Arabs rejected the offer, Israel could show the world who wanted peace and who did not.[42]

In media interviews while visiting the United States in April 1975, Begin emphasized the need for a diplomatic process based on formal negotiations toward a full peace treaty, recalling that in 1970, President Nixon wrote that Israeli withdrawal from territories depended on a signed peace treaty.[43] (Begin also called on Washington to supply Israel with weapons to prevent President Sadat from "miscalculating the situation" and starting a new war.)[44]

In June 1975, Begin elaborated on the details of his initiative, based on five principles: a complete armistice, direct negotiations toward a peace treaty, cultural autonomy for the "Arabs of Eretz Israel," Arabs freely choosing their citizenship, and resolution of the refugees' claims.[45]

As negotiations with Egypt progressed, Begin's Likud bloc became divided. The Liberal faction demanded more flexibility in the party's political position, and there were some reports that the Likud might split over this issue. The Liberals were generally more moderate than Herut in terms of possible compromises to resolve the Arab-Israeli conflict. Their chairman, Elimelech Rimalt, reflected this policy by suggesting that the Likud endorse the second agreement with Egypt. Begin did not fully reject this position, allowing the Liberals some independence. For Begin, maintaining the unity of the Likud was central. When the Suez Canal was reopened on June 5, 1975, the Likud published a response that was very moderate compared to the view Begin expressed earlier.[46]

In August, Begin realized that a majority in the Knesset would vote in favor of the second intermediate agreement. While accepting this outcome, he warned that any withdrawal would only be followed by pressure for additional withdrawals and would not bring peace.[47]

The Interim Agreement (Sinai II) was finally signed on September 4, 1975, in Geneva, following a deal between Israel and the United States. It included not only the physical presence of Americans (government civilian contractors, not troops) in the Sinai—making the United States a party in the agreement—but also a package of guarantees for Israel. This package—in the form of an agreement signed by Kissinger and Allon and letters from Kissinger to Allon and from Ford to Rabin—promised Israel significant American military and financial aid, diplomatic support in international bodies (particularly in the UN Security

Council), a guarantee not to hold talks with the PLO until it accepted 242 and Israel's right to exist, a promise not to announce new peace plans without first consulting Israel, a promise to sell F-16 combat aircraft that had been withheld until then, and other terms. It also included an oil guarantee, saying that if Israel could not purchase oil for its annual consumption on the world market, the United States would provide the oil and if Israel could buy the oil but had no means to ship it, the former would provide the tankers. The guarantee was given to substitute for the Abu-Rudeis oil fields that Israel was about to return to Egypt and was offered for five years.[48]

Upon receiving Ford's letter, Prime Minister Rabin showed it to Begin, saying that "it places the US-Israel relationship on an entirely new footing."[49] Begin, according to Yehuda Avner's account, was impressed by Ford's letter. Three years later, as prime minister, Begin took the letter to Camp David and demanded that Carter abide by the pledge not to present an American peace plan without consulting first with him. The package of guarantees that Rabin received also served as a precedent for the incentives that Begin received in 1978 and 1979. The oil guarantee of 1975 in particular was the model for the 1979 version, although under very different circumstances.

Begin's Attitude toward Sadat

Throughout this period, Begin portrayed Egyptian president Anwar Sadat, who took power after Nasser's death, as an implacable enemy whose past included collaboration with the Nazis. In June 1972, Begin quoted at length from a speech made by "the Egyptian ruler" at a mosque on Mohammed's birthday.

> The most glorious act the Prophet did was that he expelled them, the Jews, from the Arab peninsula. This is what the Messenger of God, Mohammed, did. We will never directly negotiate with them. We know our history and theirs. They are a people of liars and traitors; a people of plotters; a people born for treason. I promised last year, and I promise now, that on the next birthday of the Prophet we will celebrate not only our people's freedom, but also the thrusting of the Israeli arrogance and wild behavior, in order to humiliate them as the Koran says. We will not give that up. The issue is no longer only the liberation of our soil, but has to do with our honor and our destiny, as we believe. We will return them to their previous situation, [of poverty and humiliation, as written in the seventh century].[50]

Begin ascribed great importance to these words, noting that whatever concessions Israel might make, Sadat would interpret them as evidence of the prophesized humiliation of the Jews.

Begin saw the 1973 war as evidence that Sadat meant what he said and continued to call attention to Sadat's statements, particularly when they were at odds with the Israel government's more optimistic interpretations. For example, in

February 1975 at the World Jewish Congress in Jerusalem, Begin warned that Sadat was deceiving the world by speaking of peace while intending to annihilate Israel.

In July 1974, Begin wrote in *Maariv* that the government presented disengagement as an Egyptian step toward peace but warned that "the ruler of Egypt had not given up his two conditions: A complete withdrawal of Israel to the Rhodes (1949) lines, and the return of the well-known Palestinian people's rights." Begin concluded that these conditions together implied an aspiration to destroy Israel. "Sadat wanted, before anything else, to get rid of the Jewish soldiers in Egypt, and to achieve full control of the Canal, from both banks. Us being on the western bank was a horrible humiliation for him."[51]

During April 1976, US senator Jacob Javits visited the region, first meeting with Sadat and Assad and then coming to Israel. Javits was one of the few prominent Americans to meet with Begin to discuss policy during this period, and the senator relayed Sadat's latest peace initiative, including two preconditions: return to the June 4, 1967, lines and allow the Palestinians to establish a state with a ground link between the Gaza Strip and the West Bank. Begin told Javits that these demands were unacceptable, and he referred to Sadat as "that Egyptian ruler, a clever enemy," who appeared as if he wanted peace, even when presenting such ideas.[52] During the years following the 1973 war and the signing of the intermediate agreement with Egypt, Begin warned against Sadat's real intentions and focused on his refusal to declare an end to the state of war between the two countries.

Policy Statements on Other Foreign Policy and Defense Issues

During this period as opposition leader, Begin went on a number of speaking tours to the United States and Europe. These tours reflected his emphasis on the importance of explaining Israel's position and in reinforcing the connections between Israel and world Jewry and, according to Kadishai, also allowed him to meet powerful figures in the Jewry communities.[53]

Begin's 1972 trip to Britain was particularly noteworthy. As the former leader of the Irgun in the independence struggle, Begin was active in the uprising against British mandatory rule, including violent reprisal attacks, and his visit twenty-five years later generated a great deal of bitter comments and protests. In London, Arab ambassadors called for Begin's extradition and trial for war crimes.[54] A formal dinner scheduled by Jewish organizations in Begin's honor was canceled due to bomb threats. The British press was particularly hostile, referring to Begin as "ex-terror chief" or "nice little killer," and in this atmosphere Begin ended his planned three-day trip one day early, citing the contrasts between his reception and those given to leaders of liberation groups from other former British colonies. This discrimination, he declared, was a reflection of the particular hostility directed against him as "a Jewish warrior."[55]

Begin understood that the United States was the most important diplomatic arena for Israel, and he made frequent trips during this period. Begin was an Americophile—he saw the United States as the main champion of democracy, uncorrupted by the colonialism and anti-Semitism of the British. It was the United States that stood up consistently to fight communism and the Soviet regime that had tormented Begin and the Jewish people for many decades. For Begin, the contributions that Israel made to American security were a major source of pride, and he criticized the Meir and Rabin governments for talking about reopening the Suez Canal. Begin argued that by keeping the canal closed, Israel was assisting the Americans and preventing Soviet rearmament of the communist forces in Vietnam. (He quoted Prof. Bernard Lewis and Dean Acheson, who said that opening the Canal would only assist the Soviets in gaining political power.[56]) It was therefore difficult for him when America seemed to follow policies that appeared to be inconsistent with its own self-interest and sense of morality.

In November 1975, Begin went to Washington with a Knesset delegation for discussions with President Ford, Secretary of State Kissinger, members of Congress, and Jewish leaders. The agenda included reports circulating in Washington alleging that Israel had become strong enough to dispense with American military assistance and support. In a speech in the Knesset following this visit, Begin noted that the delegation's role was to explain that although Israel was indeed strong, the balance of power in the Middle East was not changing in Israel's favor. The Arab states were acquiring major weapons systems, thereby contributing to instability in the area and increasing the prospects of renewed war. Begin reported that the atmosphere in Washington was very friendly to Israel: "We have, these days in the United States a very supportive public opinion, perhaps more supportive than we've had for many years. But there are also many dangers and we must continue and influence it by all of the means that we have."[57]

Begin was also aware of American efforts to increase pressure on Israel to make major concessions to the Palestinians and to bring the PLO into the process, including the 1975 Brookings Plan, which was to become the basis for the Carter administration's peace efforts. In a December 1976 session of the Herut Central Committee, Begin reported on his meeting with Zbigniew Brzezinski, one of the main authors of the plan and soon to be appointed as President-elect Carter's national security advisor. In Begin's account, they agreed on the need for direct talks without preconditions, in contrast to the indirect approach of the Rogers Plan. Begin also claimed that while Brzezinski had in the past been a supporter of a Palestinian state, he no longer held this position after recognizing that such a state would become a Soviet base.

Throughout this period, Begin condemned the United Nations for attacks against Israel's legitimacy and national rights and accused the government of weakness in confronting these discriminatory resolutions. In November 1974, UNESCO adopted a highly politicized resolution calling on Israel "to desist from any archaeological excavations in the City of Jerusalem and from any alteration of its features or its cultural and historical character, particularly with regard to Christian and Islamic religious sites."[58] This followed the UN decision to invite Arafat to address the General Assembly. In the Knesset, Begin attacked the invitation to the PLO leader, saying that there were people who sensed that compared with others, Arafat sounded moderate: "My generation heard Hitler's speeches in the 1930s and they sounded very moderate." On UNESCO, Begin declared that Israel was not destroying Muslim or Christian holy sites, unlike the practice of Israel's enemies toward Jewish sites before the Old City of Jerusalem was liberated. "We respect all religions and allow free access for Muslims and Christians to their sectors and for any other religion to their holy sites. . . . We shall get along without UNESCO; we will continue to revive our past for our future."[59]

Two weeks later, the UN General Assembly adopted Resolution 3236 (November 22, 1974), asserting the right of the Palestinians to self-determination. The text "reaffirms also the inalienable right of the Palestinians to return to their homes and property from which they have been displaced and uprooted, and calls for their return." In response, Begin declared that Arafat was "rewriting history on the General Assembly's podium" by claiming that Israel initiated the 1948 war and that resolutions calling for the return of the Palestinians "means the destruction of the State of Israel." Begin reiterated his proposal that Israel absorb the refugees in its territory and the Arab states take care of those who are in their territories. He also condemned the United Nation's endorsement of violence and terrorism through the inclusion of the words "by all means" and blamed the government for its lack of vigilance as such terms became routine. "Our worst enemies are using our own words to justify the destruction of the State of Israel."[60] (UNGA Resolution 3210 "invites the Palestine Liberation Organization, the representative of the Palestinian people, to participate in the deliberations of the General Assembly on the question of Palestine in plenary meetings.")

Begin also condemned the United Nations for adopting the Arab vocabulary, noting that "liberation" implies justification of the goal of destroying Israel, while also comparing the PLO to the Nazis. He issued a call on American Jews and those around the world to demonstrate against this resolution. The UN campaign and Begin's condemnations reached their peak in UNGA Resolution 3379, which, on November 10, 1975, equated Zionism with racism and racial discrimination.

On November 30, 1975, the UN Security Council adopted Resolution 381, extending the UNDOF mandate by six months, but also invited representatives of the PLO to participate in the Security Council discussions on the Palestinian issue. Addressing the Knesset on December 2, Begin presented a six-point program of responses: stopping all cooperation with UNDOF, applying the Israeli law on the entire Eretz Israel, returning to a call for direct negotiations for peace, establishing settlements in all of Eretz Israel, announcing a state of emergency in Israel to reduce its dependence on the United States, and mobilizing the Jewish people all around the world to aid in accomplishing these objectives. As head of the opposition, he again blamed the government for the political defeat at the United Nations and called for its resignation.[61]

The 1977 Election Campaign

The combination of the 1973 war "catastrophe," the economic crisis, the tensions in Israel's complex social fabric, and spreading corruption scandals among Labor Alignment officials continued to weaken the government, while the credibility of the Likud and Begin as alternative leaders increased steadily. In retrospect, the outcome of the 1977 elections, and the Likud victory, should not have come as a major surprise. However, after decades of Labor domination, the signs of pending change, including the large and enthusiastic crowds that came out around the country to hear Begin speak, were largely ignored outside of Israel.

Although Begin was hospitalized for heart problems for most of the campaign, he quickly returned and resumed attacks on Labor policies, focusing on disengagement negotiations with the United States. Israel, he repeated, could not afford the luxury of trading territory for "non-belligerency" agreements that could soon be broken—the country needed leaders who could explain to the Americans "that the retention of the territories was a matter of life and death for Israel."[62] Labor Party officials portrayed Begin as a dangerous fanatic who would reject even the most reasonable peace offer; moreover, he would drag Israel to war.[63]

In response, at the Herut national convention in January 1977, Begin declared that his first concern as prime minister would be to prevent war and that he had a peace initiative in mind, to be negotiated directly with Israel's neighbors. He clarified that "Judea and Samaria are an inseparable part of Israel's sovereignty" and "the border between Egypt and Israel will be established within Sinai. We no longer hold all of Sinai, and there is no party in Israel, except the Communists, that is prepared to abandon all of Sinai."[64]

In its election platform, the Likud reiterated the eternal right of the Jewish people to Eretz Israel; "therefore Judea and Samaria will not be handed to any foreign sovereignty; between the (Mediterranean) Sea and the Jordan River there shall be only Israeli sovereignty."[65] The Likud declared its objection to a Palestinian State, which would endanger all of Israel and the free world, and therefore the Likud government would make this danger clear. They were ready to negotiate peace, to participate in the Geneva Conference, and to prevent war by all means. Peace talks must be "genuine and with no pre-conditions." Regarding Syria and Egypt, the Likud government would negotiate peace based on the interests and needs of the parties, but without peace, only the signed disengagement agreements would oblige the parties.[66]

During this period, Begin also appeared to soften his demand for Jewish sovereignty over the entire Land of Israel (the Revisionist platform had included "both banks of the Jordan"). According to Eliahu Ben-Elissar, who became director general of the prime minister's office after the elections, Begin held negotiations with Moshe Dayan before the elections to include him on the Likud list in 1977. Dayan demanded a pledge not to annex Judea, Samaria, and Gaza to Israel, and Begin eventually agreed as long as negotiations were deemed possible. Dayan eventually did not join the Likud list but, based on this early agreement with Begin, later accepted the position of foreign minister.[67]

In March, while the election campaign was well under way, Prime Minister Rabin was invited to meet the new US president, Jimmy Carter. He accepted and became the first Middle Eastern leader to meet with Carter. Their meeting at the White House was particularly acrimonious, and Carter's public statements immediately after this session were major departures from the established American policy of private consultation and coordination with Israeli leaders. As Stein notes, Carter and Rabin were "on a collision course."[68] Thus, when Begin took office a few months later, he inherited a relationship with President Carter that was difficult, to understate the case.

On March 16, 1977, a week after the White House clash with Rabin, Carter addressed a "town hall meeting" in Clinton, Massachusetts. In that event, in response to a question on the Middle East, he declared, "There has to be a homeland provided for the Palestinian refugees."[69] This statement was a further development of the Brookings Plan, although, according to Quandt, Vance and Brzezinski were surprised by Carter's statement, indicating that it had not been discussed with them prior to its pronouncement.[70] Quandt said later that Carter's use of the term "homeland" was his "own contribution. We certainly didn't brief him on it or suggest it."[71] As Stein notes, "Rabin and most Israelis were astounded by Carter's remarks," and a US government official is quoted as saying, "We were stunned, furious; that Carter should give his [public endorsement of a Palestinian homeland] away . . . for nothing. It was dumb, utterly stupid." Apparently, Carter had not considered the Israeli response and the degree to which this would hurt the Labor Party.[72]

The elections were held on May 17, 1977. The Likud emerged as the largest party, with forty-three seats (four more than in 1973). The Likud faction grew to forty-five when Ariel Sharon and Yitzhak Yitzhaki, elected under the Shlomtzion Party, joined Herut. (Sharon then orchestrated the formation of the Likud bloc, including the Liberal Party.[73]) Labor dropped from fifty-one to thirty-two seats. Most of the voters who left Labor voted for the centrist Democratic Movement for Change (DMC), making it the third-largest faction in Knesset with fifteen seats. With the National Religious Party (NRP), which grew to twelve seats, four MKs from Agudat Israel (the Orthodox religious party), and Dayan, who defected from the Alignment and became a single-member faction, Begin had a bloc of sixty-two, even without the DMC. The era of Labor domination had ended, and Begin became prime minister.

Conclusion: From Opposition to Decision Maker

Following the resignation from the Unity Government and the return to opposition in 1970, Begin was building the foundations for the policies that he would pursue as prime minister. But in this period, he and his views remained relatively unknown outside his circle of supporters. In his meetings with American and other officials, Begin's carefully developed approach to peace negotiations and to relations with Egypt, Jordan, and Syria brought little interest.

In the United States, Jimmy Carter entered the White House in January 1977, eager to promote a comprehensive settlement to the conflict, including the establishment of a Palestinian state, as outlined in the Brookings Report, to which Brzezinski, Vance, and Quandt had contributed actively.[74] The expanded all-party Geneva peace conference that had been initiated by Kissinger in the previous administration was to serve as the anchor for this process.[75]

But Carter and his advisors knew little about Begin, and their image focused on his "hard line views" and repeated declarations that Israel must never return to the June 4, 1967, "green line."[76] Such policies appeared to stand in sharp contrast to those of the familiar figures from the Labor Party such as Meir, Allon, Rabin, Peres, and Eban. Carter reported that he was "shocked" by Begin's victory, demonstrating the degree to which America's foreign policy officials were poorly informed regarding Israeli domestic politics.[77] To the degree that they had any impressions of Begin and Herut, these were based largely on the often distorted and hostile images presented by his political and ideological rivals in Israel. Thus, from the beginning, interactions between the Begin and Carter administrations were (dis)colored by terms such as "extremist" and "terrorist." As Yaacov Bar-Siman-Tov notes, Begin's domestic opponents "habitually maligned him as irresponsible and lacking political understanding, and persistently warned that his coming to power would entail war and bloodshed."[78]

But Begin's views were neither static nor one-dimensional. While the differences with Carter in perspectives and approaches were apparent from the beginning, he also clearly recognized that the two interim disengagement agreements with Egypt had started a process that could not be left in midair.

These negotiations began with direct discussions between Israeli and Egyptian officials—the first such contacts since the 1948 armistice agreements—and Sadat and Begin shared both the goal of a peace agreement and of detouring around Carter's vision of the Geneva Conference. These conditions and the intense debates during the previous five years set the stage for the opening of direct talks immediately after Begin took office.

Notes

1. Menachem Begin, "Halikud Vehatchalat Sofi Hapoliti," *Maariv*, September 26, 1973 [Hebrew].
2. Protocol of Mr. M. Begin's opening remarks at the Herut Center meeting, November 4, 1971, 9, BCA, file OP-85 [Hebrew].
3. Menachem Begin, "Shura Shel Ashlayot Optiyot," *Maariv*, August 28, 1970 [Hebrew].
4. Menachem Begin, "Hamemirim Shalom Bishitchiyut," *Maariv*, September 30, 1970 [Hebrew].
5. Speech at the National Committee of the Herut Party, July 22, 1973, A7-A9, BCA, file OP-111 [Hebrew].
6. Menachem Begin, "Al Timaher Mar Sisco," *Maariv*, July 30, 1971 [Hebrew].
7. Menachem Begin, "Uvvchen, Kulam Ashemim," *Maariv*, November 30, 1974 [Hebrew].
8. Berlatzky, interview with Kadishai; Bar-Joseph, *Watchman Fell Asleep*.
9. Berlatzky, interview with Kadishai; Bar-Joseph, *Watchman Fell Asleep*.
10. Menachem Begin, speech in the Knesset in response to US appeal for a ceasefire, in Lorch, *Major Knesset Debates, 1948–1981*, 5:1815.
11. Yossi Goldstein, *Golda*, 563; Medzini, *Golda*, 547–548.
12. Lorch, *Major Knesset Debates, 1948–1981*, 5:1815–16.
13. Lorch, 5:1817–18.
14. Berlatzky, interview with Kadishai.
15. Berlatzky, interview. When Meir resigned, Begin complimented her "for her contribution to the country" and added, "I respected you before, when we sat in the same Government, and I continue to respect you today" (Lorch, *Major Knesset Debates, 1948–1981*, 5:1896).
16. Matti Golan, "The Alignment's Asset," *Haaretz*, December 3, 1973 [Hebrew]; "Begin in Response to Sapir: Repetitive Wars and Continuous Bloodshed," *Haaretz*, December 18, 1973 [Hebrew].
17. Shlomo Nakdimon, "Milchemet Shnei Hagushim," *Yediot Aharonot*, December 28, 1973 [Hebrew].
18. Menachem Begin, speech with the report of the new government, *Diveri HaKnesset* 69, 589–590 [Hebrew]; Menachem Begin, "Tsiri Leida Shel Halikud," *Maariv*, August 31, 1973 [Hebrew].
19. Lorch, *Major Knesset Debates, 1948–1981*, 5:1897.
20. Menachem Begin, speech with the report of the new government, *Diveri HaKnesset* 70, 1521 [Hebrew].
21. Menachem Begin, "Confusion and whitewash," *Maariv*, December 14, 1973 [Hebrew].
22. Menachem Begin, January 14, 1976, *Divrei HaKnesset*, 75, 1197 [Hebrew].

23. Menachem Begin, "Hahachlata Leha'amin La'aravim," *Maariv,* July 5, 1974 [Hebrew].

24. Menachem Begin, "Umar Rabin Molich Lemilchama," *Maariv,* September 27, 1974 [Hebrew].

25. Begin, "Umar Rabin Molich Lemilchama."

26. Menachem Begin, request to make a discussion about the security-political situation, August 6, 1974, *Divrei HaKnesset* 71, 2647 [Hebrew].

27. Menachem Begin, "Le'hichana Oh Lo Lehichana, Zo Hashe'ela," *Maariv,* July 4, 1975 [Hebrew].

28. Menachem Begin, "Mitoch Michtavim Ve'Al Tachtivim," *Maariv,* February 28, 1975 [Hebrew].

29. Menachem Begin, "Bli Nostalgya, Bli Pachad," *Maariv,* November 12, 1976 [Hebrew].

30. Menachem Begin, "Yesodot Hahasbara Baumot," *Maariv,* May 2, 1975 [Hebrew].

31. Menachem Begin, a speech in the Knesset following UN General Assembly Resolution 3210, October 21, 1974, *Diveri HaKnesset* 72, 2 [Hebrew].

32. Menachem Begin, "HaNazism HaAravi Neged HaYeled HaYehudi," *Maariv,* May 24, 1974 [Hebrew].

33. Menachem Begin, "Lekach Mitargil Biviturim," *Maariv,* October 15, 1971 [Hebrew].

34. Menachem Begin, speech following the government announcement on the political-security situation, *Divrei HaKnesset* 69, 13 [Hebrew].

35. Menachem Begin, "Tnu'at Atsuma Amamit," *Maariv,* October 18, 1974 [Hebrew].

36. Menachem Begin, speech following the government announcement on the political-security situation. *Divrei HaKnesset* 69, 13–14 [Hebrew].

37. "Begin at Jewish Congress: Sadat Is Creating a Political Deception," *Haaretz,* February 7, 1975, 3 [Hebrew].

38. Uzi Benziman, "After Temperamental Discussions and Recess in Plenary Session, the Knesset Approved Rabin's Announcement re Suspension of Negotiations with Egypt," *Haaretz,* March 25, 1975, 2–3 [Hebrew]; Begin's speech in the Protocol of the Herut Center meeting, March 18, 1975, 6, BCA, OP-88 [Hebrew].

39. Fischer, "Turning Point on the Road to Peace."

40. Protocol of Herut Center meeting, April 24, 1975, 1–3, BCA, OP-88 [Hebrew].

41. Menachem Begin, "Persistence in Withdrawal and Rulers' Illusions," *Maariv,* July 18, 1975, 16 [Hebrew]; Menachem Begin, "Frank with Dr. Kissinger and with Ourselves," *Maariv,* August 15, 1975 [Hebrew].

42. Protocol of Herut Center meeting, January 5, 1975, 1–3, BCA, OP-88 [Hebrew].

43. Dan Margalit, "Begin in US: Nixon Told Israel in 1970 Not to Withdraw without Signed Peace," *Haaretz,* April 7, 1975, 2 [Hebrew]. In 1971, Begin had already claimed that this constituted a formal commitment by the US president to Israel's security (Protocol of Mr. M. Begin's opening remarks at the Herut Center meeting, November 4, 1971, 12, BCA, OP-85 [Hebrew]).

44. Dan Margalit, "Begin in US: Nixon Told Israel in 1970 Not to Withdraw without Signed Peace," *Haaretz,* April 7, 1975, 2 [Hebrew].

45. "Begin Sketches a Peace Initiative," *Haaretz,* June 6, 1975, 3 [Hebrew].

46. Ran Kislev, "Unity of Likud at stake," *Haaretz,* June 8, 1975, 9 [Hebrew]; Kislev, "With Major Disagreements the Likud Opened Its Political Discussion," *Haaretz,* June 9, 1975, 3 [Hebrew]; "Following the Liberals Demand, the Political Debate over Rimalt's Suggestion Was Passed to the Likud Knesset Faction," *Haaretz,* June 24, 1975, 2 [Hebrew]; Kislev, "The Liberals: Run Away from Profound Confrontation," *Haaretz,* August 22, 1975, 13 [Hebrew].

47. "Begin: There Is Majority in Favor of Agreement in Knesset," *Haaretz*, August 28, 1975, 2 [Hebrew]; Gideon Alon, "Begin in Jerusalem Rally: Withdrawal Will Intensify Our Dependence on USA," *Haaretz*, August 31, 1975, 2 [Hebrew]; "Begin: Pressure for Withdrawals Will Intensify," *Haaretz*, September 2, 1975, 3 [Hebrew].

48. *FRUS 1969–1976*, vol. 26, documents 227–234.

49. Avner, *Prime Ministers*, 298.

50. Speech at ceremony marking the transfer of Nahal Sinai settlement from the military to civilian control, June 18, 1972, 2, BCA, OP-133 [Hebrew].

51. Begin, "Hahachlata Leha'amin La'aravim."

52. Protocol of Herut Center meeting, April 25, 1976, 3, BCA, OP-89 [Hebrew].

53. Berlatzky, interview.

54. "Arabs Plan Action against Jewish Visit," *Manchester Daily Telegraph*, January 8, 1972.

55. James Wightman, "Murder Threats Stops Banquet for ex-Terror Chief," *Daily Telegraph*, January 10, 1972; Vincent Mulchrone, "The Return of a Nice Little Killer," *Daily Mail*, January 11, 1972; "Begin: Hamasa Negdi siyea Labikur Belondon," *Maariv*, January 11, 1972 [Hebrew].

56. Begin at Herut Center meeting, November 4, 1971, 13–15; speech at ceremony of "civilinization" of Nahal Sinai settlement. Begin had also said that the American emergency airlift during the 1973 war was a form of repayment for Israel's role in keeping the Suez Canal, which was a major impediment to the Soviet Union, making Israel a partner rather than a client (Protocol of the Herut Center Meeting, November 20, 1973, 7, BCA, OP-86 [Hebrew]). See also Begin's speech at Herut Center meeting, December 16, 1973, 2, BCA, OP-86 [Hebrew]; and "Impasse at Suez," *Time*, February 9, 1968. In January 1977, he repeated the claim that Israel held the Suez Canal closed and by this saved thousands of American soldiers' lives ("Main points of keynote speech by Mr. Menachem Begin, Chairman of the Herut Movement, at the opening session of the 13th Herut Convention," January 2, 1977, 2, BCA, OP-192).

57. Menachem Begin, "Mishlachat Haknesset Lakongress," *Maariv*, November 28, 1975 [Hebrew].

58. UNESCO General Conference, Eighteenth Session, Paris, November 21, 1974

59. Menachem Begin, speech in the Knesset following UNESCO's decision, November 13, 1974, *Divrei HaKnesset*, volume 72, 359–360 [Hebrew].

60. Menachem Begin, speech in the Knesset following UN General Assembly decisions, *Divrei HaKnesset* 72, 492–496.

61. Yehoshua Tira, "Begin: We Suffered One of the Worst Political Defeats Ever," *Haaretz*, December 3, 1975, 3 [Hebrew].

62. Aryeh Rubinstein, "7 Parties Launch TV Electioneering," *Jerusalem Post*, April 29, 1977, 2.

63. Labor election advertisement, *Jerusalem Post*, May 2, 1977.

64. "Main Points of Keynote Speech by Mr. Menachem Begin, Chairman of the Herut Movement, at the Opening Session of the 13th Herut Convention," January 2, 1977, 1, BCA, OP-192.

65. Likud elections platform, in Telem, Tzabag, and Neuberger, *Israel's Foreign Policy*, part A, 354.

66. Telem, Tzabag, and Neuberger, *Israel's Foreign Policy*, 354–355.

67. Ben-Elissar, *No More War*, 15–18.

68. Stein, *Heroic Diplomacy*, 192–193.

69. "Clinton, Massachusetts Remarks and a Question-and-Answer Session at the Clinton Town Meeting, March 16, 1977," *Public Papers of the Presidents, Jimmy Carter,* accessed September 17, 2017, http://www.presidency.ucsb.edu/ws/?pid=7180.

70. Quandt, *Camp David:* 48; Brzezinski, *Power and Principle,* 91; Stein, *Heroic Diplomacy,* 193.

71. Strieff, *Jimmy Carter and the Middle East,* 30.

72. Stein, *Heroic Diplomacy,* 193–94.

73. Ariel Sharon was elected to the Knesset in 1973 as part of the Liberal faction in Likud but resigned on December 23, 1974, to keep his IDF reserve rank. In June 1975, Prime Minister Rabin appointed him as his security advisor, a post he left in March 1976. Likud members saw his links with Rabin as a betrayal and rejected his attempts to return. Sharon established his own party, Shlomtzion, in late 1976 and tried to recruit moderate political figures, without success. In the 1977 elections, Sharon won two seats and immediately called Begin, who agreed on a merger, increasing Likud's faction to forty-five seats. Since the defense portfolio was promised to Weizman, Sharon was appointed minister of agriculture and chairman of the ministerial committee on settlements. See Hefez and Bloom, *Ariel Sharon,* 179–189. On the short-lived Shlomtzion Party, see also Benziman, *Sharon,* 185–98.

74. Brookings Middle East Study Group, *Toward Peace in the Middle East.*

75. As Stein notes (*Heroic Diplomacy,* 188), Carter did not realize that the 1973 Geneva conference was engineered to provide a cover to legitimize the "pre-arranged" Israeli and Egyptian disengagement agreement.

76. In January 1975, Begin quoted from his conversation with then–prime minister David Ben-Gurion on the eve of the 1956 Sinai Campaign. Begin quoted Ben-Gurion as stating that when peace agreements are reached, all of western Eretz Israel (i.e., to the Jordan River) should remain in Israeli hands (Protocol of a Herut Center meeting, January 5, 1975, 11, BCA, OP-88 [Hebrew]).

77. Jimmy Carter, *Keeping Faith,* 282.

78. Bar-Siman-Tov, *Israel and the Peace Process, 1977–1982,* 20; Perlmutter, *Life and Times of Menachem Begin,* 240–312; Weizman, *Battle for Peace,* 36–38; Sofer, *Begin,* 124–31; Naor, *Begin in Power,* 65–93.

3 Setting the Stage

May–November 1977

Prime Minister Begin's Policies and Red Lines

Menachem Begin became the prime minister-designate of Israel during the early hours of May 18, 1977, as head of the victorious Likud bloc, marking the first time in twenty-nine years of Israeli independence that a party other than Mapai (in different versions) formed the government. Begin had spent the days prior to the election in the hospital following a heart attack, but he recovered quickly to take command. Following the political *mahapach* (upheaval), Begin completed the coalition negotiations, and on June 20 he presented his government to the Knesset for approval.[1]

From the beginning, the new government had a full agenda, including pressing economic and social issues. However, the security and diplomatic dimensions quickly dominated activity, particularly in the Prime Minister's Office. On the day after the election (May 18), Begin told Ezer Weizman (who was appointed defense minister) that the primary goal of his government was to prevent war.[2] A few days later, in a meeting with the new US ambassador Samuel Lewis, Begin declared that his first task as prime minister was to enter into peace negotiations with Egypt.[3] Begin assured Lewis of his determination to reach a peace agreement and later sent President Jimmy Carter an English translation of his government's basic guidelines even before they were approved by the Knesset.

Begin's decision to appoint Moshe Dayan as foreign minister provided a level of experience and some degree of continuity. It also meant that issues in this domain would receive a high profile.[4] Yaakov Meridor, a close friend of Begin (and minister of economics and inter-ministry coordination in Begin's second government, 1981 to 1983), noted that he was worried at first because he did not know where Begin planned to lead the country. Dayan's appointment reassured Meridor and many others.[5] In the Labor Alignment, the appointment was criticized, as it was by some Likud members and others who held Dayan responsible for the trauma of the 1973 Yom Kippur War. Families of the war casualties protested his appointment as an unjustified rehabilitation. Begin explained that although Dayan's status had declined in Israel, to the nations of the region and the world, he still symbolized the "fighting Jew" and as Israel's foreign minister, he would help the new government gain respect.[6]

Dayan conditioned his acceptance of this position on Begin's agreement to refrain from discussions on annexation of Judea and Samaria and on acceptance of the Geneva framework based on UNSCR 242.[7]

At the same time, Begin took care in ensuring that Dayan would not encroach on the authority of the prime minister to set the agenda and make policy. Begin saw the foreign minister's role as being responsible for implementing the government's agreed objectives, as well as providing analyses and suggestions.

The decision to appoint Dayan disappointed many Likud activists and supporters. But beyond the official explanation that Dayan would gain international respect for the new government, Begin did not have appropriate candidate from his own party. Indeed, rejecting the views of many Likud leaders, Begin decided against replacing the wider Israeli bureaucracy appointed during the long Mapai era. Reflecting the British model, which he admired, Begin viewed civil servants as professionals and probably more capable of performing their duties than many political appointees. In his own office, Begin selected a very few confidants: cabinet secretary Arye Naor, Director General of the Prime Minister's Office Eliahu Ben-Elissar, Director of the Prime Minister's Bureau Yechiel Kadishai, and his personal secretary, Yona Klimovitsky. Begin also kept several of Yitzhak Rabin's advisors in place: spokesperson Dan Patir, advisor Yehuda Avner, political advisor (and Rabin's chief of bureau) Eli Mizrachi, and military attaché Ephraim Poran. He even asked Israel's ambassador to Washington, Simcha Dinitz—Golda Meir's and later Rabin's confidant—who had offered his resignation, to continue. Dinitz remained ambassador until late 1978, after the Camp David Summit.

In Washington, Begin was largely unknown compared to his predecessors. In a White House Policy Review Committee meeting on April 19, two weeks after Rabin's forced resignation from the leadership of Labor (he was replaced by Shimon Peres), Brzezinski, Vance, Harold Brown, Quandt, and other senior officials discussed scenarios for the Israeli elections, none of which included the possibility that Begin would emerge victorious and become prime minister.[8] The annual report of the National Security Council for 1977 acknowledged in retrospect, "The United States had not anticipated that the May elections in Israel would bring about a change in government. Our approach had been predicated on the well-known positions of the Israeli government concerning withdrawal in exchange for peace."[9] A few days after the Likud victory, Brzezinski gave Carter a few excerpts from J. Bowyer Bell's tendentious book on the prestate underground, *Terror Out of Zion.* Brzezinski highlighted some quotes from Begin and analyses based on the period thirty years prior to the book's publication.[10]

On the day after the elections, William Quandt wrote a memorandum to Brzezinski analyzing the results. He warned that the United States was about to face "the prospect of a very weak coalition, a prolonged period of uncertainty, and an Israeli leadership which may be significantly more assertive in its policies concerning the West Bank, Palestinians, settlements, and nuclear weapons." He added that the Arabs would "no doubt" see these results as the end of the chance to reach Geneva in 1977 and that "the short term looks rather bleak in the Middle East."[11]

On this basis, Quandt suggested that American policy not express disappointment with the Likud victory; Begin should be invited to Washington, but to reach its objectives, the United States should not hastily revise its policy and avoid helping Begin in new Israeli elections that were "inevitable in the near future." Quandt wrote that the Israeli public should know that a hardline government would have difficulties with the United States, but the administration "should not be seen as the bully. Begin should be allowed to make his own mistakes." Quandt also assumed that the Likud government would have less backing among American supporters of Israel than the Labor Party; therefore the administration could use the opportunity to "take some of the hard decisions on arms for Egypt and contacts with the Palestinians."[12] Quandt clearly misjudged Israeli political realities (perhaps echoing the assessments of the Labor Party officials with whom he was in contact), but this memo reflected the antagonistic prism through which Begin and his policies were viewed.

In interviews in late May 1977, Begin presented his positions and prescriptions on each of the central foreign policy issues facing Israel. Begin stated that 1977 "might be the year of political negotiations" but also said, "It is inconceivable to us to allow a Palestinian state . . . . On this we have a national consensus. . . . Under no circumstances can we agree to a so-called Palestinian state. It would be a mortal danger to us."[13]

Restating the plan that he had presented as minister without portfolio in the National Unity cabinet two weeks after the June 1967 war, Begin declared his readiness to "give the people of Samaria and Judea free options of citizenship. If they want Israeli citizenship, they will get it. . . . They can have complete cultural autonomy and social and economic advancement, living in their homes."[14]

Begin acknowledged differences of opinion with the US administration, noting that President Carter demanded an Israeli withdrawal to the 1967 borders with minor modifications, as called for in the Rogers Plan. In his diary, Carter wrote, "it was frightening to watch his adamant position on issues that must be resolved if a Middle Eastern peace settlement is going to be realized."[15]

Although largely new for foreign audiences, these policy objectives were consistent with Begin's positions over the previous decade. He continued to emphasize strengthening Israel's claim to Judea, Samaria, and Gaza while viewing the Sinai Peninsula and the Golan Heights as negotiable in the framework of a peace agreement. To promote Israeli security, he was willing to reach an agreement with Egypt in the context of a separate peace, and he gave high priority to signaling this readiness to Sadat.

Following the established practice, Begin delivered a detailed programmatic inaugural address to the Knesset on June 20, 1977, in which he again emphasized the issues of war and peace. The themes that Begin discussed, as well as his perspectives and priorities, provided the underpinning for policies in the four years that followed (and beyond). In Washington, this speech should have provided an important foundation for understanding the policies of the new Israeli government.

In this speech, Begin used his grand rhetorical style that was relatively unique in Israeli politics and stood in sharp contrast to the dry rhetoric of his immediate predecessors (Meir and Rabin). He demonstrated his detailed knowledge of Jewish sources to frame the debate, quoting from the vision of the apocalypse of the Prophet Micah (4, 3) and Prophet Isaiah (2, 4): "And they shall beat their swords into plowshares, and their spears into pruning hooks: nation shall not lift up sword against nation, neither shall they learn war anymore."[16] Begin noted that he was responding to Carter's quote from Micah (6, 8: "He has shown you, O mortal, what is good. And what does the Lord require of you? To act justly and to love mercy and to walk humbly with your God") in his inaugural speech in January. Quoting from the Bible was not only a frequent practice for Begin; he believed that this would establish a common language with the US leader. In many of the discussions with Carter, Begin included biblical citations, although it was evident—or at least should have been—that the hope for greater understanding was not succeeding.

In this speech, Begin reminded his audience at home and abroad of the position he had held since 1967, in contrast to the Labor leaders and allies who attempted to paint him and the Likud as undifferentiated hawks opposed to any and all peace efforts. As he had done in private meetings, Begin told the Knesset, "Our overriding concern is to prevent a new war in the Middle East."[17]

But lasting peace could only be achieved through direct, face-to-face negotiations, in contrast to the various shuttles undertaken by Henry Kissinger and his predecessors. Begin issued an open invitation for the Arab leaders, including King Hussein, President Anwar Sadat, and President Hafez al-Assad, "to confer with me, whether in one of our capitals or on neutral ground, whether in public or out of the public eye, to discuss making true peace." After recalling the history of "Arab intransigence" and the refusal to negotiate with the "five Prime Ministers who preceded me," Begin declared that "we will not tire of making our appeal, not for propaganda purposes but for the essential needs of our people and our country."[18]

Begin then restated his core principles based on political Zionism, Jewish sovereignty, and rights in the Land of Israel. No prizes would be given for recognition of Israel's right to exist—this was not to be used as a bargaining chip to extract security or other concessions from Israel. Thus, Begin stated,

By virtue of that ancient heritage of thousands of years, I declare that the government of Israel will not ask any nation whether near or far, great or small, to recognize our right to exist. . . . We received the right to exist from the God of our fathers at the dawn of human history, almost four thousand years ago. . . . A different kind of recognition is required between us and our neighbors, recognition of sovereignty and the mutual need for a life of peace and understanding. . . . For that recognition, we will make every effort.[19]

However, Begin clarified that Israel would not withdraw to the 1967 lines and would refuse the establishment of a Palestinian state that would threaten the lives of all Israelis. If anyone expected, now that the Likud was finally in power, that these fundamental positions would change, Begin reminded them, "We were in the desert of opposition for 29 years and did not abandon our principles for a single day. There were those who said that we lost votes because of those principles. Yet we adhered to them."[20] After the speech, Begin's government was approved by sixty-three votes, with fifty-three opposed.

Following the euphoria of the first days in office, the rhetoric and lofty declarations of principle began to be translated into policies. Begin understood that he would have to immediately address the continuing developments in the post-1973 peace efforts, particularly with respect to Egypt, and to create clear guidelines and objectives. The two interim disengagement agreements with Egypt, achieved with a great deal of effort and the direct involvement of Kissinger and the US government, started a process that could not be left in "mid-air."[21]

Begin was well aware of differences with the Carter administration, which entered office with a plan framed by the Brookings Report. This plan envisioned a very ambitious and comprehensive Middle East peace agreement, including the establishment of a Palestinian state.[22] The proposed all-party Geneva peace conference that had been developed by Kissinger in the previous administration was to serve as the anchor for this process, including the active involvement of the Soviet Union. Whereas, in the past, Moscow was viewed as a spoiler whose inclusion in peacemaking efforts would be counterproductive and Kissinger brought in Moscow in a symbolic role, the Carter administration sought to actively involve Soviet leaders in the process in an effort to neutralize their negative impact.[23]

To quickly engage with the Americans and present alternatives, Begin tasked Dayan with preparing a memorandum analyzing likely developments and conditions "considered essential for a just and lasting peace." Dayan's June 24 outline presented options for parallel tracks on each front, including a peace treaty with Egypt that would involve a major but not complete withdrawal. In contrast, in Judea and Samaria, Dayan's memo did not envision or advocate any diminution of Israeli military and political control.[24]

On June 25, Ambassador Dinitz sent Dayan a memorandum summarizing the discussions during Rabin's final visit to Washington as prime minister in

March 1977. Rabin's conditions for peace were very similar to Begin's, including a termination of the state of war, open borders, and free movement of people and commodities. Dinitz reported that the administration responded that "your standards of peace are exactly compatible with ours."[25]

However, unlike Begin, Rabin had a fallback position and was willing to discuss nonbelligerency and other options short of a full treaty. Regarding borders, Rabin accepted the principle of territorial compromise but not a return to the pre-1967 lines, particularly in the Golan Heights. On the Sinai, Rabin said that Israel did not insist on sovereignty over Sharm El Sheikh but on "control and presence," including a land connection to Israel. Carter told Rabin that the United States distinguished between legal borders and security borders and spoke of "secure lines of defense." According to the Americans, Egypt had rejected this distinction but was willing to discuss demilitarizing territories and international forces.[26]

Dinitz noted some changes in the American position since Rabin's visit. Carter now sought an Israeli withdrawal to the pre-1967 lines with minor adjustments, and Israeli security would be guaranteed through a defense treaty with the United States. Another memo to Dayan stressed the centrality of the Brookings Plan for Carter and his determination to go beyond talks and reach a comprehensive agreement by changing the previous terms and patterns of negotiations.[27]

Dinitz's assessment was reinforced by Foreign Ministry analyses of the perceptions held by Carter and other key American officials. Begin was informed that the Americans told Arab leaders that peace could not consist only of the absence of war but must include trade, cultural exchanges, tourism, normal diplomatic relations, and security arrangements for Israel. But in parallel, on June 27, a State Department official pointedly stated that in return for security arrangements, Israel would have to withdraw from territories to agreed and defensible borders on all fronts and to negotiate terms for a Palestinian homeland—all terms that Begin rejected.[28]

Begin also listened closely to Sadat's statements, which indicated the existence of a framework within Begin's parameters.

Elements of Sadat's initiative were made public already on June 6, 1977, after the Israeli election and two weeks before Begin formally took office. In a speech addressed to the Egyptian Third Army, Sadat declared, "If necessary, as I said already, I will be prepared to go to the end of the world to save the life of each soldier and officer here. But if the peaceful solution failed and if the enemy remains stubborn—it will be a different story." Shimon Shamir, who later served as Israel's ambassador to Egypt, argues that Sadat feared that 1977 would become another wasted year (after 1976 because of the US elections and early 1977 because of Israel's elections). He wanted to see results of the diplomatic track that started with the interim agreements made with Rabin's government in 1975. These agreements had been in force for three years, and Sadat needed to demonstrate some tangible results, according to Shamir.[29]

In June, Begin received a message from Sadat, delivered by Professor Irwin Cotler, head of Canadian Professors for Peace in the Middle East (and, later, the attorney general), who came from Cairo, where he was lecturing at the Al-Ahram Center's Institute of Politics and Strategic Studies. Cotler had met with the center's head, Boutros Boutros-Ghali, a professor of international law (and Sadat's foreign minister starting in October 1977), who asked whether Egypt would "be able to reach a peace agreement with the new Israeli prime minister and his hawkish government?"[30] Cotler responded affirmatively and then met with Sadat, who sent a message to Begin to be delivered by Cotler.

In Jerusalem, Cotler secured a meeting with Begin, and, reversing the process that had occurred in Cairo, the latter asked Cotler whether he thought Sadat's intentions were genuine and received a positive response. Begin then read the message, which "inquired about the possibility of opening peace talks, with two conditions: the return of Sinai, and Israeli recognition of the rights of the Palestinian people."[31]

Cotler reports, "He read the note and said these conditions are unacceptable. . . . I said, 'I didn't say the conditions were acceptable to you. I'm just conveying to you the fact that these are the conditions [Sadat] conveyed but that he would want to explore. Peace negotiations would ensue, and I believe they're worth exploring.'"[32]

As a result of these and other indications, Begin was prepared to receive further evidence of positive movement from Egypt. On July 16, three days before Begin's first meeting with Carter, Sadat spoke again, this time to the Central Committee of Arab Socialist Union. Sadat seemed to share many of Begin's views, declaring that "we are prepared to sign a treaty of just and lasting peace. . . . [W]e are willing to end the state of war, politically and legally. It means also that for the first time in Israel's history its legal existence within its borders will be acknowledged." Sadat called on Israel to follow "the principles of international law," (an apparent reference to withdrawal to the border with Egypt) to become "a Middle Eastern country living in peace."[33] Shamir interpreted this statement as an effort to prepare the Egyptian public for Sadat's initiative later that year.

Several sources sought to explore the background for Sadat's statement. Israel had allegedly warned Sadat of a Libyan plot against his regime, and he thanked Begin through this statement after his intelligence services confirmed the information. Three days later, on July 19, a six-day border war broke out between Egypt and Libya.[34] An Israeli academic, Michael Handel, reported that the head of Mossad handed the information to his Egyptian counterpart in a face-to-face meeting in Morocco in mid-July. In the context of an active border conflict between Egypt and Libya, Begin assured Egypt that Israel would not take advantage of the situation. Handel saw this as one of Begin's signals to Sadat.[35]

Begin's First Meeting with Carter

As had become customary, the first foreign trip of a new Israeli prime minister was to Washington, and on July 19, Begin met with Carter and other officials. This meeting was important for both leaders, and Stein notes that Ambassador Lewis recommended treating Begin "with honey, not vinegar." Indeed, Carter honored Begin with a red-carpet welcome, gave him legitimacy, and refrained from attacking him.[36]

However, Begin did not come only to gain legitimacy but rather to take the initiative, uproot the Brookings Plan (as well as to set firm limitations), and get Carter's support for his own peace strategy. Begin's office prepared a detailed, unsigned, single-page document dated July 13, 1977, describing Israel's willingness to make territorial concessions and the principles behind them. This central document, which was top secret until 2010, provides an important insight into Begin's strategy. The contents were conveyed directly and privately by Begin to Carter in their first meeting (and in writing to Vance) and served as the outline of all of Begin's subsequent moves and policies:

> Because of the vastness of the land, we will be prepared, in the context of a peace treaty and the determination of the permanent boundary between Israel and Egypt, for a substantial withdrawal of our forces in Sinai.
>
> We shall stay on the Golan Heights and be prepared for a withdrawal of our forces from the existing line in the context of a peace treaty and the determination of the permanent boundary between Syria and Israel.
>
> Concerning Judea, Samaria and the Gaza Strip, our position is that we shall not place them under any foreign rule or sovereignty on the basis of two factors:
>
> One, our people's right to the Land; it is our Land as of right.
>
> Two, our national security, which concerns the defensive capability of the State and the lives of our civilian population.[37]

Begin emphasized his request that the content of this document remain secret and would not be passed to the Arab states.[38] Two months later, he revealed its existence in a radio interview but refused to disclose the contents.[39]

Prior to their meeting, analysts and pundits predicted that the relationship between Carter and Begin would be tense (as was the case with Carter and Rabin), but Carter—according to his diary—claims to have found Begin "quite congenial, dedicated, sincere, and deeply religious." He sensed—as suggested in a memorandum by Robert Lipshutz from May 23, 1977, based on conversations he held with American Jewish leaders—that with American backing, Begin could be persuaded to change his policies.[40] Carter observed that Begin's strong leadership was "quite different from Rabin, who is one of the most ineffective persons I've ever met."[41] Carter's initial positive response did not extend to the substance of Begin's carefully composed statement on how to proceed in seeking peace.

In their discussions, Begin declared his willingness to participate in the proposed Geneva peace conference, with a number of significant conditions. To counter the Brookings Plan, Carter's "Palestinian homeland" speech, and the American opposition to Israeli settlements in Judea and Samaria, Begin presented his model for Palestinian autonomy that would stop far short of sovereignty.[42] He wanted Carter to understand his framework and launched into a long narrative on history. In addressing the Knesset after his return, Begin said that he had told the American president, "Palestine is the Land of Israel, and the British Mandate accorded recognition to the link between the Jewish people and Palestine. . . . When the late Dr. Chaim Weizmann made an agreement with King Feisal it stated that there should be friendly relations and understanding between 'the Arab state' and 'Palestine.' . . . Thus, anyone who uses the phrase 'Palestine problem' to refer to the Arabs of the Land of Israel is distorting the historical facts."[43]

As clearly stated in the memo, Israel was prepared to make significant withdrawals in the Sinai and Golan Heights in exchange for peace agreements. But Israel would never relinquish Judea, Samaria, and Gaza to foreign authorities while not claiming sovereignty. Begin made it clear that he had no preconditions for peace negotiations; therefore, any subject, including Jerusalem and the West Bank, could be discussed.[44] On this basis, Begin urged Carter to relay his ideas to Sadat as the foundation for a meeting.

In their summaries, Carter and Brzezinski noted that Begin showed flexibility but that the gap was very wide, and Israel would need to make major concessions.[45] The American memorandum of the conversation mentions that "Begin commented that Sadat's conditions were not conducive to peace. He was demanding total Israeli withdrawal on all fronts and a corridor between Gaza and the West Bank. If his conditions were realized, it would be the beginning of the end of the Jewish state. Sadat knew that."[46]

Yehuda Avner, a senior Israeli diplomat and Begin's advisor on Diaspora affairs, who also took notes in the meetings, reports that the president stated that his administration was abandoning the Ford-Kissinger policy of achieving "a slow, incremental, step-by-step process toward peace." The time was ripe, said Carter, for a comprehensive peace in the Middle East, and this should be achieved by convening all of the parties in Geneva as soon as possible. He made clear that Resolution 242 must be accepted as the legal basis of the conference. However, Carter added, he thought that the resolution's call for ending the state of belligerency was insufficient. Carter told Begin that he was widening the connotation to mean "a full-blown peace settlement." Begin asked how the Arabs responded to this policy, and Carter replied that they found it difficult to accept but did not reject it. Begin, according to Avner, was very pleased.[47]

Predictably, Carter and Begin disagreed on the West Bank and Palestinian dimensions. However, the US president noted in his diary that Begin "pointed out that he was making tentative plans to meet directly with Sadat."[48] Carter did not mention any follow-up on this at the time.

At the state dinner, the public toasts between Carter and Begin clearly reflected the differences of opinion. Carter complimented Begin, saying that "our guest is a strong leader. He is a man of deep convictions and unshakable principle. He is a man of truth and quiet dignity. He is a man who is polite and very modest." But he did not conceal his differences of opinion with Begin: "We have explored differences of opinion in a very blunt and frank fashion, and I think we have resolved some of the differences. Few still remain, but we have discovered and mutually recognized, in order to make them permanent the agreements that are inherent in the attitudes of our people."[49]

On the American role in the expected negotiations, Carter told aides he would be careful to avoid imposing US policy on anyone and would act as a trusted intermediary. But he also warned that the United States would not "avoid a controversial issue . . . even when at times it creates some hopefully transient dissension among people who have strongly held opposing views."[50] In playing this role vis-à-vis Begin and other Israelis, Carter created more than "transient dissension."

Begin's reply emphasized very different issues. He flattered and praised Carter (much as the president tried with Begin), calling him "a great friend of humanity, a man of great understanding and feeling . . . a great friend of Israel." Begin spoke of his own belief in divine providence and mentioned the suffering of his generation during the Holocaust and the "terror and bloodshed . . . in our own land," which he sought to end through negotiating peace.[51]

Begin then reminded Carter that "we, Israel, are a faithful ally of the United States. We do whatever we can to serve the free world. We are a guardian of human liberty and democracy in the Middle East . . . with free elections and peaceful transfer of power." He recalled his first executive order "to bring in the Vietnamese refugees into our country." As a proud democracy, he said, "This is our contribution to freedom, national security of the free world. We shall continue to do so to the best of our ability."[52]

Regarding the peace negotiations, Begin called for a sense of urgency alongside patience, stating that the conflict was historical, "not a territorial problem." He went into the history of the Arab-Israeli conflict, in which Israel "only defended [itself] against attempts, repeated, to destroy our people."[53]

He concluded by saying, "We don't hate our neighbors. . . . But we had to defend ourselves. This is the whole story, as they used to say in those ancient days, on one foot. I can only speak very shortly standing on one foot, the whole story. We are hopeful; we are optimistic. We have to be."[54]

Clearly, Carter and Begin had vastly different perceptions regarding the future of the Middle East and spoke past one another. Begin did not alter his positions or vocabulary to suit Washington's new approach. With their very different sets of reasoning, future clashes between the president and the prime minister were inevitable.

The detailed substantive response came when Begin returned home on July 25, and Ambassador Lewis handed him and Dayan a five-point document that the administration prepared as a basis for the Geneva Conference. In his memoirs, Dayan writes that Israel accepted the first three points—that the purpose was to reach peace agreements, that UN Resolutions 242 and 338 would be foundations for the negotiations, and that there should be normal relations between Israel and the Arabs and not only an end to belligerency—but rejected the fifth, concerning the establishment of a Palestinian entity. Regarding the fourth point, Israel refused to oblige itself to full withdrawal on all fronts, exempting Judea and Samaria.[55]

A few days later, Begin addressed the Knesset to report on his visit, including the efforts to convene the Geneva Conference. Begin indicated that Israel was willing to go forward in this mode but only if the terms were consistent with his long-stated requirements. He told the Knesset that Israeli participation meant that the Arab states "will not submit any prior conditions for their participation" such as Israeli withdrawal or guarantees regarding the outcome. The work of the conference would take place through three "mixed committees—Egypt-Israel, Syria-Israel, and Jordan-Israel."[56]

Most importantly, the goal could no longer be partial agreements, but rather "negotiations will be conducted for signing peace treaties between Israel and its neighbors." This point was cardinal and was repeated in significant detail to avoid any misunderstanding. "The objective of the negotiations between Israel and its neighbors is to attain peace treaties . . . i.e., ending the state of belligerency, settling permanent borders, establishing diplomatic relations with the exchange of ambassadors, setting up economic relations, etc."[57]

In addition, Begin reported that he had told Carter that any efforts to include delegates from the PLO in this process would be rejected. It is "an organization of murderers, which aspires to destroy the State of Israel and is the Jewish people's most implacable enemy since the Nazis. There is nothing to negotiate with it." Indeed, "A Palestinian state . . . in Judea, Samaria and Gaza . . . is a threat to the existence of the Jewish state."[58]

The pace of meetings and discussions was very intense, and Secretary of State Vance embarked on a ten-day tour of the Middle East, with Israel as his last stop. In meetings with Dayan on August 9 in Jerusalem, differences over the

Palestinian issue were central. According to Dayan's account, Vance conveyed Egypt's demand for the return of the Sinai and Gaza, and the latter would be transferred to the Palestinians at a later date. In the West Bank, the Egyptian plan was for an Israeli withdrawal, after which UN forces would take control for several years, during which the Palestinians would hold a referendum with self-determination as a central option.[59]

On August 10, Vance met with Begin and Dayan. Dayan stated, "If an agreement is negotiated which establishes withdrawal to a certain line which leaves outside that line a settlement, the Israeli Government will move such a settlement," knowing that this was also Begin's position. Dayan reiterated this position (apparently in the same meeting), saying "no Israeli settlement"—referring to Sinai—"will be an obstacle to any peace agreement." [60] In retrospect, this appears to be a dramatic statement vis-à-vis existing and future settlements. Nevertheless, in his report to Carter, Vance gave little emphasis to this central point, instead writing, "In concluding this part of the discussion, Dayan seemed to misjudge Arab reaction. It is increasingly apparent that the Israelis are trying to convince themselves and to base their legal case on the proposition that the Arabs will not react to settlements which do not result in displacement of Arab population."[61]

In Egypt, Sadat asked Vance whether Begin seemed serious, and Vance replied that Begin was sincere and his toughness was tactical, although Begin's opposition to any negotiations with the PLO seemed real. Sadat was interested in Begin's ideas and told Vance he wanted to meet Israel's prime minister. This message was passed to Begin.[62]

Developing an Alternative to the Geneva Conference Framework

While Begin was laying out his response to Carter regarding the Geneva framework, this approach was coming under increasing criticism, particularly from Cairo. US-Soviet comanagement of the process was increasingly undesirable. Sadat frequently explained that he did not "throw out the Russians" only to have them reenter through the political door.[63] (During his visit to Jerusalem in November, Sadat complained to Dayan, "Why did they [the United States] have to get the Russians involved that way?"[64])

Begin was also strongly opposed to involving Moscow, and in his inaugural speech to the Knesset, he attacked the Soviet leadership, demanding an end "to the persecution of and incitement against Judaism and Zionism" and freedom for "all prisoners of Zion" to enable them to immigrate to Israel.[65] In addition, as he made clear, Begin did not welcome a negotiation process based on the Brookings Plan, centered on the creation of a Palestinian state. Thus, both Sadat and Begin were more than open to explore alternative approaches and actively sought them.

Even before going to Washington, Begin started exploring other diplomatic options. The first move in what was to become the Romanian channel began on July 4, at the annual reception at the residence of the US ambassador in Herzliya. The Romanian ambassador asked the outgoing director general of the foreign ministry, Shlomo Avineri, for an introduction to the new prime minister. The ambassador immediately invited Begin to Romania (repeating the invitation that had been extended to Rabin a few months before, which Rabin did not accept, citing the election campaign). Begin immediately accepted and traveled to Romania at the end of August.[66]

On August 14, Foreign Minister Dayan met the Indian prime minister Moraji Desai in New Delhi, and on the nineteenth, after reporting to Begin in Jerusalem, Dayan traveled to Tehran and met the Shah. In both meetings, he conveyed Israel's desire to reach peace with Egypt.[67] Dayan then met secretly with Jordan's King Hussein on August 22 in London and concluded that Hussein would not agree to a separate negotiations track that would bypass the PLO. Hussein also indicated that any acceptable treaty would have to ensure the unity of the West Bank and a full withdrawal of Israel, including east Jerusalem.

On the basis of these meetings, Dayan and Begin decided to focus on the Egyptian track.[68] At this point, Begin flew to Romania to send another signal to Sadat indicating that he wanted to meet directly with the Egyptian leader.

It is unclear whether Begin knew what to expect upon arrival in Romania in terms of contacts and messages from the Egyptian government. Certainly, neither he nor anyone else could have expected that these initial steps would eventually lead to Sadat's visit to Jerusalem a few months later. Begin was known as a staunch anticommunist, and in making Romania his second international destination (after the United States), he demonstrated publicly that he was not wedded to frozen ideologies or simplistic views of the world.

Romania, the only communist bloc country that had maintained full diplomatic relations with Israel after Moscow broke off ties in 1967, had a unique status in the Israeli diplomatic framework. Nicolae Ceausescu was known to have an open and very active channel to Egypt and had been attempting to bring Egyptian and Israeli leaders together and to play a major role in the Middle East for some time. In May 1972, Ceausescu told Prime Minister Golda Meir that Sadat was ready to meet with an Israeli official at some unspecified level, following the Egyptian disappointment at the failure of the Moscow summit between Nixon and Brezhnev to produce a new Middle East initiative. In contrast to Begin, Meir chose not to pursue this possible lead, and since Sadat was "pursuing several options simultaneously" at that time, she could readily have concluded that the feelers were not serious. (Her suspicions did not diminish over the years, and a few days before Sadat arrived in Israel, she dismissed the reports as political hype, declaring, "Grass will grow in my hand if he comes to Jerusalem."[69])

In 1976, about two years after Rabin replaced Meir as prime minister, the Romanians tried again, extending an official invitation to Rabin during MFA director general Shlomo Avineri's visit to Bucharest. The Israeli Foreign Ministry and other officials did not directly link the Romanian activity and invitations to the prime minister to Sadat's visits and considered various explanations, including the possibility that Romania was acting on behalf of the Soviet Union. At the same time, Rabin treated Sadat's talk about peace "carefully and with skepticism."[70] (However, in October 1976, Rabin made a secret trip to Morocco to discuss diplomatic initiatives.[71])

Thus, it is possible that upon taking office, Begin received intelligence briefings on the Romanian and Moroccan channels and involvement in the Egyptian connection from the Mossad or another source. The evidence clearly shows that Begin moved quickly to probe the potential for a "far-reaching territorial compromise" in Sinai.[72]

In Romania, Begin asked Ceausescu to help pave the way for a direct meeting with Sadat, and he followed this up with a similar message just prior to Sadat's visit to Romania in late October.[73] According to Sadat's public testimony in the following years, the Romanian connection was a central factor in the Egyptian leader's decision to meet Begin.[74]

Shamai Kahana, Israel's ambassador to Bucharest, summarized the meeting between Begin and Ceausescu in a highly classified cable, although the most important discussion was held between Begin and Ceausescu alone, with only a translator present, and thus there are no transcripts or detailed notes. In the larger forum, the Romanian prime minister, minister of foreign affairs, ambassador to Israel, and the translator joined their president, and on Israel's part, Begin was joined by Ambassador Kahana and the new director general of the Foreign Ministry, Efraim Evron. The meeting took place on August 26, 1977, in Snagov, Ceausescu's retreat on a lake near Bucharest, where he also held official meetings.

Begin explained the peace plan he had presented to President Carter and handed Ceausescu a copy. Begin talked about the June 1967 lines to which Sadat demanded Israel to withdraw and, using a map, emphasized the dangers that he saw. He repeated that this could not be a precondition to negotiations, but Sadat could bring it up (along with anything else) during the negotiations themselves. Begin reminded Ceausescu that Israel also had critical issues to discuss in the negotiations, such as keeping Jerusalem united, but these were not preconditions.[75]

According to Kahana's cable, Ceausescu said that the Geneva course would be a good way to start negotiations but not the only one. He told Begin that Israel must understand it would not be able to base negotiations on the premise of keeping the territories captured in 1967, whether the issue came up before the negotiations or later. He also informed Begin that Assad and Sadat told him that they would not agree to not receiving their respective territories back.

Ceausescu urged Begin to regard the PLO as an organization trying to achieve a collective right to exist for three million people and to recognize the Palestinian right to self-determination. According to the Romanian leader, he learned from Arafat that the PLO had changed and understood it had to accept Israel's existence. Therefore, the structure of the Geneva Conference depended on Israel's willingness to accept the Palestinian right to participate and gain its national rights.

Begin replied that for all other countries, the role of the PLO was a political question, but for Israel it was existential. The status of the territories could be discussed during negotiations, but until a peace treaty was signed, Israel's claims were entirely legal. He told Ceausescu that in discussions with Arab leaders, Secretary Vance suggested that as part of an agreement, Judea and Samaria would be demilitarized, but this had been rejected. As expected, Begin and Ceausescu reached no agreement on characterizing the PLO (as guerrillas or terrorists). The rest of their discussion was private and therefore undocumented in the ambassador's report.

However, in a report to the members of his coalition on September 4, Begin revealed that Ceausescu had told him that Sadat was willing to hold a meeting between representatives of Israel and Egypt but not yet between himself and Begin. This, Begin emphasized, was not to be made public.[76]

After Begin left, Sadat sent his confident and in-law, Speaker of the National Assembly Sayid Mar'i (who later accepted the Nobel Peace Prize for Sadat in 1978) to Romania to receive a report.[77] Sadat's autobiography indicates that Ceausescu said that Begin was serious. When Sadat visited in late October, he received the same assessment.[78] (Begin had sent another message to Ceausescu repeating his desire to meet Sadat anywhere.)[79]

According to documents in the Israel State Archives, Begin and Dayan understood that the Egyptians told Ceausescu to proceed with a high-level meeting, and this information was passed on to the United States.[80] In parallel, Ambassador Dinitz reported to Dayan on a meeting with Henry Kissinger, who had received detailed information on the Israeli-Egyptian contacts in Romania and on Sadat's proposal for an international conference to be held in east Jerusalem. Kissinger, who opposed the Carter administration's plan to include Moscow in the Geneva Conference, expressed concern about holding such contacts in Romania, "where the Soviets have ears in every wall."[81] While the Romanian summit did not take place, the discussions indicated the direction of events that led to Sadat's visit to Israel.

The Moroccan channel arose in parallel to the Romanian track, during July to August 1977, and grew in significance, with some important successes even before Begin's trip to Romania. As noted, in October 1976, Prime Minister Rabin had secretly visited King Hassan in Morocco, where he posed two questions for Sadat: what are his parameters in terms of a possible peace treaty, and what are the expectations for a treaty of nonbelligerence? Sadat did not respond, but

Dayan, as foreign minister, suggested renewing the Moroccan track, and Begin immediately agreed.[82] Moreover, Israel's warning to Sadat in July 1977 regarding Gaddafi's plot against him was conveyed via Morocco.[83]

The head of the Mossad under both Rabin and Begin, Yitzhak ("Haka") Hofi, had established good relations with King Hassan of Morocco, and Ben-Elissar reports that on July 28, 1977, Hofi brought a message from Sadat through Morocco, which opened the door for a meeting.[84] Begin approved Hofi's trip.

Only after arriving in Morocco did Hofi learn that the Egyptian he came to meet was Hassan Tuhami, deputy prime minister and one of Sadat's closest confidants.[85] Tuhami "was known to be close to religious conservatives and the Saudis" and had "a history of involvement in clandestine activities."[86] The first meeting, in early August, was described as harsh. Hofi told King Hassan that Egypt could not have sent a worse representative due to his well-known extremism. The next day, Tuhami and Hofi met again, with an entirely different atmosphere, perhaps following a conversation with Sadat. According to Hofi, Tuhami said that Egypt did not favor a Palestinian state and preferred that Jordan resume control, fearing a "leftist country" in the region. Hofi replied that if Egypt was serious about establishing ties with Israel, he would ask Begin to send a political official to negotiate.[87]

Begin agreed and sent Dayan to, first, meet the king alone and, later, to negotiate with Tuhami.[88] Hofi joined Dayan's first trip to Morocco (September 4, after Begin returned from Romania) but not the second one (September 16), when David Kimche, his deputy, accompanied Dayan.[89]

In the September 5 meeting, Dayan again expressed Israel's interest in engaging at the highest level—Sadat or Mubarak from Egypt, Begin or Dayan from Israel. The king agreed to do his best to arrange such a meeting, and Dayan suggested involving the United States in the informal agreement that he hoped to reach, with letters that would commit the sides.[90] (At the time, the Carter administration was apparently unaware of Dayan's visit to Morocco.[91])

On September 9, four days after the meeting, King Hassan informed Dayan that the Egyptians had agreed. But while Israel sought a Begin/Sadat meeting, Cairo preferred the Tuhami/Dayan option, to take place on September 16.[92] Begin's hopes to meet Sadat face to face already at that time reflects his seriousness and deep commitment to the effort of reaching a peace agreement. But Sadat may not have been ready yet to meet Begin and commit himself to the same degree, preferring a ministerial-level meeting first.

Dayan reports that Sadat told him during his visit in Jerusalem that he did not send Tuhami to explore a direct meeting but rather to discuss the Geneva Conference and to determine whether there was enough common ground for agreement.[93]

In the meeting, Tuhami stated that Israel must accept the principle of withdrawal from all occupied territories and that Egypt would agree to any security assurances Israel demanded in return.[94] According to the summary of the meeting (apparently by Dave Kimchi), Tuhami repeated numerous times that Israel had to accept the principle of withdrawal as a first step, and then security arrangements and the substance of peace were open for discussion. Tuhami said that the Palestinians "should be left to Egypt and the Arab nations. Egypt will see [to] it that they will not become communists . . . they should have formal links with Jordan and Egypt and we [Israel] should trust Sadat to control them. Egypt will see to it that Palestinians will not become radical."[95] Tuhami also asked Dayan not to inform the United States of their discussions, citing the great risk that he, Sadat, and Mubarak took by even agreeing to meet directly.[96]

In his memoirs, Dayan claimed that he told Tuhami that he was not authorized to commit to anything, including the principle of withdrawal, and asked several questions in return: Was Sadat ready to sign a treaty, even without Assad or other Arab leaders? Was Sadat willing to begin talks if Israel's commitment to withdrawal was limited to the Sinai? According to Dayan's account, following these talks, he and Begin concluded that the answer to both questions was affirmative, while apparently Tuhami concluded that Sadat would be able to retrieve all of the Sinai.[97]

The question of what Dayan promised Tuhami has been debated by political analysts, academics, and journalists. Bar-Siman-Tov argues that Sadat came only after he already knew that Israel would withdraw from the Sinai completely, meaning that Dayan had accepted Tuhami's demand, but Dayan denied this.[98] In a rare interview with Dan Patir, published in 1987, Begin denied that Dayan had promised Tuhami a full withdrawal but acknowledged that the Egyptians might have understood otherwise.[99] Similarly, in their notes from meetings with Dayan immediately afterward, American officials concluded that Israel was willing to return all of the Sinai as part of a peace treaty.[100]

However, the *Foreign Relations of the United States* volume on the Arab-Israeli conflict (January 1977 to August 1978) offers a different account of what was promised in Morocco, presented during a meeting between Begin, Dayan, and Vance in Jerusalem on January 16, 1978, two months after Sadat's visit. During discussions about the protection of the settlements in the Sinai by an Israeli police force, the following was reported:

> The *Foreign Minister* [Dayan] said that he had discussed this with Tuhami twice and that the second time he had put it in writing. At the time, he had the impression that Tuhami did not reject the idea. He was so impressed by *Israel's willingness to cede sovereignty over all of Sinai* [italics added], that he did not react particularly to the settlements, but then he got used to the proposal and it is now taken for granted that Israel will go back to the international border, but if Israel cannot keep the settlements, we will have to return to the old position, and we will have to look for changes in the border for our security.[101]

Dayan reports that at the end of their meeting in Morocco, he and Tuhami agreed to immediately send a summary to Sadat and Begin and ask them to approve a second session within two weeks; Dayan would report Sadat's demand that Begin commit to withdraw from the territories before the next meeting, and the two countries would exchange peace proposals before the next meeting and share them with the United States.[102]

Dayan returned to Jerusalem to report to Begin, who approved a second meeting and agreed to send a peace framework but refused to commit to withdrawal before a meeting with Sadat.[103] At this point, however, the Dayan-Tuhami connection had run its course and set the stage for Sadat's Jerusalem trip two months later.

Carter's Geneva Push

While Dayan and Tuhami were meeting secretly, the Americans pressed for progress in the Geneva framework but without success. In Carter's view, Israel was deliberately blocking an agreement by being adamant on Palestinian representation and supporting the settlements.[104]

On September 19, Dayan met with Vance and repeated Israel's traditional position regarding the border with Egypt, which would leave Israel with a strip from Sharm El Sheikh to Eilat and the northeastern part of the Sinai, including the civilian settlements.[105] According to American accounts, Dayan also hinted that Israel might agree to return all of Sinai to Egypt, and this was probably passed to Egypt's foreign minister, Fahmy, on September 21.[106] Vance pressed Dayan on the details of the demilitarization in the Sinai and proposed the opening of the Suez Canal to Israeli shipping under UN supervision. On the West Bank, Dayan rejected both a return to Jordanian control and a Palestinian state. Begin's autonomy formula would provide for individual freedom, but Palestinian sovereignty would endanger Israel.[107]

Dayan also met with Carter in what he described as a very unpleasant meeting, with both Carter and Vice President Mondale blaming Israel for the lack of progress. Carter expressed anger over settlement construction, calling Israel more stubborn than the Arabs and stating that it was "putting obstacles on the path to peace."[108] Dayan replied that Israel did not accept the US position that the settlements were illegal. However, during the meeting, Dayan promised to limit the construction of new settlements for one year, as he stated in an interview on NBC's "Meet the Press" on February 12, 1978:

Q: Did you or any responsible officials in your government tell President Carter or any responsible American that there would be no new settlements for a twelve-month period?

DAYAN: I did.

Q: Why then have there been four new settlements announced in the last two weeks?

DAYAN: No, I think that we are living up to my promise exactly. We are not
doing anything against my promise. What I did promise President Carter,
I think it was in September last year [1977], was that the new settlements
that we would establish, something about one year, twelve months, would
be, would take place within military camps and that is what we are doing.
We did not say we shall not have any new settlements. We did say we will
go on with more settlements, but they would take place within the military
installations, within military camps.[109]

In his memoirs, Dayan wrote that Carter asked for his suggestions, and
he replied that while Israel "would not stop settlement in the territories," if he
(Carter) wished, Dayan could suggest a plan to Begin in which new settlements
would be in the framework of military bases, and settlers would be military personnel. Dayan reports that Carter considered the proposal and agreed, saying it
was not what he wished, but it was at least a second best.[110] In sharp contrast to
Dayan, Carter viewed the meeting as productive.

A wider meeting followed with aides, described by Dayan as no less harsh,
and then Vance told Dayan in private that the United States planned to convene
the Geneva Conference before December and was willing to give serious guar-
antees to Israel. Dayan urged Vance to let Israel consider the package quietly. On
September 26, Vance and Dayan met again, in New York, and Dayan learned that
Carter had rejected his proposal regarding settlements in military camps.[111] The
American transcript reveals that Vance suggested "a bilateral treaty between the
United States and Israel similar to treaties the US has with NATO countries."[112]
In other words, the United States considered offering Israel a defense alliance as
part of the package to offset the risks of territorial withdrawal.

On September 29, Vance handed Dayan two documents: a working paper
for the Geneva Conference and a draft of the US-Soviet joint announcement,
which had been negotiated secretly. Shortly afterward, Dayan told Vance that
Begin had spoken with Ambassador Lewis and rejected the declaration, particularly regarding the Soviet role. Dayan also rejected the working paper, saying the
government already accepted restricting settlements to military camps.[113]

According to US documents, on September 30, Dayan told Vance, "The Israelis will hang me when they hear what I say," but he suggested that "he could try to
persuade Begin to accept someone like the Mayor of Ramallah [for Geneva], even
though the man would publicly announce that he is representing the PLO. (At
this point in the conversation Dayan seemed to be saying that Israel might accept
PLO affiliated Palestinians if the word PLO is not mentioned.)"[114]

On October 1, the American-Soviet communiqué on the Geneva Conference was issued. The declaration spoke of the "legitimate rights of the Palestinian people" (a phrase that the Israelis noted had heretofore been used in the

United Nations by Arab and Soviet officials in anti-Israeli declarations) in order to encourage the participation of the PLO. Israel rejected it promptly, and the PLO endorsed it, while Egypt and Syria had reservations. US senator Henry Jackson and others strongly criticized Carter's readiness to welcome the Soviets back in the Middle East after four years of exclusion.[115] On October 4, Carter addressed the UN General Assembly, recalling UNSCR 242 and 338 and assuring Israel that the United States would not impose an agreement.[116]

Egypt's response took the form of a letter from Sadat that Fahmy delivered to Carter, urging "that nothing be done to prevent Israel and Egypt from negotiating directly with our serving as an intermediary either before or after the Geneva conference." Carter responded that Egypt was the most forthcoming and cooperative nation in the Middle East in working for peace.[117]

Carter asked to see Dayan on October 4, and Begin and Dayan quickly prepared an Israeli working paper restating the pledge (already rejected by the Americans) to restrict new settlements to existing military bases. The six-hour meeting took place in New York; Dayan rejected the joint declaration on Geneva but suggested that Israel could participate based on UNSCR 242 and 338. In his memoirs, Dayan reported that Carter agreed not to support a Palestinian state but asked if Israel would consider partitioning the West Bank between Israel and Jordan. Dayan agreed to raise it with Begin, adding that the Arab leaders would probably reject this approach. Carter again accused Israel of being inflexible and wasting time and said that he (Carter) did not understand Israel's position.[118] He told Dayan that "Israel was by far the most obstinate and difficult" in the Middle East— even Syria was more willing to cooperate.[119] In an effort to end this dispute, Vance and Dayan agreed to formulate a joint US-Israeli working paper on Palestinian representation in Geneva, but at this stage this approach had reached an impasse.

This meeting and the joint final US-Israel statement buried the Geneva track. Under Begin and Dayan, Israel, which has long opposed international conferences where it is inevitably isolated and pressured to make concessions, refused to bow to US pressure on this. The impasse also showed Sadat that Israel could change US policy, and with his own strong reservations to the proposed Soviet role in Geneva, the option of direct talks with Begin became even more important.

Sadat's Initiative and Begin's Response

The indirect discussions and exchange of messages between Egypt and Israel continued. In personal letters to Sadat on October 21 and 28, Carter asked for help in moving forward, clearly with the Geneva Conference in mind. Sadat refused to provide such help, instead developing the direct link to Israel, and on October 31, the Egyptian leader replied to Carter's request ambiguously with a promise to take a "bold step."[120]

During this period, Sadat also reportedly first broached the idea of coming to Jerusalem and speaking before the Knesset. Sadat went to Romania on October 30, following up on Begin's visit a few months earlier, and during this visit, Stein reports, Arab ambassadors in Bucharest sensed "vague evidence of momentum between Egypt and Israel."[121] Sadat asked Ceausescu several times whether he thought Begin was serious, and Ceausescu replied positively.[122] According to Mustafa Khalil, the secretary general of Egypt's ruling Arab Socialist Union, Sadat then told the Egyptian Committee on Higher Security that "Begin is ready to make peace."[123] He explained the need to speak directly to the Israelis as necessary preparation to avoid failure at the Geneva Conference.[124]

On November 3, as part of his movement away from Geneva, Sadat wrote to Carter, proposing what he called a "pre-Geneva" meeting in Jerusalem with Arab delegations, Israel, and the permanent members of the UN Security Council. He asked for a reply by the fifth and promised to make a public statement on the ninth. Carter rejected the idea, reiterating support for the Geneva track.[125]

On November 9, Sadat went public, addressing the Egyptian Parliament and publicly announcing that he was prepared to come to Jerusalem to discuss peace. In an internal memo, the political research division of Israel's Foreign Ministry quoted Sadat: "Israel will surely be surprised to hear me say now: I'm willing to go to them, to their home, the Knesset, and argue with them."[126]

In Washington, Brzezinski's memo to Carter on Sadat's speech had a similar emphasis, concluding, "All in all, a remarkable speech."[127] In contrast, from Cairo, US Ambassador Eilts was skeptical: "Sadat's offer to go to Knesset is a first for an Arab leader and should be seen as his way of dramatizing lengths to which he prepared to go to achieve peace, not as serious possibility."[128]

The evidence indicates that Begin had no advance warning of the announcement from Cairo but responded quickly. Eitan Haber, Ze'ev Schiff, and Ehud Yaari report that Begin answered a reporter's (Shlomo Nakdimon of the daily *Yediot Aharonot*) question the next morning by saying that Sadat would be welcomed respectfully. Begin was apparently unaware of the details in Sadat's speech before Nakdimon asked for his response.[129] (Opposition leader Shimon Peres dismissed Sadat's plan as mere rhetoric.[130])

For Begin, the prospect of direct peace talks validated the policies he had pursued since taking office and for many years before, and he immediately sent Sadat an oral invitation through an American congressional delegation in Jerusalem that was scheduled to meet Sadat the following day.[131] Begin acted quickly, without convening the cabinet.

Beyond ensuring that the momentum created by Sadat's announcement was maintained, Begin was also testing to determine whether "it was seriously meant or just a flight of rhetoric."[132] Begin's oral invitation assured Sadat that he would be welcomed and would receive an appropriate reception.[133] In public comments,

Begin reiterated his positive response and the hope that Sadat's declaration was substantive and not only a rhetorical flourish. On Israel Radio, Begin stated that Sadat was welcome but that the declared Egyptian conditions for peace were unacceptable. Begin also invited the leaders of Jordan, Syria, and Lebanon to Jerusalem to join in negotiating peace treaties.[134]

On Friday, November 11, Begin took another step in the developing momentum, appealing directly to the people of Egypt to end the state of war and to turn toward a lasting peace agreement.[135]

The following evening (Saturday night, November 12), Begin received a summary of Sadat's comments to the same congressional delegation that had been in Israel, in which Sadat complained that he had not received an official invitation. In a public address, again without prior consultations or analysis, Begin immediately repeated his early invitation and declared, "I hereby invite President Sadat on behalf of the Government of Israel to come to Jerusalem and to start negotiations to establish permanent peace between Israel and Egypt." On Sunday morning (November 13), the cabinet endorsed the invitation and announced that if Sadat came to Jerusalem, the speaker of the Knesset should ask him to address the assembly from the podium.[136] (Begin did not consult with Israeli military intelligence, in part due to the lack of time and also perhaps because IDF commanders concluded that Egyptian military exercises and other factors indicated that there was no change in Cairo's policy and that there was a possibility that Egypt was preparing to resume warfare in the short term.[137])

On November 15, the pace of activity increased as the US media, led by Walter Cronkite of CBS News, entered the process. After recording an interview with Sadat, Cronkite interviewed Begin and then broadcast the two sessions side by side. Begin repeated that he had sent an official invitation via the US Embassy and declared his readiness to postpone a planned visit to London if Sadat decided to come to Jerusalem in the following week. He again stated that he was prepared to meet Sadat without preconditions, such as an end to the state of war that existed between Egypt and Israel.[138]

Begin then went to the Knesset to participate in a debate on the prospective Sadat visit, and in a vote of eighty-three to three, the legislators endorsed the invitation.[139] Begin reported that he had informed Carter of the latest developments and thanked the United States for its good offices in delivering the invitation. Begin said that from Israel's perspective, there was no basis for the conflict with Cairo; it was tragic, unnecessary, and protracted. Begin also responded to Sadat's statement on CBS that the alternative to peace is horrible, saying that no threats should accompany the coming talks: "We are not making threats toward Egypt and will not do so, and we ask Egypt's President not to threaten us."[140]

After being interrupted by Members of Knesset from Hadash (an alliance of small parties led by the Israeli Communist Party) regarding the Palestinians,

Begin replied that "Israel was willing to negotiate with authorized representatives of the Arabs of Eretz Israel [i.e., the Palestinians] in order to establish a joint life based on mutual respect, social and economic progress, freedom of the individual, equal rights and peace with the entire Arab World, in Israel and abroad. . . . President Sadat and I have viewpoints, and we will bring them to the table and discuss them openly . . . but there are no preconditions."

At every step along the way, Israeli critics and opponents accused Begin of bad faith. Journalists and politicians associated with the Labor Alignment, who were watching as Begin appeared about to achieve the most important political breakthrough since the creation of the state, argued that the leader of Likud was using Sadat's initiative to "drive a wedge between the Arab countries."[141]

After receiving Knesset approval, Begin handed Ambassador Lewis the written invitation, which Lewis cabled from the American Consulate in Jerusalem directly to the office of US ambassador Herman Eilts in Cairo. The physical letter itself arrived in Cairo the next morning and was delivered to Sadat.[142] (In response to a cautious query from Eilts at Mubarak's request, Lewis also noted, "If a certain president wants to visit Israel on a Saturday, he should come any time after six o'clock in the afternoon,"[143] referring to the end of the Jewish Shabbat.)

On the next day, November 16, at a Herut caucus, Begin spoke only briefly about the invitation: "Tomorrow we will receive a note from Cairo and then we will know on what date the visitor from Egypt will arrive. This is an important event and we must not exaggerate, and on this issue we will also not do so. But of course, if the President of Egypt comes to Jerusalem, to the Knesset, to talk with us after thirty years of invitations from all prime ministers to representatives of Arab states, one cannot deny this is an event which should be appreciated." He reminded the audience that while the Labor Alignment had predicted that no one would speak with the Likud government, the United States and Romania proved them wrong. "Britain, against which we fought, is anticipating us. Tomorrow I will know when my official visit there will take place, and above all Egypt for the first time says: 'We are ready to talk with you in Jerusalem,' and its president is about to come. Such developments in five months since 'no one will speak with you' prove we are on the right track."[144]

Begin was anticipating his visit to London, his first to the United Kingdom as prime minister. His previous trip in 1972, as head of the opposition, was followed by protests, and some events were canceled. This visit in 1977 was expected to be different. But due to Sadat's visit, Begin postponed his trip to London by two weeks.

On the same day (November 16), Sadat sent a positive response, including an arrival time of Saturday evening, November 19, 1977. Sadat was visiting Damascus; therefore, Begin kept the reply secret for another day.[145] When Sadat returned to Egypt, Eilts went to visit him at his home in Ismailyia, and, in front of the media that had gathered outside, the Egyptian leader told Eilts, "Please tell Begin through President Carter, I accept."[146] Immediately afterward, Foreign Minister Ismail Fahmy submitted his resignation.[147]

With a positive reply and the historic meeting only a few days away, preparations in Jerusalem moved into high gear. However, since most of the contacts with Sadat over the previous months had been conducted in great secrecy, most of the government officials and military officers responsible for foreign and defense policy had no information on the background of what appeared a sudden and unexplained upheaval in Israel's political and security environment. Without this information, the IDF chief of staff, Mordechai Gur, suggested calling a military alert, warning of a scenario in which Sadat's visit would serve as a cover for a mass assassination operation against the Israeli dignitaries gathered at the airport to greet the Egyptian president. Even after Sadat's announcement in Cairo on November 9, and for the next week, "no thorough deliberations were conducted by the Israeli decision makers in preparation for his arrival."[148]

In this vacuum, and without authorization from Begin or knowledge of the secret contacts that preceded Sadat's announcement, and at the specific request of Defense Minister Weizman,[149] Shlomo Gazit, head of the IDF intelligence branch, prepared and circulated an assessment that portrayed "an uninviting picture of a well-laid trap." According to Haber, Yaari, and Schiff, Gazit feared the repercussions of having missed such a shift in Egypt's position regarding peace, which would be worse than the intelligence failure preceding the Yom Kippur War. In his conclusion, Gazit wrote, "Sadat has changed his approach, not his attitude or his demands."[150] In response, Begin exclaimed, "Since when did the head of military intelligence dictate policy to the government?"[151]

In an interview published on November 15, Gur said that "it should be clear to President Sadat that if he is planning another fraud like the Yom Kippur War, his intentions are clear to us." Weizman rebuked Gur for speaking without approval.[152]

On Friday, the day before the scheduled visit, Begin called a special meeting with the IDF chief of staff, the head of military intelligence, and the head of the Mossad to reveal the details of the discussions of the previous five months.[153] In contrast, according to Weizman, up to this point, "Israel's cabinet did not devote a single moment's consideration to what would happen—and, perhaps, change— the moment our archenemy set foot on Israeli soil."[154] (IDF intelligence reported that Egypt's army was placed on alert, apparently responding to Israeli moves and also in response to fears regarding threats likely to come from other Arab countries.[155])

Uzi Benziman reports that in the special cabinet meeting before Sadat's visit, Begin finally shared some secrets with the ministers, saying briefly that "we have been working on this meeting for five months" (i.e., since he became prime minister); nevertheless, "we were surprised with Sadat's decision to come to Jerusalem." He added that "King Hassan of Morocco had a major role in organizing the trip."[156] Begin appointed Eliahu Ben-Elissar to lead the preparations for the visit, including coordinating the schedule with an Egyptian advance team that had already arrived.[157]

In public statements, including radio interviews and speeches before different groups, Begin spoke about the expectations and possibilities, emphasizing that this would be the first official visit by an Arab leader to the Jewish state since it was founded. The visit to Jerusalem would also be a de facto recognition of Israeli sovereignty in Jerusalem, he declared. Begin expressed the hope that Sadat's visit would launch serious regional peace negotiations. "The opening will be in Jerusalem. I hope the continuation will be in Cairo. There is almost a certainty that the President will invite me to come to the capital of Egypt."[158]

On that day (November 18), Carter sent messages to Begin and Sadat through the respective US ambassadors in which he urged them to declare that Syria would be part of the "working group" on the West Bank.[159] Carter mistakenly believed that including Syria would "strengthen Sadat's position" regarding Geneva, but the entire scenario had changed. Middle Eastern diplomacy had entered an entirely new phase, and it was impossible to predict the outcome. The bilateral approach that replaced the Geneva Conference was unprecedented and could easily fail. The prospect of Israeli and Egyptian leaders agreeing to a separate peace deal seemed remote, and in public, Begin and Sadat continued to frame their actions as if they were part of the Geneva track, which provided a fallback if the direct meetings were unsuccessful. But it seems clear that Carter and his administration did not understand the profound depth of Israeli and Egyptian rejection of the multinational conference approach, led by Washington and Moscow.

The Red Carpet for Sadat

Sadat's plane arrived at the Ben-Gurion Airport on Saturday night, November 19, 1977, shortly after the end of the Jewish Sabbath. Begin demonstrated that despite the unprecedented nature of this visit and the relatively short time to complete preparations, he and his government could organize the reception of the Egyptian president with the appropriate mix of ceremony and substance.[160] Although Egypt had fought four wars with Israel, causing thousands of deaths and many more injuries, and Sadat had led Egypt in the bitterest and costliest battles only four years earlier, Begin led Israel in celebrating this breakthrough and revolutionary change. From beginning to end, the visit was marked by Begin's personal charm, his pride in representing the sovereign Jewish state in the first direct public meetings with an Arab head of state, and formal protocol that honored both Sadat and Egypt.

The visit included many ceremonies but few opportunities to discuss substantial issues. But when substance was discussed, the interactions were tense, emphasizing the gap between Israeli and Egyptian positions. Begin's Israeli critics would argue that this proved their point, while Begin insisted—backed by Dayan, Weizman, and Yadin—that this was a positive start and there was basis for continuation.

From the airport, the motorcade drove up to Jerusalem. Sadat held a series of closed sessions with leading Israeli politicians and the news media, and then met privately with Begin at the King David Hotel. They agreed on some critical matters, which broke through the initial fears. First, from this point forward, there would be no more wars between the two states. Second, the entire Sinai Peninsula would be demilitarized except for the stationing of Egyptian forces on a narrow strip on the eastern bank of the Suez Canal, and a multinational force would continue to be deployed. Third, they agreed to discuss the future of Israel's settlements in the Sinai.

According to Ben-Elissar, Sadat suggested, after understanding that the Sinai would return to his control, that Israel turn over the West Bank to the Palestinians and let them fight against each other. Begin replied by emphasizing that this issue was a question of life or death for Israel, and Sadat took a step back, promising to discuss it again.[161]

Bar-Siman-Tov reports that Sadat presented his peace proposal to Begin, including a full Israeli withdrawal from all conquered territories, including east Jerusalem, and a solution for the Palestinian problem (without mentioning the PLO). Sadat also stated that his visit was not a step toward a bilateral agreement, because such an agreement would not bring "a lasting and just peace."[162]

While Sadat's approach, as demonstrated the next day in his speech before the Knesset, was broad and based on the effort to "engage Begin in a discussion of general principles," the Israeli leader's negotiating style was largely the reverse.[163] Begin focused on the details, reportedly stating that Israel was prepared to return the entire Sinai to Egypt in return for a full peace agreement and demilitarization of the Sinai in the area between the Mitla and Gidi Passes and the border with Israel. Sadat reportedly accepted the idea of demilitarization as Begin presented it.[164]

Subsequently, however, differences over demilitarization became a serious source of friction. The Israeli recollection was that in "Jerusalem the President [Sadat] said, inter alia, to the Prime Minister: A. That it is his intention to declare the Straits of Tiran to be an international waterway; B. That the Egyptian army will not move eastwards of Mitla and Gidi passes and that the whole area east of the passes will be demilitarized."[165] Begin quoted this to Ambassador Lewis a month later, after the former returned from Ismailia, and it was similar to what Begin stated in his 1987 interview with Dan Patir. Ten years after the first meeting in Jerusalem, Begin said he told Sadat that Israel demanded the Sinai demilitarized, as Dayan had already told Tuhami in Morocco in September 1977, and that it was willing to return the Sinai to Egypt only under this condition and within the framework of a peace treaty.[166]

This was quite different than what Sadat told Weizman in Cairo a few days before the Ismailia summit that followed. And in the Carter-Sadat meeting at Camp David on February 4, 1978, Carter said, "President Sadat says that he never promised Begin that there would be no Egyptian forces on their own land between the passes in the demilitarized zone. He said only that there would be no main forces there. *President Sadat:* I said that they would not 'exceed' the passes. *President:* Does that mean 'not go beyond?' *President Sadat:* We will not go beyond the passes. That means that from the eastern part of the passes to the demilitarized zone is a limited armaments zone."[167]

This issue became a major obstacle to concluding the Sinai agreement. Only at the Camp David summit of September 1978 did Sadat formalize demilitarization. According to some sources, in their first meeting, Begin did not mention the future of the Israeli settlements and military airports in the Sinai, while Sadat drew the conclusion that the Israeli proposal would include both elements. Later, when Begin indicated that this was not the case, this also caused considerable friction.[168]

Sunday, November 20, marked the Muslim Eid el-Adha (the Feast of Sacrifice), and as planned, Sadat prayed at the Al-Aqsa mosque (at 6:45 a.m.), spoke briefly with the worshipers, and made a quick stop at the Church of the Holy Sepulcher in the Christian Quarter of Jerusalem's Old City.[169] Meanwhile Israel's cabinet assembled to hear first impressions from Begin, approving the points in the speech he planned to make in the Knesset later that day.[170] The cabinet also discussed the appropriate gesture Israel should make in response to Sadat's major step, but nothing was decided because Dayan said such gestures would only complicate Egypt's situation among Arab states. Later, accompanied by Begin, Sadat visited *Yad VaShem* as every foreign official does (at 11:00 a.m.). He listened carefully, asked a few questions, and wrote in the guest book a wish to put an end to all human suffering.[171]

Before going to the Knesset, Begin, Yadin, and Dayan had lunch with Sadat, Khalil, and Boutros-Ghali (at 12:00 p.m.). Begin suggested establishing a hotline between the two capitals based on the precedent between Washington and Moscow, but the Egyptians feared this might seem to indicate that they were seeking a separate agreement with Israel. Begin said that Israel does not want a separate agreement and hoped that peace with Egypt would be the first, and not the only, outcome.[172]

The special Knesset session began at 16:00 with Sadat's programmatic speech, delivered in Arabic and translated simultaneously into Hebrew. In his presentation, Sadat began on a philosophical note, talking about the brotherhood of man and the pain and futility of war. In explaining his abrupt decision to visit Jerusalem, he noted that "many months in which peace could have been brought about had been wasted over differences and fruitless discussions on the procedure for the convocation of the Geneva Conference, all showing utter suspicion and absolute lack of confidence." Instead, he declared that it was his main duty "to exhaust all and every means in a bid to save my Egyptian Arab people and the entire Arab nation the horrors of new, shocking and destructive wars." He added, "I have the same feelings and bear the same responsibility towards all and every man on earth, and certainly towards the Israeli people. Any life lost in war is a human life, irrespective of its being that of an Israeli or an Arab."[173] Turning to the specifics of the negotiations, Sadat presented his conditions for peace, the first of which was that there would not be a separate Egyptian-Israeli treaty because such a bilateral agreement would "not bring permanent peace based on justice in the entire region," especially if it did not solve the Palestinian problem.[174]

Addressing Israeli views and, in particular, Begin's long-standing position, Sadat declared, "I have not come to you to seek a partial peace, namely to terminate the state of belligerency at this stage, and put off the entire problem to a subsequent stage. This is not the radical solution that would steer us to permanent peace." More interim measures and partial withdrawals would not be useful. Instead, the Egyptian leader provided a definition of peace for Israel: "It means that Israel lives in the region with her Arab neighbors, in security and safety . . . against any aggression. . . . We declare that we accept all the international guarantees you envisage and accept."[175]

Sadat also articulated the concessions he expected from Israel, beginning with the complete withdrawal from "Arab territories that Israel has occupied by armed force . . . including Arab Jerusalem." The "City of Peace . . . will always remain as a living embodiment of coexistence among believers of the three religions. It is inadmissible that anyone should conceive the special status of the City of Jerusalem within the framework of annexation or expansionism, but it should be a free and open city for all believers."[176]

He then went on to discuss the "Palestinian cause . . . the crux of the entire problem," calling for a sovereign state for the Palestinian people. (However, as many analysts noted, Sadat made no mention of Arafat or the Palestine Liberation Organization.)[177] Upon hearing Sadat, Weizman leaned toward Dayan and handed him a note saying, "We've got to prepare for war." Begin said Sadat's words were an ultimatum. Sadat claimed to put up a mirror in front of Israel's face, saying it was isolated around the world with its position toward the Palestinians.[178]

Begin then ascended the Knesset podium, noting, "The duration of the flight from Cairo to Jerusalem is short but, until last night, the distance between them was infinite." He praised President Sadat's courage "in crossing this distance" and quoted from Israel's Declaration of Independence: "We extend our hand to all neighboring states and their peoples in an offer of peace and good neighborliness." He then addressed the substance: "We seek a true, full peace, with absolute reconciliation between the Jewish People and the Arab People. We must not permit memories of the past to stand in our way. We respect the valor of an adversary, and we pay tribute to all members of the young generation of the Arab Nation who have fallen as well." Responding to critics both in Israel and outside, Begin noted, "We did not invite you to our country in order, as has been suggested in recent days, to drive a wedge between the Arab peoples. . . . Israel has no desire to rule and does not wish to divide. We want peace with all our neighbors—with Egypt and with Jordan, with Syria and with Lebanon."[179]

Begin declared, "There is no need to differentiate between a peace treaty and the termination of the state of war. The first article of a peace treaty determines the end of the state of war, forever. We wish to establish normal relations between us, as exist among all nations after all wars." Peace meant that Egypt "will be represented by a loyal Ambassador in Jerusalem, and we, by an Ambassador in Cairo and, should differences of opinion arise between us, we will clarify them, like civilized peoples, through our authorized emissaries."[180]

Begin did not reply directly to the specifics of Sadat's speech but responded carefully and indirectly to some of the fundamental differences: "The President mentioned the Balfour Declaration. No, sir, we took no foreign land. We returned to our Homeland. The bond between our People and this Land is eternal. It was created at the dawn of human history. It was never severed." As for international guarantees, Begin recalled the painful Jewish experience in exile: "No one came to our rescue, not from the East and not from the West. And therefore we, this entire generation, the generation of Holocaust and Resurrection, swore an oath of allegiance: never again shall we endanger our people; never again will our wives and our children—whom it is our duty to defend, if need be even at the cost of our own lives—be put in the devastating range of enemy fire."[181]

Referring indirectly to borders, withdrawal, and calls for Palestinian sovereignty, he said that Sadat knew even before coming to Jerusalem that Israel had a different position concerning permanent borders. However, all the issues were open to negotiations. Concerning Jerusalem, Begin noted that in the morning, Sadat had prayed "in a house of worship sacred to the Islamic faith, and from there you went to the Church of the Holy Sepulcher. You witnessed the fact, known to all who come from throughout the world, that ever since this city was joined together, there is absolutely free access, without any interference or obstacle, for the members of all religions to their holy places." Under Jordanian occupation before 1967, "this positive phenomenon did not exist . . . and we can assure the Muslim world and the Christian world—all the nations—that there will always be free access to the holy places of every faith."[182]

In a telephone conversation with Begin after Sadat departed from Israel, Carter said he had watched the Knesset event: "The speeches were very constructive."[183] In his diary, Carter expressed satisfaction with Sadat's speech ("was very good") and disappointment with Begin's ("a rehash of what he had always said"). Carter added, "My concern and prediction is that both Begin and Sadat have an inclination to negotiate privately and to the exclusion of Syria, and we've been trying to get them, publicly at least, to disavow this inclination."[184]

The official dinner at the King David Hotel that followed was described as tense, as the differences became pointed. Dayan asked Sadat to define a "just peace" as he understood it, and Sadat replied it meant countries should settle differences in negotiations and not wars. Dayan concluded that Egypt was willing to give Israel only nonbelligerence, not peace.[185] Yadin broke the ice by suggesting to Tuhami that a joint statement should be published when Sadat leaves. They started writing a draft on a hotel napkin and passed it to Dayan, Begin, and Sadat, who approved it with some changes.[186]

Sadat stayed for another day for additional meetings. Several political figures from the West Bank came to meet him, and at 10:00 a.m. Sadat met the different Knesset factions, including the leaders of the Labor Alignment.[187] He also held two joint interviews with Begin for the American news media. At 12:00 p.m. Begin and Sadat held a concluding press conference.[188] The Geneva track was portrayed as still relevant, and Sadat's visit was framed as part of preliminary arrangements for the planned conference.

Sadat told the press that although Begin "has the full right to come and address our Parliament . . . for certain reasons" this would be postponed. When asked what he gave Sadat in return for the risks he took in coming to Israel, Begin replied that "it is not a matter of compensation. What we wanted to achieve during this visit was to make sure that we started a serious direct dialogue about the ways to establish peace in the Middle East—not only between Egypt and Israel, but also between Israel and all the other neighboring countries."[189]

Replying to peace activist and journalist Abie Nathan's question regarding his decision to come to Israel, Sadat said, "The whole situation needed action, the peace process needed momentum again."[190] He claimed that the psychological barrier was 70 percent of the conflict, leaving only 30 percent to substance, and the intention behind his visit was to break the psychological barrier.

Begin emphasized the "momentous agreement" with Sadat: "No more war, no more bloodshed, no more attacks, and collaboration in order to avoid any event which might lead to such tragic developments." Sadat thanked the Israeli people for the warm welcome and the marvelous sentiments that were shown to him. Asked if they were now convinced of the sincerity of the mutual desires, Sadat and Begin replied positively. When asked if they had set a date for the

Geneva Conference, Sadat promised to work very soon, and Begin expressed similar views but did not say it would happen soon.[191]

Regarding territorial concessions, Sadat noted that "our land is sacred," and Begin placed territory in the framework of security, explaining that for Israel this effected the lives of every man, woman, and child. "Of course, I can respect a statement as was made just now by President Sadat: 'Our land is sacred,' and because I respect it, I can say now: 'Our land is sacred.'"[192] In their concluding remarks, Begin said the visit was successful and that he hoped it would promote peace. Sadat thanked Begin and President Katzir for their "very warm welcome" and then declared, "May God guide the steps of Premier Begin and the Knesset, because there is a great need for hard and drastic decision. I already did my share in my decision to come here, and I shall be really looking forward to those decisions from Premier Begin and the Knesset." He finished by wishing the best to "my friend Premier Begin."[193]

By any measure, the visit was a major success, without embarrassing incidents or strong, unpredictable disagreements. The Egyptian leader had been received with full honor and respect, and the entire event was broadcast throughout the world. Begin and Israel had not given up any basic or core positions, and a foundation for dialogue and eventual peace agreements had been created. The predictions of calamity were shown to be unfounded, and the pressures for a grand concession to boost Sadat's position and as a concrete expression of gratitude, such as announcing a symbolic unilateral Israeli withdrawal from any part of the Sinai, were rejected.[194]

In his diary, Carter reiterated his fears concerning Begin's and Sadat's inclination to deal bilaterally. In a courtesy phone call, Begin refused to discuss contents on an open phone line. He again expressed his confidence that there would be no more war between Israel and Egypt.[195]

The day after Sadat returned to Cairo, he sent a letter to President Katzir extending him, the people of Israel, the Knesset, and the government his "most sincere appreciation and gratitude for the hospitality accorded me and my delegation during our sojourn." He added, "I would like to avail myself of this occasion to convoy, through you, to Mr. Menachem Begin my personal thanks for the invitation he addressed to me to visit your country and the constructive talks we had together with [a] view to achieving genuine peace based on justice." Sadat wrote that their "audacious step" was a historical turning point in the destiny of the Middle East and the world.[196]

After Sadat's departure, Begin, Dayan, and the Israeli leaders began to analyze these events and to consider options. They understood that Sadat's visit constituted a significant and unprecedented change in Egyptian policy and an important opportunity for Israel to gain recognition and security in the Middle East.[197] Begin also recognized that Sadat's initiative was very courageous, and the Arab world had already begun to condemn and isolate him as a result. Israel would have to be careful to avoid paying a price for this development. The Israeli leadership concluded that Sadat was motivated primarily by Egypt's dire position and economic crisis, and the opening positions he spelled out in the Knesset were negotiable. In their view, Sadat would eventually accept a separate peace agreement with Israel if there was no better alternative.[198]

In a press conference on November 23, Dayan said it was now up to Israel to make tough decisions regarding its borders but not only with Egypt, because Egypt was not seeking a separate treaty. Dayan said the direct talks with Egypt were not a substitute for Geneva and that Israel needed to prepare for the coming conference. He said the procedural difficulties in the path to Geneva were clarified when Sadat accepted the US-Israeli working paper of October 5 as the foundation, although he made it clear he was interested only in substance rather than procedure, such as the issue of PLO representation, and that the challenges were significant. Dayan noted that unlike the US approach to Geneva, which began with the process and then moved to substance, Egypt wanted the details to be agreed on before any conference began (partly because Sadat feared Soviet involvement). Dayan also stated that he was reconsidering his own opinions regarding the territories. Even so, he said that Israel still had time to make up its mind regarding the final borders.[199]

Conclusion

Begin—from his first days in office—had signaled to Sadat, through Romania and Morocco, his wish to meet in person to discuss substantial proposals. When the opportunity was presented, he moved quickly. The record shows that the meeting between Begin and Sadat and the initiation of the negotiating process at the highest level, directly between the two leaders, was spurred by a shared opposition to the Geneva framework. But to move forward, Begin recognized the need to respond and place possible Israeli concessions on the table quickly.

Sadat had an advantage in the role of initiator, and his visit to Israel was considered a major concession in and of itself, although Begin refused to acknowledge this in public. At the time of Sadat's visit, Begin had no plan that was approved by the government, and while he had shown Carter an outline, he had not formulated the details. Sadat's visit spurred Begin into immediately developing his proposal.

Sadat had opened the door to what would become Israel's first peace treaty with an Arab country. The events also served as the focus of Begin's term as prime minister, promising to consolidate his legitimacy among both internal and external audiences. But to realize these objectives and turn them into reality, Begin needed to formulate appropriate policies, navigating between his own deeply held beliefs—particularly regarding the future of Judea, Samaria, and

Gaza—the views of his own constituency, Sadat's requirements for peace, and the insistent pressure from Jimmy Carter. In the weeks and months that followed, Begin sought to balance these competing demands, working through numerous crises and eventually toward the Camp David summit and the peace treaty.

Notes

1. In addition to the Likud bloc, which won 43 seats and which Ariel Sharon joined after running on a separate ticket (the Shlomtzion Party), totaling 45, and Moshe Dayan (1), who was elected as part of the Labor Alignment (Ma'arach) list and split into a single-man faction, the government coalition included the National Religious Party (12 seats), and Agudat Yisrael (4), adding up to 62. The Democratic Movement for Change ("Dash") joined later that year with its 15 seats, stabilizing the coalition with 77 members out of 120.

2. Bar-Siman-Tov, *Israel and the Peace Process*, 21; Weizman, *Battle for Peace*, 76; Haber, Yaari, and Schiff, *Year of the Dove*, 13 [Hebrew].

3. Bar-Siman-Tov, *Israel and the Peace Process*, 23–24; Haber, Schiff, and Yaari, *Year of the Dove*, 3; Marcus, *Camp David*, 31–32. The meeting took place a few days after the elections but well before Begin formed the government. Ambassador Lewis himself had not yet officially submitted his credentials (Ben-Elissar, *No More War*, 28).

4. Dayan, *Breakthrough*, 3–6, Ben-Elissar, *No More War*, 15–18, Bar-Siman-Tov, *Israel and the Peace Process*, 22.

5. Ben-Elissar, *No More War*, 15.

6. Berlatzky, interview with Kadishai, November 3, 2002. Kadishai also points out that Begin was opposed to the other main candidate for this position, Ariyeh Dultzin of the Liberal Party.

7. Dayan, *Breakthrough*, 4–5.

8. *FRUS 1977–1980*, vol. 8, document 28.

9. *FRUS 1977–1980*, vol. 8, document 165.

10. Zbigniew Brzezinski memorandum to the president, "'Terror Out of Zion,'" June 10, 1977, Jimmy Carter Library (JCL), National Security Affairs; Brzezinski Material; Country File; Iran (Verification) 4/79—Israel 4-6/77; Box 34, Israel 4-6/77.

11. Memo, William Quandt to Zbigniew Brzezinski, "Israeli elections," May 18, 1977, JCL, National Security Affairs; Brzezinski Material; Country File; Iran (Verification) 4/79–Israel 4-6/77; Box 34, Israel 4-6/77.

12. Memo, William Quandt to Zbigniew Brzezinski, "Israeli elections," May 18, 1977, JCL, National Security Affairs; Brzezinski Material; Country File; Iran (Verification) 4/79–Israel 4-6/77; Box 34, Israel 4-6/77.

13. Donald Neff and David Halevy, "A Palestinian State: 'Inconceivable,'" *Time*, May 30, 1977, accessed April 1, 2007, at http://www.time.com/time/printout/0,8816,914951,00.html.

14. Neff and Halevy, "Palestinian State."

15. Jimmy Carter, *White House Diary*, 55–56.

16. Lorch, *Major Knesset Debates, 1948–1981* 6:2084.

17. Lorch, 6:2084.

18. Lorch, 6:2086.

19. Lorch, 6:2084–86.

20. Lorch, 6:2116.

21. On the 1975 negotiations, see Fischer, "Turning Point on the Road to Peace."

22. *Towards Peace in the Middle East*. For a critique, see Jensehaugen, "Blueprint for Arab–Israeli Peace?"

23. This strategy was already adopted in April 1977. See *FRUS, 1977–1980*, vol. 8, document 28.

24. Bar-Siman-Tov, *Israel and the Peace Process*, 23, citing Dayan, *Breakthrough*, 11–16.

25. Simcha Dinitz to Dayan, telegram no. 379, June 25, 1977, ISA, A 7054/29.

26. Simcha Dinitz to Dayan, telegram no. 379, June 25, 1977, ISA, A 7054/29.

27. Dinitz to Dayan, telegram no. 378, June 25, 1977, ISA, A 7054/29.

28. Policy Research and Planning Center, Ministry of Foreign Affairs, Expressions of US Administration Officials Concerning the Middle East Settlement, June 30, 1977, 1–3, ISA, A 7054/29.

29. Shamir, *Egypt under Sadat*, 228–231.

30. David Horovitz, "Editor's Notes: The Wisdom of 1977," *Jerusalem Post*, January 14, 2011, http://www.jpost.com/Opinion/Columnists/Editors-Notes-The-wisdom-of-1977.

31. David Horovitz, "Editor's Notes: The Wisdom of 1977," *Jerusalem Post*, January 14, 2011, http://www.jpost.com/Opinion/Columnists/Editors-Notes-The-wisdom-of-1977.

32. Lungen, "Cotler Recalls (Small) Role in Israel-Egypt Peace"; Makov, interview with Cotler.

33. Shamir, *Egypt under Sadat*, 227.

34. "Israel's Secret Contacts," *Time*, August 14, 1978.

35. Handel, *Diplomacy of Surprise*, 346–347.

36. Stein, *Heroic Diplomacy*, 199. See also quotes from the welcome ceremonies and personal impressions of them in Avner, *Prime Ministers*, 409–11.

37. Unsigned, unaddressed, and untitled document, July 13, 1977, ISA, A 4313/1.

38. Dinitz talking points with Vance, July 27, 1977, ISA, A 4313/1.

39. *IMFA*, document 45.

40. Robert Lipshutz memorandum for the president, "Israel Election and Related Matters," May 23, 1977, JCL; National Security Affairs; Brzezinski Material; Country File; Iran (Verification) 4/79–Israel 4–6/77; Box 34, Israel 4–6/77.

41. Jimmy Carter, *White House Diary*, 71.

42. Stein, *Heroic Diplomacy*, 200.

43. Prime Minister's Statement on His Visit to the US, July 27, 1977, in Lorch, *Major Knesset Debates, 1948–1981*, 6:2125.

44. Bar-Siman-Tov, *Israel and the Peace Process*, 24–25. See also Dayan, *Breakthrough*, 19–20; Jimmy Carter, *Keeping Faith*, 290–291; Brzezinski, *Power and Principle*, 98–101; Vance, *Hard Choices*, 180–184; Quandt, *Camp David*, 77–84; Katz, *Hollow Peace*, 119–127; Benziman, *Prime Minister under Siege*, 14–15.

45. Bar-Siman-Tov, *Israel and the Peace Process*, 25.

46. *FRUS 1977–1980*, vol. 8, document 53.

47. Avner, *Prime Ministers*, 412–413.

48. Avner.

49. *IMFA*, document 18.

50. *IMFA*, document 18.

51. *IMFA*, document 18.

52. *IMFA*, document 18.

53. *IMFA*, document 18.

54. *IMFA*, document 18.

55. Dayan, *Breakthrough*, 21–22.

56. Prime Minister's Statement on His Visit to the US, *Sitting 18 of the 9th Knesset*, July 27, 1977, in Lorch, *Major Knesset Debates, 1948–1981*, 6:2123.

57. Prime Minister's Statement on His Visit to the US, *Sitting 18 of the 9th Knesset*, July 27, 1977, in Lorch, *Major Knesset Debates, 1948–1981*, 6:2123.

58. Prime Minister's Statement, in Lorch, 6:2123.

59. Dayan, *Breakthrough*, 22–23.

60. *FRUS 1977–1980*, vol. 8, document 82.

61. *FRUS 1977–1980*, vol. 8, document 89.

62. Bar-Siman-Tov, *Israel and the Peace Process*, 25; Jimmy Carter, *Keeping Faith*, 296; Quandt, *Camp David*, 108.

63. Haber, Schiff, and Yaari, *Year of the Dove*, 20–21.

64. Stein, *Heroic Diplomacy*, 216.

65. Lorch, *Major Knesset Debates, 1948–1981*, 6:2084–86.

66. Quandt, *Camp David*, 108.

67. Bar-Siman-Tov, *Israel and the Peace Process*, 25; Dayan, *Breakthrough*, 26–34.

68. Bar-Siman-Tov, *Israel and the Peace Process*, 25–26; Dayan, *Breakthrough*, 35–37.

69. Stein, *Heroic Diplomacy*, 63–64.

70. Stein, 184–185.

71. Quandt, *Camp David*, 109; Haber, Schiff, and Yaari, *Year of the Dove*, 9.

72. Stein, *Heroic Diplomacy*, 202.

73. Bar-Siman-Tov, *Israel and the Peace Process*, 26.

74. Sadat, *In Search of Identity*, 306; Bar-Siman-Tov, *Israel and the Peace Process*, 276–77 (ft. 30).

75. Secret summary of PM Begin talks with Romanian President Ceausescu on Friday, August 26, 1977, in Snagov, BCA, PM 155 [Hebrew].

76. Protocol of government meeting, September 4, 1977, ISA, A 4269/6, accessed November 27, 2012, www.archives.gov.il/NR/rdonlyres/6D8D153F-279A-40AD-9F69-84167EC9C6E2/0/Egypt10.pdf.

77. Israeli, *Man of Defiance*, 226; Beattie, *Egypt during the Sadat Years*, 227.

78. Bar-Siman-Tov, *Israel and the Peace Process*, 26; Sadat, *In Search of Identity*, 305–306.

79. Bar-Siman-Tov, *Israel and the Peace Process*, 26; Yosef Harif, "Begin Was Not Surprised by Sadat's Announcement after Ceausescu Promised Him Contact with Egypt Soon," *Maariv*, November 18, 1977, 15 [Hebrew].

80. Yehuda Avner, "Prime Minster Begin and Foreign Minister Dayan's Meeting with Ambassador Lewis at the Prime Minister's Office, Jerusalem—3.11.77 at 17:00, Present Brubeck and Yehuda Avner," ISA, A 4337/10, accessed November 27, 2012, http://www.archives.gov.il/NR/rdonlyres/4EA8C304-7FEF-4691-A5C8-218F991B6150/0/Egypt13.pdf.

81. Dinitz to Dayan, telegram no. 119, November 4, 1977, ISA, A 4337/10, accessed November 27, 2012, http://www.archives.gov.il/NR/rdonlyres/A87188A5-9A0A-4232-8404-2D6ABEE99E1F/0/Egypt14.pdf.

82. Haber, Yaari and Schiff, *Year of the Dove*, 24 [Hebrew].

83. "Israel's Secret Contacts," *Time*, August 14, 1978; Handel, *Diplomacy of Surprise*, 346.

84. Ben-Elissar, *No More War*, 37.

85. Iris Berlatzky, The Begin Heritage Center oral documentation project: Interview with Yitzhak Hofi, January 11, 2002, BCA [Hebrew].

86. Quandt, *Camp David*, 110.

87. Berlatzky, interview with Hofi; Samuel Segev, *Moroccan Connection*, 173–74.

88. Haber, Schiff, and Yaari, *Year of the Dove*, 10–13.

89. Berlatzky, interview with Hofi. An account of the meetings between Dayan and the Moroccans (and, later, Tuhami) also appears in Ben-Elissar, *No More War*, 38–43.

90. Bar-Siman-Tov, *Israel and the Peace Process*, 26; Dayan, *Breakthrough*, 38–42.

91. Bar-Siman-Tov, *Israel and the Peace Process*, 26.

92. Dayan, *Breakthrough*, 42.

93. Dayan, 88.

94. Ben-Elissar, *No More War*, 40. See also Bar-Siman-Tov's account of Tuhami's presentation, *Israel and the Peace Process*, 27.

95. [Probably David Kimchi] "Highlights from Meeting of September 16, 1977, 21.00." On September 17, 1977, these were delivered via Haim Israeli (defense minister's bureau chief), and on September 18 these were delivered to Begin via Yechiel Kadishai, ISA, A 4313/4.

96. "Highlights from Meeting of September 16, 1977"; Bar-Siman-Tov, *Israel and the Peace Process*, 27.

97. Bar-Siman-Tov, *Israel and the Peace Process*, 28; Stein, *Heroic Diplomacy*, 206–7; Dayan, *Breakthrough*, 43–53; Dan, *Operation Bulrush*, 17–22; Benziman, *Prime Minister under Siege*, 18–19; Sharon, *Warrior*, 395.

98. Bar-Siman-Tov, *Israel and the Peace Process*, 29; Weizman, *Battle for Peace*, 82-83; Rubinstein, *Paths of Peace*, 14.

99. Begin interview with Dan Patir, *Yediot Aharonot*, November 13, 1987; Bar-Siman-Tov, *Israel and the Peace Process*, 29–30.

100. Bar-Siman-Tov, *Israel and the Peace Process*, 30; Quandt, *Camp David*, 115–16; Fahmy, *Negotiating for Peace in the Middle East*, 195–214.

101. *FRUS 1977–1980*, vol. 8, document 194. Italics added.

102. Bar-Siman-Tov, *Israel and the Peace Process*, 28; Dayan, *Breakthrough*, 47–52.

103. Bar-Siman-Tov, *Israel and the Peace Process*, 28; Dayan, *Breakthrough*, 53.

104. Jimmy Carter, *White House Diary*, 99.

105. Dayan, *Breakthrough*, 57; Bar-Siman-Tov, *Israel and the Peace Process*, 30.

106. Bar-Siman-Tov, *Israel and the Peace Process*, 30; Quandt, *Camp David*, 115–16; Fahmy, *Negotiating for Peace in the Middle East*, 195–214.

107. Dayan, *Breakthrough*, 58.

108. Dayan. See also Jimmy Carter, *White House Diary*, 101.

109. *IMFA*, document 122.

110. Dayan, *Breakthrough*, 60.

111. Dayan, 60–65.

112. *FRUS 1977–1980*, vol. 8, document 113.

113. Dayan, *Breakthrough*, 64–65. See also *FRUS 1977–1980*, vol. 8, document 118.

114. *FRUS 1977–1980*, vol. 8, document 118.

115. Bradley, *Camp David Peace Process*, 15.

116. Bradley; *US State Department Bulletin*, October 24, 1977.

117. Jimmy Carter, *White House Diary*, 112; Stein, *Heroic Diplomacy*, 208; Bar-Siman-Tov, *Israel and the Peace Process*, 31; Jimmy Carter, *Keeping Faith*, 294.

118. Dayan, *Breakthrough*, 67–69.

119. Jimmy Carter, *White House Diary*, 113.

120. Bar-Siman-Tov, *Israel and the Peace Process*, 31–32.

121. Stein, *Heroic Diplomacy*, 222

122. Haber, Schiff, and Yaari, *Year of the Dove*, 13–14.

123. Stein, *Heroic Diplomacy*, 222.

124. Stein, 222.

125. According to Haber, Yaari, and Schiff, Sadat discussed this idea with Fahmy on their flight from Romania to Iran and concluded it would take at least two months to arrange a pre-Geneva meeting in Jerusalem, losing time and the element of surprise (Haber, Yaari, and Schiff, *Year of the Dove*, 30–31 [Hebrew]). Fahmy claims that he suggested the world conference in East Jerusalem to Sadat "to convince him to abandon his plan to go to Jerusalem" to meet Begin (Fahmy, *Negotiating for Peace in the Middle East*, 255).

126. Political Research and Planning Center, Ministry of Foreign Affairs, "Summary of the Foreign Policy Section in Sadat's Speech (Cairo Broadcast, 9.11)," November 10, 1977, ISA, A 4313/5.

127. Brzezinski to Carter, Memorandum, "Sadat Speech," November 10. 1977, JCL, National Security Affairs; Brzezinski Material; Country File; Egypt: 7–11/77 through Egypt 7–9/79; Box 18; Egypt 7–11/77.

128. *FRUS 1977–1980*, vol. 8, document 145.

129. Haber, Schiff, and Yaari, *Year of the Dove*, 1–8, 23.

130. Bar-Siman-Tov, *Israel and the Peace Process*, 38; Haber, Yaari, and Schiff, *Year of the Dove*, 52–53 [Hebrew].

131. Bar-Siman-Tov, *Israel and the Peace Process*, 36.

132. Katz, *Hollow Peace*, 183; Benziman, *Prime Minister under Siege*, 34–35.

133. Bar-Siman-Tov, *Israel and the Peace Process*, 38; Ben-Elissar, *No More War*, 49.

134. Stein, *Heroic Diplomacy*, 223.

135. The text of Begin's message (given in Hebrew) appears in ISA, A 4313/5. It was also sent to the White House ("Address by Prime Minister Menachem Begin to the Egyptian People, Jerusalem, November 11, 1978"). JCL, National Security Affairs; Brzezinski Material; President's correspondence with foreign leaders file; India through Israel; Box 9; Israel Prime Minister Menachem Begin 11/77–6/78. See also Preuss, *Begin in Power*, 50.

136. Bar-Siman-Tov, *Israel and the Peace Process*, 39–40.

137. Bar-Siman-Tov, 36–37. See also Chief of Staff Mordechai Gur's memoirs (Gur, *Chief of the General Staff*, 299–301).

138. Bar-Siman-Tov, *Israel and the Peace Process*, 40.

139. Bar-Siman-Tov, 41. The Knesset protocol does not mention a vote but only a decision to pass the issue to the Knesset Committee on Foreign and Security Affairs (*Divrei HaKnesset* 81, 406).

140. *Divrei HaKnesset* 81, 404.

141. *Divrei HaKnesset* 81, 403–5.

142. Ben-Elissar, *No More War*, 55.

143. Stein, *Heroic Diplomacy*, 224.

144. Prime Minister speech at the Herut Center meeting, November 16, 1977, BCA, PM-158 [Hebrew].

145. Bar-Siman-Tov, *Israel and the Peace Process*, 41. Sadat made a public statement of accepting the invitation, emphasizing the pan-Arab and religious frameworks he adopted for the visit. See Handel, *Diplomacy of Surprise*, 330.

146. Stein, *Heroic Diplomacy*, 224–225. The actual letter of invitation was in Cairo since it had been given to Vice President Hosni Mubarak while Sadat was still in Damascus, but another piece of paper was folded to look like a letter, and when Sadat asked, "What do you have here?" Eilts replied, "An invitation from Mr. Begin."

147. Fahmy, *Negotiating for Peace in the Middle East*, 277; Stein, *Heroic Diplomacy*, 226.

148. Dayan, *Breakthrough*, 76.

149. Bar-Siman-Tov, *Israel and the Peace Process*, 42.

150. Haber, Schiff, and Yaari, *Year of the Dove*, 37. See also Gur, *Chief of the General Staff*, 321.

151. Weizman, *Battle for Peace*, 25, 29; Ben-Meir, *National Security Decision Making*, 78; Bar-Siman-Tov's interview with Shlomo Gazit in *Israel and the Peace Process*, 44–45.

152. Bar-Siman-Tov, *Israel and the Peace Process*, 45; Gur, *Chief of the General Staff*, 303. The interview and Weizman's response are on pp. 308–13.

153. Benziman, *Prime Minister under Siege*, 37; Ben-Meir, *National Security Decision Making*, 78.

154. Bar-Siman-Tov, *Israel and the Peace Process*, 41; Weizman, *Battle for Peace*, 24.

155. Haber, Schiff, and Yaari, *Year of the Dove*, 56.

156. Benziman, *Prime Minister under Siege*, 37.

157. Ben-Elissar, *No More War*, 58–64; Haber, Schiff, and Yaari, *Year of the Dove*, 52–56.

158. Bar-Siman-Tov, *Israel and the Peace Process*, 43.

159. *FRUS 1977–1980*, vol. 8, document 149.

160. On Thursday night, the head of the IDF band recorded the Egyptian national anthem from Cairo radio and transcribed it (Stein, *Heroic Diplomacy*, 226). See also Ben-Elissar, *No More War*, 55.

161. Ben-Elissar, *No More War*, 67–70.

162. Bar-Siman-Tov, *Israel and the Peace Process*, 52.

163. Stein, *Heroic Diplomacy*, 225

164. Bar-Siman-Tov, *Israel and the Peace Process*, 51–52, 57; Stein, *Heroic Diplomacy*, 227.

165. *FRUS 1977–1980*, vol. 8, document 180.

166. Patir, *Yediot Aharonot*, November 13, 1987, 3.

167. *FRUS 1977–1980*, vol. 8, document 211.

168. Bar-Siman-Tov, *Israel and the Peace Process*, 57; Begin's interview with Dan Patir, *Yediot Aharonot*, November 13, 1987; Benziman, *Prime Minister under Siege*, 44–47; Naor, *Begin in Power*, 147–148.

169. Hirst and Beeson, *Sadat*, 266. Time is according to Dayan, *Breakthrough*, 80.

170. According to Benziman, Begin told the cabinet that Sadat insisted on one-on-one dialogues with Begin; therefore, no protocols were to be prepared, and the only source would be Begin's reports (Benziman, *Prime Minister under Siege*, 40).

171. Haber, Schiff, and Yaari, *Year of the Dove*, 66. Time is according to Dayan, *Breakthrough*, 80.

172. Ben-Elissar, *No More War*, 71. Time is according to Dayan, *Breakthrough*, 80.

173. *IMFA*, document 73.

174. *IMFA*, document 73.

175. *IMFA*, document 73.

176. *IMFA*, document 73.

177. *IMFA*, document 73. The speech was not shown in advance to Begin. Haber, Schiff, and Yaari (*Year of the Dove*, 69; Dayan, *Breakthrough*, 81).

178. Haber, Schiff, and Yaari, *Year of the Dove*, 69.

179. *IMFA*, document 74.

180. *IMFA*, document 74.

181. *IMFA*, document 74.

182. *IMFA*, document 74.

183. *FRUS 1977–1980*, vol. 8, document 153.

184. Jimmy Carter, *White House Diary*, 139–140.

185. Dayan, *Breakthrough*, 81.

186. Haber, Schiff, and Yaari, *Year of the Dove*, 72.

187. Time is according to Dayan, *Breakthrough*, 80.

188. Time is according to Dayan, *Breakthrough*, 80; *IMFA*, document 77.

189. *IMFA*, document 77

190. *IMFA*, document 77

191. *IMFA*, document 77

192. *IMFA*, document 77

193. *IMFA*, document 77

194. Bar-Siman-Tov, *Israel and the Peace Process*, 56; Benziman, *Prime Minister under Siege*, 40–41; Weizman, *Battle for Peace*, 317; Begin's political announcement in the Knesset on November 28, 1977, *Divrei HaKnesset* 81, 520.

195. Carter, *White House Diary*, 140.

196. *IMFA*, document 79.

197. Bar-Siman-Tov, *Israel and the Peace Process*, 53; Weizman, *Battle for Peace*, 71–72.

198. Bar-Siman-Tov, *Israel and the Peace Process*, 54; Katz, *Hollow Peace*, 184–85; Benziman, *Prime Minister under Siege*, 39. See also the protocol of the government meeting on November 24, 1977, that summarized the visit. ISA, A 4270/1, November 27, 2012, http://www.archives.gov.il/NR/rdonlyres/B6777C2B-8675-4849-8472-71F6C4791661/0/Egypt36.pdf.

199. *IMFA*, document 80.

4   From Jerusalem to Camp David

December 1977–August 1978

Aɴᴡᴀʀ ꜱᴀᴅᴀᴛ's ᴜɴᴘʀᴇᴄᴇᴅᴇɴᴛᴇᴅ visit to Jerusalem and the carefully crafted speeches, discussions, and exchanges replaced the step-by-step process that had been employed since 1973. The negotiation of disengagement agreements that began with Henry Kissinger and the attempts to reconvene the Geneva Conference had reached a dead end. For Begin, Sadat, and Jimmy Carter, this meant that old conceptions and approaches had to be rethought and new policies developed. Indeed, for the diplomats, political leaders, military officials, decision makers, and other members of the foreign policy community, this was a major shift.

At the same time, although Begin and Sadat exchanged views and repeated hopeful promises of "no more war," nothing had been resolved. As the director general of the Israeli Ministry of Foreign Affairs, Efraim (Eppie) Evron, observed, "He made his speech. Then what? He took everyone by surprise, and no one had the courage to say no to him 'But then what?'"[1] Sadat left Jerusalem to face criticism at home and a political boycott in much of the Arab world as many governments broke off diplomatic relations with Egypt. In Washington, the Carter administration scrambled to catch up with events and to avoid becoming irrelevant; the key objectives that emerged were to maintain the momentum established by the breakthrough, help Sadat to overcome the Arab isolation and rejection (and to avoid losing power at home), and recover lost American influence and control over the process.

In Jerusalem, once the euphoria due to the first public visit to Israel from an Arab leader began to wear off, Begin was keenly aware of the pressures that he would face from many different directions—both external and internal—as a result of Sadat's grand gesture. Begin understood the potential benefits from this opening but also knew that if it failed to bring a peace agreement, Israel would be blamed. Having made the first move and paid a significant price in terms of his position in the Middle East, Sadat waited while Begin was pressed to make a major gesture in response.

While Sadat had indeed broken the long-standing Arab taboos, emphatically repeated in 1967 at the Khartoum summit, he had not given Israel the type of tangible assets that Begin was being pressed to provide, such as the immediate return of land in the Sinai. Three weeks after Sadat's visit, Carter urged Begin to "meet Sadat's request for a statement on withdrawal,"[2] but Begin was still developing a detailed strategy. He had objectives and a vague idea of where he hoped the process would lead but lacked a realistic road map necessary to achieve these goals. Perhaps because he was too busy managing the visit itself and was unable to devote time to a detailed plan for the next moves (beyond the West Bank autonomy outline) or because the events were unprecedented and he could not usefully predict where to go after Sadat's visit, Begin responded relatively slowly. Furthermore, the closeness with which Begin, Moshe Dayan, and Yitzhak Hofi held these developments and the broader absence of a mechanism under Begin to plan for contingencies such as this reinforced the other obstacles to a quick response. As a result of these factors, Sadat and Carter were able to take the initiative.

In addition, unlike Sadat, who, if not an entirely independent actor, did not face a powerful and well-organized domestic political opposition or free press, Begin had to deal with strong critics from both the Labor opposition and from his own party and faction in the Knesset, as well as a hostile press and angry constituents, particularly among settlers. Israeli political constraints were often ignored by the Carter administration, which preferred to deal with Begin and Sadat as unitary actors operating in a domestic political vacuum. This basic misperception fueled the tensions between Begin and Carter.

For many months, the frenetic activities and efforts to convert the initial breakthrough into a concrete and stable political relationship dominated the agendas in Jerusalem, Cairo, and Washington. Immediately after Sadat's departure, the first systematic and organized attempt to provide structure and substance to this new peace process took place in the Mena House conference in Cairo between December 13 and 15, followed immediately by Begin's trip to Washington for consultations with Carter.[3] Then, on December 25 (which happened to be Sadat's birthday), Begin's not-quite-reciprocal return visit to Egypt took place in Ismailia rather than Cairo. (Israelis speculated that Sadat may have been concerned about the security threats that would have been encountered had the meeting been held in Cairo, or, alternatively, according to at least one published account, he might also have sought to avoid the scene of crowds cheering for Begin in Cairo.[4])

In Ismailia, the leaders failed to reach a declaration of principles to guide the talks, but according to Stein, "some of the conceptual seeds for the September 1978 Camp David accords were thus planted: discussion of a framework governing Egyptian-Israeli relations and a definition of intent for Palestinian association with the negotiations."[5] This meeting marked the beginning of serious negotiations, and over the next eight months leading to the Camp David summit, Begin agreed to exchange the Israeli presence in the Sinai for a peace treaty and Egyptian acceptance of the Palestinian autonomy proposal. (In Stein's view,

"Begin eventually used Sadat's insatiable thirst for Sinai's return to dislodge and redefine Sadat's commitment to the Palestinians."[6])

They also agreed to convene the Political and Military Committees in Jerusalem and Cairo (which took place in January and February 1978). These talks highlighted important differences in approach, particularly regarding the American demand to link a peace treaty between Israel and Egypt with a resolution of the Palestinian issue. The positions adopted by Sadat and Begin on the nature of this linkage and the future of the Palestinian-Israeli relationship were very polarized, and a series of meetings and exchanges of papers at different levels in the ensuing months did not produce any openings. However, in July, the foreign ministers of both countries met at Leeds Castle in Britain and produced some common ground that set the stage for the Camp David summit.[7]

At every step in the process, the American involvement increased. Having been caught by surprise and essentially frozen out of Sadat's Jerusalem visit, the Carter administration scrambled to reinvolve itself. In part, this was the result of political self-interest—a major Middle East peace process without pivotal American involvement was unthinkable.

But there were also important substantive issues at stake, based on the perception that once the detailed negotiations began, the Israelis and Egyptians would need third-party involvement. Perhaps more importantly, the Americans continued to press for regional arrangements that would go beyond the Israeli-Egyptian dimension and incorporate a resolution of the Palestinian conflict. In a memo to Carter, William Quandt warned, "By striking out at Arab hard-liners, Sadat is paving the way for an Egyptian-Israeli separate agreement," and this was not seen as stable or sufficient in Washington.[8] From the beginning, Carter sought to steer Sadat away from a separate agreement and toward a comprehensive regional peace framework.

Publicly, Sadat emphasized the goal of tying any bilateral treaty between Egypt and Israel to a visible and significant gain for the Palestinians. Sadat called for full Israeli withdrawal to the June 4, 1967, lines and the dismantling of all settlements. He indicated a readiness to accept something short of full independence for the Palestinians and supported links to Jordan and limited self-determination but without an Israeli presence.

On this critical issue, there was little difference between the American and Egyptian positions, and the United States was determined to use the opportunity created by Sadat's visit as a springboard for resolving the Palestinian dimension of the conflict. Carter and his advisors, including Zbigniew Brzezinski, William Quandt, and Cyrus Vance, came into office with the view that the key to Middle East peace was a resolution of the Palestinian problem in the form of a homeland (sovereign state) as articulated in the Brookings Plan. After recovering from the Sadat shock and the rejection of the Geneva Conference route, the Americans began to press Israel and Begin to address these issues.

When the Carter administration understood that a quick agreement on a Palestinian state led by Arafat was unrealistic, it sought to change the status quo that had existed since the 1967 war, focusing on the concept of a transitional period for the West Bank. The process would involve autonomy for the Palestinians—a term that was presented as consistent (at least in terminology) with Begin's concepts. However, the similarities were superficial, and American pressure to achieve an objective that Begin would not, and politically probably could not, deliver was counterproductive. Begin's goal was to maintain the negotiations with Sadat while avoiding the American pressures, particularly on the Palestinian issue.

The Mena House Conference: The Other Guests Stayed Home

On November 27, shortly after Sadat's visit, Ismet Abdel Magid, Egypt's ambassador to the United Nations, handed Chaim Herzog, his Israeli counterpart, an invitation from Acting Foreign Minister Boutros Boutros-Ghali to Foreign Minister Dayan to attend a pre-Geneva conference in Egypt in early December. Dayan was abroad, and Begin replied the next day as acting-foreign minister. From the Knesset rostrum, he responded positively to the invitation, recalled the latest developments that preceded the invitation, and turned to the other Arab states, saying that "we want peace to be between ourselves and all our neighbors. . . . We do not want to drive any wedge between the Arab countries, and we did not offer President Sadat, when he was in Jerusalem, a separate peace treaty with Egypt."[9] The framework of Geneva was still relevant for all sides at the time, and Begin spoke of finding similar tracks to open negotiations with the other Arab states. However, no other Arab delegations came to the conference, although it was delayed for ten days, allowing Carter to push for wider participation.

On December 2, less than two weeks after Sadat left Jerusalem, the direct contacts resumed as Dayan and Hassan Tuhami met again in Morocco. Dayan brought the outlines of Begin's proposals for a peace treaty with Egypt that would not include removal of settlements or Israeli airbases or mention Palestinian autonomy without sovereignty or Israeli withdrawal. Dayan reportedly told Tuhami that if Egypt accepted these terms as the basis for negotiation, Begin would go ahead and raise them before the Israeli Cabinet.[10] Tuhami replied that Sadat "will not agree to a single Israeli settlement or soldier remaining in Sinai."[11] Dayan rejected these conditions, but the two agreed to explore the options, recognizing that neither government had an interest in failed negotiations. Shortly afterward, Egypt implemented an important confidence-building gesture by returning the bodies of Israeli soldiers who had been killed in the 1973 war.[12]

Following the Dayan-Tuhami meeting, the preparatory conference for Geneva was held at the Mena House in Cairo from December 13 to 15, 1977. For the first time, Israeli officials were openly invited to Cairo, along with representatives from Jordan, Lebanon, Syria, the PLO, the United States, the Soviet Union, and the United Nations. Once again, the Israelis (as well as the Americans and others) were taken by surprise, but this time Sadat's penchant for solo dramatic performances did not produce positive results. In both Jerusalem and Washington, observers concluded that Sadat either did not comprehend the degree of his isolation among Arab elites or sought to counter the official hostility from the regimes (except, to some degree perhaps, Jordan) with grand spectacles.

A few days after Sadat had returned to Egypt from Israel, the first reports on the planned conference came via radio news reports. Both Begin and Dayan reacted with alarm, fearing that the breakthrough achieved by Sadat's visit would be undermined. Dayan reported that he had no idea "what Sadat had in mind and was absolutely certain that it would fail."[13] Indeed, it appears that Sadat and the Egyptians also did not know what they had in mind. For over two weeks, and until the opening of the conference, ambiguous and contradictory reports on the details were received, including discussion of a "second phase" at the level of foreign ministers, reflecting the difficulty faced by the Egyptians themselves in defining a workable formula.[14]

None of the Arab representatives, other than Egyptians, came, and only Israelis, Americans, and UN officials were present. Eliahu Ben-Elissar was designated to head the Israeli delegation to this mysterious event, only to discover that the conference premises included a PLO flag. Since Israeli policy strictly prohibited any contact with the PLO—viewed as a pure terrorist organization—Ben-Elissar waited outside at first. (When the invitation was delivered by US ambassador Sam Lewis, the Israeli government reportedly "assumed" that the PLO would not be formally represented.[15]) Shortly afterward, the Egyptians removed the flag.[16]

However, substantively, the conference itself was a nonevent. Speeches were delivered, and, most importantly, Egyptian officials sat with Israeli officials in Cairo, while outside the conference site, the Israeli delegation visited the once-grand synagogue. El Al planes at the airport were important symbols that added to the momentum created by Sadat's initiative. The participants agreed to set up a hotline for direct communications and began discussions on security, trade, and other important issues.[17] Beyond this, there was little of substance at the Mena House conference. Instead, the focus shifted to Washington as Menachem Begin prepared to present to Jimmy Carter his model for peace with Egypt and for Palestinian autonomy.

Begin's Autonomy Plan

In the weeks following Sadat's visit, the pace of communications and exchanges increased, as did the realization that there were strong differences. Begin and Dayan were reluctant to withdraw from all of the Sinai and sought to retain settlements under Egyptian sovereignty, particularly in the Rafah border area and along the coast, in addition to Israeli military protection for them. But this was unacceptable to Sadat and the Egyptians.

More fundamentally, there were also very deep disagreements regarding the future of the Judea and Samaria regions of the West Bank and the Jewish and Palestinian populations that lived in this territory. For Carter (and, to some degree, Sadat) the issue was relatively straightforward. Israel was required to withdraw from these regions, with the possibility perhaps of minor territorial adjustments and some different arrangements for Jerusalem. The time frame was somewhat flexible and could last for up to five years, or longer in some versions, but the principle of withdrawal and dismantling of settlements was absolute. The Palestinians would receive a homeland and self-determination, with the issue of sovereignty or perhaps federation with Jordan left open for negotiation.

In contrast, Begin and most of the Israeli officials were committed to maintaining Israeli control over Judea and Samaria (Gaza was of lesser importance). In Begin's mind, these areas were vital to Israeli security and survival and contained the biblical heartland of the Jewish people; therefore, they were not negotiable. Peace was certainly important, and Begin, as much as any Israeli leader, understood the benefits of a treaty with Egypt, but the ideological commitment to Judea and Samaria was stronger.

As a result, Begin—to a greater degree than Sadat or Carter—was faced with very difficult choices throughout this process. In the effort to resolve the dilemmas, Begin quickly turned to the concept of autonomy and developed approaches that had been under some discussion long before Sadat's visit. Initially, Begin had been skeptical, and following the 1967 war, when he served in the National Unity Government, he had vigorously rejected proposals by Dayan and others to support Palestinian autonomy. At the time, Begin charged that "the concept of autonomy will lead to a Palestinian state,"[18] which was entirely unacceptable to him.

However, a decade later, as prime minister, Begin's views on this issue had evolved, at least tactically, and he accepted a framework based on personal and limited political autonomy. As noted, immediately after the 1977 elections and in the months before Sadat's visit, Begin presented an autonomy framework as an alternative to the Brookings Plan and Carter's "Palestinian homeland" speech.[19] In part, this reflected the transformation in Begin's position—from leader of the opposition to prime minister responsible for making policy. Begin realized that he had to present an alternative proposal to Carter's vision.[20] For Begin, personal, cultural, and limited political autonomy resolved the apparent contradiction between maintaining territorial control of the territories while not giving the Palestinian population Israeli citizenship. (Palestinians in Judea and Samaria were citizens of Jordan, and Begin did not expect this to change.)

But it would be overly simplistic to dismiss these changes in Begin's policy as merely instrumental, in response to the needs of the time or of the office that he held. Indeed, there is evidence that well in advance of many other Israeli leaders, Begin understood that to remain a Jewish and democratic state, consistent with the objectives of the Zionist movement that constituted its raison d'être, the Arab population in the territories could neither be integrated nor controlled by Israel. Bar-Siman-Tov quotes Begin as saying, "The Arabs of Eretz Israel, for the first time in their history, will receive autonomy. . . . They have been ruled all the time, by the Turks for generations, by the British for decades, and by the Jordanians for twenty years. And to tell the truth, by us as well. . . . Now they will really receive their self-administration. They will be administering their matters themselves—and everything through elections of their own; in short, real and absolute autonomy."[21]

In this context, Begin reviewed the examples of cultural autonomy for minorities in the Austrian-Hungarian Empire and of Jewish communities, in particular. Similar institutional arrangements had also been developed in the Ottoman Empire, through the millet system, and were applied to the Jewish community in Eretz Israel until the early twentieth century. In this, as in other areas, Begin drew on the writings of Jabotinsky, who argued that the claims of the Arabs were fundamentally and irrevocably antithetical to Jewish sovereignty and the only practical solution was to provide "minority self-rule."[22] The 1977 Likud election platform already included a reference to autonomy for the "Arabs of Eretz Israel," referring to "national cultural values, religion and legacy, as well as full economic integration, and agricultural and industrial development."[23] Begin raised this option in discussions with Secretary of State Vance in August 1977, months before Sadat's visit. Begin included Israeli citizenship and voting rights for Palestinians who chose to exercise this option.[24]

Moshe Dayan had long supported various policies and plans for the West Bank under the general concept of functional autonomy. In Dayan's proposed frameworks, the level of political autonomy was wider than in Begin's. Stein concludes that "Dayan was willing to cede to the Palestinians greater control of their daily lives than was Begin's intention."[25]

On these foundations, shortly after Sadat's visit, Begin developed a twenty-one-point autonomy plan as an alternative to the American and Egyptian demand for full withdrawal to the pre-1967 armistice lines and from all of Judea and Samaria.[26] The proposal included some of Dayan's more political dimensions such as the establishment of an elected administrative council, ending the military government, and the choice of Israeli or Jordanian citizenship (the Jordanian government was not consulted; however, Jordanian citizenship was the default option for Judea and Samaria Palestinians). The draft did not assert Israeli sovereignty over these regions, but it left the issue open.[27]

The autonomy plan suggested holding elections for eleven seats on the administrative council, dealing with all the civil dimensions—education; religious affairs; finance; transportation; construction and housing; industry, commerce, and tourism; agriculture; health; labor and welfare; rehabilitation of refugees; and justice administration and supervision of the police force. Security and foreign affairs would remain in Israel's hands; suffrage was defined as universal for those eighteen years old and up; eligibility to be elected was from the age of twenty-five; the council would reside in Bethlehem; and Palestinians could apply for Israeli citizenship through the legal system, thus having full civil rights including suffrage and the right to run for office. The plan also dealt with processes by which Jews could purchase land and settle in the West Bank and allowing West Bank Palestinians (regardless of citizenship—Israeli or Jordanian) to settle anywhere in Israel; free trade and movement rights were also universally guaranteed.

Begin presented the proposal to the Ministerial Committee on Defense for preliminary discussion on December 13, as part of a broader discussion of the core issues in the negotiations with Egypt. According to some Israeli reports, Dayan had told his colleagues that he had offered to return all of the Sinai to Egypt during his meeting with Tuhami on December 2 in Morocco and that Sadat accepted the offer and saw it as a starting point for negotiations. The withdrawal would take three to five years and would be synchronized with normalization.[28] The ministers who participated—including Defense Minister Ezer Weizman— learned the details of the proposals for the first time.

According to Weizman and additional sources, several ministers and other officials voiced strong objections to both dimensions of Begin's framework.[29] IDF Chief of Staff Gur cited Israel's traditional security doctrine, claiming that return of the entire Sinai Peninsula was too risky, and he reiterated the proposal for an interim nonbelligerency agreement in return for limited withdrawal. Gur argued that in a final agreement, part of the Sinai must remain under Israeli control, but Begin rejected this.[30] Interior Minister Yosef Burg and Agriculture Minister Ariel Sharon warned that the autonomy plan would eventually lead to a Palestinian state rather than preventing this, as Begin sought.[31] At the end of the meeting, the proposals were approved, and on the following day, Begin departed for Washington. The Cabinet's only condition was that Begin would inform Carter that the autonomy plan had not yet received the government's approval.[32]

After soliciting and receiving an invitation from the White House,[33] Begin presented the plan to Carter on December 16 and 17, in the hope of obtaining Washington's support and assistance in gaining Sadat's acceptance.[34] Begin's autonomy was far from the Brookings Plan and Carter's "Palestinian homeland" proposal, and to the Americans, this effort was interpreted as an attempt to avoid transfer of sovereignty in the West Bank by focusing on the Sinai and diverting attention from the Geneva path.[35] (Despite the fundamental changes in the environment created by Sadat's visit, Carter administration officials remained locked into the Geneva process.[36]) Brzezinski concluded that Begin's approach was "certainly not sufficient for Sadat" and recommended using the plan as a foundation for Palestinian self-rule, "making it not the final point in negotiations but a place or step along a broader continuum that would lead to something closer to Palestinian self-determination."[37] This was clearly the opposite of Begin's intention.

Even prior to Begin's arrival and based on the details that they already knew, the Americans had decided that his autonomy plan was "disappointing," and Carter declared that he was prepared to apply pressure on this issue.[38] A few days earlier, Vance had summarized his Middle East meetings in a cable in which he noted, "Begin's plan for the West Bank and Gaza would be very far from what Sadat wanted."[39] According to Quandt, "Before Begin arrived in Washington, Carter and his advisors had agreed that they should not be seen as endorsing Begin's proposals."[40]

In the meeting on December 16, Begin addressed the American demand that Israel accept Resolution 242 as the basis for negotiations. According to the minutes in the Israeli State Archives, Begin told Carter: "242 envisages secure boundaries. If we withdraw with minor modifications in the East, we lose all our security. We have the experience of nineteen years. The issue is not an army but incursions. The green line is absolutely indefensible. . . . Since we have defended the Jordan River there have been no incursions for the past two years; perhaps only one. This is for us *the* question of our lives, the men, women and children."[41]

Regarding Jerusalem, Begin floated a conceptual proposal based on open access for all and the creation of "an international religious council that would take care of the Holy Shrines of each of the respected religions." Thus, the Muslim holy places would be under a council formed by Israel's neighbors: Jordan, Egypt, Syria, Lebanon, Saudi Arabia, Iran, and Morocco. Christian shrines would be under a council of "the Vatican, the Providavians, the Protestants, including the Baptists," and Jewish shrines would be under the Israeli Chief Rabbinate. Carter replied jocularly that he invited Begin to name the chairman of the council. Begin asked Vance to sound out Arabs leaders on the idea, but there is no indication of any follow-up.[42]

Regarding the West Bank, Begin noted that his proposals provided "autonomy for Palestinian Arabs; security for Palestinian Jews. It is as simple and as profound as that." Carter replied that "the proposal on self-rule, autonomy for the region—is very positive" and then added that it all depended on what would be agreed on for it included.[43] When Begin said that the military government in the West Bank and Gaza would be abolished, Carter replied, "It is a wonderful way to say it."[44] Toward the end of the meeting, Carter said, "I think your proposal is very constructive. It is a fair basis for negotiation."[45] As became common in their meetings, Carter claimed to find Begin more flexible than he expected and complimented Begin, only to later change his mind, perhaps reacting to what Begin said publicly—usually not saying what Carter expected—or after Carter spoke to his aides and with Sadat. It is also likely that Carter's praise was a means of creating a cooperative atmosphere and not necessarily based on substantive agreement.

Two days later, as Begin was flying to meet Prime Minister James Callaghan in London, Carter sent a message to the latter on Begin's proposal: "I did not agree to accept Begin's description that it is (quote) a fair basis for negotiation (unquote)."[46] Moreover, the differences between the Israeli and American minutes of the White House meeting were discussed in a memorandum that Brzezinski wrote to Carter on January 13, 1978. He received a copy of the Israeli minutes, which he compared to the American text.[47] He told Carter that "your own comments, while supportive, did contain qualifications which are missing in the Israeli version" and suggested that "we should correct the record so that Prime Minister Begin will not interpret our silence as acceptance of his interpretation of our position."[48] Brzezinski did not refer to the question of endorsement of the autonomy plan as a "fair basis for negotiations." The American record shows that Carter indeed said, "Your proposals are very constructive and could provide a fair basis for negotiations."[49] However, he was apparently referring to the entire package—including the Sinai proposal, over which there was no dispute.

In his diary, Carter wrote that Begin presented "a proposal for the Sinai region, giving up Sharm al-Sheikh and the route from there to Eilat, withdrawal of Israeli troops, and demilitarization east of the passes by Sadat, which I think is acceptable to us and the Egyptians." Carter viewed this aspect of Begin's presentation positively, unlike the autonomy proposal, although he wrote that it was a step in the right direction. Carter met with Begin again on December 17, writing in his diary that Begin had agreed that military rule over the West Bank would be "abolished." However, Begin "had very little to offer in Jerusalem. I think the minimum is a Vatican-like autonomous area to encompass the holy places, extending as far as possible into eastern Jerusalem." Carter concluded, "all in all, he's much more flexible than we had feared."[50] In a note to Brzezinski on February 7, 1978, Carter wrote that he examined his notes from the December meeting with Begin (including the private talk which is not documented) and that settlements in the Sinai were never discussed. (On this point, Begin's version differs.) He added, "In referring to his [Begin's] general Sinai proposal I said then that it sounded reasonable."[51]

This was clearly a major misreading of Begin and his diplomatic efforts to avoid direct conflict with Carter. In praising Begin's proposals, Carter may also have sought to reduce the tension created in his contentious first meeting with Begin before the Sadat initiative.[52] At the end of the discussion, Carter phoned

Sadat to suggest "that he take Begin's proposal seriously, though it would not meet all his expectations about the Palestinians."[53] The reasons for this response remain obscure, perhaps reflecting a basic misunderstanding of the details, or perhaps to ensure the return of the United States and the president to the center of the process, or to prepare Sadat and prevent what the Americans feared would be a major rupture. (Carter also sought to avoid a situation in which Begin would gain congressional endorsement for his autonomy plan, further weakening the position of the White House.)

Indeed, a disagreement quickly erupted between the Americans and Israelis, presaging the later dispute following the Camp David summit in September 1978 over what Begin allegedly promised Carter regarding a freeze on settlement construction. According to Carter, the plan that Begin presented to Sadat one week later in Ismailia, on December 25, was not the same one that Carter had seen and "was attenuated substantially."[54] Carter's negative response was not immediate, and after the Begin-Sadat meeting, he praised Begin's "flexibility."[55] A few days later, Egyptian sources reported that Sadat was "unhappy with Carter's stand."[56]

The alleged changes are linked at least in part to an intense debate during a seven-hour meeting of the Israeli Cabinet on December 22. Begin first tried to persuade the ministers that since he had already presented the document to President Carter, who had endorsed it, no changes were possible. As noted, the plan had been discussed at the Ministerial Committee on Defense before Begin left for Washington, and it had been strongly criticized, but the committee endorsed the plan. However, in the wider Cabinet, Begin faced stronger objections, particularly from members of his own party.[57] Cabinet ministers questioned the plan in detail, warning again that "autonomy for the Arabs of Judea and Samaria" would lead to statehood, ironically echoing what Begin said about the autonomy concepts that his colleagues in the National Unity Government raised during the post-1967 war discussions.[58]

To obtain approval, Begin agreed on some changes (which Dayan presented to Lewis as clarifications, adding that Begin "had no problems with the cabinet"), including the introduction of a five-year review period, an explicit statement that the question of sovereignty would remain open, exemption of the Israeli settlers from the authority of the administrative council, and responsibility of the Israeli authorities for security and public order.[59] Eventually, Begin produced a twenty-six-point plan, including American input, such as the introduction of an official role for Jordan via participation in a joint committee to deal with refugee issues and legislation (Jordanian law was still being applied in Judea and Samaria.)[60]

However, in comparing the original plan and the revised version based on the available evidence, the differences between the two texts appear to be largely in emphasis without altering the substance. Begin's basic framework—cultural and limited political autonomy without Palestinian sovereignty, the removal of settlements, or an end to Israeli security control—remained intact. Indeed, after the Cabinet meeting, Begin reaffirmed his support for the autonomy plan, declaring that although he still believed in the Jewish historic rights in Judea and Samaria as firmly as before, he added that "certain realities" had to be taken into consideration.[61]

Israeli officials, such as Ben-Elissar, also rejected Carter's claims, concluding that no significant changes in the document had been made.[62] Indeed, William Quandt notes that "the proposals were not 'attenuated substantially' as Carter maintained. Instead, some of the hints that Begin and Attorney General Aharon Barak had made orally about the scope of authority for the Administrative Council were never acted on, and a few new points were added to the version shown to Sadat."[63]

Beyond the substantive disagreement, the allegations of changes in Begin's plan between the presentations to Carter and to Sadat ten days later became a major source of rancor in the personal and political relationships. Reflecting the American perspective, Kenneth Stein notes, "Carter thought he had obtained something more forthcoming from Begin than he had given, and Begin thought he had received Carter's endorsement for his Palestinian self-rule proposals." As a result, "Carter felt that Begin manipulated what he heard and what he did not hear for his own purposes. . . . This would not be the last time that Carter and the administration thought or claimed they heard Begin say one thing and found out later it meant something else."[64]

This conflict can also be explained as the result of Carter's inexperience, his impulsive endorsement of Begin's proposal when it was first presented, and the phone call to Sadat, followed by a greater understanding and loss of enthusiasm on Carter's part. After Begin had left, Carter and his advisors looked at the proposal's details and implications more carefully, particularly with respect to their own preferences for a radical political agreement based on Palestinian sovereignty. At this point, Carter might have realized that he had made an error by adopting the proposal uncritically, but rather than admitting this mistake, the administration blamed Begin for changing the program.

Another factor reflected the fact that after Begin left, Carter was pressed by Saudi Arabia. Simcha Dinitz reported this on December 23 from an unidentified secret source that he described as close to the administration. According to Dinitz, during the previous two days, Saudi pressure had increased. King Fahd reminded Carter of the role Saudi Arabia played in slowing the oil price increase and pushed Carter on the Palestinian issue "as was promised to the Saudi delegation when it visited in Washington" (there was no further reference to this visit). Fahd also discussed policy on "our Jerusalem."[65]

Whatever the reason, this clash between Carter and Begin damaged the relationship significantly, and Begin came back to the dispute many times. For example, over a month later, in a meeting with Vance on January 16, 1978, before the opening of the meeting of the Political Committee, Begin quoted from the record of his meeting with Carter, to which Quandt adds that it was "as if to imply that Carter had endorsed his proposals."[66] Indeed, the evidence suggests that Begin in fact believed that Carter had endorsed his proposals and then changed his mind, inventing a very weak excuse, blaming Begin in order to back away from this support.

Furthermore, this incident again highlights the Carter administration's limited understanding of the dynamics and strains of Israeli democracy. Begin's election caught Washington unprepared, and officials were still scrambling to understand the fundamental change in the Israeli leadership following the end of Labor Party domination. To some degree reflecting the attitude of Israel's old guard, the Americans tended to see Begin and the Likud government as a fluke— a passing phase that would soon be over, with power returning to the traditional Israeli leadership with whom the Americans, and the Democrats in particular, were more comfortable. Ideologues like Begin, who were strongly committed to maintaining Jewish historical rights in Judea and Samaria, were anathema to the problem-solving orientation of the Carter administration. Quandt recalled later, "We never quite figured out how to get around Begin or work through him or work over his head or behind his back. I cannot stress to you how difficult that turned out to be."[67]

Given this image, it was even harder for the United States to contend with and incorporate the fact that Begin's harshest critics were from his own party and faction in Likud and Herut. If Begin was seen as a fanatic and hard-line Zionist extremist, the Carter administration could not understand that his willingness to make compromises, including the dismantling of settlements and withdrawal from the Sinai and to accept even limited autonomy in Judea and Samaria was fiercely rejected by critics who accused him of treachery or capitulation to American pressures. At the other end of the political spectrum, the Labor Party and the Left attacked Begin for not moving quickly enough, not making generous concessions, or taking the security risks that they might have taken had they been in power. From the beginning, Begin was caught between these different pressures, and as a result, he sought to chart his political path very carefully.

The Ismailia Summit

The Ismailia summit, which took place on December 25, 1977, was, in many ways, symbolic of both the successes and weaknesses of the entire process. Only a month after Sadat's visit to Jerusalem, the euphoria was still tangible, as was the confusion about the process and goals. Begin, who emphasized protocol and reciprocity, was clearly aware of the mixed message of being the first Israeli prime minister to pay an official visit to Egypt—though to Ismailia rather than Cairo. Before departing, Begin said publicly that he was bringing a peace plan that he presented in the United States and the United Kingdom and that "everyone who saw it" said it was a fair basis for negotiations with Egypt and also "a first step towards attaining an overall peace in the Middle East."[68]

In the working sessions, Begin presented Sadat with a document containing the framework for an Egyptian-Israeli peace treaty and with the autonomy proposal. The discussions were reportedly contentious, in part because Sadat had little interest in the details (and avoided offering detailed proposals of his own) and in part reflecting a rejection of the Israeli approach. However, some of the substance, such as Begin's proposal that "when the peace agreement is signed, the Egyptian Army may be established on a line which will not reach beyond the Mitla and Gidi passes," became the basis for the demilitarization agreements in the peace treaty.[69] (Begin claimed that this was based on a discussion with Sadat in Jerusalem.) In his Ismailia proposals, Begin also sought a formula that would leave Israeli settlements in the Sinai with IDF protection.

The Ismailia summit ended with a joint statement and a press conference. Sadat indicated progress in the question of withdrawal of forces and disagreements over the Palestinian issue. Egypt had called for a Palestinian state in Judea, Samaria, and Gaza, while Israel offered autonomy.[70] He also made it clear that he was not speaking for the Palestinians or the Syrians but presenting a general framework into which the other Arab nations would enter and discuss directly with Israel. When asked by an Egyptian reporter (in Hebrew) whether Sadat's initiative changed his thinking and how he saw Israel's future in the Middle East, Begin replied (also in Hebrew) that Sadat's visit was of "historic significance" and Israel prepared a peace plan in response. Begin continued by saying Israel's future would be glorious and the Middle East would develop into "a sort of paradise on earth," quoting King Hassan of Morocco. Regarding the future role of the United States, Sadat said it would have a part to play in the Political Committee but not in the military one, which will be bilateral. The Soviets, Sadat said, had excluded themselves, so they had no part at all.[71] The meeting in Ismailia marked the end of Carter's efforts to reconvene the Geneva Conference.

The United States was not represented at this meeting (for the last time in the negotiations) and relied on secondhand reports, leading to two entirely different evaluations. According to Stein's account, Lewis reported that Begin and Sadat were close to an agreement, but Hermann Eilts reported that Sadat said, "This was the most insulting meeting. I'm never going to see this man again. He was my guest, so I had to be polite to him, but don't ever expect me to talk to him again." However, in public statements, Sadat gave no hint of friction, and a week later, in an interview on Cairo radio, he continued to refer to the talks as successful.[72] Weizman called the meeting a "blind alley."[73]

Going beyond the spin, which Sadat and Begin sought to use to influence perceptions in Washington and elsewhere, they reaffirmed establishment of the political and military committees to meet in Jerusalem and Cairo, respectively, giving the process structure. According to Kenneth Stein, the Ismailia meeting produced three points of agreement: a commitment to achieve a comprehensive peace settlement, a willingness to negotiate peace treaties based on UNSC Resolutions 242 and 338, and the fulfillment of all the specific contents of UNSC Resolution 242. "Sadat told the Israelis that UNSC Resolution 242 required Israel to return all territories taken by force and return to the pre-1967 armistice lines. There was no declaration published because a formula for the Palestinian Arabs could not be agreed upon."[74] Although they issued separate public statements, no signs of anger were apparent, as both leaders stated that they were very pleased and hopeful for the future.[75] In both public and private comments, Begin said that a declaration of principles would have been reached at Ismailia "if not for the hardline intercession at a crucial moment of Ismat Abdel-Meguid and other Egyptian Foreign Ministry men (officials), who drew Sadat away from a compromise on the Palestinian clause of the declaration."[76] According to Stein, the fundamental source of conflict was not the issue of Palestinian autonomy but rather "Egypt's non-acceptance of any continuing Israeli civilian or military presence in Sinai. Begin told Sadat, that 'not only the settlements would stay, they will be defended by an Israeli contingent.'"[77]

Israel found Egypt's proposals on security, demilitarization, and normalization between the two states to be "very disappointing."[78] The Israeli proposal included a combination of demilitarization and reduction of forces, "an Israeli military presence 'for a period of years' until final withdrawal to the international border. Free navigation in the Tiran Straits would be assured by either a United Nations force, which could only be withdrawn by agreement of both countries and the Security Council unanimously, or by joint Israel-Egyptian patrols."[79] In Ismailia, the Egyptians showed little interest in these proposals.

After Ismailia, on January 22, 1978, Begin discussed with Lewis and Alfred Atherton the problem of demilitarization and the wider concerns regarding the negotiations in Jerusalem. According to the American summary of the meeting, Begin

> was especially concerned over Sadat's penchant for making verbal agreements and then later, upon advice of his advisers, reversing himself. He cited as an example the demilitarization of Sinai. In Jerusalem Sadat had agreed on the spot not to permit any Egyptian forces east of the Sinai passes. Begin had been ecstatic over the statesmanship Sadat had demonstrated in reaching this decision. And in Ismailia when the subject came up Sadat had said nothing to indicate any change of mind. Not 48 hours later when the Israelis had communicated to the GOE [government of Egypt] through our Embassies the Israeli

plan which started "Based on promises made in Jerusalem," once again not a word had been said. It was only when Weizman and Gamasy first met in Gianaclis and Gamasy handed over a completely different plan that Begin had realized something had gone wrong. He quoted Weizman as having reminded Sadat of his commitment to Begin in Jerusalem and how Gamasy had interrupted to say that Sadat was not a military man and therefore his commitments on the issue were not relevant. Begin said this episode had badly shaken his faith in Sadat's steadfastness.[80]

The Weizman-Gamasy meeting that Begin referred to apparently created a crisis of confidence in Israel regarding the efficacy of negotiating directly with Sadat. Begin learned that other members of the Egyptian government did not always follow Sadat's lead, and, more concerning, his pledges—in this case to demilitarize the Sinai in exchange for Israel's full withdrawal—were not binding. Israel's assumption that Egypt would demilitarize the Sinai was the basis of its planning and proposals to Egypt. The sudden understanding that this had not been agreed on became a major problem for Begin and led to greater caution which he maintained until the end of the negotiation process. The issue was settled only at the Camp David summit in September 1978, where Sadat gave a formal promise to demilitarize the Sinai Peninsula.

There was strong disagreement on the issue of Palestinian autonomy. After the Ismailia talks, Sadat reportedly complained to Eilts, "What is this guy doing? He is a merchant. He is peddling me notions. I just recognized his existence and now he is going to give the Palestinians a little of this and a little of that."[81] Since the autonomy concept was no more welcome in the White House than it was in Cairo, Sadat's complaint resonated.

Begin did not change his position following the negative Egyptian reaction to his autonomy proposals, declaring that "very serious people" in the West had approved them and that international pressure "would be fruitless, because Israel was accustomed to withstanding pressures."[82] On December 28, Begin addressed the Knesset and read out his twenty-six-point proposals for self-rule in Judea, Samaria, and Gaza, as well as the foundation for a peace treaty with Egypt. Following this presentation and debate, in which the internal opposition within Begin's own constituency was intense, the Knesset endorsed his proposal by a significant majority.

While Begin could derive satisfaction from his success in the Knesset, the Carter administration was focusing on what it saw as a growing deadlock. Quandt noted, "In Ismailia, Begin and Sadat were unable to agree to anything of substance. . . . The failure of the talks in Ismailia dampened the hopes generated by Sadat's trip to Jerusalem. Not only was the substantive gap between Egypt and Israel very wide but also the atmosphere was beginning to cloud."[83] This provided an opening for active US involvement in the process.

The Challenges of Begin's Domestic Political Negotiations

As a new prime minister, the first non-Labor Party leader, and former head of the Irgun, Begin faced constant challenges and tests from the Labor-led opposition, which expected to return to its "rightful" governing position in short order. The intense political activity initiated by Sadat's visit and its aftermath increased the pressure from Labor, and its leader, Shimon Peres, was determined to bring about new elections and end the Likud-led interlude. From the moment that Sadat announced his intention to visit Jerusalem, Peres and the opposition demanded dramatic gestures and Israeli concessions and criticized Begin at every sign of friction.

At the same time, for the right wing of the Israeli spectrum, Begin's readiness to negotiate with Sadat for the return of the Sinai and to promote autonomy for Arab residents of Judea, Samaria, and Gaza was viewed with great suspicion. In response to Sadat's demand for the return of all the Sinai, ministers and leaders of the settler movement demanded increased construction. And immediately after Begin developed his autonomy concept, and before it was presented to Carter, ministers declared that they would oppose any plan that might lead to a Palestinian state.[84] Thus, throughout this period, Begin was forced to maneuver between the pressures from the left and right at home while also trying to avoid clashes with Carter and Sadat. His successes in maintaining control of the government and steering policy toward the 1978 Camp David agreement and subsequent peace treaty are testimony to his skills as a political leader, as well as to his commitment to a durable peace with Egypt.

Nevertheless, Begin bowed to pressure from the settler movement, which had powerful support from within the Cabinet—mostly the National Religious Party ministers and Agriculture Minister Ariel Sharon—and agreed to expand settlements. Throughout the negotiations, decisions to build new settlements were commonly announced by the government and routinely denounced by the United States in public statements and sometimes in personal letters from Carter to Begin expressing the president's anger and frustration. But for Begin, in addition to the ideological dimension, this was a means of offsetting political pressure from the right.

The Knesset debate on December 28, 1977, was the first to be held regarding Begin's peace plan. Until then, MKs learned the details from the press and had not been asked for their opinions. The various factions already held internal debates and staked out positions, and the extraparliamentary opposition movements (most importantly Gush Emunim) started protesting. In the Likud, Geula Cohen and Moshe Shamir led the opposition from within and questioned Begin's loyalty to his own principles. Begin responded decisively and eventually demanded a vote of confidence. The majority supported Begin's plan and his leadership.[85] The Knesset debate was an opportunity for all sides to present their views and policies, and, for Begin, it was the first test of his support. He asked all factions to allow their members to vote freely, without party discipline.[86]

Begin succeeded: sixty-four MKs voted in favor of the peace plan, eight rejected it, and forty (most of whom were from the Labor Alignment) abstained. Although they supported the peace process, as the main opposition, Labor MKs avoided voting for Begin and his plan. Most of them would later vote in favor of the Camp David Accords and the peace treaty. But the outcome of this vote was problematic as it showed Begin that he had to rely on opposition support. Although the coalition had seventy-seven seats, thirteen members did not support Begin's peace plan, and more defections were expected as the negotiations advanced. The opposition from within Likud was significant.[87]

The attacks from the ideological core of the Herut faction of the Likud Party intensified with the pace of negotiations, as was the case with the National Religious Party (NRP), whose platform emphasized a strong commitment to settlements and the Greater Israel concept.[88] To maintain support within the Likud, Begin was forced to defend his policies almost daily. Before the Ismailia summit, ministers from the Likud and NRP challenged him to explain "how autonomy for the Arabs of Judea and Samaria can be prevented from growing into statehood."[89]

In early January 1978, in a public forum sponsored by Herut, Begin spoke about the legitimacy of border changes under international law and criticized Sadat for rejecting any civilian or military Israeli presence in Egypt after the signing of a peace agreement. Begin also declared that "the Israelis do not burn settlements. They build settlements and keep them" and pledged that the IDF would stay in Judea, Samaria, and the Gaza Strip under the autonomy plan: "The only (legitimate) claim to sovereignty over Judea, Samaria and Gaza is that of the Jewish people." Begin also noted the Cabinet decision to add settlements in Gaza and the northern Sinai, to be defended by the IDF, stating, "We propose a security belt around the State of Israel, not just for this generation, but for the coming generations."[90] (To emphasize this point, Begin later declared that any prime minister who would give up these settlements would be thrown out, "but I would resign first."[91])

Such pledges and commitments did not end the criticism, and Shmuel Katz, who was very close to Begin and served as a press advisor, resigned.[92] In a subsequent meeting of the party leadership, Katz and Geula Cohen attacked the unacceptable concessions in Begin's proposals. Katz rejected the idea that the return of the Sinai would give Israel a "stronger position in Judea and Samaria," warning that this was an illusion: "what we give him, (Sadat) puts in his pocket and then he starts from scratch." Katz also rejected Begin's claim of Carter's support for autonomy, arguing (accurately) that the Americans had only accepted the plan as a basis for negotiations but "expect Israel to make further concessions in Judea and Samaria."[93] Carter's words and actions gave these predictions credibility. Within Likud, Begin again threatened to resign if his peace plan was not endorsed by the party. This tactic succeeded, and he won support for his policies by an overwhelming vote of 168 to 15 in the central committee, but the criticism remained.[94]

The attacks were led by MK Geula Cohen, who would later vote against the Camp David agreements and peace treaty and form a breakaway party known as Tehiya. In early 1978, Cohen demanded that Begin's government "drop its 'so called' peace plan and break off negotiations with Egypt." She also warned Begin that the Americans would continue to support the Egyptian position, meaning that Israel would be forced to return to the pre-1967 lines, while also claiming that Washington was driving "a wedge between world Jewry and Israel."[95]

At the same time, Begin also faced continuous pressure from the Labor-party opposition, led by Peres, who moved between criticizing the government for its uncompromising policy, on the one hand, and for offering too much, on the other. In response to Sadat's visit, Peres emphasized Labor's platform calling for territorial compromise while preserving vital security interests. He criticized the decision to "send tractors to carry out earth moving work in Sinai while peace negotiations were in progress."[96] Regarding settlements, Peres declared, "For peace, we must be ready to think everything anew."[97]

Shortly afterward, and taking the opposite ideological approach, Peres also attacked Begin for offering "too much" in the first stages of negotiations with Sadat.[98] Peres and Labor's Knesset faction seemed to join forces with Begin's hawkish Herut and NRP critics, declaring that the autonomy proposals "were tantamount to the establishment of an independent Palestinian state on the West Bank."[99] In a series of speeches and statements, Peres called Begin's position as being "worse than the Rogers Plan," demanded a Jordanian role in the West Bank "to prevent the emergence of an independent Palestinian Arab state," and warned that functional autonomy could be, at best, a temporary arrangement.[100] Pushing the Jordanian option, Peres announced, "The real alternative for the residents of the administered territories is between Jordan and the PLO . . . and whoever leaves Jordan out, even if he rejects the PLO, opens the way for the PLO's entrance through the back door."[101]

In response, Begin accused the Labor Party, which continued to have strong links with the US government, of undermining Israel's negotiating position with the Carter administration. In March, when the different interpretations of Resolution 242 became a central focus of conflict, Labor presented its own interpretation, which was consistent with Carter's. In the Knesset, Yigal Allon attacked Begin's autonomy proposal as ineffective in addressing the Palestine problem while warning that "it would lead to the 'de-Zionisation of Israel. . . . The Begin plan embodied all the negative elements of previous peace plans."[102] In response, Begin noted that the Alignment government delayed its acceptance of UNSCR 242 for a long time and referred to the Allon plan for peace (which was never officially adopted by Labor) as "a childish farce which the Arabs scorned and the US termed 'totally unacceptable.'"[103] In March, after Begin returned from another conflictual meeting with Carter in Washington, Labor called for the former's resignation.[104]

While sharp exchanges between government and opposition MKs are frequent, in this case, the position taken by MK Mordechai Wirshubski, a member of the Democratic Movement for Change, one of Begin's ruling coalition partners, agreed with Labor. In a public statement, Wirshubski declared that Begin's policy "has been a failure. The time has come to re-think our position in regard to our participation in the government. I don't say that Israel is entirely guilty, but certain government positions have served to aggravate the situation."[105]

While this small crack in the coalition did not threaten the government's position in the short term, it did provide another indication of dissent. As events developed toward the Camp David summit at the end of August, the pressure to avoid a breakdown in relations with the United States, as well as to prevent the failure of the negotiations with Egypt, served as a counterweight to pressures from Begin's right, as articulated by Shmuel Katz and Geula Cohen.

Deadlock

December's Ismailia summit helped to define the respective positions and the focus of disagreement in terms of the bilateral issues related to the Sinai (settlements, demilitarization, borders, and so forth) and the Palestinians.[106] In the eight months until the Camp David summit, this agenda provided the framework for the interactions, which took place largely through public declarations from Cairo and Jerusalem.

While the Americans focused on the Palestinian issue, Israel and Egypt began with the bilateral issues and, in particular, the question of Israeli settlements in the Sinai. Sadat issued public statements declaring that after the conclusion of a peace agreement, "I will not accept a single Israeli settlement to remain on my soil. Let them [the Israelis] demolish them."[107]

Dayan pledged that every square kilometer of the Sinai would be subject to intense negotiations and that Israeli settlements would remain while sovereignty returned to Egypt, perhaps protected by UN forces and even paying taxes to Egypt.[108] However, such pledges did not end the growing protests from Begin's core constituency. In the attempt to appease the critics, he appointed Ariel Sharon, who was closely associated with the settlement movement in both the Sinai and the West Bank as the deputy head of Israel's negotiation team.

The complexities of this balancing act were reflected in early January, when press reports indicated that the government had approved the construction of eight new settlements in the Sinai. This elicited sharp protests from Egypt, from the Labor Party opposition in Israel, and from the Americans. Quandt notes that "on day of the Aswan meeting between Carter and Sadat, Israel announced 4 [*sic*] new settlements in Sinai."[109] While holding his ground in a letter to Carter, Begin's cabinet secretary stated that "no new settlements would be established in the Sinai," noting that this decision was "identical in substance to a decision made a few days earlier, but not made public."[110]

Sadat also referred to the "clouded atmosphere" created by Begin's December 31 speech at the Herut meeting and the decisions to increase settlement construction:[111] "Begin gave me nothing. It was I who gave him everything. I gave him security and legitimacy and got nothing in return."[112] After Sadat pushed for unilateral partial Israeli withdrawal in Sinai (to the Al Arish–Ras Mohammed line), Begin rejected the proposal in a letter that reportedly "included a lecture on how Sadat could not expect to get something for nothing."[113]

At the same time, the Egyptian press resumed the political and personal attacks against Begin that had been muted since Sadat's visit in November. Several articles and editorial cartoons portrayed Begin as a fascist, and the Shylock image was common. Since the Egyptian press was seen to be tightly controlled, Begin could not avoid the conclusion that the campaign of vilification was sanctioned by, if not initiated by, Sadat or his close advisors. For Begin, these images also invoked analogies to the Nazi caricatures in *Der Sturmer* and other publications, thereby poisoning the relationship significantly.

In this context, the first meetings in January of the Political and Military Committees took place in Jerusalem and Cairo, respectively. The Military Committee involved the two defense ministers—Gamasy and Weizman—and did not include a US presence. Weizman presented a five-point agenda focusing on security arrangements in the Sinai. The Egyptian engagement on the basis of this agenda was understood as signaling a readiness for a separate peace agreement with Israel, provided that acceptable wording on the Palestinian issue could be found.[114] The Egyptians could also infer that despite the public statements and declarations regarding new settlements, Israel would be prepared to withdraw completely from the Sinai as part of a peace agreement. (Weizman became Sadat's "favorite Israeli" interlocutor and was invited to Cairo frequently, beginning in December 1977.)

In contrast, the meeting of the Political Committee on January 17, 1978, at the level of foreign ministers, including Vance, was far more conflictual. Even before the meeting opened, the disagreement over the agenda indicated that friction was likely.[115] In his speech upon arrival, Egyptian foreign minister Muhammad Ibrahim Kamel called for the return of Jerusalem to Arab control.[116] When the meeting began, he presented a five-point plan: (1) Israeli withdrawal from Sinai, the Golan Heights, the West Bank, and Gaza according to UNSCR 242 and the principle of nonacquisition of territories by force; (2) guarantees of security for the territorial and political independence of all regional states, through agreed measures based on the principle of reciprocity; (3) respect of all regional states' rights to sovereignty, territorial integrity, and political independence; (4) a just solution to the Palestinian problem, based on the right of self-determination through negotiations involving Egypt, Jordan, Israel, and representatives of the Palestinian people; and (5) an end to all claims and belligerencies and the establishment of peaceful relations between all regional states by signing peace treaties.[117] These demands were unacceptable to Begin.

In addition to the conflict in the formal sessions, the other activities were also marked by tension. In a private meeting with Kamel, Begin protested the personal attacks in the Egyptian newspapers that portrayed him "as a Shylock and fascist." (Begin presented the details in a Knesset speech on January 23, reflecting the importance he attached to this issue.) Later, in a toast during the official dinner, Begin referred to Foreign Minister Kamel as a "young man," which the latter took to be patronizing. According to Ben-Elissar, Begin did not intend to insult Kamel, but he acknowledged that Begin "was not 100 percent tactful and was a little paternalistic, as he so often was."[118]

Carter wrote in his diary that Begin "made a ridiculous and abusive speech" that embarrassed Vance and Kamel and aggravated Carter himself.[119] According to Ambassador Lewis, "Quite inadvertently, Begin insulted the poor Egyptian Foreign Minister who didn't want to be there anyway, had tried to resign at Camp David [eight months later] and was really pained by the whole experience of being in Israel. Begin referred to him as a 'young man' in his speech. It wasn't any intention to insult him, but it symbolized a cultural gap."[120]

Hours later, Sadat ordered the Egyptian delegation to return home, thereby bringing an abrupt end to the first meeting of the Political Committee, which was never reconvened afterward. An Israeli statement accused Egypt of causing the rupture by demanding Israeli withdraw from all the territories and handing Jerusalem over to foreigners. The statement recalled the support that Begin's peace plan had received just a few weeks earlier in the United States and the United Kingdom and reiterated the commitment to negotiations.[121]

Carter became involved in this crisis immediately, asking Sadat to reverse his decision and keep his delegation in Jerusalem for one more day. He warned Sadat, "At this moment there is great support for you and disappointment with Begin in this country. This can shift." Sadat replied that "the Israelis need a lesson."[122] Vance told Begin later that night that to his and Carter's plea that the discussions continue, Sadat responded that "unfortunately he had gone too far to reverse" and that "he understood the importance of continuing the process, that perhaps his decision to break off the Political Committee talks had been a mistake but that he had gone too far to reverse it immediately."[123]

Begin also discussed his talk with Kamel and the Egyptian "series of reasons for the breaking off of the talks," including the pressure the Egyptians felt themselves to be under in Jerusalem from the Israeli press. Begin told Vance that Kamel indicated he considered his recall "a suspension rather than a termination" and that Kamel expressed his hope the Political Committee could be reconvened soon. Despite the setback, Begin said that the negotiations were making good progress, but Sadat was acting on "a whim, Sadat is a whimsical man."[124]

In Cairo on January 20, Sadat told Vance "that he had been very sorry to take the decision to remove his delegation, but it appeared that the approach to the whole problem was being twisted by the Israelis. They should recognize that the fact of sovereignty cannot be negotiated. From Begin's speech yesterday, one can conclude that their main goal is land, not peace at all." Sadat told Vance of his hesitations, reinforced when disagreement arose over the agenda. But when the United States broke the impasse, he decided "to go ahead and to see what would take place." Sadat blamed Begin's speech for the reversal, complaining, "Israel's main objective is land, not security, as Begin has argued. Begin, he said, wants security, land, and peace all together. After talking about the importance of Arab recognition of Israel, Begin has now said arrogantly that he does not need Arab recognition."[125]

On January 22, in a meeting with Lewis and Atherton, Begin analyzed the abrupt termination of the Political Committee, admitting, "It was clear that Sadat and his advisers had misgivings about sending a delegation to Jerusalem from the very beginning. Even so, Begin found Sadat's decision to recall his delegation to be 'an irrational act.'"[126]

On February 4, 1978, Carter and Sadat met in Camp David. According to Carter, the discussion focused on settlements in the Sinai, including Minister Ariel Sharon's declarations about the "need for many new settlements" and then the cabinet decision to instead fortify existing settlements. These moves signaled acceptance of "the idea of keeping settlements. When President Sadat understood that, he was prepared to take his people out of the negotiations." Sadat made no mention of Begin's toast.[127]

The explanations for these developments vary widely. Sadat's words notwithstanding, Quandt blamed the incident on Begin's toast, as did David Korn, the US State Department's director for Israel and Arab-Israeli affairs.[128] Stein offers four other possible explanations: Sadat's dislike of the content and pace of the Political Committee discussions, his decision to regain control over the talks and not leave them to his underlings, a response to Saudi pressure and threats of severing relations and boycotting Egypt (Gamasy's suggestion), or Sadat's displeasure with Vance's formulations, though he did not want to embarrass Vance or Carter.[129] This range demonstrates the extreme difficulty encountered in Washington, Jerusalem, and elsewhere in attempting to understand Sadat. David

Kimche, a high-ranking official in the Mossad at the time and later director general of the Foreign Ministry, claims that Sadat drew his delegation back as soon as he understood that leaving the negotiations in the hands of Egypt's foreign ministry would be counterproductive to the goal of returning the Sinai to Egyptian control since Egypt's diplomatic establishment did not want peace.[130]

The evidence according to the US cables published in *FRUS* supports the view that Sadat sought a pretext to pull out of the talks in Jerusalem as a tactical move, and Begin's reference to Kamel as a "young man" provided the pretext. But shortly after recalling his delegation, and faced with backlash from the United States, Sadat appeared to understand that his move was a substantial public-relations error. Nevertheless, for several months the direct contact between Israel and Egypt was maintained by the Israeli military delegation based in Cairo.

Following these events, conflict between Cairo and Jerusalem escalated, although Sadat met with Weizman in March in what was officially termed a meeting of the Military Committee. (In July, after the Leeds talks, Sadat closed the Israeli military mission in Cairo.)[131] On March 1, Sadat gave US envoy Alfred Atherton a letter addressed to Begin containing "extremely critical language."[132] (By using the Americans to deliver the letter, Sadat clearly sought to involve the Carter administration in the conflict with Begin and to gain support.) Begin's reply noted that Israel did not need Egyptian recognition to exist: "Every nation has the same right to exist. . . . Indeed, we were given our right to exist from the God of Abraham, Isaac and Jacob. It is inherent; it requires no recognition. What we do expect, however . . . is the recognition of our right to our land, sovereignty, independence, and to enjoy peace with our neighbors."[133]

Begin and Carter: Round Two

Sadat's surprise visit to Jerusalem had effectively frozen the Americans out of the diplomatic action, causing concern in terms of both image and substance. The Carter administration entered office with a comprehensive plan for Middle East peace and pursued this policy.[134] From this perspective, a bilateral Israeli-Egyptian treaty that did not lead to resolution of the Palestinian dimension would be considered a failure.

On this basis, Carter hammered at the Palestinian issue and attacked the Israeli policy. As Quandt shows, the US strategy was to press Israel and Begin to change basic positions.[135] As a result, much of the negotiation activity took place in exchanges between Carter and Begin.

During a high-profile visit to Iran on January 1, 1978, Carter pointedly declared, "We don't back any Israeli military settlement in the Gaza Strip or on the West Bank. We favor, as you know, a Palestinian homeland or entity there. Our own preference is that this entity be tied to Jordan and not be a separate and independent nation."[136] A few days later, during a stopover in Aswan, in which he and Sadat made press statements, Carter repeated the position that "a lasting peace must resolve all aspects of the Palestinian problem."[137] Carter emphasized his "principles for a just peace," including normal relations (not only nonbelligerency): Israeli withdrawal from territories captured in 1967, agreement on secure and recognized borders according to UNSCR 242 and 338, and a solution acknowledging Palestinian legal rights and participation in determining their future.[138]

Carter repeatedly declared that Begin's proposal could only be acceptable as a "transitional phase" toward Palestinian self-rule and Israeli withdrawal.[139] In response, Begin stated, "The term self-determination, as it is understood in international law and practice, means a Palestinian state and we will not agree to such a mortal danger to Israel."[140]

The Israelis complained that Carter was inconsistent, tailoring his policy pronouncements to fit different audiences. For example, in January he announced, "I have never thought . . . it is advisable . . . for the world to have an independent nation located between Israel and Jordan."[141] In February 1978, Carter told Jewish leaders that Israel would be able to keep an airfield in the Sinai and maintain a military presence in the West Bank beyond five years. He also endorsed Begin's position on holding a Palestinian referendum without offering the choice of an independent state.[142] In a meeting with Weizman shortly afterward, Carter discussed keeping an Israeli military presence in the West Bank beyond the initial five years and endorsed Begin's autonomy plan as the basis for transitional arrangements. However, he also pushed for Israeli agreement on a plebiscite, which was decidedly not part of Begin's proposal.[143]

The increased American intervention was justified by the claim that without this mediation, the initiative would fail. Sadat fed this fear, periodically threatening that if no agreement was reached, war was still an option.[144] Immediately after Sadat's visit to Israel in November, the Carter administration was already issuing detailed statements and conducting extensive meetings with the main actors. The Americans continuously pressed Begin to make a dramatic gesture to Sadat and to define "what territory it is ready to surrender while urging President Sadat to specify how Israel's independence and territorial integrity would be respected."[145] Carter and Vance were concerned that Sadat was losing public esteem "by his irrational, unpredictable actions and statements."[146]

By early 1978, both Begin and Sadat tried to bring the Americans into the process to gain their support. The Americans also began to view Sadat's diplomatic style as highly problematic, fearing that "he has little idea of how to proceed and counts on us to bail him out. His impatience with details is becoming a real problem, as is his reluctance to engage in sustained negotiations."[147]

After Ismailia, Quandt reported that the American diagnosis was: "First, left to themselves, Sadat and Begin would get nowhere. Second, Sadat would insist on recovering all of Sinai, but would show flexibility on the details of a West Bank and Gaza arrangement for a transitional period."[148] The US position continued to emphasize a comprehensive peace agreement and, particularly, a solution to the Palestinian issue. In contrast to self-determination, American officials reported that Sadat privately favored Palestinian links to Jordan.[149] The official Egyptian press quoted Sadat as saying, "I have been calling for the past four years for a link between Jordan and any envisaged Palestinian state."[150] Peres also supported this position.

As the American involvement increased significantly, the structure of the negotiations gradually shifted back to the previous model of indirect exchanges. In January, Kamel asked Eilts to increase US pressure regarding the issue of settlements in the West Bank and on the Palestinian "right of self-determination."[151] The Israeli response came in many forms. On Israeli television, Dayan explained that Palestinian autonomy and a continued IDF presence were entirely compatible and that the IDF would intervene if "in violation of the agreement, the Arabs would want to establish a Palestinian state." He reiterated this point in the Knesset, declaring that "if hundreds of thousands of refugees would come from Lebanon and other countries and from the PLO—we would use the IDF."[152]

American pressure on Israel became part of Sadat's strategy, and he told journalists that "the role of the US is to exert pressure on Israel, particularly with regards to the Palestinian problem, because it is the crux of the crisis."[153] (He also spoke of the need for compromise: "We should renounce the policy of either getting everything or rejecting everything. We should get what we can until we can get all that we want."[154]) In another pressure tactic, Sadat would complain to the United States whenever he disliked an Israeli action or declaration, claiming that Israel would not act in this way without the acquiescence of the Americans and that if Carter put his foot down, Begin would listen.[155]

In response to the collapse of the Political Committee in January 1978, the US administration increased its cooperation with Sadat to extract concessions from Begin. According to Quandt, the strategy was for Sadat to propose a plan that "should include a few elements that would be unacceptable to the United States and Israel." Carter would then enter as a mediator, "but Carter would have an understanding in advance with Sadat that at a mutually agreed moment an American compromise proposal would be put forward—and Sadat would accept it."[156] In a more explicit approach, Quandt and Brzezinski pressed "a strategy of collusion with Sadat to help bring pressure to bear on Begin."[157]

In a February 4 bilateral meeting at Camp David, Carter and his aides developed what they saw as a realistic strategy. In response to Sadat's request for American leadership, Carter said, "The time has come for a US position to be presented on both sides. . . . [I]f the United States puts forward a position after our meeting, it will look like a US-Egyptian proposal. . . . It will be seen as collusion.

It is essential for me to see Begin, and to invite him, and to have a similar meeting. Then . . . I have to have the US public see that I have consulted both you and Begin first."[158]

In response, Sadat prepared a document entitled "Basic Guidelines for the Solution of the Palestinian Question," which repeated maximalist and uncompromising demands, including full Israeli withdrawal, the "right of refugees to choose return to their homes or compensation," and a Palestinian plebiscite. This was more than the Americans had bargained for, and Quandt reports that Sadat was asked to prepare another proposal ("this time spelling out more completely Egypt's views on the transitional period"), but the structure of negotiations that would continue through Camp David was set.[159]

Two months after the Carter-Sadat meeting, their joint strategy was not working. In response to an American proposal, Kamel told Vance, "If you didn't tell me these were American ideas, I would have thought they are from Begin." The Egyptians responded by revising their own plan: "Summing up his reaction to the Nine Points, Kamel observed that if such an American proposal is put forward 'it's the end of Sadat, it's the end of Egypt.' Kamel expressed his hope that, in that case, the United States would take an Egyptian revision as seriously as it does the Begin Plan."[160]

In a memorandum to Brzezinski in mid-May 1978, Quandt warned that this strategy was not working: "Sadat takes initiatives without informing us in advance; he holds back on what he is saying to Weizman; he lets his officials turn out worthless legalistic documents in the guise of serious negotiating proposals; and yet he seems to be disappointed with our reluctance to become a full partner. We do not have a satisfactory political understanding with Sadat as we enter a crucial phase of the negotiations."[161]

To implement this strategy, Carter and the Americans pressed Begin through meetings, memos, and other ploys, but they all led to the same outcome. In March, for example, during a trip to Washington, Begin and Dayan held talks with Carter and his Middle East team. As in other interactions with Begin, they attempted psychological manipulation, and before the meeting, Carter, Brzezinski, and Vance agreed to emphasize the positive consequences of peace. They would give Begin credit for some proposals but also would prepare for a probable breakdown of the negotiation, necessitating greater US involvement: "In the future it might be necessary to offer a United States-Israel security treaty."[162] Following the strategy that had been worked out with Sadat, Carter demanded concessions to match Sadat's flexibility.[163]

In the March 21 meeting, they argued again about UNSCR 242 and about the concepts and implications of Palestinian home rule and self-determination. Carter finally agreed to consider an Israeli plan that would be based on less than full withdrawal and include elements of Begin's autonomy proposal.[164]

(The meeting took place in the shadow of a major PLO terror attack on March 11 against a passenger bus on the Tel-Aviv Haifa highway. This triggered Israel's Litani Operation in Southern Lebanon. The UN Security Council adopted Resolution 425, calling for Israel's withdrawal from Southern Lebanon, and during the meeting, Carter praised Begin for implementing the terms. Regarding the peace negotiations, Carter hinted that Israel's security needs after its withdrawal would be partly met by American guarantees and that he made this known to Arab leaders.)[165]

Despite several differences, the Israeli and American protocols of the meeting did not substantially differ. Rather, the conflicts were over interpretation and analysis. During the following meeting with the Israelis, on March 22, Carter listed Israel's positions as negative on everything, which Begin and Dayan resented and tried to reframe more positively.[166] In his diary, Carter wrote, "For the first time . . . the true position of the Israeli government was revealed."[167]

In a press conference after the Israeli delegation departed from Washington, Vance said the talks were "very full, frank and candid," "difficult" but not "unfriendly or ugly." He said the main argument was over the implementation of UNSCR 242, especially in the West Bank and Gaza. A second issue was the settlements in the Sinai. When asked about a US-Israel defense agreement, Vance replied, "If that were the final item which would be required as the linchpin . . . then that is something I think we would have to seriously consider recommending to the Congress."[168]

In April 1978, as the deadlock continued, Dayan floated the idea of Israeli unilateral implementation of the self-rule proposal, which attracted American interest as a first step in breaking the deadlock.[169] On May 1, 1978, Carter again met with Begin privately, noting in his diary that "he's a small man with limited vision, and my guess is he will not take the necessary steps to bring peace to Israel—an opportunity that may never come again."[170]

In parallel to the intense interactions that were largely initiated by the Americans, in late April, they also sent a formal questionnaire to Begin and Sadat. The questions were designed to elicit focused policy responses in the effort to define and then narrow the gaps between the positions of the two parties while also indicating the areas where some agreement has been achieved.[171] (This third-party negotiating tactic can be compared to the single negotiating text process, which was employed by the Americans in Camp David a few months later.)

On June 18, 1978, Israel replied, repeating previous positions on negotiations "with participation of representatives of the Palestinians living in the region."[172] Quandt concluded that this was a "sterile exercise in diplomacy by questionnaire which produced little more than a sense of frustration."[173]

On July 5, Egypt published its plan for the West Bank and Gaza, "based on the legitimate rights of the Palestinian People and considering the legitimate security affairs of all sides." The terms included "a timetable of Israel's withdrawal" from areas "conquered since June 1967" and "methods to fulfill UN resolutions which are relevant to Palestinian refugees."[174] Israel rejected the text as "unacceptable," stating that these positions "cannot by their nature lead to the establishment of peace in the Middle East and the conclusion of peace treaties with Israel."[175]

In parallel, the Israeli delegation, led by Dayan, prepared to attend the Leeds Castle summit. On July 16, Begin spoke before the Herut Central Committee, denouncing the personal attacks he suffered from the Egyptian press. Nevertheless, he expressed hope for a positive result, regardless of his personal feelings. He also quoted the Cabinet decision from earlier that day, in anticipation of the summit, restating the goal of "negotiating with Egypt in order to make peace and sign a peace treaty." Indirectly addressing Carter and Sadat, he declared, "The only authority to negotiate with Egypt or any other state in a state of war with Israel lies with Israel's government and its authorized representatives."[176]

Opposition leader Shimon Peres met with Sadat in Austria a few days earlier, on July 10, during the Socialist International conference, led by Willy Brandt. Austrian chancellor Bruno Kreisky chaired the Middle East Committee. The conference ended with a statement of principles for achieving peace in the region. Peace should be based, according to the statement, on normal relations, Israeli withdrawal to secure borders on all fronts that would be agreed on in negotiations, and on a solution to the Palestinian problem in all its aspects, including recognizing Palestinians' rights to participate in determining their future.[177] Dayan rejected the statement as worthless because Kreisky stated that it was deliberately vague (so that "both sides could read into it whatever they wished"), and indeed the Egyptian interpretation was completely opposite that of Peres and Abba Eban.[178]

More important was the political reaction in Israel to these events. Peres, as leader of the Opposition, appeared to be negotiating with Sadat, putting pressure on Begin to moderate his policies or risk losing support. Begin accused Peres and the Alignment of weakening Israel's position and helping Sadat drive a wedge between the government and the public.[179] Bar-Siman-Tov reports that on July 16—after Peres sought to meet with King Hussein and Begin objected—the government declared the obvious: that it had sole authority to negotiate.[180]

At the end of June 1978, Vice President Walter Mondale visited Israel. According to the *FRUS* documents, Deputy Prime Minister Yigael Yadin told Mondale "that the US and Egypt seem to have given up on [Begin]. 'Yadin explained that, given these apparent feelings in the US and Egypt, Begin had become passive or intransigent. He in effect tells Weizman and Dayan to go ahead and play the game their way.'" Mondale told Yadin that Begin was the prime minister; thus, the United States would deal only with him. He added that Carter and Begin shared a "deep religious belief and understand each other."[181] There is no evidence that Mondale's visit had an impact in either Washington or Jerusalem.

The Leeds Castle Meeting and Beyond

The rhetoric of conflict and difficult bargaining often overshadowed the substantive exchanges and movement in positions that marked gradual progress. On July 17 to 19, the Political Committee, headed by the foreign ministers, reconvened in Leeds Castle in Kent County, United Kingdom. According to Stein, "At Leeds, Egyptian and Israeli officials, who had traded barbs for months previously suddenly re-energized. Dayan heard from Osama el-Baz . . . a moving understanding of Israeli security needs"; Dayan defined what was not possible, "and when the talks broke, key personalities who would become central to engineering verbal compromises at Camp David found themselves on the same negotiating page."[182] In Quandt's assessment, the talks were surprisingly productive, the gaps were narrowed significantly, and while Dayan rejected the idea of withdrawal to pre-1967 lines, he declared that "Israel would be prepared after five years to discuss the question of sovereignty and . . . an agreement would be possible." At the same time, the Egyptians agreed, for the first time, to a separate peace agreement, without insisting on Jordanian or Palestinian participation.[183]

These talks helped in defining and focusing attention on the potential trade-offs, and, as Stein reports, they provided the basis for the document prepared by Assistant Secretary of State Harold Saunders that became the basis for the Camp David negotiations. According to Atherton, "Leeds was a very important breakthrough in a lot of ways, not in terms of issues, but in terms of people getting to begin to perceive each other's points of view . . . and locking them up inside of a castle with a moat around it, symbolically the press was on the other side of the moat, and they couldn't get in."[184]

In their first meeting on July 17, Dayan told Vance (as documented in the Israeli protocol) that after the five-year autonomy talks, the situation would be reviewed and each side would be able to demand sovereignty:[185] "The government agrees that if the other side will propose a withdrawal and a territorial compromise, we will ask where exactly the line is. And if they tell us that, we will discuss it." He also told Vance, "This government might agree—I'm not convinced, but I will try to persuade them—to discuss and decide on sovereignty, provided that we agree on the mechanism." Vance asked how he saw the situation after the five-year interim period, and Dayan replied tellingly, "I speak for myself. I know that Begin thinks differently."[186]

Ambassador Lewis noted a difference between Dayan's statement—"After five years we will decide on sovereignty"—and Israel's official replies to the American questionnaire, rejecting any discussion of non-Israeli sovereignty.

Dayan and Barak replied that the autonomy plan left the question of sovereignty open for review after five years, but it was not a commitment to discuss this issue. Dayan repeated his own opinion: "If the Israeli peace proposal is accepted, Israel will be prepared to discuss after five years the question of sovereignty (or permanent status) of the areas. Although these provisions do not call for a decision on the subject, it is the personal view of the Foreign Minister that an agreement on this question is possible." In a later meeting, the Americans raised the issue of territorial compromise. Dayan cited his Knesset speech, in which he had said, "If such a proposal will come, and I mean a concrete one, not a general statement, because even negligible changes can be presented as territorial compromise—we will discuss it."[187] By telling the Americans that he made such a statement in the Knesset, Dayan implied that this was not a new position. By emphasizing this in the report to Begin, he sent the same message.

In a meeting with Atherton in Jerusalem on July 28, Begin accepted (albeit reluctantly) Dayan's position. The US record states that "Begin broke in to underscore the fact that on the matter of Israeli willingness to discuss West Bank sovereignty after five years, Dayan had spoken to the secretary at Leeds on his own behalf. The Foreign Minister of Israel cannot speak on a personal basis, Begin proclaimed, so the government gave its approval to Dayan's three points and they now constitute the Israeli position."[188] In other words, although Dayan spoke without approval from the government, Begin accepted this formulation, demonstrating a degree of pragmatism. In this case, Begin's critics could see Dayan as responsible for changing the official position, but they could also note that Begin was perhaps too weak to stop him or discharge him.

There were no bilateral Israeli-Egyptian meetings during the Leeds Castle summit. The three parties met three times, although Vance let the Egyptians and Israelis talk and was only sporadically active. The parties agreed in advance that the summit would focus on the Palestinian issue, and as noted, two weeks before the first session, Israel received Egypt's six-point plan, titled "Proposal Relative to Withdrawal from the West Bank and Gaza and Security Arrangements." This was the Egyptian counterproposal to Begin's Autonomy Plan. The Egyptians stated that the Palestinian issue was the key to peace in the Middle East, based on "the legitimate rights of the Palestinian people," with consideration to "legitimate security concerns of all the parties."[189] Negotiations would set the timetable for Israel's withdrawal, security arrangements, and a solution for the refugees.

El-Baz argued that Israel's plan was inadequate because the Palestinians did not accept its foundations.[190] While Israel remained adamant in its attempt to delay the discussion on sovereignty over Judea, Samaria, and Gaza and find practical solutions for the interim period, Egypt wanted an immediate decision on withdrawal and the right of the Palestinians to self-determination, from which all temporary arrangements would be derived. Hence, the Leeds Castle summit sharpened the disagreements.

On July 19, Dayan told Vance that Begin did not have a concrete plan for the final status of the territories, but he was certain about what he did not want (presumably, a Palestinian state). In addition, he noted "that the Arabs of the West Bank are not crazy for Hussein. The Arab Legion was brutal. As to Jerusalem—we all agree it will not be divided. Sadat suggested an Islamic flag over Islamic holy sites—I have no objection to that."[191]

In the concluding discussion that centered on a joint press statement, the issue of Jerusalem was raised. El-Baz accused Israel of annexing one-third of the West Bank to Jerusalem. Dayan replied, "We annexed—by implementing the Israeli law—part of East Jerusalem that was not under our supervision—and that is not one third of the West Bank. It is barely half a percent. . . . True, we implemented the Israeli law, but that does not mean that it is not negotiable."[192]

Although some analysts claim that Dayan's statements represented a fundamental change and even a breakthrough in Israeli policies, the record does not support this.[193] The central impact of Leeds Castle was to restore direct communications between the Israelis and the Egyptians and to establish the starting points for the next round, which was to be held at Camp David.

On July 24, 1978, Dayan delivered a policy statement in the Knesset that included Israel's readiness to discuss sovereignty in Judea, Samaria, and Gaza after five years of administrative autonomy and to also discuss territorial compromise. He declared that Israel would not accept any proposed peace treaty if it would be based on Israeli withdrawal to the pre-1967 lines and on Arab sovereignty on territories after Israeli withdrawal, even with security guarantees.[194]

Begin concluded the Knesset debate, repeating that Israel sought a peace treaty with open relations. If that could not be attained in the near future, Israel was willing to live in peaceful relations with Egypt, as Germany had with the rest of Europe before signing the peace treaties. Begin rejected pressure from the United States and the Labor opposition to give immediate territorial "gifts" to Sadat.[195]

On July 31, Sadat reportedly told Atherton (as reflected in the American documents) that this was the final stage of his initiative, and he was furious with Begin's statement that he would not make a territorial gesture or unilaterally withdraw from el-Arish. Sadat argued that the Leeds Castle summit only worsened the situation as it showed that Israel's goal was to acquire land. Land and sovereignty were not to be part of the negotiations again, he said; negotiations were on what happens after Israel's withdrawal.[196]

In early August 1978, Secretary Vance brought the invitations for Camp David, handwritten by Carter. Ambassador Sam Lewis recalled that "both principals jumped immediately to accept. . . . They were both delighted that the invitation suggested that this was the only way they were going to get any far-ther."[197] Begin could not reveal the content of the letter he received, claiming later he could not let the world know he and Sadat were invited to Camp David before Sadat received the invitation. In the press conference, Begin said he was waiting for an update from the American delegation regarding their talks in Egypt the next day.

Begin accompanied Vance as he was leaving the prime minister's office on his way to the airport. Begin was asked by Barry Schweid from Associated Press whether he and Sadat were invited to the United States. Begin said something that sounded negative. But, later, Begin felt uncomfortable that he did not tell the truth. Dan Patir, Begin's press advisor, recalled that he suggested that Begin write a personal note to Schweid explaining that the fate of the Camp David summit was hanging in the balance. Begin indeed wrote the letter, and Patir said that Schweid later recalled that, for the first time in his career, a statesman apologized to a reporter for making a false statement.[198]

Begin then held another press conference with Israeli reporters, without mentioning the upcoming summit, and repeated his rejection of demands that Israel withdraw to the 1967 lines: "No Israeli Government of any composition whatsoever could agree to such an undertaking. And President Sadat knew this—he knows it. Therefore, if he ties the meeting of the three statesmen to an undertaking by the Israeli Government to this demand, then such a meeting sim-ply cannot take place." According to Begin, "Mr. Vance accepted the mission to convince President Sadat that the meeting indeed should take place—without imposition of prior conditions. . . . Everything is negotiable—but without prior conditions."[199]

Begin's demand for no prior conditions was accepted. Sadat and particularly Carter realized that to get Begin to participate in the summit and make the deci-sions that only he, as prime minister, could make, they were obliged to accept his terms.

Conclusions

The months of negotiations following Sadat's visit in November 1977 were dif-ficult, but the process continued, although without significant progress. With international and domestic pressures on both sides, everyone involved had a great deal to lose if the negotiations failed. Moreover, with all the crises and sus-pensions, direct negotiations between Israelis and Egyptians were minimal.

The conflicts and stalemate between Begin and Sadat, and the failure to devise a realistic road map needed to reach an agreement, opened the door for the return of Carter and the Americans as essential mediators. By constantly holding meetings, sending letters, pressing the leaders, and presenting proposals, Carter kept the process initiated by Sadat's visit alive.

For Begin, the friction, frustration, and disappointment with Carter exceeded that involving Sadat. The Egyptian leader could be expected to argue intensively with Begin and to press the Israeli leader to accept his positions. But the Bible-quoting, democratically elected American leader was supposed to be an ally and to understand the Israeli fears, concerns, and historic rights.

In the months of stalemate, Begin adjusted his perception and expectations of Carter and learned how to respond to American pressure. Agreeing to send Dayan to participate in the Leeds Castle summit, accepting Dayan's independent initiative regarding future discussions on the West Bank, and then agreeing to participate in Camp David bought Begin time and kept the process going.

As the danger of being blamed for failure receded, Begin's position as prime minister stabilized. After the second Sinai disengagement, the Labor government's attempts to move the process forward proved unsuccessful, and Begin was considered the best chance for a breakthrough. For Begin's critics on the right, the numerous examples in which the prime minister rejected the American and Egyptian pressure, particularly on the Palestinian issue and the construction of additional settlements, provided reassurance that he was not going to capitulate.

At the same time, the limited contact between Israelis and Egyptians in this period demonstrated the differences between Sadat, the Egyptian military, and the officials in the foreign ministry. If the Israeli side lacked a strategy, as well as the tactics necessary to implement a strategy, the government was still largely centralized under Begin's firm leadership. In contrast, in addition to lacking a consistent strategy, the Egyptian team appeared scattered and incoherent, with Sadat stepping in and out unpredictably. Advisors and ministers came and went, without continuity.

Furthermore, in the buildup to Camp David, Sadat's incoherence provided Begin with an important advantage. While Begin's private and public statements were consistent, Sadat's were clearly not. Carter discussed this with Begin several times and tried to assure him that Sadat was merely maneuvering and would end up with positions that Begin could accept. But Begin could not accept this behavior—particularly when domestic pressure was growing, from coalition and opposition, to either push forward or cease the process.

Anticipating the Camp David summit, where the three leaders would be in the same location for the first time, Begin could envision a situation in which Sadat would be forced to make the tough decisions and commitments, thus setting the stage for an agreement.

In the months of arguments and jockeying, Begin had learned Sadat's negotiation style. It became apparent that Sadat wanted to reach peace to get the Sinai Peninsula back and was willing to pay a heavy price, but at the same time, his aides—after failing to stop him—tried to minimize that price, particularly the demilitarization of the Sinai. Begin and Dayan could see that Carter and his team were not paying much attention to the influence of Sadat's aides and were more concerned—indeed, overly concerned—with Sadat's inter-Arab difficulties. A closed-door summit in an isolated retreat could bring Sadat to the position of having to make key concessions to obtain a successful outcome, and Begin could see the advantage of this situation.

In addition, although a US-brokered summit was not what Begin or Sadat were thinking of when the direct negotiations between Israel and Egypt began, this was the only remaining option. This limited format, without the participation of all of the Arab states (unlike the Geneva model), and led by the two heads of state, was also closer to Israel's preferred structure of negotiations. Begin consistently sought bilateral negotiations, without the United States (similar to the Oslo process and the negotiations between Rabin and Hussein in 1994, which produced a peace treaty), but under the circumstances, the summit seemed a reasonable gamble.

Notes

1. Stein, *Heroic Diplomacy*, 228.
2. Quandt, *Camp David*, 153.
3. Ben-Elissar, *No More War*, 84–115.
4. David Landau and Anan Safadi, "Why 'Summit Meeting' Will Be Secluded—Sadat Fears Cheering Crowds for Begin," *Jerusalem Post*, December 19, 1977, 1. See also Ben-Elissar, *No More War*, 110–15.
5. Stein, *Heroic Diplomacy*, 239.
6. Stein, 241.
7. Stein, 232.
8. Quandt, *Camp David*, 152.
9. *IMFA*, document 83.
10. Bar-Siman-Tov, *Israel and the Peace Process*, 63–64, citing Dayan, *Breakthrough*, 91–97.
11. Bar-Siman-Tov, *Israel and the Peace Process*, 64; Dayan, *Breakthrough*, 95.
12. Hirsch Goodman, "Egypt Returns Bodies of Yom Kippur War Dead," *Jerusalem Post*, December 9, 1977, 1.
13. Stein, *Heroic Diplomacy*, 236.
14. David Landau, "Foreign Ministers to Discuss Borders at Second Stage of Cairo Conference," *Jerusalem Post*, December 9, 1977, 1; Wolf Blitzer, "Sadat: Room for ministers in Cairo," *Jerusalem Post*, December 11, 1977, 1.
15. David Landau, "Israel Accepts Offer; Assumes No PLO Seat," *Jerusalem Post*, November 27, 1977, 1; "No Mention of PLO-Official Invitations Handed to Envoys," *Jerusalem Post*, November 28, 1977, 1; David Landau, "Lewis to Deliver Invitation," *Jerusalem Post*, November 28, 1977, 1.
16. Stein, *Heroic Diplomacy*, 237–38; Ben-Elissar, *No More War*, 85–87. Ben-Elissar and Rosenne reported this incident, saying they protested to the hotel manager on raising "an

unidentified flag . . . one not representing any state" (Delegation to Cairo, telegraph to prime minister, foreign minister, and defense minister, December 14, 1977, ISA, A 4313/7).

17. Stein, *Heroic Diplomacy*, 238.

18. Oren, *Six Days of War*, 314.

19. Stein, *Heroic Diplomacy*, 200; Prime Minister's Statement on His Visit to the US, *Major Knesset Debates, 1948–1981*, 6:2125.

20. Malka Rabinowitz, "Begin Hopes to Forestall US-Egyptian Front," *Jerusalem Post*, December 16, 1977, 1.

21. Bar-Siman-Tov, *Israel and the Peace Process*, 65.

22. Haber, Schiff, and Yaari, *Year of the Dove*, 105–7; Stein, *Heroic Diplomacy*, 233; Sofer, *Begin*, 131–34; Naor, *Begin in Power*, 154–55.

23. Telem, Tzabag, and Noiberger, eds., *Israel's Foreign Policy Documents*, 355.

24. Bar-Siman-Tov, *Israel and the Peace Process*, 65.

25. Stein, *Heroic Diplomacy*, 234.

26. Bar-Siman-Tov, *Israel and the Peace Process*, 65; Quandt, *Camp David*, 155; Rabinowitz, "Begin Reveals Part of Peace Plan in CBS Interview—Self-Rule for Territories, Jerusalem Stays United," *Jerusalem Post*, December 19, 1977, 1.

27. Early drafts of the autonomy plan are in the ISA, A 4314/6.

28. Bar-Siman-Tov, *Israel and the Peace Process*, 66–69; Benziman, *Prime Minister under Siege*, 85.

29. Asher Wallfish, "Cabinet Lauds Begin's Steps, but Ministers 'Still in the Dark,'" *Jerusalem Post*, December 19, 1977, 1. Bar-Siman-Tov found that Begin did not hold any consultations regarding the peace plan, and except for Dayan and Attorney General Barak, only Begin's closest aides knew the details. According to Katz, Weizman was not consulted because Begin did not want him to pass the information to Chief of Staff Gur, who would have pressed his views regarding Israel's minimal security needs (Bar-Siman-Tov, *Israel and the Peace Process*, 62; Katz, *Hollow Peace*, 199). Begin ignored all peace plans prepared by the military establishment, some of which Weizman presented to him on December 9, 1977 (Bar-Siman-Tov, *Israel and the Peace Process*, 62).

30. Bar-Siman-Tov, *Israel and the Peace Process*, 67–68; Gur, *Chief of the General Staff*, 345–50.

31. Bar-Siman-Tov, *Israel and the Peace Process*, 68; Benziman, *Prime Minister under Siege*, 86–87; Katz, *Hollow Peace*, 194, 198; Weizman, *Battle for Peace*, 119.

32. Bar-Siman-Tov, *Israel and the Peace Process*, 69.

33. Bar-Siman-Tov claims that the trip to Washington to obtain Carter's support was Dayan's idea.

34. Begin reportedly surprised Vance by announcing that he intended to go to Washington to present to Carter his ideas on home rule, particularly considering Begin's policy of not coordinating with Washington in the period leading up to Sadat's visit (Quandt, *Camp David*, 155–157).

35. Stein, *Heroic Diplomacy*, 234.

36. Wolf Blitzer, "US Pleased Begin-Sadat Talks Stress Geneva," *Jerusalem Post*, November 22, 1977, 1; Wolf Blitzer, "US 'Reassures' Sadat after Lukewarm Response to Meeting," *Jerusalem Post*, December 2, 1977, 1.

37. Stein, *Heroic Diplomacy*, 236, 242; Carter, *Keeping Faith*, 298; Quandt, *Camp David*, 157; Brzezinski, *Power and Principle*, 115–120.

38. "Carter: Will Tell Begin if His Offer Falls Short," *Jerusalem Post*, December 16, 1977, 1.

39. Quandt, *Camp David*, 158.

40. Quandt, 154–155.

41. "Meeting between Prime Minister Begin and President Carter at the White House, Washington, D.C., Friday, December 16, 1977 @ 8:00 a.m.," 16–17, ISA, MFA 6862/11.

42. "Meeting between Prime Minister Begin and President Carter at the White House, Washington, D.C., Saturday, December 17, 1977, @ 1905 Hours," 5–6, ISA, MFA 6862/11. The name Providavians that appears in the quote appears to be an error in place of Pravoslavs, the Russian Orthodox Church (Shay Fogelman, "What Israeli, US Leaders of 1977 Hoped Would Be Jerusalem's Fate," *Haaretz Magazine*, November 4, 2011, http://www.haaretz.com /weekend/magazine/what-israeli-u-s-leaders-of-1977-hoped-would-be-jerusalem-s-fate -1.393738.) [Originally, in Hebrew, "Begin Is Dividing Jerusalem."]

43. "Meeting between Prime Minister Begin and President Carter at the White House, Washington, D.C., Saturday, December 17, 1977, @ 1905 Hours," 8–9.

44. "Meeting between Prime Minister Begin and President Carter at the White House, Washington, D.C., Saturday, December 17, 1977, @ 1905 Hours," 16.

45. "Meeting between Prime Minister Begin and President Carter at the White House, Washington, D.C., Saturday, December 17, 1977, @ 1905 Hours," 23.

46. *FRUS 1977–1980*, vol. 8, document 179. Begin and Callaghan established friendly relations, and Begin would casually inform Callaghan about the developments in the peace process. It started with Begin's visit to London in December 1977, which was rescheduled due to Sadat's visit. On the Begin-Callaghan relations, see Ashton, "'A Local Terrorist Made Good.'"

47. The Israeli minutes: "Meeting between Prime Minister Begin and President Carter at the White House, Washington, D.C., Saturday, December 17, 1977, @ 1905 Hours," 5–6. The American minutes: *FRUS 1977–1980*, vol. 8, documents 177, 178.

48. *FRUS 1977–1980*, vol. 8, document 191.

49. *FRUS 1977–1980*, vol. 8, document 178.

50. Carter, *White House Diary*, 150–51.

51. *FRUS 1977-1980*, vol. 8, document 213.

52. Avner, *Prime Ministers*, 416–27, presents the relevant section of the first Carter-Begin meeting.

53. Stein, *Heroic Diplomacy*, 235.

54. Stein, 234–35; Quandt, *Camp David*, 158; Carter, *Keeping Faith*, 300.

55. Marder, "Carter Lauds Begin's Flexibility, Sees No Reason for Pessimism," *Jerusalem Post*, December 30, 1977, 1.

56. "Sadat Unhappy with Carter's Stand on Middle East," *Jerusalem Post*, December 30, 1977, 1; "Begin Lauds Statement," *Jerusalem Post*, December 30, 1977, 1.

57. Joshua Brilliant and Asher Wallfish, "Begin May Face Serious Challenge by Supporters over His Proposals," *Jerusalem Post*, December 20, 1977, 1; Wallfish, "Begin to Lift Veil—Just Enough—at Full Cabinet Session Today," *Jerusalem Post*, December 21, 1977, 1; Joshua Brilliant, "Settlers Worried about 'Autonomy': Peres: Jordan Is Defense Line," *Jerusalem Post*, December 21, 1977, 2.

58. Wallfish, "Begin to Be Queried on Arab 'Autonomy,'" *Jerusalem Post*, December 22, 1977, 1.

59. Elyakim Rubinstein, "Foreign Minister, Lewis Rubinstein," December 23, 1977. *ISA*, MFA 6862/11.

60. Bar-Siman-Tov *Israel and the Peace Process*, 71. See Begin's speech to the Knesset, "'Real Security' and 'The Prime Minister's Self-Rule Plan,'" December 29, 1977. Dayan, *Breakthrough*, 359–61.

61. Wallfish, "'Certain Realities' Caused Begin's Changed Approach," *Jerusalem Post*, December 25, 1977, 1.

62. Stein, *Heroic Diplomacy*, 235.

63. Quandt, *Camp David*, 158.

64. Stein, *Heroic Diplomacy*, 235.

65. Telegram, Dinitz to Dayan and Chechanover, December 23, 1977, ISA, MFA 6862/11.

66. Quandt, *Camp David*, 164.

67. Quandt interview with Pressman, February 18, 2011, in Pressman, "Explaining the Carter Administration's Israeli-Palestinian Solution."

68. *IMFA*, document 99.

69. Stein, *Heroic Diplomacy*, 239.

70. The Joint Statement in Ismailia, in Gammer, *Peace Initiative*, 6.

71. *IMFA*, document 101.

72. Ari Rath, "Begin, after Meeting Sadat Sees Peace 'in Few Months,'" *Jerusalem Post*, December 26, 1977, 1; "Sadat: One of Happiest Days of My Life," *Jerusalem Post*, December 26, 1977, 1; Stein, *Heroic Diplomacy*, 242.

73. Weizman, *Battle for Peace*, 122–35; Quandt, *Camp David*, 159.

74. Stein, *Heroic Diplomacy*, 241.

75. Rath, "Begin, After Meeting Sadat Sees Peace 'in Few Months'"; "Sadat: One of Happiest Days of My Life."

76. David Landau, "Begin Cultivation Sadat's 'Instinct,'" *Jerusalem Post*, December 29, 1977, 1; Quandt, *Camp David*, 159.

77. Stein, *Heroic Diplomacy*, 241.

78. Hirsch Goodman, "Egypt's Security Proposals Seen 'Very Disappointing,'" *Jerusalem Post*, December 23, 1977, 1.

79. Asher Wallfish, "Begin's Peace Plan Wins Large Majority," *Jerusalem Post*, December 28, 1977, 1.

80. *FRUS 1977–1980*, vol. 8, document 207.

81. Kenneth W. Stein, "Sadat, Carter, Begin: A Triangle with Unequal Sides," in Fuksman-Sha'al, *Camp David Accords*, 79.

82. Wallfish, "Begin's Peace Plan Wins Massive Vote."

83. Quandt, *Camp David*, 159–60.

84. Wallfish, "Begin to Be Queried on Arab 'Autonomy.'"

85. Bar-Siman-Tov, *Israel and the Peace Process*, 72–78, 80–83.

86. Wallfish, "Begin's Peace Plan Wins Massive Vote."

87. Wallfish.

88. Joshua Brilliant, "Settlements Planned for West Bank as Criticism of Begin Plan Mounts," *Jerusalem Post*, January 4, 1978, 1.

89. Wallfish, "Begin to Be Queried on Arab 'Autonomy.'"

90. "Begin Warns: No Sinai Settlements, No Deal," *Jerusalem Post*, January 9, 1978, 1.

91. "Begin: 'I'd Quit Rather Than Give Up Rafiah Settlements,'" *Jerusalem Post*, January 16, 1978.

92. Joshua Brilliant, "Shmuel Katz Quits Post as Information Adviser," *Jerusalem Post*, January 6, 1978, 1.

93. "Herut Picks Haim Landau for Cabinet," *Jerusalem Post*, January 9, 1978, 1.

94. "Herut Picks Haim Landau for Cabinet," *Jerusalem Post*, January 9, 1978, 1.

95. "Herut Group Wants to End Peace Talks," *Jerusalem Post*, February 12, 1978, 2.

96. "Peres Queries Gov't Moves South of Rafiah," *Jerusalem Post*, January 24, 1978, 2.

97. Mark Segal, "Labour Flatly Reject Joining National Coalition Government," *Jerusalem Post*, December 2, 1977, 2.

98. Joshua Brilliant, "Peres Says Begin Has Offered Too Much Too Early," *Jerusalem Post*, December 26, 1977, 2; Mark Segal, "Negotiating from Back to Front" (interview with Shimon Peres), *Jerusalem Post*, February 10, 1978, 14.

99. "Alignment: Begin Plan Means Palestine State," *Jerusalem Post*, December 20, 1977.

100. Joshua Brilliant, "Settlements Planned for West Bank as Criticism of Begin Plan Mounts"; Joshua Brilliant, "Peres: Autonomy Means Palestinian State Unless There Is Link to Jordan," *Jerusalem Post*, December 23, 1977, 2.

101. Joshua Brilliant, "Peres Says Begin Has Offered Too Much Too Early," *Jerusalem Post*, December 26, 1977, 2.

102. "Labour Attacks before US Trip 'Irresponsible': Begin," *Jerusalem Post*, March 9, 1978, 1.

103. "Labour Attacks before US Trip 'Irresponsible': Begin," *Jerusalem Post*, March 9, 1978, 1.

104. Sarah Honig, "Labour Wants Begin to Resign Following 'Washington Failure,'" *Jerusalem Post*, March 24, 1978, 1.

105. Honig, "Labour Wants Begin to Resign Following 'Washington Failure,'" *Jerusalem Post*, March 24, 1978, 1.

106. Bar-Siman-Tov (*Israel and the Peace Process*, 85) claims that in Ismailia, Israeli leadership lost its euphoria regarding the peace process.

107. "No Israeli Civilians Can Stay in Sinai after Peace: Sadat," *Jerusalem Post*, January 8, 1978, 1.

108. *Jerusalem Post*, January 5, 1978, 1; "Dayan on TV: Autonomy and IDF Presence Compatible," *Jerusalem Post*, January 1, 1978, 1; David Landau, "Sinai Settlers Would Pay Taxes to Egypt under Peace Plan Terms," *Jerusalem Post*, January 1, 1978, 1.

109. Quandt, *Camp David*, 161.

110. Letter, Begin to Carter, January 9, 1978. BCA, PM-0072; Asher Wallfish, "Cabinet: NO New Sinai Settlement," *Jerusalem Post*, January 9, 1978, 1.

111. David Landau, "Sadat Says: 'Israel Wants Land and Not Security,'" *Jerusalem Post*, January 13, 1978, 1, 5.

112. "Sadat Says He Got 'Nothing' from Israel, Sees No Early Agreement," *Jerusalem Post*, January 15, 1978, 1.

113. Quandt, *Camp David*, 202, citing Weizman, *Battle for Peace*, 330.

114. Stein, *Heroic Diplomacy*, 244.

115. "Vance Due Here Today," *Jerusalem Post*, January 16, 1978, 1.

116. Stein, *Heroic Diplomacy*, 246.

117. Egypt's proposal for a declaration of principles as brought before the Political Committee in Jerusalem, January 16, 1978 (published in Cairo on January 19), in Gammer, *Peace Initiative*, 14.

118. Stein, *Heroic Diplomacy*, 247; Dayan, *Breakthrough*, 113–114.

119. Jimmy Carter, *White House Diary*, 164.

120. Sam Lewis, "The Camp David Peace Process," in Fuksman-Sha'al, *Camp David Accords*, 58.

121. The government of Israel's announcement following the break of the Political Committee talks by Egypt, January 18, 1978, in Gammer, *Peace Initiative*, 15–16 [Hebrew].

122. *FRUS 1977–1980*, vol. 8, document 198.

123. *FRUS 1977–1980*, vol. 8, document 200.

124. *FRUS 1977–1980*, vol. 8, document 200.

125. *FRUS 1977–1980*, vol. 8, document 204.

126. *FRUS 1977–1980*, vol. 8, document 207.

127. *FRUS 1977–1980*, vol. 8, document 211.

128. Quandt, *Camp David*, 164–65. According to another version, Kamel called Sadat, who agreed to call him back and end the talks (Stein, *Heroic Diplomacy*, 247).

129. Stein, *Heroic Diplomacy*, 247.

130. Kimche, *Last Option*, 93, 96.

131. Quandt, *Camp David*, 201.

132. Quandt, *Camp David*, 181.

133. Quandt, 182. The quote is from Begin's letter to Sadat, March 5, 1978, 2, BCA, PM 0073.

134. Brookings Middle East Study Group, *Toward Peace in the Middle East*.

135. Quandt, *Camp David*, 182–183.

136. Wolf Blitzer, "US Does Not Support IDF Presence in Areas," *Jerusalem Post*, January 1, 1978, 1.

137. "Carter Restates Stand on Palestinian Rights," *Jerusalem Post*, January 5, 1978, 1.

138. Excerpts from President Carter's speech after meeting President Sadat in Aswan, January 4, 1978, "The Aswan Formula," in Gammer, *Peace Initiative*, 13.

139. David Landau and Anan Safadi, "US Forming Bloc to Accept Begin Plan as Interim, Sharon Joining Negotiations," *Jerusalem Post*, January 3, 1978, 1.

140. David Landau, "Begin Firmly against Self-Determination," *Jerusalem Post*, January 5, 1978, 1.

141. "'Palestine State Is Inadvisable'—Carter," *Jerusalem Post*, January 8, 1978, 1.

142. Quandt, *Camp David*, 180, citing Dayan, *Breakthrough*, 119–20.

143. Quandt, *Camp David*, 183, citing Weizman, *Battle for Peace*, 260–62.

144. "Sadat Raises War Option If Parley Fails," *Jerusalem Post*, December 5, 1977, 1.

145. "US Wants Israel to Spell Out Withdrawal," *Jerusalem Post*, December 8, 1977, 1.

146. Jimmy Carter, *White House Diary*, 145.

147. Quandt, *Camp David*, 192.

148. Quandt, 162–63.

149. Blitzer, "US Does Not Support IDF Presence in Areas."

150. Anan Safadi, "Carter Supports Hussein at Teheran Meeting, Jordan to Stay Out of Talks 'for the Moment,'" *Jerusalem Post*, January 2, 1978, 1.

151. Anan Safadi, "Egypt: Israel Must Remove All Settlements," *Jerusalem Post*, January 1, 1978, 1.

152. "Dayan on TV: Autonomy and IDF presence compatible."

153. David Landau and Anan Safadi, "US Forming Bloc to Accept Begin Plan as Interim, Sharon Joining Negotiations," *Jerusalem Post*, January 3, 1978, 1.

154. Post Diplomatic Correspondent and Agencies, "Sadat: Egypt Willing to Reach Compromise," *Jerusalem Post*, January 3, 1978, 1.

155. Quandt, *Camp David*, 174.

156. Quandt, 171; Brzezinski, *Power and Principle*, 242–43.

157. Quandt, *Camp David*, 163.

158. *FRUS 1977–1980*, vol. 8, document 211.

159. Quandt, *Camp David*, 182.

160. *FRUS 1977–1980*, vol. 8, document 238.

161. Stein, *Heroic Diplomacy*, 249–50.

162. Jimmy Carter, *White House Diary*, 176.

163. In a press conference several days before Begin came to Washington, Carter declared he was about to search for some common ground on which all parties could agree in order to resume the direct talks (*IMFA*, document 130). The meeting was delayed because of a terror attack on the Tel-Aviv–Haifa highway.

164. The protocol of the meeting appears in both the US and Israeli archives: *FRUS 1977–1980*, vol. 8, document 232; *ISA* A 4173/6; see also Dayan, *Breakthrough*, 120–29; Quandt, *Camp David*, 186–87.

165. *IMFA*, document 140.

166. *FRUS 1977–1980*, vol. 8, document 234.

167. Jimmy Carter, *White House Diary*, 180.

168. *IMFA*, document 144.

169. Quandt, *Camp David*, 189–90.

170. Jimmy Carter, *White House Diary*, 193.

171. Quandt, "Camp David and Peacemaking in the Middle East."

172. Government decision, June 18, 1978 [official translation to English] (*ISA*, A 4313/13). See also Gammer, *Peace Initiative*, 22.

173. Quandt, "Camp David and Peacemaking in the Middle East," 366.

174. The Withdrawal Plan Egypt Passed to the Government of Israel, July 5, 1978, in Gammer, *Peace Initiative*, 23–24.

175. *IMFA*, document 170.

176. Protocol of the Herut Party Center, July 16, 1978, 5 [Hebrew] (BCA, PM 158).

177. Bar-Siman-Tov, *Israel and the Peace Process*, 103–4, citing Haber, Yaari, and Schiff, *Year of the Dove*, 283–84 [Hebrew], and *Maariv*, July 11–12, 1978.

178. Dayan, *Breakthrough*, 140.

179. Bar-Siman-Tov, *Israel and the Peace Process*, 104.

180. *IMFA*, document 179.

181. *FRUS 1977–1980*, vol. 8, document 258.

182. Stein, *Heroic Diplomacy*, 250.

183. Quandt, *Camp David*, 198–201.

184. The document contained concepts distilled from months of staff work, linking Begin's autonomy proposal, Carter's Aswan definition of Palestinian rights, and clarifications from Atherton's shuttles. Saunders said the talks at Leeds were "some of the freest, farthest ranging and honest discussions of underlying issues" (Stein, *Heroic Diplomacy*, 250).

185. Aharon Barak, "Conversation between American [Secretary of State] Vance and Israeli Foreign Minister Dayan, Accompanied by Lewis and Prof. Barak, Leeds Castle, 17.7.1978, Evening" (ISA, A 4313/14); Barak to Begin, July 20, 1978, ISA, A 4313/14.

186. Aharon Barak, "Conversation between American [Secretary of State] Vance and Israeli Foreign Minister Dayan, Accompanied by Lewis and Prof. Barak, Leeds Castle, 17.7.1978, Evening" (ISA, A 4313/14); Barak to Begin, July 20, 1978, ISA, A 4313/14.

187. ISA, A 4313/14.

188. *FRUS 1977–1980,* vol. 8, document 277.

189. ISA, A 4313/14.

190. Dayan, *Breakthrough,* 138–48, and protocols of the meetings at ISA, A 4313/14.

191. Barak, "Conversation between American [Secretary of State] Vance and Israeli Foreign Minister Dayan, Accompanied by Lewis and Prof. Barak, Leeds Castle, 19.7.1978, Morning," 5 (ISA, A 4313/14).

192. Meir Rosenne, "Leeds Summit: Minutes of Meeting from 19.7.1978 Afternoon," 5 (ISA, A 4313/14).

193. Shilon, *Menachem Begin,* 297–98.

194. Gammer, *Peace Initiative,* 26.

195. *IMFA,* document 179.

196. *FRUS 1977–1980,* vol. 8, document 279.

197. Stein, *Heroic Diplomacy,* 251.

198. Dan Patir, "The Relations of the Policymakers and the Press at Camp David 1978," in Fuksman-Sha'al, *Camp David Accords,* 40.

199. *IMFA,* document 183.

5 Camp David—Between Psychology and Political Realism

September 1978

THE THIRTEEN-DAY (SEPTEMBER 5 to 17, 1978) Camp David summit produced the framework agreement that had been sought from the beginning of the secret exchanges between Anwar Sadat and Menachem Begin. This framework set the agenda and parameters for the final stage of the negotiations and the peace treaty signed in March 1979. After an eight-month marathon of summit meetings, conferences, and crises, Camp David marked a critical breakthrough.

Before the summit, the general perception in Jerusalem was that, at best, Camp David would result in a broad framework for detailed negotiations on the two major sets of issues and on the linkage between them. However, after long and difficult negotiations, reaching a climax in the final Saturday night session between Jimmy Carter and Begin, Israel agreed to relinquish all settlements and air bases in the Sinai, and the United States (as well as Egypt) accepted the autonomy proposal as the foundation for future negotiations. The two central dimensions of the negotiations—the Egyptian-Israeli element, including the Sinai and the nature of the peace treaty, and Palestinian autonomy—were loosely linked, but the Camp David texts kept them separate and not directly dependent on each other.

During the summit, many different formulas were considered and discussed, and the negotiations went through several cycles of crises, reversals, and last-minute agreements. Numerous versions of events, as reported and interpreted by the participants, have been published, leaving many different perceptions and analyses.

For some, particularly in the United States and Egypt, Begin emerged as a master negotiator, gaining the most and compromising to the absolute minimal extent. According to Ambassador Sam Lewis, "Menachem Begin was a world-class negotiator. He came out ahead in Camp David, in my view, of the other two players."[1] Quandt offers the opinion that "Sadat himself almost certainly expected much more out of Camp David than he got."[2]

However, in the standard Israeli narrative, as presented by Uzi Benziman (*Prime Minister under Siege*) and Yoel Marcus (*Camp David: The Opening for*

Peace) and largely accepted by Yaacov Bar-Siman-Tov, Camp David was a difficult, high-pressure situation for which Begin and the Israeli team were poorly prepared. In the face of the Carter-Sadat alliance and relentless pressure from the Americans, Begin had very little bargaining power and was forced to make unanticipated concessions. After ten months of declarations that the Israeli settlements and the airbases in the Sinai would remain, Begin agreed to relinquish them. Begin also accepted language regarding the future status of Judea, Samaria, and Gaza and the applicability of Resolution 242 that he had emphatically rejected earlier and for which he was intensely criticized by members of Herut and the settler movement.

According to these analyses, as well as those voiced by the critics in the Likud and on the Israeli right, such as Geula Cohen, the other members of the Israeli delegation—Moshe Dayan, Ezer Weizman, Aharon Barak, and Abraham (Avrasha) Tamir—worked with Carter and Sadat behind Begin's back to obtain these concessions. The evidence supports the claim that within the Israeli delegation, each member, with his own ideological and political agenda, had a significant input. Furthermore, the absence of a coordinated strategy, systematic preparation, or simulations (in sharp contrast to the Americans, who came with briefing books, psychological profiles, and game plans) allowed individual Israelis to speak freely to Carter and the other American officials, and they became conduits of information and sources of bridging proposals.

But ultimately, as the protocols and other documents demonstrate, the difficult decisions on the Israeli side came back to Begin, who weighed the benefits of a framework agreement against the costs of failure, including being blamed by the US administration. Furthermore, Begin's behavior in the weeks and months after Camp David was inconsistent with the image of a physically and politically weak Israeli prime minister "under siege," unable to control events and forced to make concessions against his will and in contradiction to his lifelong ideology.

Additionally, after making the key concessions at Camp David, in the months of negotiations and crises that followed before the treaty text was agreed in March 1979, Begin had many opportunities to allow the process to reach a dead end. Instead, during the post–Camp David period, he stood firm against demands from Israeli opponents to reconsider the terms while also rejecting intense pressures from Carter for more concessions and to alter the understandings. Ambassador Lewis argued that Begin had "buyer's remorse" after Camp David.[3] However, there is no evidence that Begin regretted the results of Camp David, given the alternatives and their consequences. Thirty years later, Elyakim Rubinstein, who headed Dayan's office and participated in Camp David, recalled a conversation with Begin in 1982. Noting that four years had elapsed since Camp David, Begin said, "Ely, we did well for our people and our country."[4]

Indeed, the evidence indicates that for Begin, the outcome of Camp David represented the optimum and perhaps the only realistic agreement. Every central issue was considered intensively and negotiated until the final deadline, after numerous earlier deadlines had already passed. It is hard to see how different strategies, more pressure, and other measures could have extracted further Israeli concessions, and without agreeing to the removal of all settlements from the Sinai, it is likely that no agreement would have been reached.

Getting to Camp David

The Leeds Castle talks in July restored the negotiation process but also highlighted the substantive gaps on the central issues and took the discussions to the point where the direct and detailed involvement of the heads of government was required. Thus, a summit meeting was the next logical step. For many months, the Carter administration had already been considering a summit, including location and format. The Americans favored an isolated venue, in which the leaders would be cut off from journalists and their domestic political environments, in a major push to reach agreement. Under these conditions, it was hoped that both leaders would be freed from lobbies, interest groups, and pressures in response to media reports and would be able to make far-reaching concessions that would not be possible in ordinary negotiating conditions.

An agreed negotiating framework and agenda were considered necessary to prevent the collapse of the entire effort, which, it was feared, would potentially result in the resumption of hostilities and even another major Middle East war. Despite the lofty talk of "no more war, no more bloodshed," at various times during the negotiations, Egyptian and Israeli officials spoke of preparing their forces and nations for possible war if the negotiations reached a dead end. According to Chief of Staff Mordechai (Motta) Gur, discussions of scenarios in which failed peace talks would lead to war followed many of the initial stages.[5] (An explicit discussion about this within the Israeli delegation at Camp David took place on September 12.)

The American political calendar was another central factor in determining the timing and stakes involved at the summit. The Carter administration was in trouble at home, the president's approval ratings were very low, and the campaign for the midterm congressional elections was intense. The continued deadlock did not help Carter's presidency, and while he pressured Begin by threatening to blame him for failure, this would not have led to the breakthrough sought in the context of Carter's reelection campaign.[6] But a major diplomatic achievement could offset this precarious situation.

According to Cyrus Vance, Carter "momentously" came up with the idea of a summit sometime in early August (Carter's diary reports July 31), after Leeds. Vance supported the idea as the best means available to go forward, in the hope that a treaty with an interim solution for the West Bank would open the way for a general Middle East peace, which remained the administration's overall objective.[7] In his memoirs, Carter reports that he planned a three-day summit that could be extended to a week.[8]

Other than Vance, most officials in the Carter administration were unenthusiastic. Carter's political advisors attempted to talk him out of calling for a summit, telling him, "Stay as aloof as possible from direct involvement in the Middle East negotiations; it's a losing proposition." Carter, according to his diary, as quoted in his wife's book, refused to be dissuaded by the scenarios of failure.[9]

Carter's Preparations

During the week preceding the opening of the summit, Carter prepared intensively, including studying a sixty-page State Department briefing book. The section that discussed outcomes stated that the "best from our viewpoint would be both sides ready to sign a document like the joint statement . . . but that seems an unlikely outcome." In the margins, Carter wrote, "This will be our firm goal." On the section regarding applying the principles of UNSCR 242, Carter wrote that the draft text was "not ambitious enough." In his memoirs, Carter explained that his displeasure with the State Department's cautious assessment came after meeting Ambassadors Eilts and Lewis, who spoke about both Sadat's and Begin's "enthusiasm for the idea of the summit meeting."[10]

Brzezinski submitted his proposed strategy for the summit, which was much more vigorous and decisive than the State Department's version. In a seven-page document, the National Security advisor presented his views on negotiating and maneuvering the leaders of Israel and Egypt toward the desired outcome. Brzezinski discussed the expectations and red lines of both sides and provided threats for Carter to use at crucial points.[11]

Before the summit, Carter made a list of issues that, in his view, were already decided. Some of them were indeed accepted by both sides, but others were far from agreed, including the active involvement of the Palestinian leadership, meaning the PLO, headed by Arafat, which neither Begin nor Sadat would accept. The list consisted of twenty-one entries, nine of which were "agreed," such as "Jerusalem will be an undivided city, with free access to holy places" and "Egypt will have undisputed sovereignty over the Sinai." Carter's partially agreed items included references to UNSCR 242, full diplomatic recognition, Palestinian self-determination, and the future Israeli military presence in the West Bank. The eight remaining issues, such as settlements, West Bank permanent status, security guarantees, and "the Arab role in Jerusalem," were placed in the understated category of "expected problems."[12]

As reflected in Carter's lists, the main American effort at Camp David would be focused on pressuring Begin, again, to make major concessions regarding the

Palestinian issue, with less emphasis on the Israeli-Egyptian dimension. Carter's notes reflected a belief that the basic framework of an Israeli-Egyptian bilateral peace agreement had largely been agreed as Israel was prepared to withdraw from the Sinai (although the future of the settlements remained open), and Egypt was willing to sign a full peace agreement, possibly including diplomatic relations and navigation rights.

In the American assessment, Begin could afford to walk away and maintain a strong political position at home, despite the demonstrations from the Left.[13] Begin, Dayan, and Weizman probably would have disagreed with this assessment. For them, failure and its implications, including a crisis with the United States, domestic criticism for missing Israel's first and truly historic opportunity for peace, and the potential for another war with Egypt were major concerns.

On the Egyptian side, there were different accounts of expectations. According to Kamel, Sadat's advisors expected the summit talks to break down in a few days, leading to a crisis in US-Israel relations and then to the fall of the Begin government He told his American interlocutors that improving relations with the United States (including access to advanced weapons) was more important to him than any potential Egyptian-Israeli agreement.[14] However, Kamel, who resigned during the summit, may not have reflected Sadat's views accurately.

Washington and Cairo continued working on a coordinated strategy in which Sadat would present a "hard-line proposal," which Israel would reject, allowing Carter to present a bridging formula, which the Israelis would accept under duress. The US bridging proposal would focus on linking the two core issues—the bilateral Egyptian-Israeli dimension and the Palestinian dimension. Although apparently unaware of the details, the Israeli team considered scenarios of collusion between Carter and Sadat throughout the negotiations, including regarding the summit.

Vance reports that in mid-August, he, Harold Saunders, Alfred Atherton, and William Quandt reviewed different scenarios for the summit. Saunders brought the text he had begun after the Leeds Castle talks. The goal was to produce a draft of an Egyptian-Israeli treaty that would be part of a comprehensive settlement. Vance assumed that Sadat would endorse such a document and Begin would continue to object but would also understand it was the only way to reach an agreement.[15]

Beyond the discussion of scenarios and issues, Carter had the CIA prepare in-depth psychological and political profiles of Begin and Sadat.[16] He envisioned a grand brainstorming session in which the leaders would overcome "distrust" and understand each other better, while Carter's role "would be that of impresario more than mediator."[17] Presummit strategy sessions in the White House focused on personal and psychological factors rather than on interests and substance. According to Quandt, "For Carter, the psychology of the meeting seemed to be more important than the issues or the strategy."[18]

The psychological profiles of Begin and Sadat were prepared by Dr. Jerrold Post, director of the CIA CAPPB (Center for the Analysis of Personality and Political Behavior) and his associates. The section on Begin centered on the "increasing trend of oppositionism and rigidity in his personality"; a profile of Sadat, entitled "Sadat's Nobel Prize Complex," stressing his preoccupation with his role (and place) in history; and an analysis of "the implications for negotiations of the contrasting intellectual styles of Begin and Sadat," as Post characterized it. These documents were updated versions of similar analyses of Begin and Sadat prepared in 1977.[19]

Post reported basing Begin's 1977 profile on the Israeli leader's two books, *White Nights* and *The Revolt*, from the late 1940s and early 1950s, respectively. Post claims these books revealed Begin's tendency to express provocative statements, sometimes out of context and without regard to their negative political fallout. The profile emphasized Begin's focus on detail and legalism, but his long tenure as head of the opposition and his role in the National Unity Government were given little weight. Post predicted that the two leaders would not come to terms at Camp David and that Sadat's "big picture" bias clashed with Begin's "small picture" bias. The paper suggested keeping Sadat and Begin separated, leaving Carter the major role of bringing them to terms.

Rosalynn Carter wrote that Begin "liked small talk, especially about his grandchildren, and he yearned for a peaceful life with them. But when serious discussion about peace efforts arose, he would change the subject and talk for hours about his past experiences and the Holocaust—the death of his family at the hands of the Nazis, the time he had spent in a Russian prison, and his years as a leader in the underground." She wrote, "Jimmy knew that because of these beliefs and positions he would be very suspicious of any bold peace effort, and it was going to be hard for him to make the compromises necessary to reach a final agreement."[20] In his published diary, Carter commented (in 2010) that "Sadat cared little about semantics, while Begin seemed to have no regard for anything except his own people."[21]

Begin's Preparations

Begin received the invitation for Camp David from Vance in Jerusalem and accepted immediately, recognizing the potential for improving relations with the Americans and renewing the momentum for a peace agreement with Egypt.[22] Begin recognized that the negotiations with Sadat were deadlocked, and he had begun to explore alternatives, such as a permanent partial agreement, short of a peace treaty, including "termination of the state of war, but also normalization of relations, including economic cooperation and tourism."[23] Begin might have believed that this would prevent the need to dismantle the settlements in the Sinai, but at the same time, a limited agreement was inconsistent with his own long-standing demand that any Israeli withdrawal take place only in the context of a full and formal peace treaty. In any case, Sadat was not prepared to discuss a partial withdrawal from the Sinai, and within a few weeks, Begin dropped the concept. When Vance presented the invitation for the Camp David summit, Begin accepted it without consulting Dayan or Weizman and had no time to consider the various scenarios that might evolve at a Camp David summit choreographed by the American president.[24]

For Begin and his inner circle, Camp David provided a structure for reviving discussions with Sadat, but it was not expected to end with a framework for a peace treaty. The Israeli leaders were hoping that, at best, the summit would restore the framework in which substantive negotiations could resume in the months that followed. If the negotiations later failed to reach agreement, at least Begin could point to his willingness to engage in substantive talks on the terms of an agreement and avoid some of the inevitable blame that would follow failure. Prior to leaving for the United States, Begin is reported to have said, "Our people's fate does not depend on that meeting. Our people lived thousands of years before Camp David and will live thousands of years after Camp David." However, he did label it "a very important meeting."[25]

On August 31, Begin met with head of the opposition and chairman of the Labor Party, Shimon Peres, and with chairman of the Foreign and Security Affairs Committee of the Knesset, MK Moshe Arens (Likud). According to the protocol, on the issue of the West Bank, Begin said that Israel was not asking the Arabs to give Israel sovereignty over any territory but to agree to autonomy, which was "the only option" at the time.[26] Begin made a point in confirming that there was a broad consensus in Israel that the IDF must remain in the West Bank territories. In what may be a disclosure of his negotiation tactics, Begin told Peres and Arens that he would be willing to discuss a territorial compromise if Sadat raised the issue. The logic of such tactics is that as long as the Arabs (in this case, Egypt) demanded full Israeli withdrawal, Israel would refuse, but if the Arab side suggested territorial compromise, i.e., that *it* accepts that Israel may keep any territory, this would be worth exploring and negotiating.[27] Peres replied that he would be willing to discuss anything too, including Jerusalem, noting that the Labor Party "objected to returning to the 1967 borders, and not to minor modifications [in English], Jerusalem must remain united, and Israel's defense must begin on the Jordan River, including by IDF presence in Judea and Samaria." Peres added, "We are against a Palestinian State. We insist that the Rafah region [Yamit region] settlements will stand."[28]

Regarding the West Bank, there were several significant differences. Peres stated his support for a functional compromise on the West Bank, to which Begin responded, "i.e., no territorial division." Peres added that "in the future, we will divide [the territories] because we will not know what to do with the Arabs," citing a number of 1.8 or 1.9 million. Repeating the Labor Alignment position at the time, Peres stated that Jordan was already a de facto Palestinian state and that he opposed another Palestinian state, an Arafat state: "Jordan is a better partner; they will prevent the establishment of a Palestinian state; and the people of Gaza should obtain Jordanian passports." Begin added that Dayan wanted Jordan to make them citizens, and Peres replied that "he [King Hussein] will absorb the refugees and they will become Trans-Jordan inhabitants." Begin agreed, and Peres suggested that in the autonomy framework, Israel would be responsible for security and Jordan for the people because "they can do to the PLO things that we can never do."[29] For all of their differences, Begin and Peres agreed that Arafat and the PLO were not potential partners for peace or coexistence with Israel, and they also concurred on the need for strong measures against the Palestinian "armed struggle."[30]

On his way to the United States three days before the summit, Begin read Sadat's books *Rebellion on the Nile* and his autobiography. He told the press during the flight that he would do everything to make the summit succeed since "no one more than us wants peace, and since the international prestige of President Carter is at stake."[31]

Begin at Camp David

In contrast to the plan for three days or, at most, a week of meetings, the summit lasted for almost two weeks—thirteen days and twelve nights—from Tuesday, September 5 through Sunday evening, September 17. Following many intense debates, numerous drafts and responses, and crises and resolutions, as well as joint outings and attempts at social interaction, the negotiations ended with a framework agreement for a peace treaty.

The conference was closed to the media and all outsiders. As a result, in attempting to analyze what occurred, particularly from Begin's perspective, the attempt to document and verify the events, including meetings, activities, and paths that led to agreement, is unusually problematic. There were numerous meetings involving different participants on most days, and most of the official protocols and documents from the American side had not been made public as of September 2017, with the exception of documents published in *FRUS 1977–1980*, vol. 9 (documents 27–51, many of which are the editor's notes),[32] and the official White House daily log of the activities of the president, which provided information on the participants in the different meetings and the length of each session. In contrast, almost all of the protocols from the Israeli delegation meetings during the negotiation process were declassified by the Israeli State Archives.[33] The diaries and later memoirs published by the various participants, as well as journalistic accounts based on interviews, are patchy, often contradictory, selective, and embellished by personal perspectives and interests.

Many of the earlier published memoirs and diaries were written by the American participants, including Jimmy Carter and his wife, and naturally present the events from their perspectives, particularly in their analyses of Begin's strategies, policies, and decisions. Additional histories are based on material provided by members of the Egyptian delegation. In addition, Dayan, Weizman, and some of the other Israeli participants published their own versions, as well as providing partial material to journalists such as Benziman and Marcus.

Begin did not keep a diary or publish a detailed account, and in very limited interviews, he offered few details. Therefore, any effort to understand and analyze Begin's policies and actions during the Camp David summit, including those based on reports and speculations about these issues by other participants, should be undertaken with caution.

In particular, the reports and descriptions of anger, emotional flare-ups, and crises, particularly between Sadat and Begin, might reflect real conflicts or might be the controlled product of rational negotiation strategies. The repeated emphasis on psychological profiles and interpersonal conflict, particularly in reports from Carter and some of the other American participants, can also be explained by the perception (or artificial image) that without Carter acting as an intermediary, the two leaders would never have reached an agreement. Similarly, the degree of strategic coordination between Sadat and Carter remains unclear. At times, the evidence for coordination of collusion is strong, but in other instances, Carter and Sadat seemed to be moving in different directions. Thus, due to both the lack of authoritative documentation and the potential for spin, including in the firsthand reports, the details in the following descriptions of the events at Camp David, as well as the analysis, particularly with respect to Begin, must be treated very cautiously.

For the first eight days, the intensive talks in different combinations (bilateral, trilateral, full delegations and leaders only, and so on) failed to produce significant breakthroughs and generally went over the same ground and reached the same impasses as in past discussions. Daily triangular meetings involving the three leaders were scheduled, while the rest of the time was available for different frameworks, including bilateral sessions and discussions involving the various advisors and delegations that accompanied the leaders.

In the early meetings, Sadat reportedly told Carter that he did not believe Begin was really seeking an agreement and would delay progress. Sadat stated that he was willing to be flexible on all issues but two: land and sovereignty.[34] However, if Begin negotiated in good faith, Sadat told Carter that Egypt would agree to diplomatic relations and end the economic boycott of Israel. Both objectives were high on Begin's priorities in the framework of a peace treaty.

Carter's lists of agreed, disagreed, and partly agreed issues were divided into two groups—bilateral Israeli-Egyptian issues and the options for the West Bank and Gaza. In the first category, the dimensions included the future of the settlements and airbases in the Sinai, the terms of the peace framework between Egypt and Israel (ambassadors, recognition, open borders, tourism, and so forth), borders, the references to UNSCR 242, and security arrangements (which included American involvement and guarantees for Israel). (Carter notes that he had considered applying the "Shanghai method" for the points of disagreement, meaning that each party would simply express its positions as in the US-China talks.)[35]

On the Palestinian issue, the disagreements included the political framework (different forms of autonomy or a state); the presence of the IDF, including proposals for phased withdrawal; and similar questions. During the initial meetings, Carter reports, Sadat had demanded that Israel commit to withdrawing from the West Bank, beginning with a settlement freeze. Carter told Sadat that he opposed Begin's plan in which Israel's military would have authority over the West Bank autonomy's administrative council.

US-Egyptian "Collusion"?

On September 6 (the second day), Sadat introduced a draft agreement that Carter referred to as a "rigid and uncompromising" plan, which Sadat reportedly insisted upon showing to Begin.[36] Carter claims to have told Sadat, "Begin will blow up."[37] The draft blamed Israel for all previous wars and demanded indemnities for using the Sinai occupation, including payment for the oil Israel pumped out of wells, as well as a full withdrawal to the 1967 borders, enabling the Palestinians "to form their own nation, and relinquish control over East Jerusalem."[38] Sadat repeated his declaration that he could not be flexible on land or sovereignty.

However, the Americans reported that Sadat immediately provided a private three-page memo listing concessions to be made later in the negotiations, which is consistent with the "collusion strategy" discussed in February. In his diary, Carter quotes Sadat as stating that "on a short-term interim agreement I can be flexible, but any final agreement will have to include much more completely the Arab provisions that I have described."[39] Carter was then able to tell Begin that he had averted a major crisis by pressing Sadat to back down while asking Begin to make comparable concessions to be presented to Sadat.[40] According to Brzezinski, "Carter doubtless agreed with Sadat, but he admirably maintained his position as a conciliator."[41]

The crisis that Carter claims to have avoided arrived on September 8 (day four), and Sadat reportedly prepared to leave, claiming that there was no chance to reach an agreement with the Israelis. In the American narrative, Carter persuaded him to stay and continue the negotiations.[42]

In all of these actions and scenes, the degree to which this good cop/bad cop strategy was artificial, preplanned, and coordinated is unclear. Earlier in the negotiations, the Americans and Egyptians had discussed and planned to use this negotiating tactic, but Sadat's behavior was also seen as erratic, making collusion more difficult. In Quandt's words, Sadat was prone to flying off "in new, and often unproductive directions."[43]

Carter's Strategy of Separating Begin and Sadat

The triangular meetings involving Begin, Sadat, and Carter ended after three days, based on Carter's claim that these sessions were dangerously conflictual. The evidence supporting Carter's version is mixed. On the second day, when Sadat presented his "hard-line" draft treaty to Begin, Carter reported that Begin was shocked. (Afterward, Rosalynn Carter, who participated in meetings of the American team but not in the ones involving the Israelis and Egyptians, suggested that Sadat was being dramatic. She reports that Carter assured Begin it was just rhetoric and that Sadat would be flexible later, but, in her words, Begin was not convinced.[44]) According to Quandt, "Begin and Sadat are not speaking the same language and they do not get along personally at all. . . . A member of the Israeli delegation approached me in the evening and pleaded with me to find some way to get the message through to the president to keep Begin and Sadat apart."[45]

In contrast, according to Brzezinski, "the meeting with Begin and Sadat went better than expected. Although Sadat's proposals were clearly unacceptable to Begin, Begin, to some extent forewarned by the President not to expect anything forthcoming, responded rather magnanimously, indicated that he is prepared to consider any proposal, and he hopes that the Egyptians would do the same to his proposals."[46]

In the following three-way meeting (day 3) without the delegations, Carter reports that Begin and Sadat began shouting at each other over the language and terms in Sadat's draft treaty presented the previous day.[47] At lunch, Carter described the meeting to his aides: "It was mean. They were brutal with each other, personal."[48] But the next meeting, a few hours later, took place as scheduled. Begin's report to the Israel delegation claimed that Sadat did most of the shouting.

From day 4 (Friday), the Americans met with each leader separately, or, when they convened sessions involving both Israelis and Egyptians, these took place without Begin and Sadat. It is impossible to know whether Carter exaggerated the emotional dimension, but the effect was to highlight his mediation role. Whether by design or default, for the next nine days of the summit, the primary and most difficult negotiations took place between Carter and Begin.

Carter Presses Begin

In examining the White House logs for these days, the difference between the relatively short meetings between Carter and Sadat, on the one hand, and the longer Carter and Begin sessions (ninety minutes to two hours), on the other, is notable. Anticipating great difficulty in moving Begin from his long-stated and strongly held positions, Carter reportedly began the first meeting by expressing appreciation for the concessions that Begin had been willing to make and repeating American guarantees regarding Israeli security. In extending the flattery, he termed Begin's proposal for Palestinian self-government as bold and his willingness to acknowledge Egypt's sovereignty over Sinai as constructive. Begin reportedly told Carter that while he sought a full agreement with Egypt, he first needed an agreement with the United States.[49] He also reminded Carter of President Ford's security commitments to Israel under the 1975 Sinai II agreement, reflecting Begin's emphasis on ensuring Israeli security in the context of withdrawal from the Sinai.

The reports and summary documents show that the discussions returned to the points of disagreement that had repeatedly arisen. The leaders discussed a two-phase implementation of autonomy, in which, initially, the Israeli military governor would continue to be the source of authority, to be replaced later with a negotiated agreement. Begin again stated a readiness to leave the issue of sovereignty for Judea, Samaria, and Gaza open, but reminded the Americans of his position that Israel would never agree to foreign (non-Israeli) sovereignty.[50] From the first day through the final meeting, Begin's position on this core issue was unchanged despite Carter's increasing pressure.

Carter also prodded Begin to involve Jordan in the autonomy plan, "because Jordan itself is in many ways the natural homeland for the Palestinian, and the question of sovereignty over the West Bank territory naturally involved Jordan."[51] Predictably, Begin rejected this position. Carter also asked Begin how much freedom the Palestinians would have according to his autonomy plan, and Begin replied that the only excluded issues would be movement of refugees (into Israel) and security.

Begin requested that Carter ask Sadat for patience in the negotiations with Israel in order to deal with the complex issues of security, demilitarization, navigation rights, and settlements. More broadly, in this and other meetings, Carter warned that if the summit failed, there might be war, and other pro-Western regimes in the region would be jeopardized. He also told Begin that Sadat would never yield on his demand to dismantle all Israeli settlements in the Sinai and returning full sovereignty to Egypt. In his memoirs, Carter acknowledged that Begin understood the centrality of the contest between Egypt and Israel for American support, noting that Sadat had acted on this principle much earlier than Begin.[52]

The core conflicts were also expressed in the numerous arguments over Carter's insistence on including references to Resolution 242 regarding "the inadmissibility of acquisition of territory by war" (hereafter the "inadmissibility" paragraph). From the first meeting, Begin told Carter that the Arab interpretation would require full Israeli withdrawal, without reference to secure and recognized borders. Instead, in keeping with Begin's perception, he pressed for language that referred to "belligerent war," as distinct from self-defense. (In contrast, Sadat's draft text assigned blame to Israel for all previous wars and demanded payment for the oil Israel pumped out of wells in Sinai and a total withdrawal to the pre-1967 borders.[53]) These disagreements would be repeated many times during the thirteen days.

Later, Carter wrote that the meeting was discouraging since Begin brought "no new proposals."[54] Rosalynn Carter also reported this frustration: "I believe Begin will consider the summit a success if anything happens, even a very small thing, so that he can say we 'started something' . . . but I don't believe he has any intention of going through with a peace treaty."[55]

The numerous meetings between Carter and Begin (some of which included other members of the two delegations) highlighted the vast and fundamental differences between Carter's emphasis on personal relations and trust and Begin's fundamental mistrust of outsiders based on his understanding of the Jewish historical experience, including his own.

For example, on the third day (September 7), the top Americans (Carter, Vance, and Brzezinski) met with Begin, Dayan, and Weizman to discuss Sadat's draft and options to proceed. Begin wanted Sadat to withdraw the draft, while Carter pressed to move forward, even though he acknowledged that the terms were unacceptable.[56] In his memoirs, Carter reports pressing the Israelis on security, asking, "What do you actually want for Israel if peace is signed? I need to know whether you need to monitor the border, what military outposts are necessary to guard your security. . . . If I know the facts, then I can take them to Sadat and try to satisfy both you and him. . . . My greatest strength here is your confidence—but I don't feel that I have your trust. . . . I believe I can get from Sadat what you *really* need, but I just do not have your confidence."[57]

Begin clearly had no intention of trusting Carter with decisions that were vital to Israel's future, but he also wanted to avoid a rupture with the United States, as well as the blame that Carter would pin on the Israelis. Dayan reports that Begin confided, "I want an agreement with the US more than with Egypt."[58]

In his reports back to the Israeli delegation regarding these intensive meetings with Carter, Begin continued to express the same frustration resulting from their previous encounters. Similarly, Carter complained that Begin showed no sign of changing long-held positions—the informal atmosphere of Camp David and the pressure of the summit did not have the expected impact. (Vance reports that during the second week, Begin commented that "he felt he was trapped within the chain link fences and tall trees of Camp David. 'It is beginning to feel like a concentration camp.'"[59])

The Americans shifted their emphasis to Dayan and Weizman, much as they had in the previous months. Vance, like Carter, saw the two Israelis ministers as more flexible than Begin regarding removing civilian outposts in the Sinai and also with respect to the proposed moratorium on settlement construction in the West Bank. In meetings with Vance, Dayan reportedly urged the United States to submit its own proposal.[60] In a separate meeting, Weizman and Tamir brought maps of the Sinai to Carter to discuss potential withdrawal scenarios. Weizman asked whether the settlements in the Sinai were really an obstacle to peace, and Carter assured him they were. As the meeting ended, Carter thanked Tamir for teaching him more about the Sinai in two hours than his aides did in two years.[61]

Sadat and other members of the Egyptian team also began meeting with Weizman and Dayan, discussing and making progress on some of the issues related to a phased Israeli withdrawal from Sinai. According to Weizman, Sadat sent an important signal, saying that he had no claims of sovereignty over Gaza and that the Palestinian issue would not interest him once an agreement (over the Sinai) was reached.[62] In this version, Sadat insisted he could not allow Israeli settlements or airfields in the Sinai, but Israel would have two years to evacuate them.

Notwithstanding the separate meetings involving Dayan, Weizman, and others, Begin maintained close control over the Israeli delegation's activities, reminding everyone that under Israeli law and precedent, the delegation was limited in its authority. In the meeting held on Friday, September 8, Dayan, Weizman, and Barak reported on their meeting with Vance and Brzezinski in which they discussed the American proposal that was to be tabled on Sunday. Begin instructed them to tell the Americans that there were issues that he had to discuss with the government in Jerusalem because the delegation had no authority to decide.[63] This occurred more than once—including in their final meeting, when Begin explained to Carter that a decision to dismantle the settlements in the Sinai needed Knesset approval.

Since, in addition to the Egyptian draft, the Americans were writing their own version, on Sunday morning (September 10, day 6), Begin started discussing and dictating notes for an Israeli draft to his longtime aide, Yechiel Kadishai. Barak, Rosenne, Tamir, and Dinitz were assigned the task of editing the paper and preparing an English translation. The delegation decided to wait for the American proposal scheduled to be distributed in the afternoon and to turn the Israeli paper into a response.[64]

In the delegation meeting that morning, Weizman argued for more concessions in the Sinai if there were "good achievements" on Judea and Samaria, while Begin said that Sadat gave Israel nothing on Judea and Samaria. Weizman replied that he was referring to the Americans.[65] This exchange demonstrates the nature of the debates within the Israeli delegation and the challenges to Begin's position, which were duly noted.

Later that morning, the delegations went to Gettysburg, in an event that Carter and his team believed would foster informal communications and progress based on the approach to negotiations known as contact theory, which is popular among American officials and academics.[66] (According to White House press secretary Jody Powell, it was Begin who asked to see the battlefield. Carter fulfilled the request out of courtesy and to ease the tense negotiations. But this version is not confirmed by other documents.)[67] On the way, Begin and Sadat recalled their prison experiences.[68] Sadat asked about the American Civil War, and Begin recited Lincoln's Gettysburg speech from memory. American expectations notwithstanding, the excursion did not lead to any breakthroughs or changes in positions.

That afternoon, the Americans presented their draft to Begin and the Israelis.[69] The text contained the statement that the peace agreement would be based on UNSCR 242 and 338, including the preamble paragraph, which Begin had consistently rejected, in particular, the statement referring to the "inadmissibility of the acquisition of territory by war." In the section on Sinai, there was no explicit mention of the civilian outposts, reflecting Israel's request. The section on the Palestinian issues called for final status talks beginning after three years and the creation of an administrative authority operating under a joint mandate from Israel, Egypt, Jordan, and the Palestinians (replacing the military government). Jordan would have a special status in the West Bank, no new settlements would be established, and the existing ones would not be expanded; and the International Court of Justice in The Hague would be the sole decider regarding any dispute.[70]

Begin asked for four hours to study the plan, reportedly telling Carter, "There are positive elements in it; there are also some that could cause grave peril to our people." Begin did not reject the American document, and the debates with Carter resumed at 21:30 and went for many hours. Carter wrote that he returned to his cabin at 3:45 AM, telling his wife that "we had to do a song and dance with Begin over every word."[71]

The American draft included many of the terms that Begin had repeatedly rejected, including on the final status of the West Bank and Gaza, which "would be settled on the basis of all of the principles of U.N. Security Council Resolution 242, including the mutual obligations of peace, the necessity for security arrangements for all parties concerned . . . the withdrawal of Israeli forces, a just settlement of the refugee problem and the establishment of secure and recognized boundaries."[72]

Quandt reports that "Begin rejected this formulation precisely because it would have obligated Israel to withdraw. . . . This he would not do. The most that he would accept was that 'the negotiations,' not even 'the outcome of the negotiations,' would be based on 'all the provisions and principles of Resolution 242.'"[73]

At the end of the meeting, Carter asked Dayan to accompany him to his cabin and told him that he considered Begin unreasonable and an obstacle to progress. Dayan reportedly told Carter that Begin wanted an agreement, but issues such as the settlements in the Sinai and the language referring to UNSCR 242 were extremely difficult.[74] Carter might have expected Dayan to express disagreement with his prime minister, but Dayan apparently defended Begin's position.

According to Marcus, in a meeting of the Israeli delegation focused on the demands regarding the West Bank, Begin said, "It will not be accepted by the public."[75] In an early delegation meeting on Sadat's draft treaty, Begin observed, "Based on this Egyptian paper we will not sign any agreement. No party, not even Sheli [on the far left of the Israeli spectrum], would sign it. No one would accept the freeze of settlements. What they demand is a unilateral freeze. The Arabs would not be restricted during this time."[76] When Carter reportedly told Begin that polls in Israel indicated majority support for an agreement in the West Bank based on territorial compromise, Begin replied he was sure the public would support his position, and if the Knesset would not support him, he would resign.[77]

The Israeli reply that was drafted on Sunday had not been presented, and according to the Israeli protocol, during the morning meeting of the Israeli delegation on Tuesday (September 12), Begin reported that he had agreed to phrases that he had previously rejected, citing the insistent and "exhausting" pressure from Dayan, Weizman, and Barak. Begin referred to "the extreme Egyptian document," the draft Israeli reply, and an American proposal, most of which Israel accepted. "What is clear to me today—it is obvious that we cannot give in on the inadmissibility [of capturing territory by force] because this would be a verdict on our people's future. How could I agree to the 'in all parts' [of 242], because there is the opinion that the introduction is not an inseparable part of the Resolution."[78]

At the end of the meeting, Weizman asked whether it was time to talk with the Egyptians and the Americans regarding the 1974 Separation of Forces agreement that would expire in October 1978. Begin suggested waiting to raise it, but Weizman noted that Carter had repeatedly warned that if Camp David failed, Egypt would deploy five divisions east of the Suez Canal. Begin replied that there was a government to decide this and suggested a joint meeting of the government (cabinet) and the IDF general staff as this was a "political military issue." Weizman replied that starting on that day, Israel should deploy forces in Sinai, and Begin concluded the debate, again stating, "There is a national leadership to discuss that."[79]

Following Sadat's brinksmanship and threats to leave, the Israelis tried the same strategy. Begin reportedly drafted a concluding statement, and Carter rejected it. Dayan told Ambassador Sam Lewis that there was nothing more to do in Camp David and he was leaving the following day. Dayan made sure that would be public knowledge.[80] In another long meeting between Carter and Begin, Carter agreed to delay the issue of settlements in the Sinai to the end of the summit.

Thus, as the second weekend approached, the main actors were planning their departures, without an agreement but perhaps with a joint statement detailing areas of agreement and the differences that remained. Carter asked Sadat and Begin not to make any public statements between Sunday (the last day) and Monday, and they agreed. White House press secretary Jody Powell reports that Carter was planning to tell the entire story of the summit to the public, including "his explanation of why it had failed."[81]

However, in parallel, on Wednesday, September 13 (day 9), Carter and the legal advisors of both sides (Aharon Barak and Osama el-Baz) started to compose an agreed-on draft.[82] Barak reported back to Begin frequently, whereas the Americans pushed Begin, without significant success. The core conflicts had not changed and included the future of the Israeli settlements and air bases in the Sinai, the demand for a freeze on settlement construction in the West Bank, the status of Jerusalem, and the language referring to UNSCR 242.

Again on day 10, Carter met with Dayan and Weizman, seeking their help in pressing Begin on the issue of removing the Sinai settlements, which the Americans saw as a potential key to an agreement. Weizman had indicated that they were willing to make this concession as part of a peace agreement with Egypt.[83]

According to Carter, Begin frequently declared that if he agreed to a removal of the settlements and their residents from the Sinai, his government would fall.[84] However, as the negotiations focused on this issue in the final days of the summit, Begin started to make less strident statements, including the potential of leaving this issue to the Knesset to decide.

On this point, Begin spoke on the telephone to Ariel Sharon, who held the position of agriculture minister and chair of the Ministerial Committee on Settlements but whose real political influence was based on his record as a war hero. Uri Dan, who was with Sharon in Israel, reports a call on Friday, September 15 (late on Thursday night at Camp David, as reported by Weizman), in which Begin implied that he had reached the decision point and needed Sharon's help as the Sinai settlements stood between Israel and a peace treaty. The impetus for the call and gaining Sharon's support reportedly came from Weizman and Tamir, both of whom had worked with Sharon in the military, although the relations were not always cordial.[85]

Politically, Begin was vulnerable on the settlements issue, and he found himself in the situation that his Herut critics warned against. In the political arena, Sharon was a key figure who could also bring the coalition to a breaking point.

Thus, if Sharon objected to the removal of the Sinai settlements, Begin could be forced out of office. But by informing Sharon in advance and seeking his advice and support for this concession, Begin secured a powerful ally for the political struggles ahead. Weizman and Tamir arranged the phone call after confirming that Sharon would back the prime minister. Although it could be interpreted at face value that they manipulated Begin, it seems more accurate—based on the primary sources—that Begin already understood that he would need to concede the settlements, and Sharon's call assured him that he could secure sufficient political support.

On Friday (September 15) Sadat told Vance he was leaving since there was no chance for an agreement.[86] Once again, Carter reportedly dissuaded Sadat.[87] Simultaneously, Begin agreed to cancel plans to leave on Friday, September 15, to attend a concert of the Israeli Philharmonic Orchestra in the Kennedy Center on Saturday night.

According to Carter, Weizman and Sadat continued to meet and at this stage, agreed on terms of the demilitarization of the Sinai, with a small symbolic parallel zone on the Israeli side of the border.[88] Carter reports that at that point he had three views of Israel's position: Begin was not willing to commit to withdrawing fully from the Sinai, Dayan agreed to do so after an extended period (twenty-five years), and Weizman was in favor of presenting the issue to the Knesset.[89]

On Saturday morning, Sharon spoke to Begin again and expressed his support for a decision to remove the settlements in the Sinai as part of a peace agreement while stating the continued opposition to any change regarding settlement construction in Judea and Samaria.[90] This was a major change and cemented Begin's agreement later in the final meeting with Carter.

In his diary, Carter reports that he told Sadat and el-Baz on Saturday afternoon, September 16, that Begin, for the first time, had agreed that UNSCR 242 was applicable in all its parts to all the territories, including the West Bank and Gaza, but would not accept language in the preamble referring to the "inadmissibility" of acquiring territory by force. According to Carter, Begin agreed to end Israel's military occupation, accepted the principle of withdrawal on the West Bank and the Sinai, recognized the international border, and accepted removal of all armed forces, allowing Egypt to exercise full sovereignty over Sinai.

On the issue of the West Bank, according to Carter's diary, Begin reportedly accepted "full autonomy" up to the 1967 lines for five years, and during that time a permanent resolution of issues would be achieved.[91] However, Carter does not indicate the basis for his conclusion that Begin was willing to accept this (before meeting with Begin on that same night but after the meeting with Sadat). In his memoirs, these terms are not mentioned.[92] Carter does report that he had a meeting with Dayan on Saturday morning, from which he might have concluded that these concessions were in reach.[93] Quandt reports a Saturday morning meeting of

Dayan, Barak, and Vance, which could have also supported Carter's conclusion.[94] Carter's diary entry on the meeting with Begin, Dayan, and Barak includes the claim that on "the framework for peace in the West Bank/Gaza, there was a surprisingly amicable discussion," but there is no indication of Begin's concessions that Carter mentioned in his discussion with Sadat.[95]

Still unresolved were Egyptian demands for a statement on Jerusalem, the fate of Israel's civilian settlements in the Sinai, and Carter's demand for a freeze on West Bank settlement construction. In his diary, Carter wrote, "There would be no new settlements in the West Bank/Gaza Strip," although, again, the basis for this statement is unclear and might be a statement of objectives rather than one based on any Israeli concession.[96]

Carter asked to speak with Begin on Saturday night to conclude unfinished business in a small meeting in which Vance would accompany him. Begin replied that he would bring Dayan and Barak.[97] (In his memoirs, Carter referred positively to Begin's decision to include "the two best ones he could have brought."[98])

Before that final meeting, and after the phone call with Sharon, Begin reportedly told the Israeli delegation that he would tell Carter that the issue of dismantling the settlements in the Sinai could be brought before the Knesset, but that was as far as he would go.[99] This was, however, a major concession that indicated, for the first time, Begin's reluctant agreement to accept a full withdrawal from Sinai.

The Final Carter-Begin Meeting

The meeting on Saturday night began at 8:00 p.m. and ended at 12:20 a.m.—almost four and a half hours.[100] Begin agreed to put the future of the Sinai settlements to a vote in the Knesset, recognizing that it would ratify the agreement to remove them. Begin also made concessions regarding the language on West Bank autonomy, including acceptance of the terms "Palestinian people" and "legitimate rights." Begin rejected Carter's demands regarding Jerusalem, but they agreed to exchange formal letters detailing the differences as part of the framework document. Begin also agreed to freeze settlement construction on the West Bank for the duration of the negotiations to complete the treaty. In Carter's version, the agreed freeze was for the duration of the autonomy talks—a much longer timeframe than Begin's understanding. This difference was to become the basis of a major dispute between Carter and the Israelis.[101] All of the reports on this meeting point to a very difficult session. According to Marcus, Carter warned that if the meeting and summit were to end without agreement, he would publicly accuse Israel of not wanting peace or appreciating American support. He also warned Begin that he would not support Israel in the future since he would not view it as a peace-loving nation, and he threatened to stop the annual financial support.[102]

In Carter's brief diary version, it was Begin who shouted during the meeting, using terms like "ultimatum," "excessive demands," and "political suicide." Carter claims that he proposed to transfer the decision over settlement removal to the Knesset: "I said if the Sinai agreement was approved with the exception of the settlers, it would be a great step forward, and they [Begin, Dayan and Barak] agreed," he wrote. The Knesset would vote within two weeks on this question: "If agreement is reached on all other Sinai issues, will the settlers be withdrawn?"[103] Carter wrote, "[I]f the Knesset acts favorably, Camp David will have been a complete success."[104] Regarding the West Bank, Carter claimed to have been surprised by the amicable discussion and full agreement on the language from UNSCR 242.

More likely, the proposal could well have been made by Begin, given his emphasis on the Israeli constitutional process and his use of similar tactics in the past. The only Israeli documentation is provided by Barak's minutes, released in 2010 by the Israel State Archives.[105] The handwritten notes and the typed telegram that Barak sent from Jerusalem (after the summit, when Barak was back in Jerusalem, while Begin remained in the United States) show that once Begin agreed to put the future of the Sinai settlements to a free vote in the Knesset (i.e., without coalition discipline), the Sinai issues were essentially agreed, and Carter promised to gain Sadat's approval.

The discussion then shifted to the West Bank settlements, on which Begin repeatedly rejected Carter's pressure for a long freeze on construction. This had been anticipated—in the Israeli delegation's meeting on September 8, there was a long discussion on the American demand for a five-year freeze.[106]

Barak's notes from the meeting reveal that Begin told Carter that "no Israeli prime minister could take upon himself a freeze. . . . During the three months of negotiations for peace, three new settlements were to be established—one in the Golan, one in southern Israel and one in the Jordan Valley, all 'army security settlements.'" Carter asked, "What do I tell Sadat? No freeze?" Begin replied, "What does Sadat have to do with freeze in Judea and Samaria?" Carter answered that if Israel decided that Judea and Samaria were part of Israel, Sadat would have no say and "Camp David was unnecessary" (or moot). Carter then suggested different wording: "After the signing of the framework and during the negotiations, no new Israeli settlements will be established in the area, unless otherwise agreed. The issue of further Israeli settlements will be decided and agreed by the negotiating parties." Carter insisted on having this in a letter from Begin that would be publicized. Begin replied, "I will think and let you know tomorrow." According to Barak's minutes, Begin repeated this twice and did not accept Carter's suggestion, despite the US president's later claim.[107]

Beyond Barak's minutes, the Israeli sources provide little additional information. Dayan briefly mentioned the meeting in his memoirs, confirming

Barak's account on what Begin had promised Carter. The accounts of the American participants regarding the West Bank settlements differ among themselves and with Barak's minutes. Carter wrote, "On West Bank settlements, we finally worked out that no new Israeli settlements would be established after the signing of this framework. The issue of additional settlements would be resolved by the parties during negotiations."[108]

The following morning (September 17), Barak brought Carter Begin's letter stipulating a freeze for three months. According to Carter, the letter was "unsatisfactory and contrary to what we had earlier agreed." He then cited what he claimed was agreed in the meeting, and "Barak confirmed that my language was accurate."[109] In his book *The Blood of Abraham*, Carter alleges that in 1983, he spoke to Begin in Jerusalem and "explained again why we believed he had not honored a commitment made during the peace negotiations to refrain from building new Israeli settlements in the West Bank."[110]

On the other hand, in a conference at the Carter Center marking twenty-five years after the Camp David summit, Barak—then chief justice of the Israeli Supreme Court—said that he was the only one who took notes in the decisive meeting and that in his notes, he wrote "three months." He added that he called Carter to tell him that it was three months, as Begin had claimed. At that point, in response to Barak's remarks (in 2003), Carter commented, "I don't dispute that."[111]

Vance's memoirs are consistent with Carter's, claiming that Begin agreed to a five-year moratorium. However, in April 1979 (one month after the peace treaty was signed), Vance testified in a congressional hearing, "There was for a period of time a freeze. They [the Israelis] are no longer abiding by that freeze."[112] Vance's statement from 1979 thus contradicts his 1983 memoirs.[113]

Similarly, in a 2007 essay, Quandt acknowledges that "the wording of the final agreement left all parties able to read into the text their preferred positions. It did not resolve the issue, and Carter is incorrect to imply that Begin made any commitment to withdraw from the West Bank." Furthermore,

> Carter overstates the solidity of the diplomatic record regarding the status of the 1967 lines as the eventual border between Israel and Palestine. . . . He is not correct in stating that Begin accepted the obligation to withdraw to the 1967 lines as part of eventual negotiations over final status issues. We tried at Camp David to get such a commitment from him, but Begin was adamant in refusing. He would not sign anything that implied that Israel would eventually withdraw from territory that he thought of as intrinsic to Eretz Israel.[114]

Regardless of the actual agreement and the different versions, this meeting ended the summit successfully, and the leaders committed themselves to completing the negotiations on a peace treaty. At the same time, the sharp conflict that marked this final session indicated that the dispute between Carter and Begin would continue and intensify.

The Final Day

On Sunday morning, September 17, when Barak delivered Begin's signed letters, Carter immediately rejected the text on the West Bank settlement freeze. Another conflict arose over the US letter on Jerusalem, addressed to Sadat, which restated American policy that east Jerusalem was occupied territory.[115] The draft letter remains classified, but the different sources agree on its content. Dayan wrote that Mondale showed the draft to Dinitz, and "in it Carter stated that the United States considered East Jerusalem to be conquered territory."[116] Dinitz had a similar recollection.[117] Begin immediately rejected this letter, and Dinitz reports telling Mondale that in the event that the Jerusalem issue led to a failure at Camp David, American Jews would support Israel's position.[118]

Dayan immediately confronted Carter and Vance on this issue in the billiards room. According to the Israeli minutes, Carter claimed that the letter represented the long-standing US position, but Dayan replied that the timing was ill-advised and warned that Begin would leave without signing anything. Dayan told Carter that the Israeli delegates would not have come to Camp David had they known that the United States was planning to express its policy on Jerusalem. Carter said several times in the argument that he could not take back his word to Sadat to state his policy on Jerusalem. Dayan emphasized that it was the first instance when Israel had to deal with an independent American policy that concerned the most sensitive issue.[119] (In a public event in Jerusalem one year later, Dinitz said that Dayan asked a senior US official, "If Jerusalem is not Israel's capital, what is?" The official replied, "I don't know." The protocol does not show this exchange, and Shlomo Nakdimon, Begin's spokesman, told the *Jerusalem Post* that "Dinitz's revelations were 'news' to the Prime Minister's Office."[120])

The American officials then drafted a new letter simply noting that their position was well known, as stated by Ambassador Arthur Goldberg in the UN General Assembly on July 14, 1967, and by Ambassador Charles Yost in the Security Council on July 1, 1969.[121] For the Israelis, this generalized and laconic version removed the sting of the earlier one. Begin then approved the text, and Sadat followed.[122]

In his published diary, Carter attributed Begin's last-minute concessions on Sunday to the emotional reaction created by the photos Carter handed him with dedications to Begin's grandchildren.[123] There is no evidence supporting Carter's analysis, which, as in the past, was based on his interpretation of Begin's personal psychology.

At this stage, Carter reportedly told his wife, "I think we've gotten everything we wanted. I'm going to try to get Begin and Sadat together today. They haven't seen each other since we went to Gettysburg."[124] But when he sent Mondale to obtain Sadat's final approval on the language of the accords, Begin was already there with Barak.[125] Ultimately, the agreement depended on Begin and Sadat—Carter and the United States were third parties in the process.

From Camp David, the leaders flew to the White House for the brief public signing ceremony and triumphant conclusion of the summit. Carter insisted on having the event that night, and it was held at 10:30 p.m. EST, which was before dawn in the Middle East—a point noted by the Israelis. In insisting on an immediate signing, Carter also made sure that neither Begin nor Sadat would reverse course or talk to the media and create an incident.

In his diary entry for September 18, Carter (angered by the settlement dispute) wrote, "Begin was making an ass of himself with his public statements," while Sadat was depicted as responsible and moderate.[126] In the memoirs, Carter wrote that he had been advised of Begin's "negative statements to Jewish audiences concerning the arrangements for Jerusalem, withdrawal from the West Bank, new settlements in the occupied territories, Palestinian refugees, and future relationships with Israel's other neighbors."[127] There are no direct sources for such statements to Jewish audiences, but Begin did speak to Israeli journalists and on American news programs.[128] He told the *Haaretz* correspondent in Washington, Yoel Marcus, that Israel would not withdraw from the West Bank and the Gaza Strip after the five-year interim term, that Jerusalem would not be divided, and that the moratorium on settlements was limited to the three months of the final negotiations with Egypt. Begin made similar declarations in a telephone conversation with Tel Aviv mayor Shlomo Lahat (an important Likud official and ally), who repeated it publicly at a Tel Aviv mass rally in support of the agreement on September 18.[129]

In addition, the *Washington Post* reported, "Begin, who spent the day at his hotel before joining Carter and Sadat at the Capitol, told broadcast interviewers that Israel will refuse under any circumstances to change its position that Jerusalem is its 'eternal capital' and that the Egyptian differences with this view are 'their problem.'"[130] Begin also declared, in an interview with ABC's Barbara Walters, that both Egypt and the United States agreed to an Israeli military presence in the West Bank following the planned five-year "'transitional period' there," but added, "No such provision appears in the published text of the accords."[131]

Evaluating Begin at Camp David

Analyses and assessments of Begin's negotiation strategy and tactics at Camp David vary widely. Some participants and observers argue that Begin controlled the events and the outcome, maneuvering the process to the best results possible from his and Israel's perspectives and interests. Others are critical and assert that he eventually folded under Carter's constant demands and threats, as well as pressure from Dayan and Weizman, agreeing to the full withdrawal from the Sinai, including the civilian outposts, and even accepting language on the West Bank that served as a precedent for greater pressure on Israel.

Quandt is among the most vocal supporters of the first thesis, concluding, "Sadat, like Carter, was eventually worn down by Begin's adamant refusal to dilute

Israel's claim to the West Bank."[132] He also observed, "By the end, the process came to resemble an endurance contest in which the party that could least afford failure was brought under the greatest pressure to make concessions. This turned out to be Sadat." In another section, Quandt wrote, "Begin's steamroller tactics, coupled with his willingness to leave Camp David without any agreement, if necessary, proved to be more successful than Sadat's flamboyant concept of confrontation."[133]

In the words of Ambassador Samuel Lewis, Begin proved to be "a real word-smith and a very good negotiator—annoying, but extraordinarily effective. He was the best negotiator at Camp David, without question. He got much more of what he was seeking than anyone else, in my view."[134]

In contrast, a number of Israelis from Begin's Herut faction and Likud party were highly critical, arguing that he had capitulated to Carter's pressure, combined with the readiness of Weizman and Dayan to make concessions to please the Americans and Sadat. The Movement for Greater Israel declared that it was shocked by Begin's and the delegation's surrender to President Sadat's demands: "Under Carter's massive pressure, Menachem Begin reversed/abandoned the achievements of the Six Day War."[135] Israeli academic Yaacov Bar-Siman-Tov claims that until the final days, Begin believed that Carter was "an honest broker" and only at the end realized that he was cooperating with Sadat.[136] However, the evidence is inconsistent with this analysis.

As noted, the general perception of the Israeli leadership before the summit was that Camp David might create a broad framework for detailed negotiations and that American pressure for Israeli concessions would be intense. They were correct regarding the pressure, but the outcome was more substantive than had been expected, in part due to this pressure.

The evidence refutes the thesis that Begin was isolated and frozen into passivity while Dayan, Weizman, Barak, and others cooperated or conspired with Carter in manipulating the outcome. The protocols and other documents show that Begin was at the center of every stage of the negotiations, including giving instructions and receiving detailed summaries related to each meeting involving Israeli officials. He made the most difficult decisions, both in terms of concessions on the Sinai and with respect to refusing Carter's demands on the West Bank and Jerusalem. Indeed, Begin's actions after Camp David do not support the image of an Israeli prime minister "under siege." There is also no reliable source for the claim that Begin regretted the results of Camp David, given the alternatives and their consequences.[137]

Dayan stated that Begin had dealt with every detail of the negotiations, adding that "were it not for him, we would not have arrived at this agreement." Dayan explicitly said that Begin's authority as prime minister and his personal leadership were essential at Camp David, allowing the Israeli delegation to make the crucial decisions.[138]

As noted, Quandt saw Begin as the winner, adding that Sadat expected much more than he got at Camp David.[139] But Quandt's assessment is problematic. Sadat's apparent primary objective was to recover all of the Sinai, without any Israeli presence, and he achieved this. He also maintained the support of the United States throughout the talks. On the Palestinian issue, Sadat was much less enthusiastic than Carter or other members of the Egyptian delegation and appeared to be interested in Israeli concessions on the West Bank primarily for political cover. When Begin refused to go further than autonomy, Sadat accepted this, perhaps hoping for more movement in the next phase of negotiations.

For Begin, the agreement to withdraw from the Sinai settlements was clearly painful on both the personal and political levels, and there is no basis for assuming that he had anticipated making this concession before the summit. Rather, it would be consistent with Begin's record to conclude that despite Sadat's emphasis on receiving all of the Sinai from the beginning, Begin thought the thin strip with the settlements could be pried loose. This was not the case, but at the same time, he had held firm on Judea, Samaria, and Gaza. As Begin saw it, the United States and Egypt had accepted the Israeli military presence for years to come, and in any final status negotiations, Israel would maintain a veto.

Israeli internal political realities created their own limitations on Begin's options or perhaps reinforced his own preferences and red lines. For much of his core Herut constituency, the agreement to withdraw from all of the Sinai—particularly the settlements—was entirely anathema, and he was denounced as a traitor. The opposition Labor Alignment, led by Shimon Peres, who continued to seek Begin's downfall, also objected to the removal of the Sinai settlements. In this sense, the constraints on Begin were significant, and the Israeli leader went as far as he could to obtain a peace agreement.

Conclusions

Although Carter was disappointed and angry, he had received a rare foreign policy success at a crucial time in his administration and emerged, at least in the American media (backed by Begin's expressions of gratitude during the signing ceremony and later), as the hero who performed miracles to reach a successful conclusion. But on the substance, Carter was forced to settle for much less than he expected, which was a regional peace agreement anchored in a Palestinian homeland, as envisioned in the Brookings Plan.

However, this grandiose goal continued to be beyond any realistic option, and its pursuit would jeopardize the bilateral objectives that both Begin and Sadat sought. One year earlier, Carter's idea of a comprehensive Geneva peace conference had driven Sadat and Begin to exclude Washington, and Carter could not afford a repetition. Nevertheless, it is doubtful that Israel and Egypt could realistically have reached an agreement without the American sponsorship, which gave Israel security guarantees for the risks it was taking by returning the Sinai buffer zone, as well as financial aid to complete the withdrawal.

Under these circumstances, Carter's third-party role was necessarily limited yet essential and centered on cementing the bilateral agreement. Since both Begin and Sadat were satisfied with the summit's results, Carter had very little leverage to push for a wider agreement. However, after the summit and until the final stage of the negotiations, he maintained and even increased the pressure on Begin.

Begin's conduct throughout the negotiations turned out to be effective as he reached a framework for peace that would change the strategic position of Israel in the Middle East. But it also left Carter bitter and angry, which added up to more animosity and increased suspicion toward the following phase of peace negotiations. In addition, the very narrow autonomy parameters did not give Sadat much to present to the Arab world.

Finally, while Jimmy Carter failed to form the agreement he pursued and was forced to accept the deal that Begin and Sadat were willing to sign, he could present a major foreign policy success. Sadat and Begin, in contrast, returned to face their respective critics. For Begin, there was a long battle ahead, partly with the formal opposition—the Labor Alignment—but, more concerning, with his own constituency.

Notes

1. Lewis, "The Camp David Peace Process," in Fuksman-Sha'al, *Camp David Accords*, 56.
2. Quandt, *Camp David*, 208.
3. Lewis, "Camp David Peace Process," 54.
4. Rubinstein, "Thirty Years since the Camp David Accords," in Fuksman-Sha'al, *Camp David Accords*, 21.
5. Gur, *Chief of the General Staff*, 293–391.
6. Quandt, *Camp David*, 206–7. See also Herring, *From Colony to Superpower*, 829–60.
7. Vance, *Hard Choices*, 217; Jimmy Carter, *White House Diary*, 210.
8. Jimmy Carter, *Keeping Faith*, 322.
9. Rosalynn Carter, *First Lady from Plains*, 259.
10. Jimmy Carter, *Keeping Faith*, 321.
11. *FRUS 1977–1980*, vol. 9, document 21.
12. Jimmy Carter, *Keeping Faith*, 325–27.
13. Quandt, *Camp David*, 208.
14. Quandt, 208, 221.
15. Vance, *Hard Choices*, 218–19.
16. Jimmy Carter, *White House Diary*, 213.
17. Quandt, *Camp David*, 206.
18. Quandt, 218, citing Jimmy Carter, *Keeping Faith*, 322.
19. Post, *Leaders and Their Followers in a Dangerous World*, "Appendix: The Role of Political Personality Profiles at the Camp David Summit," 265–71. The original article is Post, "Personality Profiles in Support of the Camp David Summit."

20. Rosalynn Carter, *First Lady from Plains*, 243.

21. Jimmy Carter, *White House Diary*, 213.

22. Jimmy Carter, *White House Diary*, 213; Vance, *Hard Choices*, 217. White House spokesperson Jody Powell reports announcing the summit while Vance was still in the Middle East to forestall leaks from Jerusalem and Cairo, creating a situation that would have been uncomfortable for the other side (Powell, *Other Side of the Story*, 59). Vance suggested that Powell be appointed as the sole spokesperson for the summit to prevent separate and contrasting briefings (Powell, 64).

23. Bar-Siman-Tov, *Israel and the Peace Process*, 108.

24. Bar-Siman-Tov, 108–9.

25. "The Sealed-Lips Summit," *Time*, September 18, 1978.

26. A stenographic protocol of a meeting with head of the opposition, MK Peres, and chairman of the Foreign Affairs and Defense Committee, MK Arens, Jerusalem, August 31, 1978 (ISA, A 4351/9).

27. There is no such similar statement directly attributed to Begin in any other source. We cannot exclude the possibility that there was a misunderstanding or error in the protocol. However, our analysis of this statement is not entirely speculative. As discussed in chapter 5, Quandt understood that this was an option after meeting with Dayan.

28. A stenographic protocol of a meeting with head of the opposition, MK Peres, and chairman of the Foreign Affairs and Defense Committee, MK Arens, Jerusalem, August 31, 1978 (ISA, A 4351/9).

29. A stenographic protocol of a meeting with head of the opposition, MK Peres, and chairman of the Foreign Affairs and Defense Committee, MK Arens, Jerusalem, August 31, 1978 (ISA, A 4351/9).

30. A stenographic protocol of a meeting with head of the opposition, MK Peres, and chairman of the Foreign Affairs and Defense Committee, MK Arens, Jerusalem, August 31, 1978 (ISA, A 4351/9).

31. Marcus, *Camp David*, 12.

32. In May 2018, a revised edition of *FRUS 1977–1980*, vol. 9, was released (Wieland, ed., FRUS 1977-1980, vol. 9, second, revised edition). The editor added several handwritten documents by Ambassador Sam Lewis that were recently discovered. As the editor notes, they do not add much new information. Our analysis ended before these additional documents were found. All references to this volume of FRUS are to the original one from 2014.

33. ISA, A 4314/1.

34. Jimmy Carter, *Keeping Faith*, 328–29.

35. Marcus, *Camp David*, 17. The Shanghai Protocol is referenced by Jimmy Carter (*Keeping Faith*, 363) at a much later stage in the negotiations.

36. See the plan in *ISA*, A 4314/2.

37. Indeed, Carter told Begin that Sadat was introducing a proposal that Begin could not accept, as Begin reported to the Israeli delegation in their consultation at 18:00 on September 6 (transcript of the meeting sent by Elyakim Rubinstein to Yechiel Kadishai and Chaim Israeli, January 10, 1979, ISA, A 4314/1).

38. "Framework for the Comprehensive Peace Settlement of the Middle East Problem" (Egyptian proposal), September 5, 1978, 15:00. ISA, A 4314/2.

39. Jimmy Carter, *Keeping Faith*, 340–341.

40. Marcus, *Camp David*, 99; Jimmy Carter, *Keeping Faith*, 342.

41. Brzezinski, *Power and Principle*, 257.

42. Rosalynn Carter, *First Lady from Plains*, 250.

43. Quandt, "Camp David and Peacemaking in the Middle East," 366.

44. Rosalynn Carter, *First Lady from Plains*, 245.

45. Quandt, *Camp David*, 224.

46. Brzezinski, *Power and Principle*, 256.

47. Jimmy Carter, *Keeping Faith*, 351–52.

48. Rosalynn Carter, *First Lady from Plains*, 246

49. Jimmy Carter, *Keeping Faith*, 333–34.

50. Marcus, *Camp David*, 16.

51. Jimmy Carter, *Keeping Faith*, 337.

52. Jimmy Carter, *White House Diary*, 218; Jimmy Carter, *Keeping Faith*, 333–34, and on p. 366 he mentions that Sadat sought agreement with the United States more so than agreement with Israel.

53. "Framework for the Comprehensive Peace Settlement of the Middle East Problem" (Egyptian proposal), September 5, 1978, 15:00. ISA, A 4314/2.

54. Jimmy Carter, *Keeping Faith*, 337.

55. Rosalynn Carter, *First Lady from Plains*, 244.

56. Marcus, *Camp David*, 108.

57. Jimmy Carter, *Keeping Faith*, 348–49.

58. Consultation at Prime Minister's residence, September 8, 1978, 11:45, ISA, A 4314/1.

59. Vance, *Hard Choices*, 223.

60. Quandt, *Camp David*, 223–24.

61. Marcus, *Camp David*, 121–22.

62. Marcus, 125–26.

63. See transcript of consultation of September 8, 1978 (11:45 a.m.). Rubinstein to Kadishai and Israeli, January 4, 1979, ISA, A 4314/1.

64. Marcus, *Camp David*, 130–131.

65. "Consultation, 10.9.1978, 08:30," ISA, A 4314/1.

66. See, for example, Steinberg, "The Limits of Peacebuilding Theory"; Pettigrew, "Toward Sustainable Psychological Interventions for Change, Peace and Conflict."

67. Powell, *Other Side of the Story*, 76.

68. Rosalynn Carter, *First Lady from Plains*, 253.

69. Jimmy Carter, *Keeping Faith*, 373.

70. Marcus, *Camp David*, 133–37.

71. Carter, *Keeping Faith*, 373–76.

72. ISA, A 4176/7.

73. Quandt, "Review Essay: Palestine, Apartheid, and Jimmy Carter," 92–93.

74. Marcus, *Camp David*, 138.

75. Marcus, 114–15.

76. Marcus, 117–18; see transcript of the meeting of the Israeli delegation on September 8 (11:45 a.m.), ISA, A 4314/1.

77. Marcus, *Camp David*, 155.

78. Rubinstein to Kadishai, "Consultation on September 12, 1978, in the morning—Camp David," December 26, 1979, 3, ISA, A 4314/1.

79. Rubinstein to Kadishai and Israeli, December 26, 1979, ISA, A 4314/1.

80. Marcus, *Camp David*, 150–52.

81. Powell, *Other Side of the Story*, 85–86.

82. Marcus, *Camp David*, 156; Jimmy Carter, *Keeping Faith*, 387.

83. Marcus, *Camp David*, 161–65.

84. Jimmy Carter, *Keeping Faith*, 357–59.

85. Marcus, *Camp David*, 166, and Dan, *Operation Bulrush*, 252, for the details of the conversation. Weizman, *Battle for Peace*, 370; Tamir, *Soldier in Search of Peace*, 41.

86. Vance, *Hard Choices*, 224.

87. Rosalynn Carter, *First Lady from Plains*, 263.

88. Marcus, *Camp David*, 167–69.

89. Jimmy Carter, *Keeping Faith*, 395.

90. Dan, *Operation Bulrush*, 252–53. Begin and Dayan reported Sharon's phone call to Weizman during their 1:00 a.m. report on the Saturday night meeting with Carter and Vance (ISA, MFA 6913/7).

91. Jimmy Carter, *White House Diary*, 239.

92. Jimmy Carter, *Keeping Faith*, 395.

93. Jimmy Carter, *White House Diary*, 238–39.

94. Quandt, *Camp David*, 243–45.

95. Jimmy Carter, *White House Diary*, 240.

96. Jimmy Carter, *White House Diary*, 239–40.

97. Rosalynn Carter, *First Lady from Plains*, 265; Jimmy Carter, *Keeping Faith*, 395; Jimmy Carter, *White House Diary*, 240; Quandt, *Camp David*, 245.

98. Jimmy Carter, *Keeping Faith*, 396; *White House Diary*, 240.

99. Marcus, *Camp David*, 173.

100. Presidential daily schedule of September 16, 1978. Available online at https://www .jimmycarterlibrary.gov/assets/documents/diary/1978/d091678t.pdf (accessed on August 25, 2018). Vance wrote in his memoirs that the meeting took almost six hours (Vance, *Hard Choices*, 224–25).

101. Prior to this book, the only attempt to clarify these differences was undertaken by William Quandt, *Camp David*, 247–51.

102. Marcus, *Camp David*, 173–74.

103. Jimmy Carter, *Keeping Faith*, 396.

104. Jimmy Carter, *White House Diary*, 240–41.

105. Barak's original handwritten (which were typed in 2014) and telegraphed minutes of the meeting are in the ISA, A 4314/1. Dayan wrote about the meeting and confirmed Begin's version of what he had agreed to with Carter (i.e., to think about Carter's freeze proposal) and mentioning Barak's minutes (see Dayan, *Breakthrough*, 181–86). In Dayan's account, the dispute over Carter's proposal and Begin's reply is summarized in pp. 186–188.

106. See transcript of the meeting as sent by Rubinstein to Kadishai and Israeli on January 4, 1979 (ISA, A 4314/1).

107. Protocol of meeting between Carter & Vance and Begin, Dayan and Barak. 16.9.1978. *ISA*, A 4314/1.

108. Jimmy Carter, *White House Diary*, 240.

109. Jimmy Carter, *Keeping Faith*, 400.

110. Jimmy Carter, *Blood of Abraham*, 51.

111. *Camp David 25th Anniversary Forum*, 34–35.

112. Foreign Assistance and Related Programs Appropriations for Fiscal Year 1980 (FY80, Part 1 [Abstract number S181-34]), Subcommittee of the Committee on Appropriations, US

Senate, meeting of April 26, 1979, Statement of Hon. Cyrus R. Vance, Secretary of State, 1321, *Congressional Information Service* (CIS) (accessed March 8, 2010).

113. Vance, *Hard Choices*, 225.

114. Quandt, "Review Essay: Palestine, Apartheid, and Jimmy Carter," 92–93.

115. Vance, *Hard Choices*, 225; Marcus, *Camp David*, 178.

116. Dayan, *Breakthrough*, 177–78.

117. "Dinitz Tells Why Camp David Accords Mum on Jerusalem," *Jerusalem Post*, September 19, 1979, 3.

118. Dinitz conversation with Mondale, 17.9.1978. The reference to the Jews around the world is on page 2. The memo is part of Rubinstein's pack to Kadishai and Israeli, December 4, 1978 (ISA, A 4314/1).

119. Minutes of this meeting (recorded by Dinitz) in Rubinstein to Kadishai and Israeli, 4.12.1978 (ISA, A 4314/1).

120. Marcus, *Camp David*, 178; "Dinitz Tells Why Camp David Accords Mum on Jerusalem."

121. Marcus, *Camp David*, 178–79. See the similarities and differences between the two statements, as discussed in Slonim, *Jerusalem in America's Foreign Policy, 1947–1997*, 191–234.

122. Vance, *Hard Choices*, 225–26; Marcus, *Camp David*, 178–79. The letter appears in ISA, A 4314/2.

123. Jimmy Carter, *White House Diary*, 242.

124. Rosalynn Carter, *First Lady from Plains*, 265–66.

125. Jimmy Carter, *White House Diary*, 242–43.

126. Jimmy Carter, 245.

127. Jimmy Carter, *Keeping Faith*, 405.

128. In a speech that Begin delivered on September 20 before the Conference of Presidents of Major American Jewish Organizations (Begin, "Behind Camp David," *Camp David Process: Lectures*, 61–67). It includes similar and sometimes the exact same statements, but it is definitely not the statement that Carter refers to in *Keeping Faith* or in *White House Diary*.

129. Yoel Marcus, "Begin: Jerusalem will not be divided; Settlements will be frozen for only 3 months," *Haaretz*, September 19, 1978, 7 [Hebrew]; Ilan Shechori, "In a Telephone Conversation to a Rally in Tel Aviv: Begin: IDF Will Stay in Judea and Samaria and the Strip," *Haaretz*, September 19, 1978, 1 [Hebrew].

130. Edward Walsh and Don Oberdorfer, "Vance to Seek Saudi; Jordan Support," *Washington Post*, September 19, 1978, A1.

131. Walsh and Oberdorfer, "Vance to Seek Saudi; Jordan Support."

132. Quandt, *Camp David*, 211.

133. Quandt, 219.

134. Lewis, *Camp David Revisited*, 9.

135. "Greater Israel: Hero of War against the Mandate Renews White Paper Decrees," *Maariv*, September 19, 1978, 6.

136. Bar-Siman-Tov, *Israel and the Peace Process*, 120.

137. Rubinstein in Fuksman-Sha'al, *Camp David Accords*, 21.

138. *IMFA*, document 196.

139. Quandt, *Camp David*, 208.

6 The Domestic Political Struggle over the Camp David Accords

September 1978

THE AGREEMENTS AND widely publicized signing ceremony marked a fundamental transformation in the negotiations and the most positive step since Anwar Sadat's visit to Jerusalem ten months earlier. The potential for a peace treaty between Israel and Egypt had suddenly become realistic again, although by no means guaranteed. In the United States, while the success of Camp David boosted Jimmy Carter's domestic political capital, this was very short-lived, and his foreign policy success would soon be overtaken by events in Iran. Sadat left Camp David isolated and under attack in much of the Arab world.

In Israel, Begin was assailed by his core ideological and political supporters. Approval by the Knesset appeared likely but was not assured, and Begin faced extensive opposition within his own party and from noisy civil society groups such as the pro-settlement *Gush Emunim* (Bloc of the Faithful). In addition, the always problematic relationship between Begin and Carter was frayed even further, highlighting the difficulties that the United States would have in gaining more concessions from Israel.

Selling "Settlements for Peace"

In assessing the Israeli debate, it is important to understand that this would be the first time in Israeli and Zionist history that Jewish settlements were to be removed on the basis of a political agreement. The ethos of defiantly building settlements and clinging to them against all odds was central to the Zionist ideology, and the first removal on the basis of following negotiations would be painful, albeit in return for the first peace agreement in Israel's history. The need to choose between settlements and peace had never been posed so realistically before.

To make the case regarding the need to dismantle the Sinai settlements, it was necessary for Israel's most persuasive leaders—and Begin in particular—to play a central role. He needed the support of national figures and military heroes, particularly Ministers Ezer Weizman and Moshe Dayan—and, perhaps most importantly, Ariel Sharon. On the other side, the Labor Party, led by Shimon

Peres, and other opposition groups, although publicly committed to peace, would attack Begin for paying too high a price in agreeing to remove settlements.

The debate in Israel began immediately after the Sunday night signing ceremony in the White House but without Begin, who remained in the United States for meetings. Dayan and Weizman returned to Israel on September 19 and had the task of explaining the sudden and surprising outcome to the government, journalists, and other members of the Israeli foreign policy establishment, as well as to the public. The two held a joint press conference upon landing. Dayan emphasized that for the first time, Israel was dealing not with a theoretical peace but rather had the opportunity to conclude a detailed peace agreement.

He admitted that there were "very difficult times" with Carter during the summit and attributed them to the US president's desire to reach a comprehensive agreement that would include the Palestinians. Weizman reiterated Dayan's presentation, emphasizing that the benefit for Israel was a "true peace" including "diplomatic relations, freedom of navigation, the Suez Canal, open roads, trade relations, normal relations between two countries." Egypt, Weizman continued, wanted the Sinai entirely evacuated in return, and in this respect the question was indeed "settlements or peace." Dayan agreed with Weizman, adding that Egypt demanded a fundamental Israeli agreement to evacuate the settlers in exchange for its readiness to sign peace. "And if the [settlers] say that this means that the matter is being presented as if 'we [the settlers] are standing between a peace agreement [and] its absence,' their definition is correct, but it is not our definition." But, Dayan added, the government had decided to refer this most serious question to the public: "It was the Egyptians who set forth this choice, and it is the entire nation which will give the answer."[1] In Israeli politics, this is usually an indication of coming elections, but not this time.

Throughout the Israeli domestic debate, a clear distinction was made between the two frameworks agreed to at Camp David—the treaty with Egypt and the negotiation of autonomy arrangements for Judea and Samaria. It reflected the Israeli attempt to keep only a limited link between the two issues, while Egypt and the United States viewed them as closely intertwined. This central difference would continue to haunt the negotiations on the peace treaty and to be used by its opponents—primarily in Egypt and the Arab world—as a major Israeli breach. Citing this issue, the Egyptians would justify measures such as the recall of their ambassador to Israel for long periods and with regard to refusal to implement aspects of the agreements related to civil issues. The Israeli view, from the Camp David summit onward, has been consistent that the two dimensions are indeed separate, and the fact that the autonomy talks had failed does not void the bilateral agreement.

Meanwhile, in the United States, Begin gave an interview to *Maariv* (published on September 20, 1978) in which he was asked whether he was comfortable with signing a treaty acknowledging, for the first time ever, the rights of the Palestinian people. Begin replied that he did not see the agreements in this way. He admitted to having trouble with the phrase "the legitimate rights of Israeli Arabs" (referring to the Palestinians) because he used only the term "rights" during the summit. He explained that he could accept this addition after proving to the Americans that the addition "legitimate" was irrelevant. "Is there such a thing as illegitimate rights?" he asked. Begin also claimed that Israel acknowledged these rights in its peace plan of December 1977, so that nothing new had been ceded. The greatest achievement, according to Begin, was "approving our autonomy plan, and the full recognition of the IDF's continued presence in Judea, Samaria and Gaza—our people's sole defense."[2]

Begin returned to Israel on September 22 and in his airport press conference recalled debates over "not only sentences, but even on individual letters." He graciously thanked Carter for his tireless efforts and Sadat and his team for contributing to the final result.[3] But Begin prepared the citizens for "difficult days" of tests and trials, with unspecified problems to be overcome.[4]

The Knesset votes on the accords and the removal of the Sinai settlements were scheduled to take place within two weeks after the summit ended, and while a majority (including the Labor opposition) was likely to vote in favor, this was not assured due to the latter issue. During most of the thirteen-day summit, the Israeli public had not received any official information, but the media reported rumors of intense disagreements. Therefore, the sudden announcement of a framework agreement, followed by a remarkable signing ceremony, constituted a major political surprise. When Begin left Israel before the summit, he pledged to retire to one of the Israeli settlements in the Sinai, and two weeks later, this settlement, along with the rest of the Israeli presence, was to be evacuated as part of a peace treaty.[5]

Three Arenas

To gain approval, Begin and his government aides (Dayan and Weizman, in particular) had to contend with three distinct arenas in which varying levels of opposition were anticipated: the government coalition, the Knesset, and the wider public debate. The three were closely interconnected, and a significant loss of support in one could trigger erosion and perhaps defeat in the others.

Within the coalition, opposition to the agreement, particularly from Begin's political and ideological allies, was fierce and immediate. Hostility from cabinet ministers was mainly centered on symbolic and political terms, but Begin opted not to exert pressure on the ministers to vote for the government's policy, and eventually most joined the majority, and only Minister of Industry, Trade and Tourism Yigal Hurwitz and Minister of Education Zevulun Hammer abstained.

Hammer stayed in the government, while Hurwitz resigned several days after the Knesset vote, declaring that he foresaw grave developments following Camp David: "This is only the beginning, and there will be withdrawals on other fronts. Settlements on the Golan Heights will be—God forbid—dismantled. I foresee a shriveling presence in Judea and Samaria. The Americans will pour money that will first cause a sense of prosperity. But our dependence will grow and eventually the damage would be great and the country will shrink and weaken. I cannot be a partner in such a move. I do not share the general ecstasy."[6]

Outside the cabinet, other coalition MKs also expressed intense ideological opposition to the Camp David framework, and in some low-probability scenarios, the possibility of a defeat for the government could not be ruled out. Begin could assume the parliamentary opposition, led by the Labor Party, would support the Camp David Accords, but he could not have been sure, and some of the Labor hawks such as Yigal Allon harshly criticized the terms of the agreement. Most of the settlements, including in the Sinai, were built or approved under Labor governments, and many settlers were Labor supporters. In his speech at the Knesset debate on the Camp David agreements, Allon assured Begin that the opposition would "save the peace plan today, despite its failings." But he also questioned the degree to which Israel's security requirements would be met. He recalled that the Rafah area was intended to be a "defensible border" and that the settlers were sent there as "a keystone of our political struggle to create a defensible border." He added that if Labor would have conducted the negotiations, "we would not have relinquished the Rafah area."[7]

On September 24, the government approved the Camp David Accords after a heated debate. In spite of concerns that Begin and his entourage might have had, only Yigal Hurwitz of the La'am faction (originally from Mapai and who later followed David Ben-Gurion in Rafi and the National List) and Eliezer Shostak from the Free Center faction (originally from Herut)—both part of the Likud—voted against. Four other ministers from the coalition—Yitzhak Modai of the Liberal faction (of the Likud) and Yosef Burg, Zevulun Hammer, and Aharon Abu Hatzeira of the National Religious Party—did not take part in the vote.

To gain a tactical advantage, Begin decided to bring the two questions to the Knesset as a single package, which meant that the vote on the painful issue of dismantling the settlements in the Sinai would not go to a separate decision. In this way, perhaps not deliberately, Begin indicated acceptance of the terms of land for peace with Egypt—a position he repeatedly refused to state clearly at Camp David. On this basis, the government asked the Knesset to adopt a text stating: "The Knesset approves the Camp David agreements signed by the Prime Minister at the White House on September 17, 1978—if during the negotiations for the conclusion of a peace treaty between Egypt and Israel all outstanding issues are completely agreed upon and the agreement is expressed in a written document—the Knesset authorizes the Government, within the framework of the peace treaty, during a period to be agreed by the parties, to withdraw the Israeli settlers from Sinai, and to resettle them."[8]

At Camp David, Begin had outlined a plan which would give the Knesset the responsibility for authorizing the government to proceed with the agreement involving the dismantling of the Sinai settlements. But by the time he returned to Israel, Begin had basically accepted the role of leading this process, subject to Knesset approval. Begin explained that although he considered the two issues separate, to meet concerns of the Labor Alignment, he would present them as a single item.[9] But the strategy of separating the issue of the settlements from the vote on the accords was strongly criticized by ministers and coalition MKs.[10] During his final remarks during the Knesset debate (on September 28, 1978), Begin elaborated on why he decided to submit one statement for the Knesset to vote on. He explained that at Camp David, the delegation suggested submitting the question of removing the Sinai settlements separately from the Accords, but he added, "Upon returning to Israel and finding scathing attacks in the papers on our decision to vote on two separate proposals, one regarding the peace negotiations and the other regarding the issue of the settlements, indicating that the government was evading responsibility for making a difficult decision, I decided to combine the two."[11] However, these statements do not fully explain the change and may reflect a fear that the government could lose in the Knesset vote on the settlements if it was to be brought separately from the Accords. Based on statements made in the Knesset debate, it seems reasonable to assume that Begin was worried that defections might increase if there had been a separate vote on the settlements.

On September 25, immediately after the cabinet decision, the Knesset debate began, and Begin stated that unless the legislature authorized withdrawing the settlements, the final peace negotiations with Egypt could not start.

In making his case, particularly against critics who argued that an agreement could have been reached without the dismantling of settlements, Begin referred to two key documents whose contents he could not reveal "for psychological-political reasons": Sadat's first draft presented to Carter and Begin at the first meeting during the summit and the first American draft. He assured the Knesset that these documents would be made public in the future and would show what Israel gained and sacrificed for peace.

Recalling his long commitment to a full peace treaty, in contrast to previous interim agreements and nonbelligerency proposals, Begin declared, "No more partial agreements. No more interim agreements in which the state of war remains as it was." He praised the Accords for assuring security by providing demilitarized zones and early-warning facilities. Regarding the airfields, Begin admitted that he had failed to keep these in Israeli hands.

Begin rejected the claims that he gave up the Sinai settlements prior to Sadat's visit in November 1977 in order to make it possible in the first place. He added,

> This is a very painful matter, and not only will I not hide my pain, but I will express it in every way in which I can express human feeling. But today, as I well know, we are faced with the following choice: To accept the resolution as the government will table it in the Knesset. Or that the negotiations on a peace treaty will not even begin and all the things agreed at Camp David will be completely done away with. That is the choice. . . . I shall recommend opting for the possibility which we chose yesterday at the cabinet session because that is the way that leads to peace. That is the supreme national interest including that of my settler friends.[12]

Concerning the autonomy talks, Begin stressed that there would be no plebiscite in Judea, Samaria, and Gaza; no Palestinian state would be established under any circumstances; and the PLO would have no part in the negotiations. Regarding Jerusalem, Begin recalled the last-minute struggle, Carter's letter, and the response.[13] Begin repeated the promise he made to Carter that "during the period of the negotiations for the signing of a peace treaty—and today we are engaged in just one negotiation: with Egypt—that is, during the estimated three-month period, we would not establish new civilian settlements." He added, "This matter caused misunderstanding," citing notes from the September 16 meeting proving that he was correct and promised "to write the appropriate letter to President Carter this week."[14] (On September 27, Begin sent an oral message to Carter, again quoting Aharon Barak's notes.)[15]

The debate was one of the longest (two full days, September 25 and 27) in Knesset history. Peres criticized Begin for paying too high a price but added that as a responsible opposition, the Alignment decided to support the agreements. In the debate, 84 of the 120 MKs—including six ministers (Erlich, Burg, Sharon, Yadin, Weizman, and Dayan)—spoke, and, eventually, Begin replied. He reiterated that the issue was permanent peace instead of armistice agreements. He pointed to the security benefits of this agreement by claiming that with Egypt out of the cycle of hostilities, Syria would not wage war on Israel since it would be "tantamount to suicide." King Hussein would also not risk war for fear for his crown. Regarding the painful issue of the Sinai settlements, Begin said he and his team had tried to explain their importance to Carter and his aides, who then tried to persuade Sadat, but they were unsuccessful. Begin thanked Carter for trying and quoted the reply he brought back from Sadat: "I shall not be able to return. The Egyptian people will not accept that. I shall not be able to sign any agreement."[16] Begin said he could not accept this, and while repeating his personal belief that settlements should remain, he had agreed to turn the decision over to the Knesset, as the body vested with final sovereignty in Israel's parliamentary democracy.

Begin ended by saying that Israel could have rejected Sadat's position regarding the settlements, but it would have brought an end to the summit with no agreement, and "Israel could not stand up in the face of it. Not in America, not in Europe. Not before American Jewry. Not before the Jews of other lands. . . . All blame would have befallen us."[17] Begin acknowledged that he was influenced by the pressure, largely in terms of the international (particularly American) public opinion that he foresaw turning against Israel had it not agreed to dismantle the settlements, and he implied that the price that Israel was about to pay was the minimum to reach the overriding objective of a peace agreement with Egypt.

The vote of eighty-four in favor, nineteen opposed, and seventeen abstentions gave Begin a solid majority that reflected a wide public consensus willing to make sacrifices for peace. But on closer inspection, only two-thirds of the coalition members (forty-six of sixty-nine) supported the Accords, and they constituted only 55 percent of the total supporters. To gain approval, Begin needed the opposition. Furthermore, in his Likud party, less than two-thirds (twenty-nine of forty-five) supported Begin; in the NRP, only five of twelve voted yes. The centrist Democratic Movement for Change, which had divided into three factions with only one still in the coalition, supported the Accords unanimously, and three-quarters of the Labor Alignment (twenty-four of thirty-one), led by Peres, voted in favor.

The Impact of Demonstrations and Protest Movements in Israel

The third arena encompassed wider public opinion. The outcome of Camp David surprised the Israeli public and most of the politicians who had no reliable information throughout the summit. As a result, when the far-reaching framework agreement was revealed, the reactions in Israel were intense on all sides. For supporters of the peace process, this was a major breakthrough, and groups such as Peace Now organized demonstrations in support.[18] But for the settler movement and *Gush Emunim*, the withdrawal from the Sinai and the future autonomy agreement for the West Bank were betrayals of core religious and ideological principles. Thus, while Peace Now promised Begin "an enthusiastic welcome" with flowers, his opponents—most of whom were from his own constituency—called him a traitor and promised to greet him with black umbrellas, recalling Neville Chamberlain after signing the Munich Agreement with Hitler in 1938, and "peace in our time."[19]

When Begin returned from the United States on Friday afternoon, September 22, two hundred members of *Gush Emunim* and Herut organized a prayer vigil near his residence, noting that this took place shortly before the Jewish New Year and during the period of individual and collective soul-searching. Yehuda Etzion told a reporter that Begin should ask for forgiveness from God and from the Jewish people for betraying them and abandoning the Sinai settlements.

Demonstrators also gathered at Interior Minister Yosef Burg's home and clashed with the police.[20]

Protests also took place on September 25, when the Knesset debated the Camp David agreements. The Sinai residents and their supporters drove their tractors to Jerusalem, blocking traffic near the prime minister's residence, and the large community of Maale Adumim, located in the West Bank on the outskirts of Jerusalem, was emptied.[21] The protesters assembled outside the main convention center at the entrance to Jerusalem, and all speakers denounced Begin's and the government's betrayal. Several MKs participated in the demonstrations, including Haim Druckman, Moshe Shamir, Yigal Cohen-Orgad, and Ehud Olmert.[22]

A group called Loyalists to the Herut Principles asked the party's internal court to order Begin to either annul the agreements or resign on the grounds that the texts were contrary to the Herut Party Constitution, a breach of trust, and deceit of the Likud voters.[23] Veterans from the Lehi underground group (from the pre-1948 struggle to evict the British) "declared war on the accords," hinting at a willingness to use violence.[24] On the final day of the Knesset debate, about two thousand demonstrators protested outside the Knesset, which was interpreted as a weak show of force.[25]

On the other side, before the summit, Peace Now rallies in Tel Aviv were critical of Begin and pressed him not to forego the opportunity for peace and not to be an obstacle to peace.[26] Afterward, Peace Now fully embraced the outcome and helped to push the opposition Labor Alignment to support Begin's agreement.[27] In a meeting on September 19 with Peace Now, Peres and Allon assured them of support for the dismantling of the Sinai settlements as part of the peace framework, despite their party's role in establishing these settlements. Peace Now later explained that they supported Begin's decision to concede the Sinai and suspend settlement in the West Bank, and they would continue to support him if he also made concessions in the negotiations on the future of the West Bank. Otherwise, they warned, their confrontation with Begin would resume.[28] In January 1979, when the government announced the establishment of a new settlement in Nablus on the West Bank, Peace Now staged protests and demanded that this decision be canceled, with a freeze on all settlement activities during the negotiations.[29]

However, there were also some splits in the peace camp. The leftist Sheli party (Left Camp of Israel) denounced Peace Now's "hypocritical dancing," declaring, "Menachem Begin is from Herut, leader of the Likud, and not the spiritual father of the peace movement. It is necessary to support his positive moves and to criticize the negative ones, without cursing him bitterly two weeks ago and now giving him a victory parade on his return. Some sanity will do no harm."[30]

In contrast, the anti–Camp David protests were vocal and attacked Begin on personal and political grounds but failed to mobilize large crowds. Contemporary reports repeatedly mention MK Geula Cohen, Rabbi Moshe Levinger from Gush Emunim, the Movement for Greater Israel, and settlers from the Sinai and the West Bank. In addition to Cohen, the main opponents from Herut were Moshe Shamir and Shmuel Katz, after the latter had already resigned from his position as an advisor to Begin in January 1978. Katz published a book against the agreement with Egypt, *The Hollow Peace* (1981). Cohen and Shamir later left the Likud and established the *HaTehiya* party. However, most of the Likud leadership supported Begin.

There were also a number of extraparliamentary protest movements involving the settler community (both in Sinai and in Judea and Samaria) led by *Gush Emunim* and the Movement for Greater Israel, which was created in July 1967 as a cross-party movement with members from Labor, Herut, and other groups to promote Israeli settlements in the territories taken during the Six-Day War. Their protests against the Camp David framework began on the day after the signing. Levinger called that "a day of mourning for the Jewish people, a day that does not bring peace closer but war" and called those who signed the agreements traitors: "It must be stated clearly that the decision to concede parts of Eretz Israel, even by giving autonomy in Judea and Samaria and definitely by ceasing settlement activity, is a form of national treason. The land was always called Eretz Israel, and any agreement that gives up on this name and its meaning is treason."[31] MK Geula Cohen said that "this is a treaty for war, not peace. It is national suicide and wiping Judea and Samaria off the map. Begin must resign. . . . He is bringing war. . . . Peace Now can list Begin among its founders. I will demand a meeting of the Herut central committee in order to vote non-confidence in Begin."[32]

Settlers from the Sinai and Judea and Samaria participated in the protests outside the Prime Minister's Office during the government meeting that voted in favor of the Camp David agreements (on September 24, 1978), holding signs warning, "Today Yamit—tomorrow Jerusalem," and outside the Knesset during the following debate. But in both demonstrations, newspapers reported many fewer participants than expected by the organizers.[33] The demonstrators explained the sparse participation as the result of "the state of shock" that the Sinai settlers were in. However, opinion among the settlers, who came from a wide range of political and ideological backgrounds, was mixed. A press report quoted one saying that "it is hard to accept [the situation] . . . but if Israel will decide that we must leave for peace—peace is stronger and we will not [oppose it]," while another is quoted saying that "we will not leave. . . . I am shocked, if they evacuate us it will be a breach of public trust. No one spoke of complete evacuation."[34]

Two days after the signing ceremony, a joint committee to coordinate the protests was formed in Tel Aviv, led by MKs from the coalition parties—Geula Cohen of Herut, and Haim Druckman and Eliezer Valdman of the NRP.[35] The action committee of the Yamit region settlements met, and its chair "expressed hopes of getting 90 MKs to oppose the dismantling of the Yamit settlements."[36]

On the following day, Geula Cohen and a group of settlers barricaded themselves in the Elon Moreh settlement in the West Bank while security forces surrounded them. The protestors pledged that they "will resist the evacuation forcefully, will fight against it like a person that fights for his house."[37]

The Moshavim Movement (confederation of the cooperative communities in Israel, including some settlements beyond the Green Line—demarcating the 1949–1967 armistice boundary) also declared its opposition to evacuation of the Yamit region settlements: "Israel's governments viewed the establishment of Jewish settlements on Israel's security boundaries a vital and imperative factor in our security, also in peaceful times. The Movement holds to this view even today." It promised to fight the resolution using legal means and to stand with the settlers.[38] There was also a protest meeting in the community of Nahalal, with four hundred participants (estimated) who joined the Movement for Greater Israel in calling to continue struggling against the dismantling of settlements in the Sinai and expressing concerns regarding settlements beyond the Green Line. They called on Knesset members to vote against the dismantling of settlements and to make this vote overt and separate from the Sinai accord.[39]

After Rosh Hashana (October 2 to 3) and before the negotiations resumed at Blair House in Washington, DC (on October 12), opponents increased their activities to demonstrate "opposition to the Camp David policy across the country and to prevent abandoning settlements in Judea and Samaria, the Jordan Valley and the Golan Heights, and against the danger to Jerusalem."[40] In late October, former MK Yohanan Bader, who was part of the Herut core group and sat next to Begin in the Knesset for many years, declared, "These are very difficult days. Apparently, none of the party principles was violated and nowhere is it written that we give up on Judea, Samaria, the Golan or Gaza. But the Government destroyed all the safeguards that ensured our control over Judea and Samaria. I think that the day will come that it will be clear to all, maybe also to this Government, that we must not take this path."[41]

A student group called Disappointing Peace (in Hebrew *shalom achzav*, a play on words on Peace Now [*shalom achshav*]) demanded that Begin refrain from signing a peace treaty before new elections were held in which core issues would be debated.[42]

On November 19, 1978, a demonstration was held outside the Likud headquarters (Jabotinsky House) in Tel Aviv during the Herut Central Committee meeting that marked a year since Sadat's visit to Israel. During the demonstration, one participant jumped on Begin's car.[43] Begin referred to the demonstration, complaining bitterly that he was called a traitor and eggs were thrown at him. (Sarcastically, Begin congratulated Minister of Agriculture Ariel Sharon for the many products of the Holy Land.) He threatened to resign in response to the harsh attacks on his policy and on him, mentioning his fifty years of public service: "Why should I accept the insults in the Knesset and here? Why do I need to hear this word t-r-a-i-t-o-r?"[44] It was reported later that Begin said in a private session that "since the *Saison* [referring to the conflicts among the different underground movements prior to independence] I wasn't hurt so deeply by the incitement and the irrational hatred by those who were my best friends."[45]

After mentioning the heated demonstration outside the building, Begin told his critics that there were two things on which he needed no lecturing: Jabotinsky's doctrine and what Eretz Israel is. He said no one in the Herut Party had suffered more pain than he did over the Sinai. Regarding Judea and Samaria, Begin recalled there was no deadline for ending Israel's presence ("and beyond" was the phrase in Camp David)—"based on the Camp David Accords, Israel's army will be in Judea, Samaria and Gaza forever!"[46]

Begin emphasized that while removing the settlements was necessary, he did so reluctantly, particularly with the background of Zionist history and practice. It was also important for Begin to refute the argument that the Sinai would become the precedent for subsequent agreements regarding the Golan Heights, Judea, Samaria, and Gaza. The intense Knesset debate reflected the broader public concerns, highlighting the hopes in peace and the understanding that dismantling settlements was the unavoidable price while also acknowledging the costs and dangers. Press reports indicated that Peace Now and seemingly an overwhelming majority of the left and right (including thousands of Herut members and many Etzel veterans, among them Yaakov Meridor, Eliyahu Lankin, and others from the Etzel command) provided strong support to Begin.

After these difficult battles, the Camp David frameworks were confirmed in the government, in the Knesset, and in public opinion, but Begin's domestic battles were far from over. He recognized that any additional concessions on the key issues in the negotiations toward a peace treaty would give the critics from within Herut and allied parties important ammunition. The danger was and remained less from the Knesset and the possibility of being forced into new elections than from Begin's core constituency.

Notes

1. *IMFA*, document 196.
2. *IMFA*, document 197.
3. *IMFA*, document 198.
4. *IMFA*, document 198.
5. Abraham Rabinovich, "Begin's Bitter—but Finest—Hour," *Christian Science Monitor*, March 23, 1982, https://www.csmonitor.com/1982/0323/032327.html.
6. Bina Barzel, "Minister Yigal Hurwitz Resigned," *Yediot Aharonot*, September 29, 1978, 1 [Hebrew].

7. Lorch, *Major Knesset Debates, 1948–1981* 6:2269–70.

8. *IMFA*, document 199.

9. Yosef Waxman and Avraham Tirosh, "Begin Agrees to Unite the Knesset Votes on Approving the Accords and Dismantling the Settlements," *Maariv*, September 24, 1978, 1 [Hebrew].

10. Avraham Tirosh, "Likud Ministers Object to Begin's Proposal to Separate His Statement to the Knesset from the Discussion of Settlements," *Maariv*, September 20, 1978, 4 [Hebrew].

11. Lorch, *Major Knesset Debates, 1948–1981* 6:2271–72.

12. *IMFA*, document 200.

13. Begin's letter to Carter regarding Jerusalem, September 18, 1978, was one of the letters annexed to the Camp David Accords (*IMFA*, document 192).

14. *IMFA*, document 200.

15. "Oral Message from Prime Minister Begin to President Carter," September 27, 1978, BCA, PM 0072.

16. *IMFA*, document 201.

17. *IMFA*, document 201.

18. Peace Now was established in March 1978 following a public letter to Prime Minister Begin, signed by 348 IDF reserves officers and soldiers from combat units. They called on him not to miss the opportunity to make peace, and they opposed settlements in the West Bank.

19. "Thousands Will Applaud Begin with Flowers, the 'Gush' with 'Chamberlain Umbrellas,'" *Maariv*, September 22, 1978, 1, 11 [Hebrew].

20. Yosef Waxman, "At Dawn Gush Emunim Demonstration Near Begin's House Was Dissolved," *Maariv*, September 24, 1978, 1, 11 [Hebrew].

21. Yosef Zuriel, "Yesterday Maale Adumim Was a Ghost-Town and 'Symbol for Abandonment of Jewish Settlements,'" *Maariv*, September 27, 1978, 3 [Hebrew].

22. Baruch Meiri and Zvi Singer, "Police Horsemen Advanced towards the Tractors and the Protesters Moved Back," *Maariv*, September 26, 1978, 1, 16 [Hebrew].

23. Avraham Tirosh, "Demands to expel Begin from Herut," *Maariv*, September 27, 1978, 4 [Hebrew].

24. "Lehi Veterans: Begin Will Use the 'Holy Cannon' against 'Gush Emunim,'" *Maariv*, September 27, 1978, 4 [Hebrew].

25. Baruch Meiri and Zvi Singer, "A Relatively Quiet Demonstration Near the Knesset," *Maariv*, September 28, 1978, 4 [Hebrew].

26. Roni Eshel, "In 'Peace Now' Rally in Tel Aviv: About 100 Thousand People Expressed Their Yearning for Peace in a Prayer by R. Nachman of Breslov," *Maariv*, September 3, 1978, 4 [Hebrew].

27. Avraham Rotem, "At the Malchei Israel Square in Tel Aviv: 40 Thousand Sang 'Heveinu Shalom Aleichem' Hoping for 'Secure Peace Now,'" *Maariv*, September 19, 1978, 4 [Hebrew]; "'Peace Now' Arranges Welcome to Begin," *Maariv*, September 19, 1978, 4 [Hebrew].

28. Yosef Waxman, "Peres and Allon: We Will Not Position the Rafah Salient Settlements as an Obstacle to Peace," *Maariv*, September 20, 1978, 4 [Hebrew].

29. Yosef Waxman, "'Peace Now' to Demonstrate on Saturday Night," *Maariv*, January 10, 1979, 6 [Hebrew].

30. "Sheli to 'Peace Now': Stop the Dancing around the Prime Minister," *Maariv*, September 20, 1978, 4 [Hebrew]. Sheli was a short-lived bloc based on small parties on the Left with several leaders

of the Black Panther social protest movement from the early 1970s. They received two seats in the Knesset in the 1977 elections and were not elected in 1981.

31. Yosef Waxman, "Rabbi Levinger: This Is a Mourning Day for the Jewish People—Those Who Signed the Agreements Are Traitors," *Maariv*, September 18, 1978, 2 [Hebrew].

32. Moshe Maizelss, Avraham Tirosh, and Yosef Waxman, "Peres: I Bless the Breakthrough," *Maariv*, September 18, 1978, 2 [Hebrew].

33. Yosef Waxman and Zvi Zinger, "Yamit Region Settlers and 'Gush Emunim' Will Protest Today before the Knesset," *Maariv*, September 25, 1978, 1, 15 [Hebrew]; Baruch Meiri and Zvi Singer, "A Relatively Quiet Demonstration Near the Knesset," *Maariv*, September 28, 1978, 4 [Hebrew].

34. Ezra Yaniv, "Yamit Settlers: We Are Shocked," *Maariv*, September 18, 1978, 2 [Hebrew].

35. Avraham Tirosh, "A Headquarters of the Opposition to the Accords Was Formed in Tel Aviv Yesterday," *Maariv* September 19, 1978, 6 [Hebrew].

36. "I Want to Cry, We Will Not Live under Egypt's Flag," *Maariv*, September 19, 1978, 6 [Hebrew].

37. Yosef Walter, "Gush Emunim: We Will Resist Any Attempt to Evacuate, Fear of Clashes between IDF, Settlers," *Maariv*, September 20, 1978, 1, 15 [Hebrew].

38. Eli Danon, "The Moshavim Movement Opposes Evacuation of Rafah Plain Region," *Maariv*, September 21, 1978, 4 [Hebrew].

39. Meir HaReuveni, "If Yamit Is an Obstacle for Peace with Egypt, HaHula Will Be an Obstacle for Peace with Syria," *Maariv*, September 24, 1978, 4 [Hebrew].

40. Avraham Tirosh, "The Opposition to the Accords: We Will Organize an Active Resistance," *Maariv*, October 5, 1978, 4 [Hebrew].

41. Avraham Tirosh, "Bader: Israel Is Giving Security and Received Only Promises," *Maariv*, October 26, 1978, 4 [Hebrew].

42. "'Disappointing Peace' Will Hold Protest Shifts Near Begin's Home," *Maariv*, October 24, 1978, 4 [Hebrew].

43. Yosef Ahimeir, "'Begin a Traitor' vs. 'Long Live the Prime Minister': The Protesters Spoke in Eggs," *Maariv*, November 20, 1978, 4 [Hebrew]; Ada Cohen, "The Perennial Protestor Who Jumped on Begin's Car," *Maariv*, November 24, 1978, 30 [Hebrew].

44. The Herut Center Meeting, November 19, 1978, BCA, PM 158, 84–93; Ahimeir, "'Begin a Traitor' vs. 'Long Live the Prime Minister.'"

45. Yosef Harif, "Dayan: I Told Ambassador Lewis That the Choice Whether to Sign or Not Was Egypt's—We Will Settle," *Maariv*, November 24, 1978, 15 [Hebrew].

46. The Herut Center Meeting, November 19, 1978.

7 From a Framework to a Peace Treaty
October 1978–March 1979

AFTER THE CAMP DAVID framework was adopted by the Knesset, the process of closing the remaining gaps began in order to turn the guidelines into a formal peace treaty. Following months of stalemate prior to the summit, the next stage was characterized by constant movement, with numerous direct meetings, letters, and phone calls between the leaders.

This effort was ultimately successful, culminating in a peace treaty signed in Washington on March 26, some six months after Camp David. But this outcome was by no means a foregone conclusion, and the negotiations were characterized by frequent disputes and crises, particularly between Jimmy Carter and Begin. In addition, domestic politics in Israel and the United States continued to influence events, adding to Carter's zeal on the one hand while creating obstacles for Begin on the other.

This crucial stage of negotiations was consistent with the two-level model, in which external and internal factors need to be addressed simultaneously, and constrained the principle actors.[1]

In Israel, despite intense opposition from some members of Herut, the Accords received broad support in the media and the general public. On this basis, Begin and his government prepared for the final stage of negotiations toward a treaty, expected (in the Camp David framework) to last no more than three months. Begin did not hesitate in moving forward based on the language agreed at Camp David, and there is no evidence to support the theory, advanced by some American officials such as US ambassador Samuel Lewis and other analysts, of regret or buyer's remorse. Lewis argued that Begin's policies on autonomy and, in particular, the limited mandate given to Moshe Dayan on this issue reflected such remorse.

Indeed, at Camp David, Begin had made difficult concessions to achieve an agreement with Egypt, and he reluctantly conceded to the terms of the negotiation on Palestinian autonomy. Begin repeatedly and explicitly rejected Carter's pressure to go further on linkage, particularly toward a commitment to withdraw from the West Bank and Gaza and the establishment of a Palestinian state.[2] He agreed to autonomy talks but rejected repeated demands for a timetable on implementation and for giving Egypt a special role in Gaza.

Instead, it was Anwar Sadat who initially sought to back away from the terms agreed to at Camp David. William Quandt reports that the Egyptian leader began to "retreat from the idea of a peace treaty," fearing increased isolation.[3] From Begin's perspective, one of the central expressions of this reversal concerned Article 6 of the Camp David draft that gave precedence to the peace treaty over existing treaties and security obligations, such as between Egypt and the Arab League or any individual Arab state. Begin voiced concerns that after the Israeli withdrawal from Sinai, Egypt, whether under Sadat or a successor, would then resume its role in warfare against Israel. For much of the six months between Camp David and the final agreement, Begin, Sadat, and Carter exchanged numerous formulations of Article 6 and the accompanying Agreed Minutes. The record shows that in the end, Begin accepted compromise language that provided sufficient assurances on this central issue, as reflected in his speech to the Knesset on March 20, 1979. In this presentation, as elsewhere, Begin referred to Article 6 as "the soul of the agreement."[4]

In addition, throughout the negotiations after Camp David, the erosion of the Iranian regime became a major concern for all three parties, particularly during the chaos leading to the shah's exile in January 1979. American decision makers understood that "the spectacle of a pro-American regime in a Muslim country being swept aside by religious extremists did little to increase Israeli confidence in the long-term value of Sadat's promises."[5]

The Iranian Revolution also had an immediate impact on Israel's ability to import oil and increased dependence on the Sinai petroleum sources that would be returned to Egypt. As a result, the agenda of the negotiations now emphasized the need for terms by which Israel would be able to purchase Egyptian oil and by which the United States would guarantee Israel's energy security.[6]

For Carter and his administration, the events in Iran colored "American thinking about the Camp David negotiations" and "made it increasingly important to conclude the peace negotiations between Begin and Sadat successfully." As Quandt notes, a treaty was important for both strategic reasons in terms of American interests in the region and in the domestic political arena prior to the midterm congressional elections in November 1978: "Carter needed a political success to offset the enormous failure in Iran." [7]

Carter's increasing desperation was translated into more pressure on Begin for the concessions that were rejected at Camp David, and for six months, these pressures and the resulting conflict between the two leaders dominated the negotiations. Finally, in March, after many meetings and exchanges, Carter came to Cairo and Jerusalem to hammer out the final text. On all of the major issues that were raised, and on Palestinian autonomy in particular, Begin refused to accept major changes. Given the choice of no agreement or accepting Begin's terms, Carter and Sadat chose the latter.

The Carter-Begin Confrontation Continues

Immediately after Camp David, on September 19, 1978, Carter met with Jewish leaders, initially reporting, "All of us were happy about the Camp David accords." But then he launched into an intense attack on Begin, claiming, as reported in Carter's book, that the Israeli leader "continued to disavow the basic principles of the accords relating to Israel's withdrawal of its armed forces and military government from the West Bank, negotiations on an equal basis with the Palestinians and other Arabs, and the granting of full autonomy to the residents of the occupied areas. His statements, which were in sharp contrast to those of the American and Egyptian delegations, soon created understandable confusion among those who were intensely interested in the Middle East."[8]

Shortly afterward, Jody Powell (identified as a senior official) gave a background briefing that expressed the administration's impatience with "the continued haggling over details," and Dayan referred to an "atmosphere of imminent crisis" in bilateral relations.[9] For Begin, the use of terms such as "haggling over details" to describe positions on critical issues of Israeli security and historic rights added further insult. Quandt wrote that Carter sought ways to press Begin to agree to freeze settlements for the duration of the autonomy negotiations, including waiting for a letter to this effect before sending confirmation to help construct the two airfields in the Negev.[10]

Begin was aware of Carter's effort to increase the pressure. For example, in a meeting with Saunders, as reported in the Israeli transcript, Begin asked why US officials showed great understanding for the political problems of Arab leaders but had none for his own. He had been bitterly attacked by some of his oldest friends in the Irgun. The Americans should appreciate the concessions he had already made for peace. Saunders replied that the United States understood his difficulties and the Israeli procedures better than it understood Egypt's procedures. Begin told Saunders to convey to Carter his "deepest sadness that the answers [to the questions from Jordan] were sent without any consultation with us."[11]

Begin was referring to Carter's reply to King Hussein's questions concerning the outcome of the Camp David summit, in which the American president stated a position that seemed inconsistent with the texts.[12] Prof. Aharon Barak (legal advisor during Camp David) was also very critical, accusing Carter of falsely linking the "legitimate rights" of the Palestinians that was part of the Judea and Samaria question to the security question that is relevant (based on UNSCR 242) to bilateral relations between Israel and Jordan:[13] "This is a confusion and I'm sure it is deliberate."[14] In the reply to a question regarding Jerusalem, Barak noted that the Americans refer to "Jerusalem" and "East Jerusalem," commenting that "it may be an error, but it may be intentional. I feel it is intentional."[15] (The difference is very important, as the term East Jerusalem suggested a redivision of the city, which was anathema to the Israelis.) Barak added a general comment that the Accords allowed both Israel and Egypt to maintain their interpretations of UNSCR 242, but the United States adopted the Arab interpretation in its reply to the Jordanians. Barak continued to criticize many American positions in the reply that differed from the wording agreed on at Camp David. He concluded, "The serious matter is that on all of the issues we have a legitimate argument with the Egyptians on interpreting the [Accords]—East Jerusalem, the application of 242 to the discussion on Judea and Samaria [Israel's position was that 242 does not apply], the source of authority for autonomy, application of the arrangement to Israelis—the Americans interpret in a manner that is unacceptable to us, and identify with the Arab interpretation."[16]

The Blair House Talks

After Camp David, Begin appointed Dayan to head the delegation that would continue the negotiations (with Ezer Weizman) at Blair House in Washington. Eliahu Ben-Elissar was to head the steering committee on autonomy, and Minister of Agriculture Ariel Sharon (also responsible for settlements) was given the task of preparing for the relocation of Israeli civilians living in the Sinai. In this way, Begin was preparing for both the substantive talks and the internal political conflict.[17] However, Begin and the government did not authorize Dayan and Weizman to make any significant decisions without approval. They needed to return home several times during the Blair House talks to report and convince their colleagues that they were not "selling out," as charged by Minister of Education Zevulun Hammer.[18]

The formal negotiations resumed at Blair House in Washington on October 12 and quickly reached an impasse. The Egyptian delegation (headed by Kamal Hasan, who replaced Gamasi as war minister) demanded a public statement of Israel's commitment to the Camp David precedent (total territorial withdrawal) as the basis for future agreements with Syria and Jordan.[19] This undermined Begin domestically and strengthened the position of his critics who argued that the Egyptian model would become the basis for negotiations with Syria and on the West Bank.[20] As Bar-Siman-Tov noted, Israeli officials "had the impression that Egypt had withdrawn from previous understandings and was asking Israel to make additional concessions."[21]

Another point of friction arose when Israel demanded "that Egypt's obligations under the treaty should take precedence over any obligations that Egypt has as a member of the Arab League."[22] Israel was concerned that the Camp David formula might allow Egypt to give priority to inter-Arab commitments, such as the 1950 Collective Arab Defense Agreement, which pledged mutual aid in the event of a military confrontation. (Tamir reports that Carter responded angrily when Aharon Barak presented a legal argument that highlighted the difficulty with the Camp David terminology on this issue.[23]) Similarly, the Camp David framework stated that all "economic boycotts" and "discriminatory barriers" would end, but Israel wondered whether Egypt will halt its adherence to the Arab economic boycott of Israel.[24]

Negotiating the details of West Bank autonomy proved similarly difficult. The Americans and Egyptians had built their concept of autonomy on the assumption that Hussein would be deeply involved. However, Jordan stayed away. In an earlier meeting, Sadat had declared, "If he [Hussein] wished, he can participate; if not, then we will blaze the trail."[25]

Egypt again demanded that the autonomy talks be completed during the nine-month period stipulated for the first Israeli withdrawal in Sinai and the exchange of ambassadors. (At different times during the negotiations, a deadline of one year was also raised.) Furthermore, the Egyptian delegation continued to insist on Israeli "gestures"—unilateral moves outside of a formal agreement that would advance the date for implementing autonomy. Although Begin agreed to start the autonomy talks one month after signing and ratifying the peace treaty, he rejected a deadline or additional links between the bilateral relationship with Egypt and Palestinian issues.[26]

Thus, these core US/Egyptian demands were back on the negotiating table, even though Israel had rejected them at Camp David on the grounds that this would give others (Jordan or the PLO, for example) leverage for bringing the entire process to a halt.

To overcome these obstacles and initiate the post–Camp David phase of negotiations, the United States presented a draft treaty at the Blair House meetings, but difficulties occurred immediately. Egypt proposed a five-year review provision and demanded the return of "the coastal strip of Eilat" (apparently referring to Taba, southwest of Eilat) within three months. As Tamir notes, "We rejected these demands and insisted that the Camp David arrangements should stay as they were."[27] Both the Israeli and Egyptian delegations were dissatisfied with the American draft of the military annex and presented their own texts.

But Carter pressured both sides to accept his draft and to make the concessions necessary to reach the deal that he envisioned. In a letter to Begin sent on October 22, 1978, Carter wrote of good progress while continuing to press for major and quick concessions on Palestinian autonomy. Carter also wrote that Israel's delegation to the Blair House talks was constructive, accepting a treaty that was "fair and balanced." He urged Begin to endorse the draft, mentioning that he was making the same appeal to Sadat. He wanted the two to exchange letters "agreeing to begin negotiations within one month of signing the treaty to establish the self-governing authority." Carter added that he was willing to take necessary steps to ensure that a UN or multinational force would remain in Sinai on a permanent basis. Carter informed Begin that he had asked Sadat for three concessions: to leave the dismantlement of the Neot Sinai settlement to the last phase of the withdrawal, to limit deployment of surface-to-air missiles in Sinai, and to send Egypt's ambassador to Israel within one month of the completion of the interim withdrawal.[28]

Begin accepted Carter's proposal on exchanging letters with Sadat but changed the date for the start of autonomy negotiations to a month after the treaty came into force rather than from the date that the agreement was signed.[29]

In late October 1978, the cabinet voted to expand Israeli settlement activities in the West Bank—a significant point that Begin's letter to Carter had omitted.[30] As proposed by Dayan in the context of gaining approval for the treaty draft, hundreds of families would be added to existing settlements in the Golan Heights, the Jordan Valley, Judea, Samaria, and Gaza.[31] (Begin told the Likud faction that Dayan had notified Cyrus Vance of this decision.[32]) When this was revealed, Carter immediately sent an angry telegram to Begin:

> No step by the Israeli Government can be more damaging although I know you have mentioned in our earlier conversations the possibility of some small increases through family reunification. I do not believe that the reported decision is what we have discussed. . . . I have to tell you with the greatest concern and regret that taking this step at this time will have the most serious consequences for our relationship. Moreover, I believe that it may also jeopardize the conclusion of peace treaty which we are negotiating.[33]

Carter continued to argue that under the Camp David framework, Israel had agreed to a freeze on settlements other than "for humanitarian reasons—wives and children to rejoin husbands and fathers." And once again, the Israelis told US officials that "nothing of the kind had ever been said at Camp David, and [they] would do well to examine the transcript of our talks." Carter repeated the claim that he had been "led astray on the settlement issue," but as Israeli officials noted at the time, "if the President wanted clear and specific commitments from us, he should have demanded and tried to get them before the signing of the Camp David accords. Since he was then satisfied with the limited commitment Begin was prepared to give, he could not now blame us but only himself."[34] (This exchange, in different forms, was repeated many times in subsequent interactions.)

The impact on Begin was reflected in three letters he wrote to Carter on the same day, October 29. In the first, he recalled that while he promised not to establish new settlements for three months, he also stated that "we shall add several hundred families to the existing settlements"; therefore, the cabinet's decision was fully consistent with the positions taken at Camp David. He summarily rejected the possibility, raised by Assistant Secretary Saunders and Ambassador Lewis, that some or even all of the settlements might be removed from the West Bank and urged Carter to understand Israel's position.

In the second letter, Begin thanked Carter for congratulating him on receiving the Nobel Peace Prize with Sadat. The third letter, labeled "Personal for the President's Eyes Only," was Begin's response to the accusation of blocking progress. Begin complained that Carter repeatedly sided with Sadat, emphasizing the Egyptian leader's isolation, but never considered Begin's political environment.

> Today may I ask: What about my situation, my difficulties? To prove the point, I will inform you of the following facts: The men of the Irgun whom I led from the underground into a fight for liberty for five years are my most beloved friends. . . . Now, for the first time, in thirty-four years a group of them is in "revolt" against their brother and former commander. Nearly half of my own party members in the Knesset either voted against or abstained. Some young people dabbed on the walls of Zeev Jabotinsky House the words: "Begin—traitor!"

Begin reminded Carter that Sadat was a dictator who controlled the media in Egypt, in sharp contrast to Israel's democracy. He recalled that Golda Meir responded to the Rogers Plan by stating that "an Israeli government that would accept such a plan would commit treason to our people," and asked Carter to avoid proposals that would compel him to repeat Meir's statement.[35]

Carter responded with a handwritten letter on November 11, warning, "The successful conclusion of an Israeli-Egyptian peace treaty is in doubt." He praised Begin for the success at Camp David and noted that the Nobel Peace Prize recognized Begin's contribution,[36] but he added that both Israel and Egypt should be more flexible. Carter wrote that other issues needed his attention (in particular, the deteriorating situation in Iran) and urged Begin to approve the drafts that Vance would be bringing, pledging to ask the same of Sadat.[37]

However, in their respective internal political arenas, Begin and Sadat faced growing opposition to continuing negotiations toward a peace treaty. On November 2 to 5, 1978, a summit meeting of the Arab League in Baghdad condemned Sadat, and this was repeated in a March 1979 meeting of the Arab foreign ministers, also in Baghdad. The Arab regimes offered Sadat massive economic assistance in return for abandoning the peace process with Israel. As Dayan noted, "Contrary to their hopes and to America's assumptions, Saudi Arabia and Jordan had joined their opponents" in isolating Sadat and working to prevent an agreement.[38]

Within Egypt, criticism of the Camp David agreements became increasingly vocal and personal. As Stein observed, "The Egyptian press was merciless against Begin. Articles, anecdotes, and cartoons in the Egyptian media depicted Jews as immoral, hypocritical, unreliable, unmanly, intransigent, insecure, greedy, ill-intentioned, and chronically suspicious of everyone."[39] Begin and the Israeli political leadership were very disturbed by the media campaign in Cairo and passed their concerns to Sadat and to the Americans, who took note of the Israeli complaints.[40]

In parallel, Carter increased pressure on Begin regarding the proposed linkage between the treaty with Egypt and autonomy. Statements of American positions on Jerusalem, potential PLO participation in the negotiations, and apparent backing away from funding commitments to move the airbases from the Sinai were seen as inconsistent with Camp David.[41] In Israel, reports on Harold Saunders's tour of Arab capitals referred to the American envoy's statements that Israel would give up settlements in the West Bank and would be forced to transfer sovereignty within five years and that the United States considered east Jerusalem to be occupied territory.[42] Dayan asked, "Did the United States Government think we would accept them in silence? What had happened was that at the very moment that we were negotiating over the desired pattern of living with the Arabs, the Americans declared that we would be withdrawing from the West Bank Gaza and east Jerusalem."[43]

These reports added to the domestic criticism directed at Begin for claiming that the concessions to Carter at Camp David would reduce rather than increase the pressure on Israel. In response, as the negotiators completed the preliminary version of a draft treaty in Washington, Dayan, Weizman, and Barak returned to Israel for consultations from October 22 to 26.[44] Dayan recommended "advancing the date of our evacuation of western Sinai," extending the time from the first to the final move of the withdrawal process. "This additional time was highly important to us, since this was the very period when it would be possible to gauge Egypt's behavior."

However, Dayan expressed strong opposition to any agreement that would give Egypt a foothold in Gaza: "We had to be careful not to lose what we had gained—recognition of the international border as the boundary line between Israel and Egypt." Dayan noted that at Camp David, the Egyptians had agreed that "the border ran west of Gaza and was to be guarded by Israel Army forces, so that anyone wishing to cross the frontier into the Gaza District had to behave in accordance with the laws of the State of Israel. We should on no account depart from this formula."[45]

The Blair House negotiations resumed, covering the same grounds, although this time Dayan's mandate was limited to discussing the modalities of the elections for the Palestinian autonomy but not its "powers and responsibilities," as Quandt reported.[46] But he did tell the Egyptians that Israel was willing to accelerate the first Sinai withdrawal from nine months to two.

On November 1, on the way to Los Angeles, Begin met in New York with Vance and other officials who raised the issue of linkage between Israeli concessions and American economic assistance to cover the huge costs of relocating bases from the Sinai.[47] Begin surprised his own delegation (which included Dayan and Weizman, who came from Washington) by telling Vance that he wanted the $3.37 billion aid that Israel requested to be provided as a loan and not a grant: "We shall repay," he stressed, "every penny that we receive!"[48] He argued that this was imperative for approval of the deal by his government.[49] Given Israel's dire economic situation and the high costs of repayment, Begin was later convinced to withdraw this gesture and to request a grant, which was eventually negotiated but not before Begin apologized to Vance and appealed directly to Carter.[50]

The Blair House negotiations had reached a stalemate, and no direct talks between the Israelis and Egyptians took place at the senior level. On November 11, Carter introduced a new draft, at which point Dayan and Weizman then returned to Jerusalem for consultation. Quandt claims that Dayan had agreed to set a date for the autonomy elections.[51] However, on November 12, on Begin's return trip from Canada, he met again with Vance and stated that Dayan had exceeded his authority regarding elections.[52]

The Americans again pushed for direct linkage by rejecting the key sentence in the Israeli position, stating "that the autonomy negotiations were not to be dependent upon the implementation of the Egypt-Israel peace treaty."[53] This meeting also featured another American effort to divide the Israelis by asking for Dayan's views after Prime Minster Begin had made his position clear, at which point Begin asked Vance if the United States was also in charge of the Israeli delegation.[54]

The Israeli Debate on the Blair House Draft

The Egyptian and Israeli teams returned home for consultations on the text of the draft treaty, although important differences remained. For example, in a press conference on November 17, Carter spoke about "ancient distrusts and disputes," repeating America's central role, as he saw it, in creating trust and bridging the gaps.[55]

On the same day, Dayan said in a television interview that "the peace treaty between us and Egypt [is] complete, with respect to its wording." The disagreements were also clear. If both sides "[did] not stubbornly insist on reopening the disputed issues but compromise[d] instead," a treaty could be signed.[56] The main obstacle was autonomy, with the Egyptians and Americans demanding an explicit linkage to implementation of the peace treaty. This would have bound Israel to a fixed and short timetable on the West Bank, which was unacceptable to Begin, and would have increased protests and the opposition to the entire package among Herut members. As a result, the draft treaty did not include explicit linkage.

In two cabinet sessions (November 19 and 21), a meeting of the Knesset Foreign Affairs and Defense Committee, and a session of the Likud's Knesset members, members of the coalition sharply attacked Dayan regarding the draft treaty and the terms he and the negotiators had tentatively accepted.

The cabinet debates during this period were very intense, with strong opposition to further concessions and to the draft treaty. Dayan's account states,

"I warned my colleagues that unless they approved the agreement as it stood, in all its parts, Israel would be blamed for the failure to achieve peace. Begin understood this, and though he wanted certain changes he threw his full weight behind approval."[57]

In this atmosphere, and as a direct response to Saunders, Dayan proposed an immediate declaration regarding resumption of settlement construction, which he explained as important in showing the futility of pressuring Israel.[58] Begin agreed and, to counter American statements on Jerusalem, announced that Israel would build and move government offices to Sheikh Jarrah, the area below the Hebrew University on Mt. Scopus in Jerusalem, beyond the 1949 armistice line. On this basis, and after some changes designed to further decouple the peace with Egypt from the issue of the West Bank, the cabinet overwhelmingly endorsed the draft treaty, and Begin also received the support of the Likud Knesset faction, over the vociferous objections of his critics.

Although Dayan and Weizman—with Begin's powerful support—were successful in gaining cabinet approval for the text that they had negotiated, some of their recommendations were rejected. For example, the government rejected Dayan's suggestion to advance the scheduled withdrawal to the El Arish line in the Sinai to six months after the signing of a treaty.[59] The opposition to Begin within the government and the Likud party did not block the negotiations, but it did cause delays.

As Begin had pledged, the draft was brought before the cabinet on November 19, 1978. Later that day, in the Herut Central Committee, Begin said that Egypt was suggesting erasing Article 6 (5), which stipulated that if another country was involved in a conflict with Israel, Egypt would be legally bound to maintain the peace treaty with Israel. This article was clearly of central importance to Israel and reflected Begin's long-held understanding of the foundations for "real peace."[60]

In this session (an open forum, unlike the cabinet meetings), Begin focused on autonomy. He repeated Israel's three conditions: (a) maintaining the IDF presence in Judea, Samaria, and Gaza, as agreed in Camp David, (b) general security, and (c) the continuation of Jewish settlement activity. These conditions, he promised, would be presented when the autonomy talks began, after the peace treaty with Egypt was signed.[61] In this way, Begin was able to overcome much of the criticism he faced at home.

Carter versus Begin (Again) on Linkage

The draft treaty based on the American text and subsequent talks included detailed procedures regarding the Israeli military withdrawal from the Sinai and security details based on the Camp David framework. Israel and Egypt agreed that the multilateral force would be formed by states that were not permanent members of the UN Security Council, or, in the absence of agreement, the United States would lead.[62]

Egypt raised more objections regarding Article 6 (5) in the draft, which cited Article 103 of the UN Charter, stating that "in the event of a conflict between the obligations of the Parties under the present Treaty and any of their other obligations, the obligations under this Treaty will be binding and implemented." This was a key point as it highlighted the preeminence of treaty obligations to Israel over Arab League commitments, including mutual defense. Another passage stated, "The parties undertake to fulfill in good faith their obligations under this treaty without regard to action or inaction of any other party and independently of any instrument external to this treaty."[63]

On November 20, Dayan told Ambassador Lewis that assuming the government approved the current draft, Israel would be willing to sign the treaty, but the Egyptian demands for changes were unacceptable. He reiterated that the autonomy talks would start only after the treaty with Egypt was ratified, perhaps one month later. Dayan warned that if Egypt insisted on starting the autonomy track before, there would be no treaty. Israel was committed to implementing every word agreed at Camp David. Dayan informed Lewis that he had no authority to discuss autonomy and therefore would not return to Washington. Lewis replied that this position was problematic since Israel was, in practice, demanding that Sadat sign a separate peace and only later discuss autonomy.[64] In a November 21 memo to Carter, Zbigniew Brzezinski noted that Israel's position regarding the priority article in the treaty was also the American position but that Egypt insisted on more assurances regarding autonomy, including a "general target date."[65]

The United States then proposed a letter addressed to Carter, jointly written by Begin and Sadat. It would include a call on Hussein to join the negotiations, a declaration of intent to hold elections for the autonomy institutions by the end of 1979, and a statement that Israel's forces would withdraw to agreed security positions immediately after the establishment of the autonomy institutions. Egypt's counterproposal was published in the daily *Al-Aharam* on November 22, accepting the call for Jordanian involvement and for autonomy elections to take place six months after the exchange of the articles of ratification for the peace treaty. Israel was to dismantle the military civil government two weeks after autonomy was established, and "in order to facilitate the passing of authority to the autonomy establishment, the two sides would agree that a limited Egyptian police force and Liaison Officers will be present."[66] This public statement was understood as primarily designed for political impact in Egypt and the Arab world rather than as a negotiating position, and the central points were incorporated in the official letter that Begin and Sadat addressed to Carter with the signing of the peace treaty four months later.

In a November 21 phone conversation with Carter, Begin reiterated the position that Israel was ready to negotiate on autonomy soon after signing peace but would not accept a target date. Carter asked if Begin was willing to postpone the withdrawal in the Sinai until the autonomy was underway. Begin understood that Carter was suggesting suspending the implementation of the treaty pending progress on West Bank autonomy, and he replied that he needed to consult with the government before responding. Carter tried again, telling Begin that Israel would still have access to the Suez Canal as well as a commitment to diplomatic relations. Begin replied, "A commitment, yes, but not the relations themselves."[67] (Begin was not surprised by Carter's probe; the same scenario was raised in a meeting with Carter, Vance, and Weizman on November 14.[68])

On November 30, Brzezinski warned Carter that "the agreements were coming apart": Camp David had left the false impression that Carter and Sadat had agreed to a separate peace between Israel and Egypt, Begin did not want an agreement on the West Bank and "might be genuinely intimidated by his domestic opposition (though he is also doubtlessly exploiting it)," Sadat was frightened by the Baghdad conference, and Sadat and the Saudis had detected US weakness on keeping the Soviets out of the Middle East and on pressing Israel. Brzezinski recommended pressuring Sadat to accept the Blair House draft and pushing Begin to accept the target date and initiate autonomy talks. The military and economic relations between Israel and the United States would not "be allowed to perpetuate a stalemate which will inevitably radicalize the Middle East and reintroduce the Soviets into the region."[69]

A week later, Brzezinski again recommended that Carter warn Begin that the quality of peace with Egypt and relations with the United States would "be influenced by how the full range of commitments at Camp David [were] carried out." He also proposed reducing annual aid by any amount spent on settlement activities, reporting on this to the US Congress and voting against Israel on settlement issues raised in the United Nations.[70] He raised the option of holding another summit, in which Begin would be forced to make decisions on the spot and not refer back to the government in Jerusalem.[71]

The Begin-Sadat Exchange on Linkage

On November 30, Sadat sent a long letter to Begin "with full awareness of the historic responsibility we both share . . . to build a solid structure for peace." This was not a time for "scoring points" in "a contest of oratory" or "in futile arguments and discussions about issues of little or no real significance." Egypt had proved its "willingness to look seriously and sympathetically to [Israel's] need to feel secure."[72]

Sadat reconfirmed that he offered Israel full recognition and accepted Carter's request to begin implementation before the final phase of the withdrawal.

On autonomy, the Camp David framework was a good basis for a solution, and he asked Begin to accept a timetable, just as Begin insisted on a timetable for implementing the agreement with Egypt: "If the implementation of [the steps regarding the West Bank and Gaza] [was] hindered because of reasons beyond your control, you will not be held responsible for that."[73]

Sadat repeated his opposition to the proposed revisions of Article 6, giving the peace treaty priority over other Egyptian obligations: "It is inappropriate for any of us to attempt to interfere with the way the other party conducts its relations with third countries. It is the responsibility of each party to reconcile its commitments to various partners." He also criticized Begin for opposing an exchange of letters on the West Bank and Gaza and "a tangible Egyptian presence in the Gaza Strip."[74]

This was a significant development, and Begin replied on December 4, repeating Israel's goal of a comprehensive peace with its neighbors, beginning with the treaty with Egypt. He claimed that he "never suggested to you [Sadat] to conclude a separate peace with Israel. The envisaged peace treaty between our countries constitutes the first indispensable step towards the broader settlement we seek." Begin wrote that Israel's government agreed "a fortnight ago" to sign the current draft, but it was Sadat who was preventing the signature by insisting on "changing or deleting sections of Article VI and, I am informed, also Article IV." This latter article stated that the multilateral peacekeepers to be stationed in the Sinai could only be removed by the UN Security Council or agreement of the two parties. It addressed Israeli concerns regarding a repetition of the 1967 scenario, in which Nasser suddenly ordered the immediate departure of peacekeepers in the Sinai, and the UN Secretary General complied.[75]

Begin again rejected demands to shorten the interim withdrawal period in the Sinai to six months. Israel did not object to an exchange of letters concerning Judea, Samaria, and Gaza but rejected a "tangible Egyptian presence in the Gaza Strip," which was not part of the Camp David Accords. He concluded that "we shall carry out our commitments fully under the Camp David agreement. We signed the Framework. Our signature is the commitment."[76]

On the Palestinian "self-governing autonomy (administrative council)," Begin emphasized the desire to negotiate in good faith despite the Jordanian refusal to participate. Setting a timetable for the autonomy talks was pointless, he argued, since all relevant elements were out of Israel's control, in contrast to the negotiations with Egypt regarding the Sinai. Israel would be prepared to start negotiations on West Bank elections one month after exchanging the instruments of ratification of the peace treaty with Egypt.[77]

As Begin repeatedly reminded Sadat and Carter, he had no intention of sacrificing his core positions regarding Jewish rights and history or the risks of a Palestinian state.

Carter versus Begin—the Next Round

When the Jordanians and Saudis stayed away and other "moderate allies" joined the attacks on Camp David and the negotiations, Carter stepped up the pressure on Begin for more concessions in order to assist Sadat.[78]

The Israelis viewed Carter's confrontation with Begin as, in part, the result of his administration's precarious domestic political standing. The best hope for reviving Carter's floundering presidency depended on reaching the next stage in the peace process, particularly as the images of successes of Camp David began to fade amid the turmoil and impending disaster in Iran. Demonstrations in Tehran increased daily (the shah fled on January 16, 1979), and Carter needed an Egyptian-Israel treaty even more.[79] Quandt wrote, "Carter left Camp David with a feeling of real satisfaction. The reaction in Congress, the press, and the public at large to the news of agreement between Begin and Sadat was overwhelmingly positive. Carter received much of the credit, and his political fortunes appeared to improve significantly as a result. To sustain this political boost, however, Carter needed to make sure that the Camp David frameworks did not remain dead letters."[80]

The midterm congressional elections in the first week of November 1978 were crucial. Brzezinski reports, "We had hoped to obtain a peace treaty by Election Day (of 1978), but toward the end of October it was clear that no agreement was in sight." The president began referring to the likelihood of "a showdown" with Israel.[81]

The election results were not as bad as the White House had feared. The Democrats maintained their large majorities in the House of Representatives and the Senate, although with a reduced margin. In the House, the Democrats lost 15 seats, resulting in a majority of 277 versus 158 Republicans. In the Senate, the Democrats lost three seats but kept a majority of 58 to 41. Several analysts contend that the Camp David Accords had a positive effect on the voters' view of the Democratic president's resolve merely six weeks before Election Day.[82]

Nevertheless, the crisis in the US-Israel relations worsened as Vance returned to the region in early December in another effort to reach an agreement. The Carter administration sought to set December 17 as the date for signing the treaty, which was the original date set at Camp David. But even before Vance arrived, it was clear that that was entirely unrealistic. Dayan notes that "Vance's mission turned out to be an unfortunate one. Not only did it fail to shift the peace ship off the shoals but it almost shattered it. . . . We could not avoid the feeling that the Americans had misled us, and were applying a double standard, one for the Egyptians and another for us."[83] This was communicated to Vance in Jerusalem.

In Cairo, Vance told Sadat of Begin's angry reaction to American support of Egypt's position, at which, at least according to Quandt, "Sadat smiled and expressed his pleasure." Vance reportedly agreed with the Israeli assessment that the Egyptian position had hardened since the Camp David framework was negotiated, attributing this to Sadat's growing fear of the Arab rejectionists, led by Syria, Iraq, and Libya. At the same time, officials such as Quandt claimed that "Sadat was still convinced that a confrontation between the US and Begin was necessary. He was prepared to accommodate Carter on any number of details in order to keep the American president on his side for the eventual showdown with Begin." Quandt reports that "Vance said he had told Begin in private that the United States supported the Egyptian position." In response, Begin (and the Israeli cabinet) declared, "The Government of Israel rejects the attitude and the interpretation of the US government with regard to the Egyptian proposals." Carter then retaliated, again delaying implementation on some bilateral commitments and supporting Egypt's refusal to send an ambassador until the autonomy issue was resolved.[84]

As attention shifted further toward the collapse of the shah's regime, the tension and conflict between Carter and Begin continued to grow. According to Carter, time was running out, and he and Vance had other matters to take care of—the SALT talks, Nicaragua, and Nigeria, as well as coming meetings with European leaders.[85] Carter publicly blamed Israel for the deadlock. Once again, he complained that the peace process was distracting him from other important international matters.

On December 15, the Israeli government issued a statement placing the blame on Egypt's new conditions. The statement referred to the conditioning of exchanging ambassadors upon implementation of autonomy, changes in security arrangements in the Sinai after five years, the "unacceptable" interpretation of Article 6, and a target date for implementing autonomy. To keep the talks going, Israel offered to reformulate its autonomy arrangements.[86] Dayan explained that Egypt had to decide whether it was ready to continue negotiating with Israel's objections as a given fact. He said it was a realistic possibility that a peace treaty would not be signed, and that might reopen the way to the Geneva Conference.[87]

Vance left the Middle East with no noticeable achievements, and the talks were deadlocked. He told his staff to prepare a white paper to increase public pressure on Begin and Israel, but this document was never made public.[88] Once again, failure was followed by a series of US background briefings by senior officials, blaming Israel for the failure and leading to a confrontation between the Jewish community and the president. The strategy of driving a wedge between Begin and the Jewish leadership continued but without success.[89] Israel forcefully rejected accusations that it "misled the world" by saying it was willing to sign the peace treaty.[90] Vance expressed his disappointment with Israel's rejection of the "reasonable proposals" that he brought from Cairo. He said two of the four proposals were only clarifications.[91]

In the Knesset debate on December 19, Dayan suggested practical actions: (1) to restlessly promote peace with all Arab neighbors, (2) "to examine ways to give more independence to the Arabs of the [territories] in the running of their affairs, even if we don't reach agreement with Egypt on the Autonomy," (3) to examine the reciprocal dependence on water sources and other mutual affairs, and (4) to strengthen the Israeli settlements to prevent both friends and foes from removing Israel's military and settlements from the territories.[92]

In early January 1979, Edward Sanders, Carter's liaison to the Jewish community, warned the president that the pressure on Israel was indeed influencing the Jewish community's and Israeli public opinion for the worse. The United States appeared biased against Israel, and without trust in the United States, Israel might decide not to proceed on the Palestinian track. Sanders suggested two sets of reassurances to Israel: In the short term, inviting an Israeli team to discuss aid required for the withdrawal from the Sinai, avoiding further delays to Secretary Brown's visit to Israel, and reaffirming the commitment to Israel's energy needs. In the long term, he suggested exploring Begin's suggestions for bilateral and regional arrangements that would increase Israel's sense that it was still an important strategic and military asset and also considering a series of measures to improve military cooperation.[93] Public opinion polling conducted in mid-January and reported to the White House in early February 1979 showed that Israelis trusted the United States much less after Camp David than before.[94]

Between February 20 and 24, 1979, Dayan and Egyptian Prime Minister Mustafa Khalil met with Vance at Camp David. Whereas Khalil was seemingly authorized to conclude an agreement, Dayan was directed only to explore possibilities for progress and report back to Begin and the cabinet.[95] According to Israeli accounts, no progress was made as the "Egyptians hardened their demands. They demanded a clear statement that the treaty does not supersede other treaties and that it entirely depends on implementation of the entire autonomy plan. . . . 'We will not budge from these demands,' Khalil told Vance and Dayan."[96]

At this stage, the Americans proposed that Begin meet with Khalil, again claiming that Sadat had given Khalil the authority to reach an agreement. Begin, however, understood that this was not the case and that such a meeting, in which Khalil could only make demands but not offer concessions, would not be useful. Dayan and Weizman pressed Begin to go, claiming that this might be the last chance for peace. Begin replied that he could say no from home.[97]

At this point, Carter wrote, "I was in a quandary about Israel, so I asked both Begin and Sadat to come to see me, with Begin to make the first trip."[98] (When Sadat was invited, he declined.) Begin's visit to Washington in early March took place as the conflict with Carter continued to grow. Quandt reports,

"In preparation for his meeting with Begin, on February 28, 1979, Carter called together his top advisers—Mondale, Vance, Brzezinski, and Hamilton Jordan. Brzezinski bluntly stated that Israel seemed to want a separate peace and wanted Carter not to be reelected. Jordan agreed."[99] The Americans assumed that Begin would continue to delay the talks on autonomy until the upcoming elections would force Carter to reduce the pressure on Israel. According to Quandt,

> if Begin was attentive to the rhythms of American politics, and surely he was, he must have realized that it would be increasingly difficult for Carter to play a strong role in the negotiations as 1979 unfolded. At some point the pre-election atmosphere would take hold, and Carter would have to turn to shoring up his political position. He would not then want to engage in confrontations with Israel. . . . It would be far better, then, not to begin talks on autonomy until sometime well into 1979, when Carter would have other preoccupations.[100]

In sharper tones, Brzezinski describes the friction, reporting that Carter, Vance, and Mondale told him to "make certain that Sadat perceived the wider strategic purpose of our initiative, so that we wouldn't get drawn into fruitless legalisms of the kind in which Begin excelled. The President . . . suggested that Begin's inclination was to stall and perhaps even to contribute to the President's political defeat. This made it all the more important that the United States and Egypt cooperate closely so as to make it more difficult for Begin to prevent the implementation of the Camp David Accords."[101]

According to Brzezinski, Sadat showed great concern for Carter's position and with real emotion, affirmed his determination to help Carter overcome Begin's obstacles: "I have to give the President items with which to hammer at Begin."[102]

In their meeting on March 2, Begin rejected Carter's pressure for major concessions. He observed that American mediation had become little more than complete support for the Egyptian side. Reporting the meeting by telegram to Yadin, Dayan, and Weizman, Begin wrote that the two-hour private meeting was "very cordial," despite the clash and that Carter told him, "America's most important friend in the Middle East is Israel." According to Begin, Carter assured him that Israel "had nothing to fear concerning American pressure. Even if we have disagreements, they will absolutely not bring about pressure." Begin ended the secret report by admitting that in public statements he intentionally said that there was "a profound crisis in the negotiations" with Egypt.[103]

On the following day (Saturday, March 3), before the next meeting with Begin, Brzezinski offered two contrasting scenarios to Carter, one with carrots and the other emphasizing sticks. To provide reassurance to Israel regarding Egyptian refusal to change Article 6 of the draft treaty (on the precedence of collective defense agreements with Arab states), Brzezinski suggested committing the United States to significant enlargement of its security relations with

Israel but stopping short of a mutual security treaty. In addition, Begin would be pressed to accept "an informal <u>de facto</u> settlement freeze" (emphasis in the original) during the entire period of negotiations over the West Bank and Gaza. If Begin accepted this, Brzezinski suggested, Carter could then commit himself to a visit to Cairo and Jerusalem to wrap up the negotiations.

In the negative scenario, if the talks with Begin did not end with an agreement, Carter should tell Begin that he regrets the failure, while creating a sense of crisis in Israel and Egypt. A trip to the Middle East under this scenario should put more pressure on Israel, according to Brzezinski.[104]

Begin summarized the Saturday night meeting in a telegram to Yadin, Dayan, and Weizman. He reported telling Carter that

> the US made a serious mistake by making the impression with the Egyptians that it was siding with all of Egypt's positions. You totally surprised us with [State Department legal adviser Herbert J.] Hansel's legal opinion and a few weeks later the Secretary went to Cairo. Not only did he not consult with us, he didn't even hear us out. He brought documents from Egypt and recommended that we accept them. And Mr. Jody Powell, sitting in Washington, announced publicly that we must accept the Egyptian suggestions. If that is the American position, why would Egypt change its attitude? It is no coincidence that Dr. Khalil and others brag about the total agreement between Egypt and the US.[105]

Begin reminded Carter of the risks he had taken and the sacrifices Israel had already made for peace, including the painful agreement to remove settlers from their homes in the Sinai. He repeated the Israeli position that a treaty would be "worthless" if Egypt would be able to join another war against Israel.[106]

Begin expressed concern about Israel's energy situation following the Iranian revolution, which increased dependence on the oil from the Sinai fields. The United States was obligated by the 1975 agreement to provide emergency oil supplies, if necessary, to Israel.[107] According to an Israeli account, "Begin did not budge from this position, and hardened his demand for guarantees for oil from the Sinai, a claim he justified as a result of the new Iranian government's decision to cease supplying oil to Israel."[108]

In further sessions with Begin the next day, Carter presented a new American proposal on giving precedence to the peace treaty over other obligations, as well as a target date for agreement on autonomy (within one year), with elections to take place "at an early date." Begin agreed to both revisions, as did the cabinet, and the positive conclusion of the long debate, particularly on Article 6, seemed to be within reach, while other issues remained open.[109]

Based on the results of Begin's visit, Carter embarked on a trip to the region, hoping to secure an agreement on a treaty long before the November 1980 elections. Begin and Carter continued to disagree on the content of the

Palestinian autonomy, but the efforts to change the Israeli leader's core positions had reached a dead end.

End Game

Carter arrived in Cairo on March 7 for what was seen as the final phase of the long negotiation, but a successful outcome was still not assured. Quandt reports that at this point, "Carter found that the United States and Israel were now in agreement on most issues," not because Begin persuaded Carter or vice versa "but rather that the new American formulations went just far enough to overcome his suspicions."[110] This is an understatement—after six months of intense debate and pressure on Begin following Camp David, Carter (and Sadat) had the choice between signing a treaty that accepted the core Israeli positions on autonomy and the priority of the peace treaty (Article 6) or being left without an agreement. They chose the former option. Begin's refusal to bow to pressure appeared to be succeeding, particularly while regional developments—namely, the Iranian Revolution—created a sense of urgency in all three capitals. This pushed Carter to reach an agreement quickly with hopes of restabilizing the region.

Brzezinski preceded Carter to Cairo and reports that the tone in his meetings with Sadat was very hostile to Begin. But Carter reports that the tone in his meetings was very different as he cajoled Sadat: "I reminded Sadat that Begin . . . had gone much further than the other Israeli government leaders who had preceded him; that in Begin's mind he went too far at Camp David. Sadat understands that Begin may wish to back out if he gets a chance, or wait until after 1980 when there is a president in the White House who may not be so equally balanced between the Israeli and Arab interests. Sadat understands that it's important to conclude the negotiations now."[111]

In Cairo, Carter presented the latest drafts to Sadat, who again inserted revisions, particularly attempting to restore the Egyptian presence to Gaza. These included demands that autonomy be implemented in Gaza, even if there was no agreement on the West Bank, and the opening of an Egyptian liaison office there.[112] (During the negotiations, including at Camp David, Sadat had periodically included a renewed Egyptian role in Gaza—apart from the West Bank—which Begin consistently rejected. He was adamantly opposed to any special status for Gaza and considered it as part of Eretz Israel, identical to Judea and Samaria. Nevertheless, there were distinct differences that remained ambiguous in Begin's autonomy plan and in his positions during negotiations. One such significant example was that the Palestinians of Judea and Samaria had Jordanian citizenship, while those from Gaza did not have any citizenship.) Regarding the Sinai oil fields, Sadat rejected preferential treatment for Israel but agreed to treat

Israel without discrimination, "like any other customer."[113] The United States supported these changes, and Sadat accepted the "troublesome texts" (reportedly over the opposition of some of his close advisers). Carter reports that "within an hour he and I resolved all the questions which still had not been decided after all these months."[114]

But, as in previous episodes, Carter's version is inconsistent with other sources. For example, Quandt reports that Sadat again proposed a change to Article 6 after Begin and the Americans agreed on wording for the peace treaty that "will not derogate" other commitments. The Egyptians sought to add the phrase "comprehensive peace"—which, in Begin's interpretation, would again open the door for nullifying the treaty and joining a regional conflict.[115]

Carter arrived in Israel on March 10, seeking Begin's immediate signature. In the private meeting without advisors, Begin reminded Carter that he (Begin) had pledged to bring the peace treaty to the Knesset for ratification, which led to yet another "heated conversation" between the two. (No protocol of this meeting exists in the Israeli archives or the Carter Library. The available accounts are Carter's memoirs and diary and, partly, Begin's report to the government the next morning.[116]) Carter asked Begin why, at Camp David, he signed first and then asked the Knesset for ratification, while now he was insisting on going to the Knesset first. Begin reportedly replied, "During Camp David I informed you that I would not initial the peace treaty before it was ratified by the Knesset. My promise was widely noted. Why is this so hard for you to understand? Had you done your homework you would know what I promised, to whom I promised, and you would know how I promised."[117] Begin also rejected Sadat's new demands, repeating concerns that an Egyptian liaison office in Gaza would be followed by demands for Egyptian sovereignty.

Carter needed a success, and his memoir reflects the desperation: "We decided that our only hope was to present the facts to the Israeli cabinet the next day. . . . I was convinced that Begin would do everything possible to block a treaty and to avoid having to face the problem of the full autonomy he had promised to the Palestinians on the West Bank. He was obsessed with keeping all the occupied territory except the Sinai, and seemed to care little for the plight of the Arabs who [had] to live without basic rights under Israeli rule."[118]

Carter's diary indicates that months after Camp David, he was still trying to force Begin's hand by appealing directly to the Israel cabinet and the Knesset: "Ham [Hamilton Jordan, White House chief of staff] and the others advised me not to take my frustrations with Begin out on the Cabinet, that I must stick with my original plan or reason for coming to Israel—that is to go over Begin's head to the cabinet, the Knesset, and to the Israeli people."[119] Carter was scheduled to address the Knesset directly on March 12. He would quickly learn that going over Begin's head was impossible.

According to Vance's report to Dayan, Begin rejected all of Carter's proposals and declared he would not sign the treaty prior to Israeli cabinet approval. Vance told Dayan that Carter came specifically to make sure that the treaty was signed. In his diary, Carter described the tense quarrel with Begin, concluding, "We had an extremely unsatisfactory meeting, equivalent to what we'd had the previous Saturday night at the White House. I have rarely been so disgusted in all my life. I was convinced he would do everything possible to stop a treaty, rather than face the full autonomy he had promised in the West Bank/Gaza."[120]

At the March 11 meeting, Begin again insisted that the cabinet and the Knesset must approve the treaty before he would sign it. Dayan explained that the new draft, which Carter brought from Cairo, was significantly different from what Begin had agreed to in Washington a week earlier, requiring additional cabinet consent. Moreover, to reach an agreement, the cabinet needed to retract certain decisions it made a few days prior to Carter's visit, and time was short—Begin did not want to rush, but Carter demanded immediate results.[121]

A long debate on the wording of Article 6 ended with a statement that the agreed note is "not to be construed as contravening the provisions of Article 6."[122] Carter accepted this language, and Begin announced that the cabinet would formally consider this and other changes in the evening. If they voted to approve the text and the Egyptians agreed, the Knesset would be able to debate and vote on this historic agreement, and the signing ceremony could take place in two weeks.

Regarding the letter on autonomy, to be cosigned with Sadat, Begin objected to the term "West Bank" and again rejected Egypt's demand to station liaison officers in Gaza. Carter said that the Gaza issue was of "extreme importance to the US," adding that there must be access to the people of Gaza and that the omission of the liaison officers was a "serious loss" to the United States and Egypt.[123] Quandt reports that during this discussion, Sharon "intervened with his standard lecture on 'Jordan is Palestine'" and told the Americans that "within twenty years one million Jews would be living in the West Bank and Gaza."[124]

Carter continued to press the Israelis to accept the draft text so that the treaty could be signed immediately.[125] The intense animosity that had characterized the relationship from the beginning was again on display. According to Quandt, "Begin replied that he was very tired and that the meeting should now be adjourned. Once again, the Americans felt Begin was deliberately trying to keep Carter from enjoying the fruits of his high-stakes trip to the Middle East."[126]

Begin and the cabinet then met through the night (until 5:30 a.m.), discussing (and rejecting) the American proposal that, if necessary, Israel would be able to purchase Egyptian oil through American companies but approving the changes to the notes on Article 6. For Begin, after the long debate with Carter and the numerous formulations that were considered, the inherent risks of the entire peace process were now outweighed by the benefits. The long-standing fear remained that after the Israeli withdrawal from the Sinai, Egypt, whether under Sadat or a successor, would then resume hostility and warfare against Israel. However, after eighteen months of negotiations and numerous layers designed to reduce the probability of this scenario, Begin accepted the proposed language as maintaining the core meaning of Article 6 but continued to reject other demands from Carter.[127] When the two teams met again on March 12, the conflict continued.

The negotiations recessed so that Begin and Carter could address the Knesset as planned, but, as Quandt notes, "That event turned out to be somewhat less than edifying," particularly when Carter "undiplomatically implied that the Israeli public wanted peace more than its leaders did."[128] Carter told the Knesset that "no people desire or deserve peace more than the Jewish people," praised the Camp David Accords, and pledged that the United States would guarantee Israel's oil supply and its economic situation by strengthening its economic ties with the United States.[129]

In his speech, Begin again expressed Israel's concerns regarding Article 6, saying that this was the issue that would make the peace treaty real. The speech was interrupted by Geula Cohen and Moshe Shamir, who attacked Begin for his concessions that jeopardized, in their view, Israel's control of the West Bank and Gaza. Then the Communist Party (Hadash) MKs accused Carter, Begin, and Sadat of "conspiring against the Palestinians."[130] Carter privately acknowledged that these disruptions highlighted and clarified the limits on Begin's power and his political constraints. Afterward, the American and Israeli teams resumed discussions, reiterating the previous positions without any further movement on the remaining disagreements. Carter prepared to depart the following day without an agreement, "a bitterly disappointed man."[131]

The meetings adjourned, with the American team entrenched in Jerusalem's King David Hotel while the Israelis caucused at the Prime Minister's Office. The Israelis discussed if and how they should reach out to Carter without appearing submissive; should Begin ask for another meeting, or wait for Carter to ask?[132]

Minister Eliezer Shostack suggested discussing the Gaza liaison office in the context of the wider autonomy issues to avoid the impression that Israel was attempting to block any agreement. Begin sharply rejected his suggestion, restating the core principle: "No foreign force will enter Eretz Israel. That's the whole point. We do not want a foreign force in Western Eretz Israel and we shall not draw a border through it. We gave up Sinai and Rabbi Goren said that Sinai was not [part of] Eretz Israel. . . . We made a sacrifice, including the settlements, that I bear the pain of 24 hours a day, but any foreign force inside Israel—[absolutely not]."[133] Begin also rejected the proposal on strategic grounds: "We cannot permit a single Egyptian. . . . To do so would be to recognize Egyptian claims to it. . . . They will turn the Gaza Strip into a volcano. Those are the instructions and that is how they are talking, the first step to Palestinian independence."[134]

Begin also told his cabinet, "I must admit, I know how to keep calm, and I have proved that today. This makes my blood boil. To confront us today with such a demand? A need to fulfill the whimsy of Sadat or the Americans—this is why we have to accept this? Certainly not. . . . If he [Sadat] is willing to say that if such and such happens then there won't be an agreement, then we can say that too. . . . I want this peace with all my heart, and wish to sign this peace agreement according to the terms we discussed together."[135]

Later that evening, Dayan and Vance met informally and discussed several compromises. Dayan suggested that Israel would accept the US guarantee on oil supplies, and the Americans would convince Egypt to drop their requests regarding Gaza. In addition, Israel would consider moving up the withdrawal from the El Arish-Ras Mohammed line in the Sinai in return for Egypt's agreement to exchange ambassadors one month afterward.[136] (Dayan noted that this formula had been suggested by Weizman during the Blair House talks, but it was rejected at the time.[137]) This signaled to the Americans that, despite the earlier pessimistic assessment, Begin was ready to conclude the negotiations and sign the treaty.

The following morning (March 13), Carter, Vance, Begin, and Dayan met to formalize the terms the foreign ministers discussed the night before. Begin told Carter that he would consider making confidence-building gestures regarding the Palestinians to help ease Sadat's isolation.[138] Regarding oil supplies, Egypt would treat Israel the same as other potential customers, and if this was violated, the United States agreed to extend its pledge to ensure Israel's oil needs for fifteen years.[139]

With this agreement, Carter flew to Cairo, and Sadat quickly accepted the text. Quandt reports, "At 5:00 P.M. Carter said that full agreement had been reached, and he placed a call to Begin from the airport to tell him so. Begin agreed to go to the cabinet the next day for final approval, but the outcome was no longer in doubt."[140] According to Brzezinski, in that final Cairo discussion, while debating the meaning of Article 6, Carter suggested to Sadat "that you should interpret the language as your victory. The Israelis always do that."[141]

From Cairo, Carter sent a telegram to Begin through the embassy in Tel Aviv saying that Sadat had accepted the texts without mention of Gaza or the liaison offices and also the compromise regarding Article 6 as he (Carter) had discussed with Begin. Sadat accepted the plan to exchange ambassadors one month after the first interim withdrawal on the condition that Israel reaffirms the timetable drafted at the Blair House meetings. On oil, Sadat offered to construct an oil pipeline through the Sinai to Eilat if Israel requested this, but it would remain a secret. Carter ended the telegram by expressing the hope of seeing Sadat and Begin shortly in Washington for a signing ceremony.

The next day, March 14, Begin called Carter to report on the cabinet approval of the final draft. Begin said, "I have good news for you, Mr. President. The two outstanding issues were resolved by an overwhelming majority of the Cabinet." He was referring to the compromise on the oil supplies and the timing of Israel's first withdrawal in the Sinai. Carter replied, "That is the best news of my life, wonderful news."[142]

Ratification

The ratification debate and vote in the Knesset was relatively long (twenty-eight hours over two days, ending at 4:10 a.m. on March 22) and intense, but the outcome was never in doubt. Begin's opening speech focused on autonomy and not on the details of the agreement with Egypt. In general, in their responses, most MKs (except for Begin's Herut opponents, such as Moshe Arens) accepted the concessions regarding the Sinai, including the dismantling of the settlements. Instead, the representatives from across the spectrum focused on concerns raised by the autonomy talks as well as the hopes created by the historic breakthrough of a peace treaty with Egypt.

However, the proceedings were not entirely devoid of drama. As the second day of the debate began, the MKs learned from the media and a State Department announcement that the treaty text that they were debating was not the final one but rather the final working draft that the delegations produced. Begin was asked to explain and reported that when the debate began, the cabinet had only the draft and not the official treaty, which included several "insignificant" modifications. Within an hour, he promised, the correct and complete treaty would be submitted to the Knesset. Likud MK Moshe Shamir interrupted, accusing Begin of deceiving the Knesset by claiming that the autonomy would apply to the inhabitants, while the State Department insisted it was for the territory (thus having a national character). Begin responded that he insisted that the word *inhabitants* be included in the joint letter to Carter and that the Americans were forced to add it, thereby demonstrating that the United States had accepted Begin's interpretation that the autonomy would be personal and not national.

Begin's concluding remarks again focused on the autonomy plan and reiterated that this was the key to peace with Egypt, without which even the negotiations would not have been possible. Autonomy, however, would only proceed if Israel's security requirements could be met; without security, there would be no autonomy.

In the vote, 95 of the 120 MKs supported the agreement (including five from Likud, who had abstained in Camp David), 18 were against, two abstained, and 3 did not participate. The results were an overwhelming victory for Begin—the majority was larger than the vote on the Camp David Accords six months earlier.

But with 12 coalition MKs voting against him, Begin still needed assistance from the opposition, primarily the Labor Alignment.

With the final approval, Begin flew to Washington to sign the treaty. Until the very last moment, the friction continued, as demonstrated in a telegram Begin wrote to Ambassador Ephraim Evron in Washington on March 22. Begin instructed Evron to tell Vance before he arrived that he would not sign the joint letter to Carter on the West Bank if the comment that Israel perceived the term "West Bank" as "Judea, Samaria, and the Gaza Strip" was erased. This was a principled issue for Begin, and the term "West Bank" was a complete forgery, geographically, historically, and truthfully. "West Bank," Begin wrote, was the "entire territory from the Jordan River to the Mediterranean Sea" (i.e., Israel and the disputed territories). Begin added his insistence on correct terminology in the signed documents, even if in daily language people used other terms. He also recalled that Sadat used the term "Judea, Samaria, and Gaza" in Ismailia and could not reject the same term now. Begin ended his long telegram by instructing Evron—according to Dayan's suggestion—to tell Vance that "if the Egyptians continue with their improper method of suggesting changes to agreed issues (recently, about Santa Catherina and the withdrawal from the oil fields) they might bring [the Israeli] delegation to be unable to sign the treaty itself. The Americans are [demanded] to put an end to this unbelievable Egyptian extortion."[143]

Analysis: Negotiation by Attrition

The marathon Camp David talks created the foundation for a possible peace treaty but also highlighted the difficulties and divisions that remained, particularly on autonomy. For most of the primary actors, the optimism projected at the signing ceremony in Washington on September 17, 1978, barely masked the concerns that the conflicts might not be resolved successfully. Although the Camp David meetings resulted in compromise and agreement on most of the issues between Israel and Egypt, except for Article 6, they also exacerbated the friction between Carter and Begin at both the political and personal levels.

The six months of talks that took place between the framework agreements and the final treaty were essentially negotiations between Washington and Jerusalem regarding autonomy on the West Bank. Indeed, instead of serving as active and effective third-party mediators, as envisioned in theories of international diplomacy, Carter and the American officials became the main protagonists sitting across the table from Begin and the Israelis.[144] After securing the return of Sinai in Camp David, Sadat continued (albeit sporadically) efforts to bring a Palestinian dimension into the framework, but the Egyptian objective could be achieved through ambiguous language and arrangements that Begin was also willing to accept. However, this was not the case with Carter.

Throughout this period, in meeting after meeting and letter after letter, as well as numerous phone conversations, Carter continued, until the final moments, to demand, cajole, and threaten in the effort to achieve his initial objective of a comprehensive peace framework centered on a "Palestinian homeland" in some form. Exhibiting the same determination (and, indeed, eventually prevailing), Begin refused to consider any proposal that would endanger Israeli sovereignty in Judea, Samaria, and Gaza. As Begin had said many times over the years, any foreign (non-Israeli) sovereignty in these parts of the Jewish homeland was unthinkable. The issue was not open to negotiation, and Begin remained impervious to Carter's pressure.

In terms of the main theories and models of international negotiations, the post–Camp David process centered on Carter and Begin reflects the rational analysis approach in that the main actors pursued their objectives in a consistent and determined manner, shaped by the objectives that they adopted early in the process. Begin's Israeli critics, such as Moshe Arens, argued that Begin could (and should) have "insisted on a better deal . . . on a compromise in Sinai, without giving up everything. . . . Sadat received everything that he asked for," but the evidence also does not support this assessment.[145] The compromises that were made to reach an agreement were based on the analysis of costs and benefits. Both Carter and Begin were determined to prevail, but both recognized the dangers of losing the opportunity of sealing the Israeli-Egyptian peace treaty. In the end, Begin proved more determined than Carter.

Domestic politics also played a central role in this process, reflecting the two-level game approach in the theory of negotiations. In the United States, Carter's domestic crises and the midterm congressional elections in November 1978 increased the pressures he brought to bear against Begin on Palestinian autonomy. But Carter's leverage over Begin remained limited—excessive pressure, such as a total arms embargo, for example—was seen as domestically too costly in light of the 1980 presidential elections, in which Carter sought re-election.

In Israel, intense opposition from Begin's inner circle in the Herut faction of the Likud party, and the calls of "t-r-a-i-t-o-r," were very painful and marked the border of his willingness to take risks and to compromise. Every step in the negotiation process, particularly between Camp David and the final steps in writing the peace treaty, was taken within the bounds set by the domestic political frameworks.

While Begin was careful to preserve the perception of collective responsibility as vested in the cabinet and in Knesset, he also ensured that his own authority would be maintained. When some cabinet members expressed opposition to concessions related to autonomy during the Blair House talks and blamed Dayan and Weizman, Begin visibly restricted the freedom of action of his most senior ministers.

In the process of negotiations by attrition, particularly during Camp David, Begin demonstrated full control over the Israeli position, successfully blocking Carter's attempts to use Dayan and Weizman, in particular, as sources of pressure. At times, particularly during the Blair House phase, Begin gave Dayan and Weizman the flexibility to make small changes in the text in order to move forward. However, at every critical juncture, and especially on the two core issues of this period—Article 6 and autonomy—Begin made the decisions.

During this process, Sadat was largely on the sidelines, letting Carter take the lead in pressing for Palestinian autonomy. In responding to criticism, particularly from other Arab leaders, he sought to demonstrate (without a need to show results) that he was seeking more than a separate peace with Israel and the return of the Sinai. (Begin tried to assist Sadat on this point, repeatedly referring to the breakthrough with Egypt as the first in a series of future peace settlements with Israel's Arab neighbors and not an isolated treaty.) Similarly, the Egyptian efforts to maintain flexibility and avoid Begin's demand to subordinate other commitments, including to the Arab League, to the peace treaty with Israel (Article 6) were based on image rather than substance. In the end, the compromise satisfied the requirements of both Israel and Egypt.

For Sadat, failure to reach any agreement or to regain the Sinai would have been an unacceptable result after he had embarked on a solo campaign, without any wider Arab backing, in traveling to Israel and recognizing the Jewish state. He could also not risk the wrath of the Americans, which would have left Egypt with no superpower support. Sadat recognized that Israel held all the tangible assets required for a positive conclusion of the peace process, and after the United States had already proved incapable of forcing Begin to make more concessions, Sadat had no other options.

While analysts and policy makers speculated on what might have happened under different circumstances, such as if Begin were more flexible regarding the future of the West Bank, including acceptance of a Palestinian state, or if Carter had used maximum leverage against Israel to force such a change, these were not realistic options. The three leaders recognized the parameters of a potential agreement and continued to focus on the attainable objective—from Sadat's visit in November 1977 through the signing of the peace treaty eighteen long and difficult months later.

Notes

1. Putnam, "Diplomacy and Domestic Politics."
2. See Lewis's comments at the Camp David 25th Anniversary Forum.
3. Quandt, *Camp David*, 291.

4. Lorch, *Major Knesset Debates, 1948–1981* 6:2319.

5. Quandt, *Camp David*, 291.

6. On the role of oil in the peace negotiations, see Rubinovitz and Rettig, "Crude Peace."

7. Quandt, *Camp David*, 291.

8. Jimmy Carter, *Keeping Faith*, 405.

9. Dayan, *Breakthrough*, 238.

10. Quandt, *Camp David*, 264.

11. Quandt, 275; transcripts of the Begin-Saunders meeting are in the telegram from Avner to Dinitz from October 21, 1978 (ISA, A 4314/5).

12. Ashton, "Taking Friends for Granted."

13. After Camp David, Barak began his term on the Israeli Supreme Court but was given special leave to continue to advise the Israeli delegation to the Blair House talks.

14. Barak's secret telegram to Begin, October 19, 1978 (ISA, A 4314/5). Barak made it clear that his analysis should remain strictly secret since Chief Justice Yoel Zusman had agreed to allow him to continue to advise the negotiating team but ordered that he avoid dealing with any West Bank matters while a member of the delegation.

15. Barak's secret telegram to Begin, October 19, 1978 (ISA, A 4314/5).

16. Barak's secret telegram to Begin, October 19, 1978 (ISA, A 4314/5).

17. Dayan, *Breakthrough*, 209.

18. Dayan, 238; Weizman, *Battle for Peace*, 381.

19. Tamir, *Soldier in Search of Peace*, 26.

20. Bar-Siman-Tov, *Israel and the Peace Process*, 156–57, Begin interview in *Yediot Aharonot*, October 1, 1978, 5.

21. Bar-Siman-Tov, *Israel and the Peace Process*, 157.

22. Tamir, *Soldier in Search of Peace*, 40.

23. Tamir, *Soldier in Search of Peace*, 45.

24. Camp David Accords, Framework for Peace in the Middle East, article C (2), and Framework for the Conclusion of a Peace Treaty between Egypt and Israel. IMFA, vols. 4–5, document 192.

25. Tamir, *Soldier in Search of Peace*, 42.

26. Dayan, *Breakthrough*, 237–242.

27. Tamir, *Soldier in Search of Peace*, 45.

28. Letter Carter to Begin, October 22, 1978, BCA, PM-0072.

29. Letter Begin to Carter, October 25, 1978, BCA, PM-0072.

30. Yosef Harif, "Begin Notified Carter Last Night of the Decision," *Maariv*, October 26, 1978, 1, 15 [Hebrew]. The article mentions that the decision on settlements was not passed to Carter.

31. Yosef Zuriel, "22 Billion Israeli Liras—The Price of Thickening in Judea and Samaria," *Maariv*, October 26, 1978, 16 [Hebrew].

32. Yehoshua Bitzur, "Begin: We Notified the US on the Settlement Thickening in Judea, Samaria, Golan, the Valley and the Strip," *Maariv*, October 26, 1978, 3 [Hebrew]. Begin reportedly said at a Herut meeting that Dayan would notify Vance of the decision (Gideon Reicher, "Begin: Dayan Notified the US of Our Immediate Densification; Hundreds of Families Will Join Settlements,'" *Yediot Aharonot*, October 26, 1978, 3, 6 [Hebrew]).

33. Telegram Carter to Begin, October 26, 1978, BCA, PM-0072.

34. Dayan, *Breakthrough*, 226–29.

35. Letters Begin to Carter, October 29, 1978, BCA, PM-0072.

36. In his diary, Carter wrote when the Nobel Prizes were announced that "Sadat deserved it; Begin did not" (Jimmy Carter, *White House Diary*, 256).

37. Letter Carter to Begin, November 11, 1978, BCA, PM-0072.

38. Dayan, *Breakthrough*, 235.

39. Stein, *Heroic Diplomacy*, 260–261.

40. Begin's letter to Sadat, December 4, 1978. *BCA* PM-0073, and *FRUS 1977–1980*, vol. 9, document 144.

41. Dayan, *Breakthrough*, 213–20.

42. Haber, Schiff, and Yaari, *Year of the Dove*, 283.

43. Dayan, *Breakthrough*, 226–27.

44. Dayan was back for the government meetings on November 19 and 21, after which the Blair House talks were not resumed. Dayan and Weizman met Begin in Toronto (November 10) and New York (November 12) (Dayan, *Breakthrough*, 201–3; Benziman, *Prime Minister under Siege*, 218). The details on Dayan and Weizman's visits to Jerusalem during the Blair House talks are from Bar-Siman-Tov, *Israel and the Peace Process*, 157–67.

45. Dayan, *Breakthrough*, 224–25.

46. Quandt, *Peace Process*, 215–16.

47. This was one of the major issues in the post–Camp David negotiations. Several drafts of Israel's needs were prepared by the Ministry of Finance, followed by a formal request to the Carter administration. Calculations considered the military redeployments, the construction of new infrastructures for the new bases in the Negev, and for the resettlement of the Israelis who were to be evacuated from the Sinai. In November 1978, the amounts were $2.33 billion for force redeployment, $0.74 billion for special military procurement, and $0.3 billion for civilian needs, for a total of $3.37 billion. See "Special Aid Requirements, Preliminary Estimates," November 12, 1978, ISA, A 4997/5, and the document prepared by the economic advisor to the minister of finance, October 30, 1978, file A 4997/4.

48. Dayan, *Breakthrough*, 232.

49. Telegram to Yadin, "Meeting Prime Minister Vance," November 2, 1978, ISA, A 4314/3.

50. Dinitz, "Meeting of the Prime Minister with Secretary of State Vance," November 13, 1978; Avner, "Telephone Conversation between Prime Minister Begin and President Carter," November 21, 1978, ISA, A 4314/10.

51. Quandt, *Peace Process*, 216–18.

52. Telegram to the MFA, "The negotiations" (meeting of Begin, Dayan, and Weizman with Vance at JFK Airport, New York), November 12, 1978, ISA, A 4314/10.

53. Dayan, *Breakthrough*, 244; Dinitz, "Meeting of the Prime Minister with Secretary of State Vance," November 13, 1978, ISA, A 4314/10.

54. Dayan, *Breakthrough*, 246; Dinitz, "Meeting of the Prime Minister with Secretary of State Vance," November 13, 1978, ISA, A 4314/10.

55. *IMFA*, document 211.

56. *IMFA*, document 212.

57. Dayan, *Breakthrough*, 224–25.

58. Benziman, *Prime Minister under Siege*, 220; Bar-Siman-Tov, *Israel and the Peace Process*, 159.

59. Dayan, *Breakthrough*, 233.

60. The Herut Center Meeting, November 19, 1978, BCA, PM 158, 1–5.

61. The Herut Center Meeting, November 19, 1978, BCA, PM 158, 1–5.

62. "Treaty of Peace between the Arab Republic of Egypt and the State of Israel," November 11, 1978, BCA, PM-129.

63. Itonut (press officer) to MFA, telegram no. 409, November 24, 1978, 4, ISA, A 4314/10.

64. Deputy director general of the MFA, Eliakim Rubinstein, to director of the PM Bureau, Yechiel Kadishai, top-secret letter, November 20, 1978, BCA, PM-0071.

65. Brzezinski to Carter, memo, "Talking Points with Prime Minister Begin," November 21, 1978. JLC, National Security Affairs; Brzezinski Material; Country File; Israel 7/77 through Israel 7-12/78; Box 35, Israel 7/78-12/78.

66. Gammer, *Negotiations for Peace between Israel and Egypt*, 31–32.

67. Yehuda Avner, "Telephone conversation between Prime Minister Begin and President Carter, from the Prime Minister's Home, Tuesday, November 21, 1978, at 4.30 p.m.," 8, ISA, A 4314/10.

68. Weizman to Begin, Dayan, Zipori, and Eitan, November 14, 1978, 3, ISA, A 4314/10.

69. Memorandum for the president from Zbigniew Brzezinski, "Initial reaction to the latest Middle East difficulty," November 30, 1978, JCL, Donated Historical Material, Zbigniew Brzezinski Collection, geographic file, Middle East—negotiations [9/78–12/78] through Southern Africa [5/77-5/79], box 14, ME negotiations 9.7.78–12.78.

70. The United States made periodic estimates on Israel's spending on the settlements. See Brzezinski to the president, memo, "Cost of Israeli Settlements," June 12, 1979; "Estimated Cost of Israeli Settlements in the Occupied Areas Since April 1977," October 16, 1979; "Israel Ministry of Agriculture Budget Submissions, Investment in Israeli Settlements in Occupied Areas FY1974/75 through FY1979/80," JCL, National Security Affairs, Brzezinski material, country file, Israel 1–4/79 through Israel 4/25–30/80, box 36, folder NSA 6-36-3.

71. Memorandum for the president from Zbigniew Brzezinski, "Strategy for the Vance Trip to the Middle East," December 6, 1978, JCL, Donated Historical Material, Zbigniew Brzezinski Collection, geographic file, Middle East—negotiations [9/78–12/78] through Southern Africa [5/77–5/79], box 14, ME negotiations 9.7.78–12.78.

72. Letter Sadat to Begin, no date (from Begin's reply, it was delivered on November 30), BCA, PM-0073.

73. Letter Sadat to Begin, no date (from Begin's reply, it was delivered on November 30), BCA, PM-0073.

74. Letter Sadat to Begin, no date (from Begin's reply, it was delivered on November 30), BCA, PM-0073.

75. Letter Begin to Sadat, December 4, 1978, BCA, PM-0073. According to Lewis, Sadat was concerned that sovereignty over the Sinai would be permanently "mortgaged," as took place "in the Versailles Agreement." Egypt did not want "anything that recalls the past such as capitulations, mixed tribunals etc." Full peace would make "elaborate and rather one sided security arrangements . . . anachronistic." The Americans suggested that the article be changed to say that the security arrangements would be subject to mandatory review "if one of the States demands it" (conversation at the Ministry of Foreign Affairs on December 11, 1978 at 1130, initiated by the Americans, 1–3, ISA, A 4314/12). Lewis had made a similar presentation a week earlier. See Rubinstein to Kadishai, "Discussion of the Foreign Minister with Ambassador Lewis Today," December 4, 1978, ISA, A 4314/12.

76. Letter, Begin to Sadat, December 4, 1978, BCA, PM-0073.

77. Letter, Begin to Sadat, December 4, 1978, BCA, PM-0073.

78. Jimmy Carter, *Keeping Faith*, 405.

79. The Camp David summit improved Carter's approval rating moderately, but the disapproval declined dramatically. See Carter's presidential job approval trends at the American Presidency Project, accessed October 1, 2016, http://www.presidency.ucsb.edu /data/popularity.php?pres=39&sort=time&direct=DESC&Submit=DISPLAY).

80. Quandt, *Camp David*, 260.

81. Brzezinski, *Power and Principle*, 276.

82. Quandt, *Peace Process*, 206.

83. Dayan, *Breakthrough*, 250.

84. Quandt, *Camp David*, 289–290.

85. *IMFA*, document 219.

86. *IMFA*, document 221.

87. *IMFA*, document 222.

88. Quandt, *Camp David*, 292.

89. Dayan, *Breakthrough*, 250.

90. *IMFA*, document 223.

91. *IMFA*, document. 224.

92. *IMFA*, document 226.

93. Edward Sanders to the president, memo, "Observations on Where We Stand," January 3, 1979, JCL, National Security Affairs, Brzezinski material, country file, Israel 1–4/79 through Israel 4/25–30/80, box 36, NSA 6-36-1.

94. Harold F. Schneidman (associate director, International Communication Agency) to David Aaron (Brzezinski's deputy), memo, "Israeli Public Opinion," February 9, 1979, JCL, National Security Affairs, Brzezinski material, country file, Israel 1-4/79 through Israel 4/25 -30/80, box 36, NSA 6-36-1.

95. Jimmy Carter, *Keeping Faith*, 413; Dayan, *Breakthrough*, 260

96. Haber, Schiff, and Yaari, *Year of the Dove*, 292. For accounts of these meetings, see Dayan, *Breakthrough*, 259-267; FRUS 1977–1980, vol. 9, documents 174–177; and ISA, A 4174/9.

97. Haber, Schiff, and Yaari, *Year of the Dove*, 292–93.

98. Jimmy Carter, *Keeping Faith*, 413.

99. Quandt, *Camp David*, 298.

100. Quandt, 261.

101. Brzezinski, *Power and Principle*, 282.

102. Brzezinski.

103. Begin to Yadin, Dayan, and Weizman, "PM-Carter," March 2, 1979, ISA, A 4314/6.

104. Memorandum, Brzezinski to Carter, "Middle East Scenario," March 3, 1979, JCL, Donated Historical Material, Brzezinski Collection, geographic file, box 12, folder ME President's and Brzezinski's trips, 1.

105. Begin to Yadin Dayan and Weizman, "The negotiations," March 4, 1979, ISA, A 4314/6. Begin made a similar complaint to Brzezinski and Vance in Jerusalem on March 12 (Carter was not present): "You started by making the following statement—it is very important to Sadat that he has a solution to his problem. With all due respect, from time to time I have to pose this question. Why do you always consider so seriously and accept the apprehensions or considerations or the position or delicate situation of President Sadat? What about us?" (transcripts of meeting between the secretary of state of the United States, Mr. C. Vance, and delegation and the prime minister of Israel, Mr. Menachem

Begin, and delegation, Prime Minister's Office, Jerusalem, March 12, 1979, 4:45 PM, 29, ISA, MFA 6868/7.

106. Begin to Yadin Dayan and Weizman, "The Negotiations," March 4, 1979, ISA, A 4314/6.

107. Jim Schlesinger to the president, memo, "US Oil Supply Commitment to Israel," January 8, 1979, JCL, National Security Affairs, Brzezinski material, country file, Israel 1–4/79 through Israel 4/25–30/80, box 36, NSA 6-36-1.

108. Haber, Schiff, and Yaari, *Year of the Dove*, 293. See also Rubinovitz and Rettig, "Crude Peace."

109. Telegram, Begin to Yadin and Dayan, March 4, 1979, ISA, A 4314/6.

110. Quandt, *Camp David*, 301.

111. Carter, *Keeping Faith*, 418; Carter, *White House Diary*, 300.

112. Checklist for Initial Meeting with Begin, JCL, Donated Historical Material, Brzezinski Collection, geographic file, box 12, folder ME President's and Brzezinski's trips, 1.

113. Haber, Schiff, and Yaari, *Year of the Dove*, 295.

114. Jimmy Carter, *Keeping Faith*, 417.

115. Quandt, *Camp David*, 305.

116. Carter, *Keeping Faith*, 420–421; Carter, *White House Diary*, 301; *FRUS 1977–1980*, vol. 9, document 196 ("Summary of meetings," undated). See also the protocol of Carter's meeting with the Israeli government on March 11, 1979, ISA, A 4174/10.

117. Haber, Schiff, and Yaari, *Year of the Dove*, 296; Quandt, *Camp David*, 303.

118. Jimmy Carter, *Keeping Faith*, 421.

119. Jimmy Carter, *White House Diary*, 301.

120. Jimmy Carter, *White House Diary*, 301.

121. Dayan, *Breakthrough*, 271–272.

122. Quandt, *Camp David*, 306–307.

123. Zbigniew Brzezinski to the president, memorandum, "Your meetings in Cairo and Jerusalem," March 15, 1979, JCL, Donated Historical Material, Brzezinski Collection, geographic file, box 12, folder ME President's and Brzezinski's trips, 1.

124. Quandt, *Camp David*, 305.

125. Zbigniew Brzezinski to the president, memorandum, "Your meetings in Cairo and Jerusalem," March 15, 1979, JCL, Donated Historical Material, Brzezinski Collection, geographic file, box 12, folder ME President's and Brzezinski's trips, 1.

126. Quandt, *Camp David*, 307.

127. Protocol of meeting between the President of the United States, Mr. Jimmy Carter, and delegation and the Prime Minister of Israel, Mr. Menachem Begin, and delegation, March 11, 1979, 11:30 a.m., Prime Minister's Office, Jerusalem, *ISA*, MFA 6868/7.

128. Quandt, *Camp David*, 308.

129. *Divrei HaKnesset* 85:1825–28.

130. *Divrei HaKnesset* 85:1828–35.

131. Quandt, *Camp David*, 308–309.

132. Protocol of Israeli Government meeting, March 12, 1979, 13:00, ISA, A 4273/1.

133. Protocol of Israeli Government meeting, March 12, 1979, 13:00, ISA, A 4273/1, 16–21.

134. Protocol of a government meeting, March 12, 1979, 7–9, ISA, A 4273/1

135. Protocol of a government meeting, March 12, 1979, 7–9, ISA, A 4273/1

136. Quandt, *Camp David*, 309–310.

137. Dayan, *Breakthrough*, 273.

138. Dayan, 276–77; Quandt, *Camp David*, 310.

139. Cy Vance to the president, March 13, 1979, 3, JCL, Donated Historical Material, Brzezinski Collection, geographic file, box 12, folder ME President's and Brzezinski's trips, 1.

140. Quandt, *Camp David*, 310.

141. Zbigniew Brzezinski to the president, memorandum, "Your meetings in Cairo and Jerusalem," March 15, 1979, JCL, Donated Historical Material, Brzezinski Collection, geographic file, box 12, folder ME President's and Brzezinski's trips, 1, 9.

142. "Telephone conversation between Prime Minister Begin and President Carter, March 14, 1979 at 16:20, from the Prime Minister's Bureau, Jerusalem," ISA, A 4174/11.

143. Prime Minister telegram to the Ambassador [Evron], March 22, 1979, ISA, A 4174/15.

144. Zartman, *Negotiation and Conflict Management*.

145. Moshe Arens, "Begin's Gamble: Could Begin Have Insisted on a Better Deal, on a Compromise in Sinai, without Giving Up Everything?" *Haaretz* English edition, January 3, 2012, http://www.haaretz.com/begin-s-gamble-1.405174.

8 Implementation

A Glass Half Full

Implementation of the Peace Treaty

The signing ceremony in the White House on March 26, 1979, marked the end of the negotiations and the beginning of the implementation phase. This was scheduled to last for three years, from the day of exchange of the Articles of Ratification (April 26, 1979).

From the Israeli perspective, in particular, implementation was very different than negotiation. With the exception of Begin, many of the main actors—particularly Moshe Dayan and Ezer Weizman—left center stage, while others entered or became more prominent. The political dynamics were also distinct, with greater focus on internal Israeli dimensions, while factors such as relations with the United States and the wider international frameworks became secondary.

For Begin, the fulfillment of his personal commitments and of those made by the government that he headed was a top priority. It was important to demonstrate that Israel was indeed delivering on its obligations, however painful. Just as every aspect of the negotiations was carefully weighed, implementation was based precisely on the agreed terms—no more and no less.

Fulfilling the obligations, particularly concerning the withdrawal from the settlements in the Sinai, was traumatic. Military installations were a much easier task since dismantling was done within and by the IDF and defense establishment without emotional attachment, in contrast to the neighborhoods, houses, schools, and synagogues of civilians.

The construction of the new airbases in the Negev to replace those in the Sinai was the responsibility of the United States and was scheduled to continue for two years.[1] On the ground, the phased military withdrawals were coordinated, and Israel implemented the agreement without objections or significant logistical difficulties. The gradual withdrawal process over three years also allowed Israel to test Egypt's fidelity to its own promises and gave the necessary time to redeploy as agreed.

The major difficulties for Begin were, as expected, the settlements in the Sinai. Although some of the civilians left by agreement (including compensation, although the Compensation Law was not approved by the Knesset until March 1982), most ignored the deadlines. With ideological and financial support from *Gush Emunim* and other supporters (primarily from the settlements in the West Bank, who feared the precedent), many Sinai residents attempted to prevent the evacuation and demolition of their homes. The leveling of the settlements was delayed until the last days of the implementation (April 1982) and ended in forced and violent evacuation of the protesters.[2]

Israel returned the Sinai to Egypt according to the agreed timetable, after many intense domestic confrontations. Begin was forced to expend major political capital to placate his core constituency, whose members argued that he and his party were betraying their voters and values.

Domestic Political Developments

Begin's government had weathered many political crises during the negotiations, such as the breakup of the more centrist Democratic Movement for Change party and the resignation of Minister Yigal Hurwitz. The turmoil increased, particularly with the resignations of Dayan and Weizman within a year after the treaty was signed. The Likud bloc suffered several defections and by the end of the Ninth Knesset, in June 1981, was reduced to forty members (it started with forty-five—forty-three plus Sharon's two-man faction that joined immediately after the 1977 elections). Begin's coalition began to lose members in late 1978 and dropped from seventy-seven to sixty-nine and then to sixty-eight when Dayan resigned.

Immediately after the peace treaty was signed, negotiations over autonomy were scheduled to start. Begin appointed Minister of Interior Yosef Burg, the perennial leader of the National Religious Party, to head the delegation, visibly bypassing Foreign Minister Dayan, who would have been the natural candidate. By appointing Burg, Begin indicated that he saw the autonomy talks more as a domestic issue than an international one. In this way, Begin attempted to consolidate his right-wing coalition and to reassure his constituency, indicating that the autonomy negotiations would give precedence to ideological objectives (maintaining full control in Judea and Samaria) over foreign policy.

This move also isolated and weakened Dayan, contributing to his decision to resign in October 1979, accusing Begin of failing to pursue the autonomy he had promised. (Dayan's health was also a major factor.)[3] In his letter of resignation, Dayan mentioned his "reservations over the way in which the autonomy negotiations were being conducted."[4] He told Begin that "it is no secret to you that I differ over the technique and the substance whereby the autonomy negotiations are being conducted, and this applies, too, to a number of activities performed in the field."[5]

But Dayan's resignation shored up Begin's standing within the Likud and the right wing, where Dayan was viewed as too dovish and lacking ideological commitment. In the peace treaty with Egypt and withdrawal from the Sinai, Begin went as far as he apparently calculated that he could go without endangering his position and government.

Moreover, by the end of 1979—two years after the elections and with the peace treaty signed—Begin no longer needed Dayan as a legitimizing partner and could function without him and not endanger the coalition. Throughout the negotiations, the prime minister had significant disagreements with Dayan on the Palestinian issue, and as foreign minister, the latter would have demanded flexibility in the autonomy negotiations, which Begin would not accept. Six months later, Weizman also resigned, citing grounds similar to Dayan's.

For several months after Dayan's resignation, Begin was also acting foreign minister as several cabinet ministers struggled for the prestigious appointment (the Liberal faction demanded that its leader be appointed), but Begin rejected them all.[6] Eventually, on March 10, 1980, he appointed Speaker of the Knesset Yitzhak Shamir to be foreign minister. Shamir had been a leader of the Lehi underground group during the struggle against the British, served in the Mossad (1955–1965), and was elected to the Knesset on the Likud list as a Herut member. Shamir had abstained in the vote on the Camp David Accords in September 1978 and on the peace treaty in March 1979, and Begin's decision to appoint him as foreign minister reinforced the conclusion that further core compromises were unlikely.

After Weizman resigned in mid-1980, Ariel Sharon demanded to be appointed minister of defense, but Begin was not comfortable with this prospect and refused. He offered the position to Moshe Arens, a former aeronautical engineer, who was chair of the Knesset Committee on Foreign and Defense Affairs and voted against the Camp David Accords and the peace treaty. Arens refused. He would become minister of defense only in 1983, replacing Sharon after the Lebanon War and the Kahan Committee's report on the massacres in the Sabra and Shatila refugee camps in Beirut. Begin decided to keep the defense portfolio for himself until the elections of 1981 (held nearly six months earlier than scheduled), after which Sharon, whose political standing had increased now that he was a full member of the Herut faction in the Likud, was appointed.

Stressing the Treaty: Osiraq, the Assassination of Sadat, the Lebanon War, and Taba

A major test of the durability of the agreement with Egypt took place in June 1981, with the Israeli attack against the Iraqi nuclear reactor. The planning began in late 1980, when, as prime minister and minister of defense, Begin ordered the Israeli Air Force to prepare a strike on the Osiraq reactor complex that, according to intelligence estimates, would soon produce plutonium for conversion into weapons.[7] The operation on June 7, 1981, was launched from the Etzion base in the Sinai, west of Eilat—one of the three airfields Israel was to depart.

When the attack became public knowledge, it was a major test for the peace treaty and relations with Egypt. Begin calculated correctly that Sadat would not break diplomatic ties or postpone any step in implementing the treaty. Receipt of the trophy, meaning the return of the Sinai, was then just ten months away (April 25, 1982), and Sadat did not want to disrupt the process. The rivalry between Egypt and Iraq for regional hegemony was bitter, and Iraq was one of the leaders of the opposition to Sadat's opening toward Israel. Saddam Hussein hosted the Arab leaders who condemned Sadat in 1978 after Camp David (the Baghdad Summit). Nevertheless, Sadat was reportedly upset that Begin had not even hinted that such an operation was forthcoming shortly after their most recent meeting, just days before the operation. The meeting took place in Ismailia, three weeks before the elections in Israel, and was widely interpreted to be part of the Likud's election campaign.[8]

On June 30, the Likud narrowly won the elections, which were among the most contentious in Israel's history. Under Begin's leadership, Likud overcame the preelection polls that had predicted a Labor Alignment victory, making Shimon Peres prime minister. However, Begin retained the office, with a minimal majority of sixty-one to fifty-nine in the Tenth Knesset, in which the Likud received forty-eight seats in the Knesset (compared to forty-three plus two in the Ninth Knesset), and the Alignment received forty-seven (compared to thirty-two). Begin reestablished his coalition, but due to the political circumstances—the narrowing of his majority—he became even more dependent on his partners. Sharon became minister of defense during the critical period of withdrawals from the Sinai, assuring Begin that he would implement the terms of the treaty. However, the cost of Sharon's independence became apparent shortly afterward with the decision to launch the Lebanon War.[9]

The most serious test of the treaty was posed in Egypt on October 6, 1981, when Sadat was assassinated by Egyptian Islamists, and his deputy, Hosni Mubarak, became Egypt's leader. Begin expressed his grief upon Sadat's death in a special statement, saying that "the people of Israel share in the mourning of the people of Egypt," and sent condolences to Jihan Sadat and her family. He added that Sadat was "murdered by the enemies of peace" and recalled Sadat's visit to Jerusalem and the Camp David Accords that were celebrated by peace-loving people all over the world. He ended by saying he had lost a friend and expressed his hope that "the peace process, despite the cruel act of his enemies, will continue."[10] He then headed Israel's delegation to Sadat's funeral a few days later.[11]

Mubarak had supported the peace efforts and was among Sadat's few confidants during this process. However, he minimized the bilateral relationship, and during his three decades as president, he refrained from visiting Israel except for a brief visit to attend the funeral of Prime Minister Yitzhak Rabin in November 1995. Nevertheless, his relations with most of Israel's leaders were generally good, and during crises, Egypt acted as a mediator between Israel and the Palestinians.[12]

Most importantly for Begin and Israel, the peace treaty and the relationship survived Sadat's assassination and the transfer of power. As president, Mubarak marked the full restoration of Egyptian control in the Sinai, following the final Israeli withdrawal on April 25, 1982.

Nevertheless, the deep hostility toward Israel remained a major part of the Egyptian discourse. In May 1979, Pinchas Eliav, director of the internal research framework of the Israeli Ministry of Foreign Affairs, circulated a very hostile document written two months earlier (March 1979) at the Egyptian Ministry of Foreign Affairs. The Egyptian paper emphasized the enormous gap on Israel between Sadat and "his blind yes-men, such as Mubarak" and the political establishment, such as Khalil and El-Baz.[13]

Perhaps of greater concern for Israel was the deep antipathy from the professionals in the Egyptian Foreign Ministry, which, the Israelis feared, was likely to hinder the implementation of the normalization dimensions of the treaty. The Egyptian document argued that Ashkenazi Jews were not Semites, Hebrew, or Israelites but rather "German Huns" who had no right to the land; that Zionism, like communism, was invented by East European Jews to escape from the Czar's persecution; and that the USSR supported Zionism in order to establish a communist nucleus in the Middle East.[14]

Just six weeks passed between the final withdrawal from the Sinai and the beginning of the next crisis—the Lebanon War (Operation Peace for the Galilee)—which was triggered by a series of Palestinian terror attacks from Lebanese territory, culminating in the critical wounding of Ambassador Shlomo Argov in London. For Begin, this was another crucial test of the treaty and specifically on the question of whether the Egyptians would invoke Arab League mutual defense agreements and come to the aid of Lebanon. Consistent with the terms of the peace treaty on this issue, which Begin had repeatedly demanded, Egypt did not intervene.

Although Cairo did not respond militarily, the government, now led by Mubarak, recalled its ambassador from Tel Aviv, and diplomatic relations remained strained for many years. A new ambassador was appointed only in 1986, after another major test over the disputed area of Taba.

Taba is an area southwest of Eilat where Israelis had vacationed while they controlled the Sinai beginning after the 1967 war. Israel claimed that based on Ottoman maps from 1906, Taba was part of Israel and therefore was not covered by the peace treaty. Egypt rejected the claim and presented British maps that included Taba in its territory. The two countries agreed to an international arbitration that ruled in Egypt's favor, and in 1989, Taba was returned to Egypt.[15]

The Economic Dimension of Peace

After Camp David, teams from Israel and the United States discussed the American pledge of increased financial aid to offset the costs of relocation and other dimensions of the agreements. According to Israeli documents, on November 12, 1978, the government submitted its initial estimate for redeployment from the Sinai to the Negev—a total sum of $3.37 billion.[16] After detailed discussion, an agreement was reached, along with the oil supply guarantee and other bilateral issues. This US-Israel agreement was signed minutes before the peace treaty was signed—on March 26, 1979. (The US assistance package to Egypt was negotiated separately.)

In April, one month after the signing ceremony, Secretary Vance came to Capitol Hill to present the administration's annual request for foreign aid budget for 1980. In his remarks, he asked to amend the 1979 budget to finance implementation of the peace treaty—a total of $4.8 billion. Vance argued that the request would show American "firm support" of the treaty and to the economic and security needs of Egypt and Israel and that it would allow Israel to meet the commitment to withdraw military forces from the Sinai within three years.[17] An amount of $800 million was to be granted for the establishment of the two new airbases in the Negev. (Vance noted that the cost to the United States of Middle East wars prior to the treaty was between $55 and $70 billion.[18])

The Autonomy Negotiations

The autonomy talks for the West Bank that were agreed to in the treaty, after many intense negotiation sessions during which every word was a battleground, never went beyond the initial stage, in which both sides presented their distinct positions. There was no agreement on the foundations of the proposed autonomy framework—territorial or personal—or on the legislative powers of the new political structure.[19] Other areas of disagreement included responsibility for internal security, the status of the Israeli settlements, and the division of powers.[20]

Following several sessions of futile deliberations, after which both sides presented their fundamental differences in public, the Egyptians decided to suspend the negotiations over Basic Law: Jerusalem, Capital of Israel, which was introduced in May 1980 and passed on July 30, 1980, and also over accusing Israel of undermining the process through declarations of new settlement activity.[21] There were several attempts, Egyptian and American, to modify the language of UNSCR 242 or to pass a new resolution on Palestinian rights, as well as attempts to expand the spectrum of issues discussed in the autonomy discussions, but Israel insisted on the precise language and terms agreed to at Camp David and in the treaty and nothing more.[22] As reflected in a government resolution of August 5, 1979, Israel "learned that the Government of the United States considers this to be a 'propitious time' for the Security Council to adopt a new resolution regarding the Palestinian Arabs, inhabitants of Judea, Samaria and the Gaza District. This, obviously, is tantamount to a material change of Resolution 242." The government warned the United States that changes in 242 after it was agreed as the basis of the Camp David Accords would undermine the Accords, and it threatened to announce all of the articles that were derived from 242 as null and void.[23] Israel demanded that the United States implement the guarantees made during negotiation of the Sinai disengagement talks in 1975 and also from the Camp David Accords to prevent any changes in Resolutions 242 and 338. The fact that Begin, who resisted the use of Resolution 242 for many years since it was adopted by the Security Council in November 1967 and attempted at times to avoid it as the basis for peace with Egypt, became the champion of 242 is ironic.

At the same time, Israel's West Bank settlement activity irritated the United States and Egypt, causing several crises in the talks. During August 1980, Sadat and Begin exchanged letters over their differences—namely, Sadat demanded that Israel accept a moratorium, allegedly based on the understandings of Camp David, and Begin refuted this line of argument by quoting his own letter to Carter from September 18, 1978, on the three-month settlement freeze, and these conflicts continued.[24]

The 1980 US election campaign and the ongoing hostage situation in the US Embassy in Iran consumed the White House agenda, and the autonomy talks were pushed far down the list of priorities. While occasional clashes between Carter and Begin continued over settlements, these had little or no impact on Begin, who had no interest in pushing forward. Egypt was dependent on American pressure on Israel and had little leverage, particularly prior to regaining sovereignty over the Sinai. After Carter was defeated by Ronald Reagan, the US administration had less interest in the autonomy talks. Reagan was much more sympathetic to Israeli concerns than his predecessor.

Egypt's position on autonomy consistently pushed for application to all territories, including east Jerusalem, and regarding a wide spectrum of issues, including security. Cairo also demanded that after five years, the autonomy framework was to be replaced by a final status agreement.[25] In contrast, Israel came to the table with a position that left almost all dimensions (security, police, elections, taxation, water, infrastructures, unsettled territory, etc.) effectively in Israeli control. From the Israeli perspective, each area touched on sovereignty and therefore was non-negotiable.

After several rounds of negotiations, the legal advisor for Israel's Foreign Ministry, Ruth Lapidoth, prepared a list of differences among Israel, Egypt, and the United States.[26] But this document was not followed by compromise and progress toward agreed positions. The negotiations were suspended by Egypt in mid-1980, citing Israel's adoption of the Basic Law: Jerusalem, Capital of Israel.

The talks resumed briefly but were terminated in September 1982 due to the Lebanon War.

End of an Era

At this point, the Egyptian-Israeli peace process that began with informal messaging and then secret meetings, followed by Sadat's dramatic visit to Jerusalem in November 1977, had run its course. Sadat was no longer alive, and his successor, Hosni Mubarak, showed little interest in pursuing the Palestinian autonomy issue. Throughout his thirty-year tenure, he maintained a policy of cold peace with Israel.

Mubarak's only visit to Israel was to attend the funeral of Prime Minister Rabin in 1995. While it is possible and indeed likely that progress on the Palestinian issue, based on the mechanisms agreed to in the treaty, would have eased the friction reflected in the cold peace, internal conflicts within Egypt and the region also played a role in maintaining hostility toward Israel.

On the Israeli side, by 1982, Begin showed signs of fatigue; he announced his intention to resign on August 28, 1983 (saying, "I can no longer continue"), resigned on October 10, and was replaced by Yitzhak Shamir, who, as a member of Begin's Herut faction, had been a leading critic of the treaty terms. Shamir, who continued also as foreign minister, inherited the agreement, including the withdrawal from the Sinai, as a *fait accompli*, and did not seek to reverse any of its terms. However, he also was not interested in pursuing the autonomy framework.

But the peace treaty forged by Sadat and Begin showed remarkable resilience. Although the relationship went through several significant crises, the pledge of "no more war, no more bloodshed" has been honored. The United States, as the supposed essential actor and guarantor of the treaty, including the Sinai MFO, has acted when necessary to reinforce the treaty and prevent ruptures. The treaty survived major upheavals, such as the internal protests in Egypt and during the Muslim Brotherhood's short-lived rule following Egypt's 2012 elections. The network of links, both formal and informal, that were opened through the peace treaty has continued to function throughout this period. Indeed, the accomplishment achieved by Begin and Sadat remains a unique one that has long outlasted its creators.

Notes

1. Schubert, *Building Air Bases in the Negev*.
2. Kliot and Albeck's *Sinai—Anatomy of Settlement Evacuation* provides a detailed description of the whole process. They focus on the government's confused and inconsistent manner. The result, they argue, was that the settlers received a much higher compensation from the state than what was justifiable.

3. Shilon, *Menachem Begin*, 318.

4. Dayan, *Breakthrough*, 312.

5. IMFA, vol. 6: 1979-1980, document 52.

6. Shilon reports that Begin offered the foreign ministry to Yigael Yadin, who refused to take responsibility for the settlement policy (reflecting Dayan's views on this issue) and to Yosef Burg, but his party refused to exchange the interior ministry for the foreign ministry. Eventually, Begin offered it to Shamir (Shilon, *Menachem Begin*, 320).

7. Aviezer Yaari, "Intelligence Aspects of the Attack on the Iraqi Nuclear Reactor," in Fuksman-Sha'al, *Israel's Strike Against the Iraqi Nuclear Reactor 7 June 1981*, 39–44; Nakdimon, *First Strike*; Vandenbroucke, "Israeli Strike Against OSIRAQ"; Aronson with Brosh, *Politics and Strategy of Nuclear Weapons in the Middle East*, 167–84; Feldman, "Bombing of Osiraq—Revisited," 115–18; The Iraqi Nuclear Threat—Why Israel Had to Act, ISA PUB 3570; Snyder, "Road to Osiraq."

8. The meeting was recorded by the Israel Broadcast Association, but due to the elections law that prohibited showing candidates in the weeks before the elections, Begin was cut out of the frame in the evening news, and only Sadat was shown. Absurdly, a few minutes later, in the elections advertisement, the Likud showed the whole frame (Caspi and Leshem, "From Election Campaigning to Political Advertising," 120).

9. On the decision-making related to the Lebanon War, see, for instance, Evron, *War and Intervention in Lebanon*.

10. See Begin's statement in Hurwitz and Medad, *Peace in the Making*, 244–45.

11. "Israelis Add Delegates for the Sadat Funeral," *New York Times*, October 9, 1981, http://www.nytimes.com/1981/10/09/world/israelis-add-delegates-for-the-sadat-funeral.html.

12. Aran and Ginat have another view of Mubarak's attitude toward Israel (Aran and Ginat, "Revisiting Egyptian Foreign Policy towards Israel under Mubarak").

13. P. Eliav to director general, "Opinions in Egypt's Foreign Ministry," May 8, 1979, ISA, MFA 6864/8.

14. P. Eliav to director general, "Opinions in Egypt's Foreign Ministry," May 8, 1979, ISA, MFA 6864/8.

15. Kemp and Ben Eliezer, "Dramatizing Sovereignty"; Joel Brinkley, "Signing of Agreement with Israel Turns Over Last of Sinai to Egypt," *New York Times*, February 27, 1989, http://www.nytimes.com/1989/02/27/world/signing-of-agreement-with-israel-turns-over-last-of-sinai-to-egypt.html (27.3.2016). The UN Arbitration report is available at http://legal.un.org/riaa/cases/vol_XX/1-118.pdf (27.3.2016)

16. ISA, A 4997/5. The preliminary request was prepared in late October 1978. See file A 4997/4.

17. Foreign Assistance and Related Programs Appropriations for Fiscal Year 1980 (FY80, Part 1 [Abstract number S181-34]), Subcommittee of the Committee on Appropriations, US Senate, meeting of April 26, 1979, Statement of Hon. Cyrus R. Vance, Secretary of State, 1321, *Congressional Information Service* (CIS) (accessed March 8, 2010), 1286–87.

18. Foreign Assistance and Related Programs Appropriations for Fiscal Year 1980 (FY80, Part 1 [Abstract number S181-34]), Subcommittee of the Committee on Appropriations, US Senate, meeting of April 26, 1979, Statement of Hon. Cyrus R. Vance, Secretary of State, 1321, *Congressional Information Service* (CIS) (accessed March 8, 2010), 1317–19. The cost of the air-bases was questioned by Senator Inouye (1321).

19. See the description of the autonomy talks by Prof. Ruth Lapidoth, legal advisor to the Foreign Ministry (Lapidoth, "Autonomy Talks"). See also Rabinovich, "Autonomy Plan."

20. Lapidoth, *Autonomy*, 155–56.

21. On the law, see Zank, "Jerusalem Basic Law (1980) and the Jerusalem Embassy Act (1995)"; Naor, "Menachem Begin and 'Basic Law: Jerusalem, Capital of Israel.'"

22. Richard N. Viets, deputy chief of mission in the US embassy in Tel Aviv, sent a long telegram on how this suggestion for a UN Security Council resolution on Palestinian rights would affect US-Israel relations. His telegram was sent on August 6, a day after the Israeli government made its sharp rejection known (*FRUS 1977–1980*, vol. 9, document 274). See also McGarr, *Whole Damn Deal*, 255–57; Jimmy Carter, *White House Diary*, 349–50; Spiegel, *Other Arab-Israel Conflict*, 373–75; Strieff, *Jimmy Carter and the Middle East*, 167–73.

23. Government resolution, August 5, 1979 (in Hebrew and English), ISA, A 2025/4. Interestingly, in the Hebrew text, the source of this information was Ambassador Robert Strauss, Carter's envoy to the autonomy talks, and this disclosure is marked off in pencil, though it is clearly readable.

24. Sadat's letter to Begin from August 15, 1979, and Begin's reply from August 18 are at the BCA, PM-0073.

25. Gammer, *Negotiations on Establishing the Autonomy*, 3.

26. "Main points of an internal document on the differences of opinion between Israel, Egypt and the United States, prepared for Prime Minister Begin by the legal advisor for the Foreign Ministry, Ruth Lapidoth, as broadcast by Kol Israel [Voice of Israel], January 3, 1980," in Gammer, *Negotiations on Establishing the Autonomy*, 28–29.

9   Analysis and Implications

THE EGYPTIAN-ISRAELI PEACE treaty remains a singular achievement more than forty years after Anwar Sadat's visit to Jerusalem. Other treaties and diplomatic agreements in protracted international conflicts have been reached, including the Jordanian-Israeli treaty of 1994 and the Dayton Agreement (1995) in the Balkans, while in other cases, such as Cyprus and Sri Lanka, the efforts have failed.[1] The same is true for the numerous attempts to broker agreements between Israel and the Palestinians after the collapse of the Oslo framework. But even among the limited examples of success, the Egyptian-Israeli case is uniquely significant in terms of positive regional impact, durability, obstacles that were overcome, and other dimensions. However, the successful outcome was by no means a foregone conclusion or inevitable.

Precisely because of this success, there have been numerous attempts to duplicate the model, or at least what have been perceived as the essential factors that contributed to the outcome. Most of these attempts have failed. For example, the Camp David precedent was used in July 2000 by President Bill Clinton in the effort to broker an agreement between Israeli prime minister Ehud Barak and the head of the Palestinian Authority, Yasir Arafat, but the setting and methods of 1978 (including at least partial isolation, including from the media) were insufficient. Similar examples include the US-hosted Shepherdstown summit (January 2000) between Prime Minister Barak and Syrian foreign minister Farouk al-Shara, the Palestinian-Israeli (October 1998) talks at the Wye Plantation (which ended in the Wye River Memorandum that resumed the implementation of the 1995 Oslo II Agreement, signed by Prime Minister Benjamin Netanyahu and Arafat), and the Annapolis Conference (November 2007) under the George W. Bush administration with Israeli prime minister Ehud Olmert and Palestinian Authority president Mahmud Abbas (Abu-Mazen).

While the original Camp David summit in 1978 was indeed pivotal to the success of the Egyptian-Israeli peace process and provided a great deal of drama, it is also clear that this dimension has been overemphasized in subsequent analyses, in part due to the narrative shaped by Jimmy Carter and his associates.[2] Without the events that preceded Camp David, as well as the crucial decisions made by both Begin and Sadat, Camp David could not have occurred or succeeded. Furthermore, it took months of often difficult talks after Camp David to seal the treaty.

In attempting to assess the negotiation process and derive broader lessons from these events forty years after they took place, the new information and documentation provides an opportunity to reexamine the conventional wisdom. By analyzing the key dimensions of this case—decision-making, ideology, psychology, domestic politics, and mediation—we can suggest lessons that are potentially useful in other international negotiations.

Begin as Chief Decision Maker

According to the standard analysis of the negotiations, Begin was a stubborn ideologue who, while attracted to the abstract image of peace, was unwilling to accept the necessary concessions and tradeoffs and had to be coaxed and pressured into agreeing to withdraw from the Sinai and negotiate, even nominally, on the future of the West Bank. At Camp David, he was described as a reluctant participant, at best—a "prime minister under siege," in the words of prominent journalists and commentators.[3] The real Israeli decision makers, according to this version, were Moshe Dayan and Ezer Weizman, with input from Aharon Barak and other advisors.

But the detailed history, including documents and the transcripts of the meetings at Camp David, in particular, tell a different story. According to this evidence, Begin was in full control of the process from the Israeli side, giving Dayan and Weizman freedom to explore options but also restraining them when they seemed to push in directions that he was unwilling to go. Although tactics changed, his core objectives remained unchanged: a full "normal peace" and demilitarization of the Sinai and preventing any foreign sovereignty (or hint of such) in Judea, Samaria, and Gaza. He was willing to be flexible and to compromise until the point at which concessions would jeopardize these goals.

From Begin's first day as prime minister, he was seized with the urgency of concluding a peace treaty and immediately responded to the communications from Sadat that indicated the potential for reaching an agreement. As Kenneth Stein noted in the chapter on Begin in *Heroic Diplomacy*, the veteran Herut leader responded quickly and positively to the direct messages delivered through the Romanian channel, as well as to the note from Sadat brought directly by Prof. Irwin Cotler. Begin also sent Mossad head Yitzhak Hofi and, later, Dayan to Morocco to follow up on messages sent via King Hassan, creating the basis for the breakthrough talks with Hassan Tuhami. When Sadat indicated that he was ready to fly to Israel to open direct public talks, Begin immediately sent a formal invitation, despite knowing that Sadat's declared terms for an agreement were unacceptable.

Taking the responsibility of leadership seriously, and deciding to reject the advice of those (including IDF chief of staff Mordechai [Motta] Gur) who warned that the overture was a trap, Begin showed no hesitation in seeking these meetings and opening the process. When the negotiations reached an impasse, requiring departures from previously stated core positions, Begin dealt with them—eventually accepting some painful concessions and compromises, such as full withdrawal from the Sinai, including the civilian settlements—and rejecting others related to Judea and Samaria. Begin deliberated slowly; Stein argues that he "was great at making a point, but less successful at making compromises and tradeoffs,"[4] but success is highly subjective. Begin compromised enough to reach an agreement, which has endured for four decades despite numerous tests.

As the record shows, Begin weighed the difficult questions, potential concessions, and tradeoffs in private and not in discussions with aides or in more formal settings. Throughout the negotiations, Begin worked closely with a handful of people but rarely if ever in joint strategy sessions. The transcripts and other documentation show that Dayan generally took the lead in government strategy sessions and in presenting the Israeli position to the media. Ben-Elissar, who was a longtime member of Begin's inner circle, was generally in the background, speaking for Begin in the steering committee, but had little impact on decision-making. Yechiel Kadishai, Begin's loyal chief of staff, was not officially involved in any aspect of the negotiations but had a central informal role as a sounding board, similar only to Begin's family.

The Israeli records and protocols also demonstrate that in this as in other key issues, Begin compartmentalized tightly and kept everyone else at a distance from his calculations unless it became vital to share information with them. This was true not only concerning cabinet members who may have been kept in the dark for political reasons but also with the IDF chief of staff, Gur, and senior officers, including the head of the intelligence branch, Shlomo Gazit. The decision-making structure was strikingly different from Yitzhak Rabin's conduct of the negotiations on the 1975 Interim Agreement with Egypt, where Gur and other officers as well as senior officials (director generals of the Prime Minister's Office, the Foreign Ministry, and others) were always in the negotiation room. (Sadat did the same, though he left the decisions on many details to Osama El-Baz, unlike Begin, who took charge of all aspects, down to the minute phrasing of all texts.)

Thus, Begin's leadership role was essential to the outcome. He drove the process in the first phases, agreed to send Dayan to the Leeds Castle talks, and led the Israeli delegation at Camp David. Begin consistently rejected the pressure, primarily from Carter but also at times from Sadat and from within the Israeli political system, to go beyond his red lines, particularly with respect to the Palestinian dimension. It is possible that had Begin agreed to negotiations with Jordan on the future of Judea and Samaria or gone further with the autonomy framework, this conflict might have been resolved or at least reduced, but the transfer of sovereignty was unthinkable, and this was also part of Begin's leadership.

Once the agreements were reached, first at Camp David and then on the terms of the treaty, Begin used all of his political capital to gain support and acceptance in Israel. He angrily rejected the attacks from Herut hard-liners and the label of traitor and refused to back away from the terms that had been negotiated. This was also a fundamental aspect of his leadership role. In drawing wider conclusions for other cases, Begin's determination was clearly indispensable in directing the negotiations to a positive outcome. One of the reasons—indeed, perhaps the essential reason—for the failures of efforts to imitate the success of the Israeli-Egyptian negotiations was the absence of leaders with Begin's sense of history and the burden that he accepted of making the decisions, including taking significant risks, required to reach an agreement. As the charismatic leader of Herut, Gahal, and then Likud who led the parties through almost three decades in opposition and then, in 1977, to power at the head of the Israeli government, Begin felt this historic responsibility weighing heavily on him. Whether other leaders, including Begin's successors as prime minister, can rise to the occasion when the opportunity presents itself remains to be seen.

When Yitzhak Rabin was a candidate for prime minister as head of the Labor Party in 1992, one of his election promises was to establish a system of autonomy in the West Bank and Gaza within nine months.[5] In many aspects, Rabin's autonomy plan was similar conceptually to Begin's proposal. But when Rabin took office, he first tried the Syrian track, which failed to produce an agreement. Rabin was unaware of the Oslo negotiations that began as an informal track-two exercise sponsored by the Norwegian government, but he later agreed to the government's participation. The 1993 Oslo Accords, which established the Palestinian Authority, went beyond the parameters that Rabin had intended and certainly Begin's red lines. A major deviation—perhaps the most important— was that the Oslo framework included a territorial dimension, meaning that the authority received a territory to control—the Gaza Strip and Jericho—and that this territory could potentially expand. In 1995, Rabin was assassinated, and by 2000, the Oslo process had failed. Whether he would have been able to advance the negotiations to a peace agreement cannot be known.

Strategy, Realism, and the Rational Actor Model

Begin's decisions throughout the process can be largely explained on the basis of a strategy designed to reach the core objectives and interests that he had established at the outset and that remained unchanged, though mediated by domestic political considerations. Under Begin's guidance, Israel's behavior and actions in the negotiations were consistent with political realism and the rational actor model. Carter failed in his efforts to manipulate Israeli decision-making processes and domestic politics by going around Begin, particularly at Camp David, and in his attempts to force Begin into accepting fundamental changes on Judea and Samaria. As the evidence indicates, Carter's final attempt at the central meeting on the last night of the Camp David summit did not change Begin's objectives or his cost-benefit calculations.

In negotiations with Egypt, Begin gave up all of the Sinai, including the coastal communities that were very important to him emotionally and symbolically, although not strategically. In return, Begin brought Israel the full peace treaty, including diplomatic relations and cross-border tourism that he had long envisioned. While it is difficult to know what terms Sadat had expected when the process began, based on numerous public statements and the negotiation record, it appears that the final results were closer to Begin's image than that of Sadat.

At the same time, Begin and his government went further than initially sought regarding the autonomy negotiations for Judea, Samaria, and Gaza. This was a tactical decision made to finalize the treaty with Egypt, and Israeli sovereignty was unaffected. However, by accepting the principle of autonomy, Begin's successors, including Shamir, who was strongly opposed, opened the door, with important long-term implications. Similarly, Shimon Peres, who preferred the Jordanian Option, eventually sought a solution within the framework of the Palestinian Option that was opened through Begin's autonomy framework.[6] In 1993, the Oslo Accords, which did relinquish some Israeli sovereignty through the creation of the Palestinian Authority, were justified in part by Peres and the Labor Party as an extension of Begin's autonomy framework.

At the same time, Begin's goals, which were the basis for his decision-making, including the compromises and concessions as well as the red lines, were determined by an unwavering set of ideological principles that he brought with him to the office of prime minister.

Immovable Ideological Constraints

If, as William Quandt writes, "Begin was a puzzle to the Americans who met him," this was partly because they, and Carter, as an engineer by training, did not comprehend the powerful role of ideology as the basis for policy. Although Quandt and presumably other Carter advisors recognized that Begin was a Revisionist, a disciple of Jabontinsky's, and deeply influenced by the Holocaust, the "puzzle" resulting from ideological commitment remained. In contrast, in his book *Heroic Diplomacy*, Kenneth Stein gives this dimension its central position in explaining the negotiations. For Stein, the fact that Begin "was from the Holocaust generation" explained his behavior, noting that "he was driven by an emotional fervor to guard against a future holocaust. The image and memory of the Nazi destruction of Jews was always paramount in his decision making." Indeed, Stein concludes, "That Begin made any agreement [involving] the Palestinians is truly remarkable."[7]

Begin's deepest convictions could not envision or accept an agreement that would divide Eretz Israel or concede Israeli sovereignty over any part. For Begin, the boundaries of Eretz Israel were those decided by the League of Nations in 1920 as Palestine and then subject to British mandate. These boundaries coincide with the territory controlled by Israel after 1967, as well as Gaza and Trans-Jordan (and excluded the Golan Heights).[8] Within this framework, Begin eventually accepted the British partition of 1922, which separated Jordan from Palestine as a fait accompli.[9] However, Begin firmly rejected any further partition west of the Jordan River. This position was given partial governmental approval during Begin's tenure as minister without portfolio in 1967, when the government made its secret decision to treat the Sinai and Golan Heights as deposits to be exchanged for real and permanent peace. The decision explicitly excluded Judea, Samaria, or Gaza, reflecting Begin's strong stand. Hence, when the opportunity for peace with Egypt arose, Begin saw himself as implementing the 1967 decision.[10] At the same time, Begin rejected any and all formulations that impacted on sovereignty in Judea, Samaria, or Gaza. The evidence consistently indicates that if forced to choose, he would have rejected further concessions beyond the autonomy talks, even if this would have meant the failure of the peace initiative.

For the same ideological reasons, and in sharp contrast to Labor leaders such as Peres and Rabin, Begin had no interest in the Jordanian Option or a federation between the Hashemite Kingdom and the Palestinians. While Begin frequently called on King Hussein to join the negotiations, including in his inaugural Knesset speech on June 20, 1977, he never met the Jordanian ruler and was the only Israeli leader who did not meet him. To Begin, a peace agreement with Jordan was an end (although of lesser importance) in itself and not a means of dealing with the Palestinian issue.

To secure Israel's control over Judea, Samaria, and Gaza, Begin sought to break the linkage Carter and Sadat pursued between the Egypt-Israel bilateral track and the Palestinian autonomy talks. He rejected all pressures to accept even a symbolic presence of a foreign force in these territories (especially the Egyptian liaison officers in Gaza). Begin also would not agree to any element of Palestinian autonomy that might be considered to provide independence in foreign policy or a military capability. Begin welcomed autonomy on domestic matters because, in his view, this had no implications for sovereignty, but any external signs of independence were entirely unacceptable.

Begin was far from the only significant Israeli actor for whom ideology was central; colleagues and friends whose ideological commitment extended farther than Begin's severely criticized him for his concessions. They accused him of weakness and betrayal of the core principles, rejecting the distinctions between the Sinai and Eretz Israel. When Begin criticized Rabin for the interim agreement with Egypt (Sinai II) in 1975, he did not focus on the significant return of territory but rather on the concept of withdrawal from territory without obtaining a full peace treaty. Thus, ideology determined the basis for considering different formulations and negotiating positions, and in this dimension, Begin was entirely consistent.

The Overemphasis on Psychology

Throughout the course of the negotiations, and as a consequence of the failure to understand the role of ideology in Begin's policy making, as well as the domestic political constraints, Carter sought to use psychology to overcome what he and the Americans viewed as irrational inflexibility. The emphasis on individuals and personalities is reflected in many memoirs and analyses of the outcome and has spilled over into subsequent shaping of Israeli-Palestinian negotiations by third parties, including the United States.

Carter's stress on personality factors in his relationship with Begin was consistent with a wider trend focusing on personal and social interactions between leaders in efforts to forge mutual understanding and, on this basis, reach peace agreements.[11] In the academic realm, this approach was led by Prof. Herbert Kelman, a social psychologist at Harvard University with a deep personal interest in peace efforts in the Middle East (including meeting with PLO leader Yasir Arafat in 1983).[12] Kelman sought to transfer the theories of interpersonal and family conflict resolution to international relations and raised considerable funds from governments and private foundations to hold peace workshops with the objective of establishing personal links between Israeli and Arab leaders during the 1970s.[13] In his view, which he promoted in popular publications, the main obstacle to peace was the failure of the leaders to "overcome their psychological obstacles" and the impediments created by "cognitive styles."[14] Other academics involved in the development of this approach include Roger Fisher, joined by practitioner-diplomats such as Burton, Montville, and many others.[15]

Supporters of this model assumed (and continue to assume) that through psychological techniques and manipulations, the perceptions and positions of political leaders involved in protracted conflicts can be changed, leading to breakthroughs. At a basic level, such manipulation consists of flattery, including red-carpet receptions and excessive praise, and sharing of ostensibly private observations and experiences in the effort to establish personal commitments.

In attempting to implement this approach toward Begin and the negotiation process, Carter and his team invested considerable resources in preparing psychological profiles. Pre-summit strategy sessions in the White House focused on personal and psychological factors rather than interests and substance. According to Quandt, "For Carter, the psychology of the meeting seemed to be more important than the issues or the strategy."[16] In this framework, and based on a one-dimensional dichotomy between optimists and pessimists, Begin was portrayed as the latter, obsessed by the Holocaust, and in contrast to Sadat's ostensible optimism. Begin was also seen as having a "rigid personality," requiring continued attention to cause him to shift his positions.[17]

Begin's emphasis on the lessons of Jewish history and the Holocaust (unlike David Ben-Gurion, Rabin, and other Mapai leaders who grew up as Israelis, Begin was shaped by his experiences in Eastern Europe) was more a matter of ideology than psychology, although the two are sometimes difficult to separate. Ideology is a belief system that can be traced to personality traits, but individuals, including political leaders, sometimes change their ideological commitments, while personality traits, based on personal experience, family upbringing, genetics, and other factors, are more constant.

In examining the record of the negotiations, there is little or no evidence that Carter's emphasis on psychology was justified or that it worked. The use of exaggerated flattery at the beginning and what might be called bullying at Camp David and afterward to force a change in Begin's positions came at the expense of focusing on interests, ideology, and domestic politics. When Begin changed his positions and accepted compromise, such as at Camp David regarding dismantling of the Sinai settlements and later in accepting language on the Palestinian issue and on the precedence of the treaty over other obligations, it was due to the weighing of these factors.

Domestic Politics in Begin's Negotiation
Strategy: Two-Level Games

In the academic literature on international negotiations, Robert Putnam's two-level model, which examines the interaction between the internal and external political dimensions, is widely used to analyze processes and outcomes. According to Putnam, successful outcomes require synchronization of the domestic political requirements with the solutions (or win-sets) that also meet the needs of the external actors.[18]

This framework is clearly important to the analysis of Begin and the negotiation process and presents another set of factors that contributed to the successful outcome. Throughout the negotiations, Begin had to maneuver between conflicting demands in the key domestic arenas—the Knesset, Likud party, Herut faction, and Israeli cabinet—and the pressures from the Egyptians and, more importantly, the Americans.

The dominant image that was held by Carter, Quandt, and other key advisors was of an Israeli political system that was controlled by the prime minister, much like the American president made foreign policy. They were aware of the Labor opposition and, at least in the early months, were influenced by the view that the Likud government was likely to be short-lived and that Begin would not last. As reflected in his speeches, statements, and actions, Begin was also acutely aware of the efforts to deprive him and his government of legitimacy and to bring him down.

In this context, a successful peace process with Egypt would counter these efforts by providing legitimacy and cementing the coalition—particularly the continued participation of the Dash Party, headed by Yigael Yadin, which had fifteen seats. Although Begin had a bare majority of sixty-two seats without Dash, a failure in negotiations with Egypt and the subsequent defection of this crucial coalition partner would be a very painful and perhaps fatal blow. In September 1978, Dash split, and eight of the MKs left the coalition, and the continued support of the seven that remained was uncertain. In this sense, Begin had a strong domestic political interest in the success of the negotiations or, at least, the absence of a failure. From this perspective, the two levels—internal and external—largely coincided.

However, Begin faced another and potentially more dangerous political threat from his right, which he could not reconcile readily with the external dimension of the negotiations. Compounding and exacerbating this threat, Carter and the US administration had little understanding of the ferocity of the opposition that Begin faced, particularly from his core Herut constituency. The deep hurt that Begin expressed upon being called a traitor by his former comrades in the underground, particularly for agreeing to uproot the settlements in the Sinai as well as for what they considered to be the "dangerous" West Bank autonomy plan, did not register with Carter. Similarly, although to a lesser degree, Begin's willingness to include a reference to UN Security Council Resolution 242 in the peace treaty also alienated this group. For Begin, the attacks from Geula Cohen and others, and the resignations from his cabinet in protest, were very hurtful. If Begin was considered an inflexible right winger, there was no room for significant political players who were even more rigid in their ideological commitment.

But for Begin and his government, a win-set that satisfied both the core domestic political constituencies and was acceptable to Sadat required complex negotiations. The concession made at Camp David to withdraw from all of the Sinai, including the civilian settlements, needed the approval of Ariel Sharon to ensure support from the right (although Sharon was never part of the ideological core of Herut).

Tactically, Begin used numerous public political platforms at his disposal in justifying his concessions and also in gaining support and expanding the base of public and parliamentary support. The record reflects the steady stream of Knesset appearances, presentations before party frameworks, and media interviews. Similarly, Dayan was a ubiquitous figure in the Israeli media during the negotiations, defending and explaining the government's positions.

On this basis, Begin went to the Knesset to gain approval, first for the Camp David Accords and later to ratify the peace treaty. What Carter dismissed as a tactical move by Begin to avoid committing himself to the compromises reached in the negotiation was in fact an important means of gaining domestic political approval. The model set by Begin in negotiating peace based on resistance to concessions and rejection of American pressure became the standard for other Likud leaders and accounts, to some degree, for the success of the right in Israeli politics.[19]

As in this case, the failure to understand Israeli domestic political dynamics has continued to plague US peace efforts. The image of the Israeli prime minister as comparable in powers to an American president, with a fixed term of four years and in control of the agenda, continues to distort interaction with Israeli society.

At the same time, even if American leaders were to understand and account for domestic political constraints, in many ways the situation that Begin faced and managed successfully—consisting of pressure from within his government both to make concessions necessary to reach an agreement and also to avoid going beyond the minimum—was unusual or perhaps unique. This situation consisted not only of a right-wing government leading the peace process but also of a charismatic leader who was determined to reach peace as an expression of his own values and, to this end, was willing to take domestic political risks.

The Role of the United States: Impresario versus Mediator

In describing the American preparations for Camp David, Quandt mentions that Carter saw his role as the "impresario more than a mediator."[20] In the language of the academic literature and models of international negotiation, Carter attempted, from the beginning of the process, to be a very active third-party participant, going well beyond the relatively passive roles of communicator, facilitator, and formulator and promoting his goals and American objectives as a powerful manipulator.[21]

This approach was only partly successful. While Camp David produced the framework, and after additional months of American-led negotiations, the peace treaty was signed, the result fell far short of Carter's goal of a solution to the Palestinian issue and a comprehensive regional peace. Indeed, in examining the evidence, it appears that by continuously pushing this issue with Begin to a greater degree than with Sadat and attempting to manipulate the Israelis through intense pressure, Carter extended the time that it took to reach the treaty text and endangered the outcome.

The dominant image of Carter's role is that of mediator and indispensable peacemaker. The evidence in this dimension, as well as in the others, reflects a more complex and changing reality. For many years, US mediation determined the framework and content of negotiations, particularly after the 1973 war and the disengagement agreements that Kissinger obtained with Egypt and Syria. The Carter administration's effort to extend this process through the Geneva conference mechanism was seen as building on this foundation.

But Sadat and Begin both feared the results of a US-led Geneva conference, with the active participation and co-sponsorship of Moscow. In the shadow of this shared concern, the two leaders began to negotiate directly, and Sadat's Jerusalem visit solidified the alternative route to peace without the direct participation of Carter and the US State Department.

However, shortly afterward, the need to translate the symbolism of the breakthrough into specific terms facilitated the return of deep American involvement. This was also important to Carter. The role of the mediator and peacemaker is highly sought after, bringing prestige and honors, including the possibility of the Nobel Peace Prize. Political leaders and governments compete for this role, and for the Carter administration, resolving the Arab-Israeli conflict was an important objective from the beginning, as reflected in part by the adoption of the Brookings Plan.

At the same time, the requirements for successful third-party mediation in international conflicts are the subject of intense dispute in the academic literature and among practitioners. Political leaders and governmental officials seek to promote their interests and prestige by providing their good offices in the service of peace, as well as more tangible assistance, and in some cases using pressure and manipulation to press the parties into an agreement.

In this dimension, the Israeli documentation and the resulting process raises questions about the American role. At the beginning, the effort to detour around Washington and the Geneva conference led Sadat and Begin to develop a direct channel. Later, when the talks reached an impasse, the Americans provided the mechanisms for maintaining communication and restoring momentum, as in the case of the Leeds Castle talks and by issuing the invitation for the Egyptian and Israeli delegations to meet at Camp David.

In these tasks, the actions of Carter and the United States were consistent with Zartman's communications and facilitation model of mediation.[22] The United States was central in providing side payments and guarantees and in putting together the Multilateral Force in the Sinai. By agreeing to cover the costs of the transfer of the Sinai airbases to Israel, Carter helped convince Begin and the Israelis, particularly from the defense establishment (whose opposition, had it existed, would have prevented any agreement) that the security risks of withdrawal from the Sinai would be acceptable. In parallel, by pledging to provide the politically powerful Egyptian military with large-scale assistance, Carter helped Sadat gain the agreement of his country's security elite. Thus, in terms of facilitating and providing side payments, the role of the United States as a third-party mediator was of central importance in securing the treaty.

But when Carter attempted to go beyond this role and intervene directly (the persuasion and manipulation models of third-party involvement),[23] particularly at Camp David, to force Begin to accept the basis for an independent Palestinian state, he failed. While Sadat saw Carter as an ally (and the White House saw Sadat in the same role), for Begin, Carter was a disappointment. Begin had expected the American leader with the deep religious background to empathize with the struggle of the Jewish people in regaining national sovereignty in their homeland and repeatedly sought to find the key to the connection that he was sure must be hidden somewhere within Carter. Instead, during frequent meetings and appearances, particularly before closed party forums, Begin expressed frustration over the American role. More than mediating between Israel and Egypt, Carter sat opposite the table in the difficult negotiations with Begin, particularly regarding the status of the West Bank and the question of autonomy. The main confrontation at Camp David on the issue of settlement activity (in Judea and Samaria, not the Sinai), took place with Carter—not Sadat.

Concluding Observations

The success of the peace treaty is highly unusual in the history of the Middle East and indeed in the wider context of international relations. Two countries that had fought five bitter wars reached an agreement that has been honored for four decades. On core issues such as security, cooperative relations between Egypt and Israel continue, reflected in the emergence of a strategic understanding based on shared interests between Cairo and Jerusalem. With the chaos and conflict extending throughout the Middle East, as long as the Egyptian regime is stable, the two countries have more incentives to cooperate.

Begin would likely have been satisfied with this outcome and viewed it with pride as a singular achievement for Israel and the Jewish people. Regarding the status of Judea and Samaria, it is difficult to see him accepting the Oslo framework of 1993 despite claims that this was the logical or perhaps inevitable continuation of his autonomy framework. Oslo transferred limited sovereignty over the cities in the West Bank (Area A) to a quasi-governmental Palestinian Authority, headed at the time by Arafat. However, Israel maintains control, including security, over a significant part of the territory (Area C) and full military control over Area B. For better (in the view of Begin's ideological and political heirs) or worse (in the view of their opponents), the Palestinian state that Carter sought and that Begin adamantly rejected has yet to arise.

Begin's time in office ended shortly after the implementation of the treaty. He had pledged to resign at the age of seventy, and he announced this on August

28, 1983, passing the premiership in October to Yitzhak Shamir, after this was ratified in the internal Likud elections. Instead of spending his final years in Neot Sinai settlement, which had been dismantled under the terms of the treaty, Begin retreated to an apartment in Jerusalem, where he closed himself up (except for rare events) for nine years until he passed away at the age of seventy-nine on March 9, 1992. Begin expressed his wish to write his memoirs and the history of his generation but was unable to do so.

As noted throughout this volume, Begin's objective in negotiations with Egypt was consistent—a full peace treaty—and he achieved this goal. While the return of the entire Sinai Peninsula to Egypt was painful and somewhat risky, the formula of land for peace succeeded and brought an end to the cycle of wars between Israel and the most powerful country in the Arab world. This was and remains a singular achievement.

Notes

1. Schiff, "On Success and Failure."
2. See, for example, Quandt, *Camp David.*
3. Benziman, *Prime Minister under Siege.*
4. Stein, *Heroic Diplomacy,* 26.
5. Rabinovich, *Yitzhak Rabin,* 174, 193.
6. The Jordanian Option said to hand over to Jordan the management of daily life, the civilian affairs. The Palestinian Option said that Jordan is out of the picture and the Palestinians will run their civilian affairs. Peres's views had changed in the late 1980s. As foreign minister in the National Unity Government, he signed the London Agreement with Hussein, which should have activated the Jordanian Option. But he did so behind the back of Prime Minister Shamir, who immediately rejected the agreement. That was the final accord of the Jordanian Option, and since then Peres concluded that there was only a Palestinian Option. On Peres's changing views, particularly on this topic, see Ziv, *Why Hawks Become Doves.* On the London Agreement, see Podeh, *Chances for Peace,* 184–195.
7. Stein, *Heroic Diplomacy,* 25.
8. On the boundaries of Eretz Israel/Palestine in modern times, see Biger, *Boundaries of Modern Palestine, 1840–1947.*
9. In a speech at the graduation ceremony of the National Security College (Michlala Lebitachon Leumi) in 1982, Begin attributed the giving up on Jordan by the Jewish people to the Holocaust, which weakened the Jewish people, preventing them from fighting further to the east.
10. The Golan Law in December 1981 appears to challenge this argument, and the UN Security Council passed Resolution 497, saying that this annexation was null and void. But, in fact, the terminology shows that the law did not annex the Golan Heights but removed the martial law and civilized life there. The only exception is the forcing of Israeli permanent resident cards on the Druze population. But there are arguments that if Begin would have entered peace negotiations with Syria, he could have easily revoked the law. In fact, only

when Prime Minister Yitzhak Rabin began speaking of peace with Syria that would include full withdrawal from the Golan Heights did the opposition begin the legislation of a referendum over the question of withdrawal. It was completed only in 1999. The Basic Law: Referendum was completed as recently as March 2014.

11. Steinberg, "Limits of Peacebuilding Theory."

12. Kelman, "Conversations with Arafat."

13. Kelman, "Role of the Scholar-Practitioner in International Conflict Resolution."

14. Kelman, "Conversations with Arafat."

15. Fisher and Ury, *Getting to Yes*; Burton, *Conflict and Communication*; Montville, "Psychoanalytic Enlightenment and the Greening of Diplomacy."

16. Quandt, *Camp David*, 218, citing Jimmy Carter, *Keeping Faith*, 322.

17. Post, "Appendix: The Role of Political Personality Profiles."

18. Putnam, "Diplomacy and Domestic Politics."

19. Rynhold and Steinberg, "Peace Process and the Israeli Elections."

20. Quandt, *Camp David*, 206.

21. Bercovitch, "Mediation in International Conflict."

22. Zartman and Berman, *Practical Negotiator*.

23. Zartman and Touval, "International Mediation."

Bibliography

Primary Sources

Archives

United States

JIMMY CARTER LIBRARY, ATLANTA, GA [JCL]

Howard, Adam M., ed. *Foreign Relations of the United States, 1969–1976.* Vol. 26, *Arab-Israeli Dispute, 1974–1976.* Washington, DC: United States Government Printing Office, 2012.
———. *Foreign Relations of the United States, 1977–1980.* Vol. 8, *Arab-Israeli Dispute, January 1977–August 1978.* Washington, DC: United States Government Printing Office, 2013.
Wieland, Alexander R., ed. *Foreign Relations of the United States, 1977–1980.* Vol. 9, *Arab-Israeli Dispute, August 1978–December 1980.* Washington, DC: United States Government Printing Office, 2014.

Israel

BEGIN CENTER ARCHIVES (BCA)

Israel's Ministry of Foreign Affairs—Israel's Foreign Relations. [IMFA] Vols. 1–2, 1947–1974. http://mfa.gov.il/MFA/ForeignPolicy/MFADocuments/Yearbook1/Pages/TABLE%20 OF%20CONTENTS.aspx.
Israel's Ministry of Foreign Affairs—Israel's Foreign Relations. Vols. 4–5, 1977–1979. http:// mfa.gov.il/MFA/ForeignPolicy/MFADocuments/Yearbook3/Pages/TABLE%20OF%20 CONTENTS.aspx. [IMFA]
Israel's Ministry of Foreign Affairs—Israel's Foreign Relations. Vol. 6, 1979–1980. http://www .mfa.gov.il/MFA/ForeignPolicy/MFADocuments/Yearbook4/Pages/TABLE%20OF%20 CONTENTS.aspx.

ISRAEL STATE ARCHIVES (ISA)

Freundlich, Yehoshua, ed. *Documents on the Foreign Policy of Israel.* Vol. 5, 1950. [In Hebrew.] Jerusalem: Government Printer, 1988.
Lammfromm, Arnon, and Hagai Tsoref, eds. *Levi Eshkol—Third Prime Minister, Selected Documents (1895–1969).* [In Hebrew.] Jerusalem: Israel State Archives, 2002.
Medzini, Meron, ed. *Israel's Foreign Relations.* Jerusalem: Ministry of Foreign Affairs, 1972.
Naor, Arye, and Arnon Lammfromm, eds. *Menachem Begin: The Sixth Prime Minister, Selected Documents (1913–1992).* [In Hebrew.] Jerusalem: Israel State Archives, 2014.

Autobiographies and Memoirs

Avner, Yehuda. *The Prime Ministers: An Intimate Narrative of Israeli Leadership.* Jerusalem: Toby, 2010.
Bader, Yohanan. *The Knesset and Me.* [In Hebrew.] Jerusalem: Idanim, 1979.

Begin, Menachem. *The Revolt: Story of the Irgun*. Tel Aviv: Steimatzky, 1977.
———. *White Nights: The Story of a Prisoner in Russia*. 1st US ed. New York: Harper & Row, 1977.
Ben-Elissar, Eliahu. *No More War*. [In Hebrew.] Jerusalem: Keter, 1995.
Boutros-Ghali, Boutros. *Egypt's Road to Jerusalem: A Diplomat's Story of the Struggle for Peace in the Middle East*. New York: Random House, 1997.
Brzezinski, Zbigniew. *Power and Principle: Memoirs of the National Security Adviser 1977–1981*. New York: Farrar, Straus, Giroux, 1983.
Carter, Jimmy. *The Blood of Abraham*. Boston: Houghton Mifflin, 1985.
———. *Keeping Faith: Memoirs of a President*. New York: Bantam Books, 1982.
———. *White House Diary*. New York: Farrer, Straus, Giroux, 2010.
Carter, Rosalynn. *First Lady from Plains*. Boston: Houghton Mifflin Co., 1994.
Dayan, Moshe. *Breakthrough: A Personal Account of the Egypt-Israel Peace Negotiations*. London: Weidenfeld and Nicolson, 1981.
Eban, Abba. *An Autobiography*. New York: Random House, 1977.
Fahmy, Ismail. *Negotiating for Peace in the Middle East*. Baltimore: Johns Hopkins University Press, 1983.
Gur, Motta (Mordechai). *Chief of the General Staff (1974–1978)*. [In Hebrew.] Tel Aviv: Maarachot, Ministry of Defense, 1998.
Katz, Samuel. *The Hollow Peace*. Jerusalem: Jerusalem Post, 1981.
Kimche, David. *The Last Option: After Nasser, Arafat & Saddam Hussein: The Quest for Peace in the Middle East*. New York: Charles Scribner's Sons and Maxwell Macmillan, 1991.
Powell, Jody. *The Other Side of the Story*. New York: William Morrow, 1984.
Rubinstein, Elyakim. *Paths of Peace*. [In Hebrew.] Tel Aviv: Ministry of Defense, 1992.
el-Sadat, Anwar. *In Search of Identity: An Autobiography*. New York: HarperCollins, 1978.
Sharon, Ariel. *Warrior: An Autobiography*. New York: Simon & Schuster, 1989.
Tamir, Avraham. *A Soldier in Search of Peace: An Inside Look at Israel's Strategy*. London: Weidenfeld and Nicolson, 1988.
Vance, Cyrus R. *Hard Choices: Critical Years in America's Foreign Policy*. New York: Simon and Schuster, 1983.
Weizman, Ezer. *The Battle for Peace*. New York: Bantam Books, 1981.

Oral History

Berlatzky, Iris. The Begin Heritage Center oral documentation project: Interview with Yechiel Kadishai, February 10, 2002, and November 3, 2002. [In Hebrew.] BCA.
———. The Begin Heritage Center oral documentation project: Interview with Yitzhak Hofi, January 11, 2002. [In Hebrew.] BCA.
Makov, Herzl. The Begin Heritage Center oral documentation project: Interview with Irwin Cotler, July 11, 2017. [In Hebrew and English.] BCA.

Knesset Discussions

Divrei HaKnesset, vols. 58, 69, 71, 72, 75, 81, 85. [In Hebrew.]
Lorch, Netanel, ed. *Major Knesset Debates, 1948–1981*. Vol. 5, *Seventh Knesset 1969–1973 and Eighth Knesset 1974–1977*. Lanham, MD: University Press of America and Jerusalem Center for Public Affairs, 1993.

———. *Major Knesset Debates, 1948–1981*. Vol. 6, *Ninth Knesset 1977–1981*. Lanham, MD: University Press of America and Jerusalem Center for Public Affairs, 1993.

Other

The American Presidency Project (approval ratings for President Jimmy Carter): http://www.presidency.ucsb.edu/data/popularity.php?pres=39&sort=time&direct=DESC&Submit=DISPLAY.

Begin, Menachem. *Basic Outlines of Our Life-Worldview and Our National Outlook*. Jerusalem: Menachem Begin Heritage Center, 2007.

Brookings Middle East Study Group. *Toward Peace in the Middle East: Report of a Study Group*. Washington, DC: Brookings Institution, 1975.

The Carter Center and the Woodrow Wilson International Center for Scholars, Washington, DC, *Camp David 25ᵗʰ Anniversary Forum*, September 17, 2003. Atlanta: Carter Center, January 2004.

Congressional Information Service.

Gammer, Moshe, ed. *The Negotiations for Peace between Israel and Egypt (September 1978–March 1979): Important Documents*. [In Hebrew.] The Shiloah Institute of Study of the Middle East and Africa, Tel Aviv University, December 1979.

———. *The Negotiations on Establishing the Autonomy (April 1979–October 1980): Important Documents*. [In Hebrew.] The Shiloah Institute of Study of the Middle East and Africa, Tel Aviv University, March 1981.

———. *The Peace Initiative: The Political Negotiations (November 1977–July 1978), Major Documents*. [In Hebrew.] The Shiloah Institute for Research of the Middle East and North Africa, Tel Aviv University, September 1978.

Heikal, Mohamed. *The Road to Ramadan*. London: William Collins Sons and Co., 1975.

Hurwitz, Harry, and Yisrael Medad, eds. *Peace in the Making: The Menachem Begin-Anwar el-Sadat Personal Correspondence*. Jerusalem: Gefen, 2011.

Public Papers of the Presidents, Jimmy Carter. Available online: http://www.presidency.ucsb.edu/jimmy_carter.php.

Telem, Inbal, Shmuel Tzabag, and Benjamin Neuberger, eds. *Israel's Foreign Policy: Documents*. [In Hebrew.] Ra'anana, Israel: Open University Press, 2004.

United Nations. "Implementation of the Resolutions of the General Conference and Decisions of the Executive Board concerning the Protection of Cultural Property in Jerusalem." UNESCO. General Conference, Eighteenth Session, Paris, November 21, 1974. https://www.un.org/unispal/document/jerusalem-cultural-heritage-unesco-gen-conference-resolution-4/ accessed August 25 2018.

US State Department Bulletin.

Secondary Sources/Research

Abu Odeh, Adnan, Nabil Elaraby, Meir Rosenne, Dennis Ross, Eugene Rostow, and Vernon Turner. *UN Security Council Resolution 242: The Building Block of Peacemaking*. Washington, DC: Washington Institute for Near East Policy, 1993.

Aran, Amnon, and Rami Ginat. "Revisiting Egyptian Foreign Policy towards Israel under Mubarak: From Cold Peace to Strategic Peace." *Journal of Strategic Studies* 37, no. 4 (2014): 556–83.

Aronson, Shlomo. *Conflict and Bargaining in the Middle East: An Israeli Perspective.* Baltimore: Johns Hopkins University Press, 1978.

Aronson, Shlomo, with Oded Brosh. *The Politics and Strategy of Nuclear Weapons in the Middle East: Opacity, Theory, and Reality, 1960–1991; An Israeli Perspective.* Albany, NY: SUNY Press, 1992.

Ashton, Nigel. "'A Local Terrorist Made Good': The Callaghan Government and the Arab-Israeli Peace Process, 1977–79." *Contemporary British History* 31, no. 1 (2017): 114–35.

———. "Taking Friends for Granted: The Carter Administration, Jordan, and the Camp David Accords, 1977–1980." *Diplomatic History* 41, no. 3 (2017): 620–45.

Bar-Joseph, Uri. *The Watchman Fell Asleep: The Surprise of Yom Kippur and Its Sources.* Albany, NY: SUNY Press, 2005.

Bar-Siman-Tov, Yaacov. *Israel and the Peace Process, 1977–1982: In Search of Legitimacy for Peace.* Albany, NY: SUNY Press, 1994.

Bartal, Shaul. *The Fedayeen Emerge: The Palestine-Israel Conflict, 1949–1956.* Bloomington: Author House, 2011.

Beattie, Kirk J. *Egypt during the Sadat Years.* New York: Palgrave, 2000.

Ben-Bassat, Yuval, and Yossi Ben-Artzi. "The Collision of Empires as Seen from Istanbul: The Border of British-Controlled Egypt and Ottoman Palestine as Reflected in Ottoman Maps." *Journal of Historical Geography* 50 (2015): 25–36.

Ben-Meir, Yehuda. *National Security Decision Making: An Israeli View.* [In Hebrew.] Tel Aviv: HaKibbutz HaMeuchad, 1987.

Benziman, Uzi. *Jerusalem—A City without a Wall.* [In Hebrew.] Jerusalem: Schoken, 1973.

———. *Prime Minister under Siege.* [In Hebrew.] Jerusalem: Adam, 1981.

———. *Sharon: An Israeli Caesar.* [In Hebrew.] Tel Aviv: Adam Publishers, 1985.

Bercovitch, Jacob. "Mediation in International Conflict." In *Peacemaking in International Conflict,* edited by I. William Zartman and J. Lewis Rasmussen 125–53. Washington, DC: United States Institution of Peace Press, 1997.

Biger, Gideon. *The Boundaries of Modern Palestine, 1840–1947.* London: Routledge Curzon, 2004.

Bradley, C. Paul. *The Camp David Peace Process: A Study of Carter Administration Policies (1977–1980).* Grantham, NH: Tompson & Rutter, 1981.

Burton, John W. *Conflict and Communication.* London: Macmillan, 1969.

Carmel, Amos. *It's All Politics.* Vol. 2. [In Hebrew.] Lod: Dvir, 2001.

Caspi, Dan, and Baruch Leshem. "From Election Campaigning to Political Advertising: Changes in the Election Systems and Their Research." [In Hebrew.] In *Media and Politics in Israel,* edited by Dan Caspi, 110–33. Jerusalem: Van Leer, 2007.

Dan, Uri. *Operation Bulrush.* [In Hebrew.] Tel Aviv: Maariv, 1981.

Eldad, Arieh. *How Things Are Seen from Here.* [In Hebrew.] Or Yehuda: Kinneret, Zmora-Bitan, Dvir, 2016.

Evron, Yair. *War and Intervention in Lebanon: The Israeli-Syrian Deterrence Dialogue.* Baltimore: Johns Hopkins University Press, 1987.

Feldman, Shai. "The Bombing of Osiraq—Revisited." *International Security* 7, no. 2 (1982): 114–42.

Fischer, Louise. "Turning Point on the Road to Peace: The Government of Yitzhak Rabin and the Interim Agreement with Egypt (Sinai II)." *Israel Studies* 19, no. 3 (2014): 55–80.

Fisher, Roger, and Willaim Ury. *Getting to Yes: Negotiating Agreement without Giving In.* New York: Houghton Mifflin Harcourt, 1981.

Fuksman-Sha'al, Moshe, ed.. *The Camp David Accords: A Collection of Articles and Lectures.* Jerusalem: Carmel and Menachem Begin Heritage Center, 2010.

———. *Israel's Strike Against the Iraqi Nuclear Reactor 7 June 1981: A Collection of Articles and Lectures.* Jerusalem: Menachem Begin Heritage Center, 2003.

Gluska, Ami. *The Israeli Military and the Origins of the 1967 War: Government, Armed Forces and Defence Policy 1963–67.* London: Routledge, 2007.

Golan, Aviezer, and Shlomo Nakdimon. *Begin.* [In Hebrew.] Jerusalem: Idanim, 1978.

Gold, Dore. "U.S. Policy toward Israel in the Peace Process: Negating the 1967 Lines and Supporting Defensible Borders." *Jewish Political Studies Review* 24, no. 1/2 (2012): 7–22.

Goldstein, Amir. "Crisis and Development: Menachem Begin's Leadership throughout the 1960s." *Israel Studies* 20, no. 1 (2015): 110–33.

———. "Menachem Begin during the Six Day War and the Rebirth of the Israeli Right." [In Hebrew.] *Cathedra* 163 (2017): 131–162.

Goldstein, Yossi. *Eshkol—Biography.* [In Hebrew.] Jerusalem: Keter, 2003.

———. *Golda: Biography.* [In Hebrew.] Beer Sheba: Ben-Gurion University Press, 2012.

———. *Rabin: A Biography.* [In Hebrew.] Jerusalem and Tel Aviv: Schoken, 2006.

Gordis, Daniel. *Menachem Begin: The Battle for Israel's Soul.* New York: Nextbooks/Schocken, 2014.

Grosbard, Ofer. *Menachem Begin: A Portrait of a Leader—A Biography.* [In Hebrew.] Tel Aviv: Resling, 2006.

Gruweis-Kovalsky, Ofira. "The Map as an Official Symbol and the 'Greater Israel' Ideology." *Middle Eastern Studies* 53, no. 5 (2017): 782–801.

Haber, Eitan. "*Hayom Tifrotz Milchama*": Memories of Yisrael Lior. [In Hebrew.] Tel Aviv: Yediot Aharonot, 1987.

———. *Menachem Begin: The Legend and the Man.* New York: Delacorte Press, 1978.

Haber, Eitan, Zeev Schiff, and Ehud Yaari. *The Year of the Dove.* New York: Bantam Books, 1979.

Haber, Eitan, Ehud Yaari, and Zeev Schiff. *The Year of the Dove.* [In Hebrew.] Tel Aviv: Zmora, Bitan, Modan, 1979.

Handel, Michael I. *The Diplomacy of Surprise: Hitler, Nixon, Sadat.* Cambridge, MA: Center for International Affairs, Harvard University, 1981.

Hefez, Nir, and Gadi Bloom. *Ariel Sharon: A Life.* New York: Random House, 2006.

Herring, George C. *From Colony to Superpower: U.S. Foreign Relations since 1776.* New York: Oxford University Press, 2008.

Hirst, David, and Irene Beeson. *Sadat.* London: Faber and Faber, 1981.

Hoffman, Bruce. *Anonymous Soldiers: The Struggle for Israel, 1917–1947.* New York: Knopf, 2015.

Israeli, Raphael. *Man of Defiance: A Political Biography of Anwar Sadat.* London: Weidenfeld and Nicolson, 1985.

Jensehaugen, Jørgen. "Blueprint for Arab-Israeli Peace? President Carter and the Brookings Report." *Diplomacy & Statecraft* 25, no. 3 (2014): 492–508.

Kelman, Herbert C. "Conversations with Arafat: A Social-Psychological Assessment of the Prospects for Israeli–Palestinian Peace." *American Psychologist* 38 (1983): 203–16.

———. "The Political Psychology of the Israeli-Palestinian Conflict: How Can We Overcome the Barriers to a Negotiated Solution?" *Political Psychology* 8 (1987): 347–63.

———. "The Role of the Scholar-Practitioner in International Conflict Resolution." *International Studies Perspectives* 1 (2000): 273–88.

Kemp, Adriana, and Uri Ben Eliezer. "Dramatizing Sovereignty: The Construction of Territorial Dispute on the Israeli-Egyptian Border of Taba." *Political Geography* 19, no. 3 (2000): 315–44.

Kliot, Nurit, and Shemuel Albeck. *Sinai—Anatomy of Settlement Evacuation.* [In Hebrew.] Tel Aviv: Ministry of Defense Publication House, 1996.

Kriesberg, Louis. "Mediation and the Transformation of the Israeli-Palestinian Conflict." *Journal of Peace Research* 38 (2001): 373–92.

Lapidoth, Ruth. *Autonomy: Flexible Solutions to Ethnic Conflicts.* Washington, DC: United States Institute of Peace Press, 1997.

———. "The Autonomy Talks." *Jerusalem Quarterly* 24 (1982): 99–113.

Lewis, Samuel W. *Camp David Revisited: Lessons for Negotiators.* Discussion Papers no. 4 (The second annual Rebecca Meyerhoff memorial lecture). Jerusalem: Harry S. Truman Research Institute for the Advancement of Peace, Hebrew University of Jerusalem, 1997.

Lungen, Paul. "Cotler Recalls (Small) Role in Israel-Egypt Peace." *Canadian Jewish News,* March 25, 2015. http://www.cjnews.com/news/israel/feature-cotler-recalls-small-role -israel-egypt-peace.

Mann, Rafi. *It's Inconceivable.* [In Hebrew.] Tel Aviv: Hed Artzi, 1998.

Marcus, Yoel. *Camp David.* [In Hebrew.] Jerusalem: Schoken, 1979.

McGarr, Kathryn J. *The Whole Damn Deal: Robert Strauss and the Art of Politics.* New York: Public Affairs, 2011.

Medzini, Meron. *Golda: Golda Meir and the Vision of Israel, a Political Biography.* [In Hebrew.] Tel Aviv: Miskal—Yedioth Ahronoth Books and Chemed Books, 2008.

Montville, Joseph V. "Psychoanalytic Enlightenment and the Greening of Diplomacy." *Journal of the American Psychoanalysis Association* 37 (1989): 297–318.

Nakdimon, Shlomo. *First Strike: The Exclusive Story of How Israel Foiled Iraq's Attempt to Get the Bomb.* New York: Summit Books, 1987.

———. *Toward H-Hour: The Pre–Six Day War Drama.* [In Hebrew.] Tel Aviv: Ramdor, 1968.

Naor, Arye. *Begin in Power: A Personal Testimony.* [In Hebrew.] Tel Aviv: Yediot Aharonot, 1993.

———. *Greater Israel: Theology and Policy.* [In Hebrew.] Haifa: University of Haifa Press and Lod: Zmora-Bitan, 2001.

———. "Menachem Begin and 'Basic Law: Jerusalem, Capital of Israel.'" *Israel Studies* 21, no. 3 (2016): 36–48.

Oren, Michael B. *Six Days of War: June 1967 and the Making of the Modern Middle East.* New York: Random House, 2002.

Pedatzur, Reuven. *The Triumph of Embarrassment: Israel and the Territories after the Six-Day War.* [In Hebrew.] Tel Aviv: Bitan Publishers, 1996.

Perlmutter, Amos. *The Life and Times of Menachem Begin.* Garden City, NY: Doubleday, 1987.

Pettigrew, Thomas F. "Toward Sustainable Psychological Interventions for Change, Peace and Conflict." *Journal of Peace Psychology* 17, no. 2 (2011): 179–92.

Podeh, Elie. *Chances for Peace: Missed Opportunities in the Arab-Israeli Conflict*. Austin: University of Texas Press, 2015.

Post, Jerrold M. *Leaders and Their Followers in a Dangerous World: The Psychology of Political Behavior*. Ithaca, NY: Cornell University Press, 2004.

Post, Jerrold. "Personality Profiles in Support of the Camp David Summit." *Studies in Intelligence* 23 (1979): 1–5.

Pressman, Jeremy. "Explaining the Carter Administration's Israeli-Palestinian Solution." *Diplomatic History* 37, no. 5 (2013): 1117–47.

Preuss, Teddy. *Begin in Power*. [In Hebrew.] Jerusalem: Keter, 1984.

Putnam, Robert D. "Diplomacy and Domestic Politics: The Logic of Two-Level Games," *International Organization* 42, no. 3 (1988): 427–60.

Quandt, William B. "Camp David and Peacemaking in the Middle East." *Political Science Quarterly* 101, no. 3 (1986): 357–77.

———. *Camp David: Peacemaking and Politics*. Washington, DC: Brookings Institution Press, 1986.

———. *Peace Process: American Diplomacy and the Arab-Israeli Conflict since 1967*. 3rd ed. Washington, DC: Brookings Institution Press and Berkeley: University of California Press, 2005.

———. "Review Essay: Palestine, Apartheid, and Jimmy Carter: Reading Past the Title." *Journal of Palestine Studies* 36, no. 3 (2007): 89–93.

Rabinovich, Itamar. "The Autonomy Plan." *Middle East Contemporary Survey* 3 (1978–1979): 167–83.

———. *Yitzhak Rabin: Soldier, Leader, Statesman*. New Haven: Yale University Press, 2017.

Raz, Avi. "The Generous Peace Offer That Was Never Offered: The Israeli Cabinet Resolution of June 19, 1967." *Diplomatic History* 37, no. 1 (2013): 85–108.

Reiter, Yitzhak. *Jerusalem and Its Role in Islamic Solidarity*. New York: Palgrave, 2008.

Rubinovitz, Ziv, and Elai Rettig. "Crude Peace: The Role of Oil in the Israeli-Egyptian Peace Negotiations." *International Studies Quarterly* 62, no. 2 (2018): 371–82.

Rynhold, Jonathan, and Gerald M. Steinberg. "The Peace Process and the Israeli Elections." *Israel Affairs* 10, no. 4 (2004): 181–204.

Schiff, Amira. "On Success and Failure: Readiness Theory and the Aceh and Sri Lanka Peace Processes." *International Negotiation* 19, no. 1 (2014): 89–126.

Schubert, Frank N. *Building Air Bases in the Negev: The U.S. Army Corps of Engineers in Israel, 1979–1982*. Washington, DC: Office of History, Corps of Engineers and Center of Military History, United States Army, 1992.

Segev, Samuel. *The Moroccan Connection: The Secret Ties between Israel and Morocco*. [In Hebrew.] Tel Aviv: Matar, 2008.

Segev, Tom. *1967: Israel, the War, and the Year That Transformed the Middle East*. New York: Metropolitan Books, 2007.

Shamir, Shimon. *Egypt under Sadat: The Search for a New Orientation*. [In Hebrew.] Tel Aviv: Dvir, 1978.

Shapira, Anita. *Yigal Allon, Native Son: A Biography*. Philadelphia: University of Pennsylvania Press, 2008.

Shelef, Nadav G. "From 'Both Banks of the Jordan' to the 'Whole Land of Israel': Ideological Change in Revisionist Zionism." *Israel Studies* 9, no. 1 (2004): 125–48.

Shilon, Avi. *Menachem Begin: A Life*. New Haven: Yale University Press, 2012.

Shragai, Nadav. *The Temple Mount Conflict.* [In Hebrew.] Jerusalem: Keter, 1995.

Silver, Eric. *Begin: A Biography.* London: Wiedenfeld and Nicolson, 1984.

Slonim, Shlomo. *Jerusalem in America's Foreign Policy, 1947–1997.* The Hague: Kluwer Law International, 1998.

Snyder, Jed C. "The Road to Osiraq: Baghdad's Quest for the Bomb." *Middle East Journal* 37, no. 4 (1983): 565–93.

Sofer, Sasson. *Begin: An Anatomy of Leadership.* Oxford: Basil Blackwell, 1988.

Spiegel, Steven L. *The Other Arab-Israeli Conflict: Making America's Middle East Policy, from Truman to Reagan.* Chicago: University of Chicago Press, 1985.

Stein, Kenneth W. *Heroic Diplomacy: Sadat, Kissinger, Carter, Begin, and the Quest for Arab-Israeli Peace.* New York: Routledge, 1999.

Steinberg, Gerald M. "The Limits of Peacebuilding Theory." In *Routledge Handbook of Peace-building,* edited by Roger Mac Ginty, 36–54. Oxon: Routledge, 2013.

Strieff, Daniel. *Jimmy Carter and the Middle East: The Politics of Presidential Diplomacy.* New York: Palgrave MacMillan, 2015.

Talmai, Efraim, and Menachem Talmai. [In Hebrew.] *Zionist Lexicon.* Tel Aviv: Maariv, 1982.

Telhami, Shibley. *Power and Leadership in International Bargaining: The Path to the Camp David Accords.* New York: Columbia University Press, 1990.

Temko, Ned. *To Win or to Die: A Personal Portrait of Menachem Begin.* New York: William Morrow, 1987.

Touval, Saadia. *The Peace Brokers: Mediators in the Arab-Israeli Conflict, 1948–1979.* Princeton, NJ: Princeton University Press, 1982.

Tovy, Jacob. *Israel and the Palestinian Refugee Issue: The Formulation of a Policy, 1948–1956.* New York: Routledge, 2014.

Vandenbroucke, Lucien S. "The Israeli Strike Against OSIRAQ: The Dynamics of Fear and Proliferation in the Middle East." *Air University Review* (September–October 1984).

Wazana, Nili. *All the Boundaries of the Land: The Promised Land in Biblical Thought in Light of the Ancient Near East.* Winona Lake, IN: Eisenbrauns, 2013.

Zank, Michael. "The Jerusalem Basic Law (1980) and the Jerusalem Embassy Act (1995): A Comparative Investigation of Israeli and US Legislation on the Status of Jerusalem." *Israel Studies* 21, no. 3 (2016): 20–35.

Zartman, I. William. *Negotiation and Conflict Management: Essays on Theory and Practice.* New York: Routledge, 2007.

——. *Ripe for Resolution: Conflict and Intervention in Africa.* New York: Oxford, 1989.

——. "Ripeness." In *Beyond Intractability,* edited by Guy Burgess and Heidi Burgess. Boulder: Conflict Information Consortium, University of Colorado, August 2003. https://www.beyondintractability.org/essay/ripeness.

Zartman, I. William, and Maureen R. Berman. *The Practical Negotiator.* New Haven: Yale University Press, 1982.

Zartman, I. William, and Saadia Touval. "International Mediation: Conflict Resolution and Power Politics." *Journal of Social Issues* 41, no. 2 (1985): 27–45.

Ziv, Guy. *Why Hawks Become Doves: Shimon Peres and the Foreign Policy Change in Israel.* Albany, NY: SUNY Press, 2014.

Newspapers

Israel

Davar
Haaretz
Jerusalem Post
Maariv
Yediot Aharonot

United States

Christian Science Monitor
Time
Washington Post

United Kingdom

Daily Mail
Daily Telegraph
Manchester Daily Telegraph

Canada

Canadian Jewish News

Index

Abdel-Meguid, Ismat, 101, 112
Abu Hatzeira, Aharon, 173
Agranat Commission, 39, 43
airbases: in Negev 185, 216, 221, 224n18, 236;
    in Sinai, 101, 122, 141, 148, 153, 174, 190, 219
al-Assad, Hafez, 49, 62, 72, 75
Allon, Yigal, 12–15, 17, 19, 21–25, 28, 32, 34n30,
    36n91, 46–47, 54, 116–17, 173, 177
Allon Plan, 28, 117
al-Shara, Farouk, 226
Amit, Meir, 13
anti-Semitism, 30, 50, 118, 119, 189
Arab League, 20, 184, 186, 189, 193, 209, 220
Arafat, Yasir, 28, 46, 51, 73, 86, 101, 143, 147,
    226, 232, 237
Arens, Moshe, 146, 206, 208, 218
Atherton, Alfred, 112, 120, 121, 127, 128, 129,
    138n184, 144
autonomy 1967: discussion on 4, 18–20, 32, 108
autonomy 1977–82: Begin's plan for x, 3,
    4, 18–20, 32, 47, 61, 67, 76, 99, 102–16,
    123–24, 127–29, 138n184, 151, 157, 158, 172,
    183–87, 191, 195, 197, 201, 203–04, 206, 217,
    230, 237; at Camp David, xi, 140, 146–47,
    149, 151, 157–58, 165, 171, 183, 207; Carter
    administration on, 101, 105–10, 115–16, 122,
    140, 151, 158, 186–87, 190–91, 193–95, 197,
    199–203, 209, 222, 237; Dayan-Tuhami
    meetings on, 74–76, 101, 105; domestic
    opponents of, 114, 116, 170, 176–78, 206,
    208, 234; Egyptian proposals, 111–14,
    128–29, 187, 191, 198, 201, 222; Jabotinsky
    on, 32; on Jewish settlement activity, 115,
    192; Jordanian participation in, 3, 146–47,
    151, 187, 193, 228; Palestinian statehood in,
    4, 18–19, 45, 61–64, 67, 103, 105, 108, 114–16,
    146–47, 151, 175, 231; Rabin and, 229; talks
    on 3, 171, 175, 183, 185, 192–94, 206, 217–18,
    221–23, 225n19, 225n23, 231; sovereignty
    and, 128, 146, 151

Avidan, Meir, 20
Avineri, Shlomo, 71, 72
Avner, Yehuda, 48, 60, 67, 68

Bader, Yohanan, 179
Baghdad Summit (Arab League), 189, 194,
    219
Balfour Declaration, 87
Barak, Aharon: xi, 227; on application of
    Resolution 242, 186; on the authority of
    the Administrative Council, 109; on the
    autonomy plan, 128, 133n29; Blair House
    talks, 185–87, 190, 210,13, 210n14; Camp
    David summit, 141, 153, 155, 156, 158,
    159–60, 161, 163, 168n105, 175
Barak, Ehud, 226
Bar-Siman-Tov, Yaacov, 54, 75, 84, 104, 126,
    141, 163, 186
Basic Law: Jerusalem, Capital of Israel,
    35n72, 221, 222
Begin, Aliza, 1
Begin, Menachem: on American financial
    aid to Israel, 48, 190–91, 211n47; American
    intervention in peace process, 42, 44–45,
    48, 119–25, 138n163; attacks on, 50–52,
    54, 115–17, 176–80, 185, 189, 204, 208, 229,
    234; background of, xii, 1–2, 4, 11–12; in
    Britain, 49–50, 81; Carter's relations with,
    x, 8, 48, 53–54, 60–63, 66–68, 108–10,
    131–32, 152–53, 161–62, 165, 202, 187–88,
    194, 230, 237; Ceausescu's meeting with,
    71–73, 79; domestic criticism of, 5, 44,
    114, 116–17, 126–27, 131–32, 141, 157, 164,
    170, 175, 176–79, 180, 185, 188, 189, 217, 234;
    foreign policy of, 49–50, 115, 140, 154–55,
    162–63, 172–74, 199, 207; framework for
    peace, 41, 46–47, 66, 103, 111; on Geneva
    Conference, 55, 60, 67, 69, 83, 88–89, 106,
    236; Holocaust imagery used by, xi, 1,
    37n106, 45, 46, 51, 68, 87, 145, 230, 233,

GERALD M. STEINBERG is Professor of Political Science at Bar Ilan University and founder of the Graduate Program on Conflict Management and Negotiation. He is author of *Satellite Reconnaissance: The Role of Informal Bargaining* and author (with Anne Herzberg and Jordan Berman) of *Best Practices for Human Rights and Humanitarian NGO Fact-Finding.*

ZIV RUBINOVITZ is Israel Institute Teaching Fellow at Sonoma State University.

FOR INDIANA UNIVERSITY PRESS

Tony Brewer *Artist and Book Designer*
Dan Crissman *Editorial Director and Acquisitions Editor*
Julie Davis *Marketing and Publicity Manager*
Anna Garnai *Production Coordinator*
Katie Huggins *Production Manager*
Nancy Lightfoot *Project Manager/Editor*
Dee Mortensen *Acquisitions Editor*
Dan Pyle *Online Publishing Manager*
Paige Rasmussen *Assistant Acquisitions Editor*
Michael Regoli *Director of Publishing Operations*
Pam Rude *Senior Artist and Book Designer*
Stephen Williams *Assistant Director of Marketing*